CHANGING GEOPOLITICS OF GLOBAL COMMUNICATION

Changing Geopolitics of Global Communication examines the rapidly evolving dynamics between global communication and geopolitics.

As an intersection between communication and international relations, it bridges the existing gap in scholarship and highlights the growing importance of digital communication in legitimizing and promoting the geopolitical and economic goals of leading powers. One central theme that emerges in the book is the continuity of asymmetries in power relations that can be traced back to 19th-century European imperialism, manifested in its various incarnations from 'liberal' to 'neo-liberal', to 'digital' imperialism. The book includes a discussion of the post–Cold War US-led transformation of the hardware and software of global communication and how it has been challenged by the 'rise of the rest', especially China. Other key issues covered include the geopolitics of image wars, weaponization of information and the visibility of discourses emanating from outside the Euro-Atlantic zone.

The ideas and arguments advanced here privilege a reading of geopolitical processes and examples from the perspective of the global South. Written by a leading scholar of global communication, this comprehensive and transdisciplinary study adopts a holistic approach and will be of interest to the global community of scholars, researchers and commentators in communication and international relations, among other fields.

Daya Kishan Thussu is Professor of International Communication at the Hong Kong Baptist University and President of the International Association for Media and Communication Research (IAMCR). Author or editor of 20 books, he was Inaugural Disney Chair in Global Media at Schwarzman College, Tsinghua University, Beijing. Prior to that, for many years he was Professor of International Communication at the University of Westminster in London. A PhD in international relations from Jawaharlal Nehru University in New Delhi, he has been since 2005 the managing editor of the journal *Global Media and Communication*.

Communication and Society
Series Editor James Curran

This series encompasses the broad field of media and cultural studies. Its main concerns are the media and the public sphere: on whether the media empower or fail to empower popular forces in society; media organisations and public policy; the political and social consequences of media campaigns; and the role of media entertainment, ranging from potboilers and the human-interest story to rock music and TV sport.

Gender and Media second edition
Representing, Producing, Consuming
Tonny Krijnen and Sofie Van Bauwel

Journalism, Culture and Society
A Critical Theoretical Approach to Global Journalistic Practice
Omega Douglas and Angela Phillips

Journalism and Crime
Bethany Usher

Beyond Mainstream Media
Alternative Media and the Future of Journalism
Stephen Cushion

Changing Geopolitics of Global Communication
Daya Kishan Thussu

For a complete list of titles in this series, please see: www.routledge.com/Communication-and-Society/book-series/SE0130

CHANGING GEOPOLITICS OF GLOBAL COMMUNICATION

Daya Kishan Thussu

LONDON AND NEW YORK

First published 2025
by Routledge
4 Park Square, Milton Park, Abingdon, Oxon OX14 4RN

and by Routledge
605 Third Avenue, New York, NY 10158

Routledge is an imprint of the Taylor & Francis Group, an informa business

© 2025 Daya Kishan Thussu

The right of Daya Kishan Thussu to be identified as author of this work has been asserted in accordance with sections 77 and 78 of the Copyright, Designs and Patents Act 1988.

All rights reserved. No part of this book may be reprinted or reproduced or utilised in any form or by any electronic, mechanical, or other means, now known or hereafter invented, including photocopying and recording, or in any information storage or retrieval system, without permission in writing from the publishers.

Trademark notice: Product or corporate names may be trademarks or registered trademarks, and are used only for identification and explanation without intent to infringe.

British Library Cataloguing-in-Publication Data
A catalogue record for this book is available from the British Library

ISBN: 978-1-138-28079-3 (hbk)
ISBN: 978-1-138-28080-9 (pbk)
ISBN: 978-1-315-27169-9 (ebk)

DOI: 10.4324/9781315271699

Typeset in Times New Roman
by Apex CoVantage, LLC

For Liz

CONTENTS

About the Author   x

Introduction: geopolitics and global communication   1
    Hong Kong: 'Asia's World City' caught in a global
       geopolitical game 2
    Trumpism and the erosion of US global influence 4
    The imperial origins of the concept of geopolitics 5
    Critical geopolitics 7
    How global geopolitics is changing 9
    Calibrating the China challenge 10
    The Russian invasion of Ukraine: geopolitical rifts and
       shifts 13
    The myth of the EU as an autonomous geopolitical
       actor 15
    The 'Rise of the Rest' 16
    How global communication is changing 19
    The digital 'Cold War' with China 23

1   Communication, globalization and empire: legacies and leverages   28
    Control over cables 30
    Communicating the news 32
    Radio and the geopolitics of propaganda 33
    Propaganda in 'gentlemanly' tones 34
    The global 'voice' of America during the Cold War 36

Challenging the Western narrative 37
Communicating a cultural Cold War 38
*The Cold War battle for 'hearts and minds' in the
  'Third World' 41*

2 Globalization of communication – constructing and
  servicing a neo-liberal world   48
  *Infrastructure for the internet: US domination of space
    and sea 51*
  Cabling the world for the internet age 53
  Policy infrastructure: who controls the internet? 56
  Challenges to the US-led communication infrastructure 57
  *Epistemic communities: providing the software for the
    global communication system 61*
  Think tanks: how the fifth estate influences the fourth 62
  Intellectual infrastructure: universities and publishing 67

3 Digital democracy vs. digital imperialism   74
  Digital capitalism 78
  Digitally enabled capitalism 79
  Platforms for digital imperialism? 83
  Digital empires and democracy? 85
  *The 'authoritarian' BATS: digital capitalism with Chinese
    characteristics 87*
  *Checking digital imperialism? Cyber sovereignty vs free
    data flows 90*
  The authoritarian challenge 95

4 Geopolitics of communicating conflict: wars and image wars   100
  Growth in global conflict 101
  Exporting democracy by war and peace 103
  The invasions of Iraq and strategic communication 105
  The chemical attack in the Syrian civil war 111
  Public relations and image wars 112
  Afghanistan: the geopolitics of 'the forever war' 115
  Africa's invisible wars 118
  *The Russian invasion of Ukraine – covering the 'white
    man's war'? 121*
  Ukraine's propaganda blitz 123
  Privatization of conflict management 126

5   Weaponizing global communication: cyberwars,
    surveillance and spying   130
    Digital warfare: the weaponization of information in the
        Ukraine war 130
    Cyberwars 136
    Global covert spying and overt surveillance 140
    China spying 143
    Disinformation dilemmas 148
    Covid-19 as a global 'infodemic' 155
    Information weaponization on steroids – AI 158
    Wider dangers of AI 161

6   Emerging contours of a new global communication order   167
    Is BRICS building an alternative geopolitical order? 169
    Towards de-globalization? 174
    Sino-globalization via the Belt and Road Initiative 175
    Communicating Sino-globalization 177
    Changing geopolitics of 'digital for development' 182
    The Chinese model of development 183
    An Indian model in the making 185
    Decolonizing the study of geopolitics and global
        communication 190

Bibliography   *196*
Index   *253*

ABOUT THE AUTHOR

Daya Kishan Thussu is Professor of International Communication at the Hong Kong Baptist University and President of the International Association for Media and Communication Research (IAMCR). In 2018–2019, he was a visiting distinguished professor and Inaugural Disney Chair in Global Media at Schwarzman College, Tsinghua University, Beijing. Prior to that, for many years he was Professor of International Communication at the University of Westminster in London, where he was also founder and co-director of India Media Centre as well as research advisor to the China Media Centre. With a PhD in international relations from Jawaharlal Nehru University in New Delhi, he is the author or editor of 20 books, notably *International Communication: Continuity and Change*, third edition published in 2019 by Bloomsbury Academic. Since 2005, he has been the managing editor of the Sage journal *Global Media and Communication*. He is also series editor for two book series for Routledge: *Internationalizing Media Studies* and *Routledge Advances in Internationalizing Media Studies*.

INTRODUCTION

Geopolitics and global communication

The genesis of this book coincided with fundamental changes in global geopolitics. Its aim – a pioneering effort to connect global geopolitics with global communication – was to examine how the 'rise of the rest', especially China, was changing the global order, at a time when the US-led West was in decline and its globalization project on different levels was unravelling. During the course of writing the book, a succession of new and unforeseen developments rapidly reshaped the global geopolitical terrain and its mediatization: from the US-China trade war to a global pandemic, the Russian invasion of Ukraine and its aftermath, in parallel with turbo-charged technological advances, such as artificial intelligence (AI). Processing this vast amount of information and trying to analyse its multiple and multi-layered geopolitical implications was a daunting intellectual enterprise.

Having spent a quarter of a century researching and writing about international communication in London, arguably the best place to study such a field, I was fortunate to be offered, in 2018, the Disney Chair in Global Media at Schwarzman College in Tsinghua University in Beijing. During that academic year, I taught a course with the same title as this book to a small group of Schwarzman Scholars, who joined this prestigious college after a rigorous and highly competitive selection process to prepare them for 'global leadership'. The interactions with such a highly skilled and talented group of young minds provided fresh ideas and perspectives for the book. It is rare for academics to experience geopolitics as it unfolds and to have the opportunity to record and to reflect on the import of such events. This is precisely what happened as I started a new job at a university in Hong Kong in August 2019, at the height of the anti-Beijing unrest. I realized that this protest movement had much wider geopolitical implications: in effect, the beginning of what came to be known as a 'new' Cold War, between the United States and China.

Hong Kong: 'Asia's World City' caught in a global geopolitical game

The massive protests in summer 2019 against a proposed extradition bill that would allow criminal suspects in Hong Kong to be tried on the mainland received blanket coverage in the mainstream Western media, almost coinciding with the advent of the US-China trade war. With hundreds of thousands of mostly young protesters paralysing normal life from June 2019 to the end of the year, the Hong Kong story was headline news internationally. Fortunately, despite regular and consistent reporting of police atrocities in the Western media, though many were injured in the regular and often violent confrontations, only one protester lost his life (that too in an accident) in those six months. In contrast, during the same period, anti-government protests in other parts of the world – in Chile, France and most tragically in Iraq – received scant international coverage, including the fact that in October 2019, more than 100 protesters were killed in anti-regime protests in Baghdad.

Such double standards in reporting clearly demonstrate the geopolitical priorities of the dominant global media outlets. The protests in Hong Kong provided a perfect opportunity to point out the repressive policies of China in terms of ruthlessly crushing dissent and asserting its control over the Special Administrative Region. For their part, the overwhelmingly young protestors cleverly used their digital tactics to amplify a local protest into a global media event. Skilfully avoiding a digital footprint, they used anonymous and encrypted social networking platforms such as Telegram, as well as ubiquitous live streams (Hui, 2019) and projected the protests as spontaneous, even leaderless, aware that the authorities had prosecuted and imprisoned the leaders of the 79 days of protests in 2014, known as the Umbrella Movement (Lee and Chan, 2018; Dapiran, 2022).

Nevertheless, 'media faces' such as Joshua Wong were given extensive coverage in the Western media: he later wrote a book about his experiences which received considerable traction in US–UK media (Wong and Ng, 2020). Another leader, Nathan Law – the youngest Legislative Councillor, now in exile in London – also received extensive media coverage. In 2018, Nathan, Wong and another student leader Alex Chow were nominated for the Nobel Peace Prize by US congressmen and British parliament members. In 2020, Law was an invited speaker at the Oslo Freedom Forum, described by the *Economist* as the 'Davos for human rights,' and *Time* magazine included his name in the 100 most influential people in the world. His book, written with journalist Evan Fowler (Law, 2021), was reviewed extensively, and he even spoke at the 'Summit for Democracy' hosted by the Biden administration, the only speaker from Hong Kong.

The protesters were able to 'appeal to the global media directly (not least of all in English)' and conscious that they were 'the "chosen," free people of China whose messages about tyranny and "communist colonization" will be well received' (Vukovich, 2020: 202). Images of British and American flags being waved in many demonstrations, as well as of the protesting leaders with US consulate officials, were distributed widely by the Chinese government propaganda machine, suggesting in hardly subtle terms that the protesters were being manipulated by 'foreign forces', demonstrating the wider geopolitical dimensions to the protests. In November of that year, US President Donald Trump signed the Hong Kong Human Rights and Democracy Act, further escalating the tension. The coverage of the protests in the Chinese official media was declared by Britain's broadcasting regulator Ofcom in breach of the broadcasting code, citing five programmes broadcast on the China Global Television Network (CGTN) between 11 August 2019 and 21 November 2019. CGTN's licence was revoked so that it is no longer available in the United Kingdom.

Media freedom in Hong Kong was under threat even before the protests: in 2016, for example, a senior editor of *Ming Pao Daily News* was dismissed after the newspaper took part in the International Consortium of Investigative Journalists' publication of the Panama Papers leaks, which exposed the offshore wealth of some of China's elites, a very Chinese version of 'media capture' (Frisch et al., 2018). The arrests of journalists, notably Jimmy Lai, the founder and owner of the pro-Western *Apple Daily*, Hong Kong's most popular newspaper, in operation since 1995, reinforced the Western discourse about growing authoritarianism in what was considered an oasis of freedom and democracy. In December 2021, staff at *Stand News*, one of the few remaining independent voices, were arrested on suspicion of 'conspiracy to print or distribute seditious materials', forcing the pro-democracy online outlet to cease publication. In 2021, the Hong Kong broadcaster TVB did not broadcast the Academy Awards for the first time in more than half a century of this annual gala event, ostensibly because a documentary on the protests 'Do Not Split' had been nominated for an Oscar in the 'documentary short' category (Zeitchik, 2021). Accounts from veteran British (Vines, 2021) and Australian (Clifford, 2022) journalists with long associations with Hong Kong media, as well as academic work (Luqiu, 2021; Hung, 2022, among others), attest to this trend.

It is worth recalling that, as a British colony and a major hub for Western media organizations, Hong Kong was and remains a significant territory geopolitically, apart from its position as a financial centre. During the Cold War years, it was a nodal point for Western news organizations covering the region: US weekly newsmagazines such as *Asiaweek* and *Far Eastern Economic Review* were based in the territory, as were, for a period, clandestine US propaganda networks like Radio Free Asia. While the Western and more specifically the British media extolled the virtues of their rule in the territory, the grim reality was that structural discrimination was rife, as elsewhere in British empire, in terms of how the 'natives' were barred from certain premises and public facilities and how they were treated in judicial proceedings. It was only in 1989 that a Chinese person was appointed as the commissioner of police, while the post of attorney general was held by a Briton until 1997. The question of censorship, too, is revealing; as a recent study has shown, the media were 'pervasively' censored during much of the colonial period (Ng, 2022).

While Hong Kong's economic and financial systems remain distinct, in the Beijing-installed new government of Hong Kong, only 'patriots' can serve in positions of authority. Politically, the space for civil society has contracted and media freedoms have been curtailed. A US government report provided examples 'of doxing and malicious cyber activities', to 'intimidate Hongkongers and silence pro-democracy speech online', adding that the state broadcaster RTHK has been tamed too and the Hong Kong authorities have threatened foreign media outlets with legal consequences over the content of their editorials (Department of State, 2023). An editorial in *China Daily* rebutted these arguments, suggesting that by admitting that the measures were 'directly threatening US interests in Hong Kong', the US State Department revealed the true nature of its complaint: 'What China has done is to remove the US tumours that had been growing in Hong Kong and strengthened its institutional resistance to any reappearance' (*China Daily*, 2023a).

What the West failed to understand was why a large section of the Hong Kong elite might be keen to be aligned with Beijing for pragmatic rather than ideological reasons. One commentator has labelled the Hong Kong elite as '*kuashang*' (straddling businessmen), whose strategies reflect 'a pragmatic style of thinking in which private-sector Hong Kong elites continuously read the shifting international terrain of power' (Hamilton, 2021: 12). They also recognized that their future lay with Beijing and not with the West, despite verbal and material support from Washington, Brussels and London. One researcher claimed that the 'Hong Kong issue' heralded the arrival of the geopolitical 'new cold war', as it led to US-imposed sanctions on China (Toru, 2020: 95).

Trumpism and the erosion of US global influence

The election of Donald Trump as the president of the United States in 2016 – a business tycoon and a rank outsider to the public life, whose sole claim to fame was hosting for years a popular NBC reality television show *The Apprentice* – eroded the status of arguably the most important public office in the world. Apart from the controversy associated with his campaign and election, including alleged support from Russia and business interests in many other countries, Trump's attitude towards mainstream media in the United States was indicative of the changing relationship between discourse creators (the political elite) and its distributors (the media). On several occasions, Trump accused the leading liberal media, including the CNN and the *New York Times*, of promoting 'fake' news, instead using social media platforms – notably Twitter (now X) to communicate. Making an intellectual case for Trump were conservative think tanks, such as the California-based Claremont Institute, whose quarterly journal *The Claremont Review of Books* published an 'anti-anti-Trump' essay in December 2016, arguing that 'such a flawed contender could be a front-runner tells us more about what's wrong with the country than about what's wrong with his followers' (quoted in Zerofsky, 2022).

Trump's assault on the integrity of news media at a time when the journalism industry in the United States and elsewhere is struggling to sustain itself was welcomed by a large number of news consumers, increasingly cynical towards the mainstream media and looking for myriad alternative voices available online (Carlson et al., 2021). This new media ecology encouraged the circulation of unedited, unsubstantiated content, with scant regard to facts, on digital networks and contributing to the new genre of 'fact-checking' (Walter et al., 2020).

For his political campaigning, Trump depended on such conservative cable networks as One America News Network (launched in 2013) and Newsmax, started on cable in 2014. Some scholars saw, in the political ascent of Trump, a deeper malaise afflicting American democracy (see essays in Tucker and Persily, 2020), while others viewed this as a sign of the 'degeneration' of the cultural and moral foundations of liberal societies, with growing inequalities and stagnation and the breakdown of social institutions, exacerbating political polarization (Calhoun et al., 2022).

> As Biden took office in 2020, he wrote in *Foreign Affairs* that Trump had belittled, undermined, and in some cases abandoned U.S. allies and partners. He has turned on our own intelligence professionals, diplomats, and troops. . . . Most profoundly, he has turned away from the democratic values that give strength to our nation and unify us as a people.
>
> *(Biden, 2020)*

Under the Trump presidency, the United States withdrew from such international bodies as the World Health Organization (WHO) and UNESCO, as well as abandoned the Paris Climate Agreement.

Writing to mark the 30th issue of the *Journal of Democracy*, a journal associated with the National Endowment for Democracy, Francis Fukuyama noted two opposite trends – social fragmentation and the decline of the authority of mediating institutions, primarily in democracies, and the rise of new centralized hierarchies in authoritarian states (Fukuyama, 2020). Some have argued that the most dangerous form of threat to modern democracies is not the military coup but rather the steady, gradual erosion of norms and institutions (Levitsky and Ziblatt, 2018), while others were concerned about the alleged threat from 'sharp' powers (Walker, 2018) like Russia and China (Diamond, 2019), subverting the liberal democratic foundations of global geopolitics.

The imperial origins of the concept of geopolitics

Geopolitics is the study of the effects of geography (human and physical) and economics on international politics/relations, with a focus on the relationship between the physical environment (territory, locations, resources and so forth) and the conduct of foreign policy. 'The study of geopolitics', it has been suggested, 'is the study of the spatialization of international politics by core powers and hegemonic states' (Tuathail and Agnew, 1992: 192). Geopolitics should 'be viewed as the effects of space, topography, position and climate on political behaviour' (Starr and Siverson, 1990: 235). Critical readings of geopolitics suggest that it is an imperfect expression, as it

> names not a singularity but a multiplicity, an ensemble of heterogeneous intellectual efforts to think through the geographical dimensions and implications of the transformative effects of changing technologies of transportation, communications, and warfare on the accumulation and exercise of power in the new world order of 'closed space'.
>
> *(Ó Tuathail, 1996: 12)*

The so-called geopolitical tradition can be attributed to the work of Western intellectuals who helped to 'codify a mode of reasoning about international affairs' that would, in the context of the World War II, 'come to be organized and categorized as constituting a geopolitical tradition' (Ó Tuathail, 1996: 16). Coined by Swedish political scientist Rudolf Kjellén at the turn of the last century, the term *Geopolitik* became popular in Europe after World War I and gained global currency after World War II, primarily as an analysis of the geographic influences on power relationships. Kjellén's influence was particularly strong in Germany, where *Geopolitik* took on an ideological meaning during the Nazi regime. Karl Haushofer, a German army officer, widely recognized as the 'father of geopolitics', was a political geographer and leading proponent of geopolitics, who, in 1924, founded and was the editor of *Zeitschrift für Geopolitik* (*Journal for Geopolitics*), as well as the director of the Institute of Geopolitics at the University of Munich. As a recent biography notes, Haushofer's theories of *Autarky* and *Lebensraum* were a crucial influence on the Nazi regime with the rationale for Germany's control of Europe and the world. He and his colleagues propagated the theory of the 'pan-region', encompassing an industrial centre and a periphery, and suggested that four regions – pan-Europe dominated by Germany, pan-Asia by Japan, pan-America by the United States, and pan-Russia by the Soviet Union – were likely to emerge as an intermediate stage before global German dominance. As Herwig has counselled, the 'demon' of *Geopolitik* demands closer scrutiny in this new age of geopolitics (Herwig, 2016).

Britain, too, saw geopolitics as an imperial project: the industrial capabilities of transportation, communication (railroads, steamships, airplanes and telegraphy) interacting with the geographical features of the earth, would shape the emerging global international system. Alfred Mahan argued that the control of sea routes was central to the rise of the British Empire, while his compatriot political geographer Halford Mackinder suggested that land power would trump sea power, arguing that the interior regions of Eurasia ('the heartland') had become the strategic centre of the 'World Island,' as a result of the relative decline of sea power. Mackinder's 'heartland' theory suggested that any state that was able to control the heartland would control a worldwide empire. Mackinder is the source of many of the ideas of geopolitics that have been repeatedly rediscovered and reinvented to comprehend the ideology and practices of the US Empire (Kearns, 2009). The popularity of geopolitical theory declined after World War II, partly because of its association with Nazi Germany and mostly because of the emergence of nuclear warfare, reducing the significance of geographical factors in the global strategic balance of power. However, geopolitics continued to influence international politics, serving as the basis for the United States' Cold War policy of containment as a geopolitical strategy to limit the expansion of the Soviet communism.

In the Soviet Union, the victory over Germany was presented by party propagandists as a victory for all humanity, in contrast with the Western powers who fought it for their own geopolitical interests and to save their imperial possessions. The third edition of the *Great Soviet Encyclopedia*, published during the regime of Leonid Brezhnev, defined 'geopolitics' as a 'bourgeois, reactionary conception' based on the idea of the nation-state as a geographic and biological organism seeking to expand, the opposite of the ideology of borderless international socialism, and noted that geopolitics 'became the official doctrine of Fascism' (quoted in Petrov, 2018: 20). Commentators retrospectively defend expansionist policies of the Soviet Union, for example the forced 'Sovietization of neighbouring countries' with reference to geopolitics. Russian political analyst Alexander Dugin is credited with helping revive the concept of *Novorossiya* or 'New Russia' – the term invoked in the 18th century for lands the Russian empire had captured from the Ottomans as a nationalist driver for Russian ambitions. He is also the lead propagator of the idea of *Russky Mir* or 'Russian world' anchored in both imperial nostalgia and Orthodox Christian identity. In his 1997 best-selling book, *Foundations of Geopolitics*, Dugin argued that Russia as a civilization-state should be at the heart of a 'Eurasian empire', stretching from Vladivostok to Europe to challenge the maritime power of the US 'liberal empire'.

Critical geopolitics

Much of traditional geopolitical theorizing emerged in Europe during the age of empire (Agnew, 2003). Geopolitical thought – a view of the world that can be captured from one (European) viewpoint – emerged as a part of European exploration and colonialism and later evolved into legitimizing the balance-of-power politics of the 19th and 20th centuries (Ó Tuathail, 1996).

Such Eurocentric expositions of geopolitics have led to accounts of world history that leave out most of the world (Slater, 2004). More recently, a more global world history is being reclaimed. One historian has shown how the sea routes of Asia transformed a vast expanse of the globe during the past 500 years, powerfully shaping the modern world. The volume of traffic across Asian sea routes – an area stretching from East Africa and the Middle East to Japan – grew dramatically, eventually making them the busiest in the world. The result was a massive circulation of people, commodities, religion, culture, technology and ideas (Tagliacozzo, 2022).

As one Indian commentator noted:

> The classical geopoliticians were children of their age and looked at Asian geopolitics through a late nineteenth-century European or British lens, concentrating on the European hegemony that followed the breakup or decline of the classical Asian empires, namely, the Mughals in India, the Ming and early Qing in China, the Ottomans in Türkiye, and the Safavids in Iran.
>
> *(Menon, 2021: 20)*

The Indian subcontinent was 'both the pivot of the Indian Ocean world and also a self-contained geopolitical unit and could choose its engagement with the rest of the world' (ibid.: 13). The first Prime Minister of India Jawaharlal Nehru, in his book, *The Discovery of India*, saw geopolitics and power politics as the handmaidens of fascism, national socialism and imperialism. For him, geopolitics was 'the anchor of the realist', and 'its jargon of 'heartland' and 'rimland' was a 'partial truth [which] is sometimes more dangerous than a falsehood'. He argued that 'the old policy of expansion and empire and the balance of power ... inevitably leads to conflict and war' (cited in ibid.: 29).

In more recent years, the trend towards critical geopolitics has challenged the notions of space and spatiality, arguing that it is not confined to territoriality but includes popular geopolitics (Ó Tuathail and Agnew 1992: 190). This strand of analysis approaches geopolitics not as a neutral consideration of pregiven 'geographical' facts but as a deeply ideological and politicized form of analysis. Critical geopolitics seeks to unpack the rigid territorial assumptions of traditional geopolitical thinking. Post–Cold War geopolitics reveals the continued reliance on binary understandings of power and spatiality, on notions of East and West, security and danger, freedom and oppression, for example how the 'war on terror' works with these same binaries (see essays in Ó Tuathail and Dalby, 1998). Beyond nation-states, geopolitics operates also at a supranational level: positive claims about European integration overcoming nationalist narratives of territory and identity are premised on deep assumptions about Europe as a privileged territorial and cultural unit, while the European Union (EU) considers itself as a geopolitical entity. Much of critical geopolitics focuses empirically on the core states of the West, especially the United States. This is not surprising given that US foreign policy, scholarship and popular culture have been hegemonic in the exercise of geopolitics.

Outside the elite realms of state power, there are other agents of geopolitics: popular media, cartoons, films and social activists (Power and Crampton, 2005). The representations of popular geopolitics in relation to the 'war on terror' (Dodds and Ingram, 2009) constitute what has been variously described as the 'Military Industrial-Media-Entertainment Network' (Der Derian, 2009), 'militainment' (Stahl, 2010) and the 'Military-Entertainment Complex' (Lenoir and

Caldwell, 2018). Also significant is the 'feminist geopolitics', which engages with actors and locations outside the formal sphere of the state, emphasising the 'personal is also geopolitical' (Dixon, 2015). Others have proposed a framework of 'meta-geopolitics', adding new dimensions of geopolitics to offer a multidimensional view of power – soft and hard power – and its exercise in maintaining or enhancing international relations (Al-Rodhan, 2009).

Another important shift is the increasing role of digital diasporas in a 'new wave of human geopolitics' (Gamlen, 2019: 7), increasingly connected on the internet which enables geographically dispersed members to connect with one another and negotiate their identity (Brinkerhoff, 2009). The 'domestic abroad' has a crucial role in international relations (Varadarajan, 2010), indicated by the growing profile of the Indian-American diaspora – the second-largest immigrant group in the United States. From CEOs of major global corporations to highly educated professionals and even White House power brokers, their ascent reflects their economic, political and social influence, which the successive Indian governments have tried to encash as a soft power resource (Thussu, 2013a; Chakravorty et al., 2017; Badrinathan et al., 2021).

The Chinese government and the communist party engage actively with their diaspora, especially the influential Chinese communities in the United States and in Britain (Liu, 2022). China has consistently deployed – though not always successfully – 'diaspora statecraft' to promote the country's geopolitical and strategic interests (Wong, 2022). For the Russian government, Russians or Russophones living abroad are conceptualized as *sootechestvenniki* (compatriots), and the Russian language is considered one of the most salient markers of their identity rather than ethnicity or nationality (Cheshkin and Kachuyevski, 2018). Geopolitically *Russkiy Mir* was conceived as a Russian 'diaspora empire', with particular importance continually placed on the 'Russian enclaves' in its 'near abroad'.

How global geopolitics is changing

Thirty years after the end of the Cold War, the US-shaped world order is changing: there is a perceptible decline in US power and a corresponding rise in the influence of large non-Western nations, primarily China. Some see this seismic shift indicative of the fall of the neoliberal order (Gerstle, 2022). Others have raised doubts about the phenomenon of globalization itself for its failure to live up to its much-hyped potential to create a globally interdependent society, witnessed in the rise of right-wing populism and religious fundamentalism (Hafez and Grüne, 2022). As historian Paul Kennedy has surmised in the epilogue of his sweeping history, a 500-year survey of rise and fall of great powers:

> so far as the international system is concerned, wealth and power or economic strength and military strength are relative . . . and since all societies are subject to the inexorable tendency to change, then international balances can *never* be still, and it is a folly of statesmanship to assume that they ever would be.
>
> *(Kennedy, 1988: 536, italics in original)*

Others have suggested that in contrast to Western notions of liberal universalism, China and Russia define themselves as civilizational states, with unique cultural values and political institutions as a form of cultural exceptionalism (Copeland, 2022). This is already having 'a profound impact upon the physical realm of international relations and the informational representations of it' (Chifu and Simons, 2023: 5). A Bloomberg analysis declared the end of 'great age of globalization' as China and Russia joined hands (Micklethwait and Wooldridge, 2022), while a US think tank report argued that the speeches and writings of Chinese President Xi Jinping and Russian President Vladimir Putin emphasize the superiority of autocratic systems and the failings of democracy (Kroenig, 2020). Some even detect vestiges of an imperial revivalism among former Eurasian empires such as China and Russia, exploiting new opportunities engendered by a polycentric world to project power within and beyond their borders in patterns shaped by their respective imperial pasts (Mankoff, 2022). This recalling of an imperial legacy is also relevant to the 'liberal' West: British colonialism was, above all, the business of corporations, what a recent study has described as 'venture colonialism', which has survived the end of empire (Stern, 2023). The emergence of China and Russia has ended the period of unipolarity and ushered in an era of multipolarity, which is more reminiscent of those earlier eras (Mearsheimer, 2018).

Calibrating the China challenge

The geopolitical rivalry between the United States and China, triggering the so-called new Cold War (Li and Fang, 2022), resembles the inter-imperial rivalry among the great powers at the turn of the 20th century (Hung, 2022). Hung argues that this was provoked by the global expansion of China's state-backed corporations, coupled with the export of industrial overcapacity. Both the United States and China are seeking to establish positions of centrality in the networks of trade, production and consumption, through which power will be projected (Schindler and DiCarlo, 2023).

The 2018 National Security Strategy of the United States defined the long-term, strategic competition with China as the central challenge to US prosperity and security (Wang and Tanner, 2021) and indicated that China was a significant threat to the 'liberal international order' (Ogden, 2022). The CIA director William Burns announced a new mission centre focused on China, which he called 'the most important geopolitical threat we face in the 21st century' (Harris, 2021). It was argued by security hawks in the United States that 'decoupling with China – first in trade and then in technology and finance – would reduce China's economic growth potential significantly, and thus contain its power' (Pei, 2019: 1). China is already the world's second-largest economy: in 2023, for the fifth consecutive year, China topped the *Fortune Global 500* list in terms of the number of companies – 142 (including Hong Kong), followed by the United States at 136 (Fortune, 2024).

China's global ambitions are best represented by its Belt and Road Initiative (BRI), which is the central plank of its strategy 'to implement the Global Development Initiative, the Global Security Initiative and the Global Civilization Initiative' and build 'a global community of shared future' (Government of China, 2023). Scholars have argued that BRI is a geopolitical rather than economic project, in which political elites from the global South have been coopted by Beijing with the aim of creating a new China-led global order in the form of a non-territorial 'empire' (Tudoroiu, 2024).

BRI at 10: the geopolitics of the world's largest infrastructure project

Coined in the 19th century by the German geographer Ferdinand von Richthofen, the phrase 'the silk roads' (*die Seidenstrassen*) has been revived by China in recent decades as the BRI (Frankopan, 2018). Marking the tenth anniversary of setting up the BRI, it is officially defined as the

> long-term, transnational and systematic global project of the 21st century. It has succeeded in taking its first step on a long journey . . . [it] will demonstrate greater creativity and vitality, become more open and inclusive, and generate new opportunities for both China and the rest of the world.
>
> *(Government of China, 2023)*

Launched in 2013 by President Xi as 'One Belt One Road', this has morphed into the largest and the most influential infrastructural and investment initiative in modern history (Schneider, 2021; Ahmed and Lambert, 2022). By 2023, as many as 152 countries as well as 32 international organizations were involved in the BRI, generating trade and investment in the past decade in the range of more than two trillion dollars (although Italy was the only G-7 country to join BRI, it announced its withdrawal as the 'de-risking' discourse became dominant in the West). The geopolitical significance of such a massive and global infrastructural project can be gauged by comparing it with the post-Second World War Marshall Plan, undertaken by the United States between 1948 and 1951 with $13.3 billion to rebuild war-torn Western Europe. Seventy years later, the United States is very much still present in Europe – militarily, politically and culturally – and arguably shaping its foreign policy. The BRI has a much wider geographical range, ambition and investment, and it will hardly be surprising if it leaves an indelible Chinese mark on large parts of the globe (Frankopan, 2018; Maçães, 2018; Freymann, 2020; Carney, 2023).

Apart from constructing heavy infrastructure – roads, ports and airports – the BRI is increasingly focusing on 'digital silk roads', with ambition to dominate the physical infrastructure underlying global digital communications and a potential advantage in internationalizing its formidable tech sector (Freymann, 2020). In this expansion, China's digital corporations such as Tencent (Tang, 2019; Chen,

2023) and Alibaba (Wong, 2022) have played a crucial role. Researchers from a Berlin-based think tank Mercator Institute for China Studies note that this digital outreach is 'fundamentally linked to competition between systems, and China's differences with the principles of the liberal market economy, free trade and liberal democracy' (Shi-Kupfer and Ohlberg, 2019: 46).

The BRI forms part of China's concerted efforts to focus on the global South (Tudoroiu and Kuteleva, 2022). India opposes the BRI due to the fact that parts of its flagship programme, the China-Pakistan Economic Corridor, cross the disputed border between the two Asian giants. China is now the largest aid giver to the developing world (Dreher et al., 2022), giving it unprecedented power to influence geopolitics in the global South including challenging the existing rules of the liberal international system (Murphy, 2022).

In 2021, the US magazine *Politico* published a 5,000-word article attributed to Anonymous, a 'former senior government official with deep expertise and experience dealing with China', which suggested that one of China's key priorities was to transform the BRI 'into a geopolitical bloc as an infrastructural foundation for a Sino-centric global order' (Anonymous, 2021). In the same year, China announced its intention to construct a 'Polar Silk Road' – to extend its BRI project and participate in the development of Arctic shipping routes (Doshi et al., 2021). Despite being a non-Arctic state, China became an observer member of the Arctic Council in 2013, and its presence is increasing in the resource-rich region with huge potential for exploration as 'longer periods of an ice-free Arctic make the Arctic attractive' (Nilsson and Christensen, 2019: 5).

The view of China as the main source of challenges to the global system was heightened during another world-changing event, the global pandemic of Covid-19, which emerged in China in late 2019 and spread across the globe. It has been argued that this altered the global order, slowing processes of globalization and even promoting de-globalization: 'The pandemic has prompted an anachronism, a revival of the walled city in an age when prosperity depends on global trade and movement of people' (Kissinger, 2020). It was also framed as another example of the geopolitical contest between the United States and China (Ameyaw-Brobbey, 2021; Kahl and Wright, 2021), and textbooks on geopolitics now take on board the geopolitical implications of the global pandemic (Flint, 2022).

The geopolitics of a global pandemic

From the outset, China's image was damaged by its reluctance to share information about the most serious health emergency in a century (Cosentino, 2023). Although the first documented location of community spread was the wet market in Wuhan on 17 November 2019, it was not until 31 December that the Chinese government formally notified the WHO of this outbreak. The authorities sought to control the Covid-19 narrative to defend the Party's actions. Dr. Li Wenliang, who on

December 30 informed colleagues that he had treated several cases resembling SARS, was publicly reprimanded and forced to sign an apology for 'disturbing the social order'. Li subsequently contracted Covid-19 and died, becoming a folk hero on Chinese social media (BBC, 2020a). A *Washington Post* editorial cast doubts about 'China's ability to mount an effective response to a transnational crisis emanating from within its borders' and questioned what 'key leaders knew, and when they knew it' (*Washington Post*, 2020). Trump repeatedly accused Beijing of not maintaining an open, transparent and responsible approach to the pandemic, publicly referring to the virus as the 'Chinese virus' or 'Wuhan virus', and demanding compensation from China for the economic costs of the pandemic (White House, 2020).

For their part, the Chinese media highlighted how the Chinese lockdown model was superior to the more laissez-faire approach of the West, which was slow to respond and where many more people succumbed to the pandemic than in China. It used the pandemic to demonstrate leadership in global health, deploying 'mask diplomacy' (distributing face masks and other personal protective equipment [PPE]), followed by 'vaccine diplomacy' (sending Chinese-made vaccines, especially to the global South). 'Such attempts to project soft power and expand international influence (and garner goodwill) were accompanied by aggressive tactics to shape the global health agenda in China's favour' (Huang, 2022: 2). Despite this, China received a negative coverage in the Western media, with the suggestion that it was manipulating the functioning of the WHO.

The geopolitics of the vaccine economy was evident from the fact that Western pharmaceutical companies did not allow India and South Africa to develop generic vaccines (Desai, 2023), rejecting their appeal to the World Trade Organization (WTO) to provide a waiver to 'intellectual property related to Covid-19 drugs, vaccines, diagnostics and other technologies for the duration of the pandemic, until global herd immunity is achieved' (WTO, 2020). Subtle and not-so-subtle pressures – directly and indirectly – were exerted on the countries in the global South to use the vaccines developed by the United States, despite its exorbitant cost. The first country actually to develop its own vaccine against the virus was Russia – whose Sputnik was released in August 2020, but the WHO and other medical bodies discouraged its distribution globally, partly for commercial reasons. As the world emerged from the crisis of the pandemic, in February 2022, Ukraine was invaded by Russia, in clear violation of international law, which had major geopolitical reverberations.

The Russian invasion of Ukraine: geopolitical rifts and shifts

The Russian invasion of Ukraine in February 2022 has demonstrated the limits of Western powers to shape the global agenda, as large sections of the world saw it as a regional not a global crisis. It also exposed the extent to which the EU – without a coherent defence or foreign policy – was dependent on the United States. The conflict witnessed the most stringent sanctions imposed by the West on any country, an act of 'economic warfare' with a long history, going back to the inter-war years, and which, a new study notes, created 'the structure of the political and economic order that we inhabit today' (Mulder, 2022: 3). In the past 80 years, the United States has deployed economic sanctions against the Soviet Union, China, Cuba, Vietnam, Iran and Iraq as well as against South Africa's apartheid system.

The United States and the EU blocked major Russian banks from using SWIFT (Society for Worldwide Interbank Financial Telecommunication), the financial-communication system that facilitates the transfer of money around the world, a move which was described by the French finance minister as a 'financial nuclear weapon' (Leali, 2022). Despite dire predictions from Western experts that the Russian economy would collapse in three months, it not only survived but also experienced modest growth, while Europe's biggest economy, Germany, was in recession. What the West did not take fully into account was how the forging of new geopolitical and economic ties outside the Euro-Atlantic zone, between Russia and other large economies, notably China and India, would undermine the sanctions regime.

The communications aspect of the event followed the usual Western narrative in media coverage: the invasion was led by an 'irrational' and 'unwell' leader of an authoritarian state, who threatened use of weapons of mass destruction – 'nuclear war' (Zajec, 2022). This was used to justify the enormous military aid given to Ukraine, the United States spending more than $100 billion, while the EU pledged $96 billion – a windfall for defence companies – supplying sophisticated weaponry, including the Patriot missile system. The *Washington Post* revealed in an exclusive report that the Central Intelligence Agency (CIA) was working closely with Ukrainian intelligence service, the SBU, and its military counterpart, the GUR, having spent since 2015 'tens of millions of dollars' to transform these services into potent allies against Moscow. Intercepted communications from Russian military and intelligence units, it reported, are relayed through the new CIA-built facility to Washington, where it is 'scrutinized by CIA and NSA' (Miller and Khurshudyan, 2023).

Any pretence of this being not a proxy war was dispelled by the German Foreign Minister Annalena Baerbock when she claimed at the Parliamentary Assembly of the Council of Europe in January 2023 that European nations were 'fighting a war against Russia' and must do more to defend Ukraine. She went on to comment at the Munich Security Conference that Russian President Vladimir Putin must 'change by 360 degrees' for Ukraine to be safe. Such unprofessionalism provoked much derision among commentators and not just in Moscow.

Some of these ideas stem from a stream of thought deeply rooted within Europe, which views Russia as 'the Other', and Russophobia fundamental to propaganda (Gleeson, 1950). The conflict in Russia's 'near abroad' is projected by the West as a contest between democracy and authoritarianism and between European integration and Russian 'imperialism' (Diesen, 2022). One account, originally in French, and translated into Russian, Italian and German, has argued that Russophobia was supplanted after 1917 by 'Sovietophobia' (Mettan, 2017), while another scholar argues that anti-Soviet/Russia sentiment in the United States – including Reagan's 'Evil Empire' jibe – emanates from the myth that Russia is intrinsically anti-Western, illiberal and expansionist (Tsygankov, 2009: 14–15). Given such a history, the West's role in contributing to the conflict in Ukraine is often ignored in mainstream Western media: its support for toppling President Viktor Yanukovych in February 2014 sparked a crisis in eastern Ukraine, while the Minsk-2 agreement, a year later, which offered a compromise, was undermined by the United States, followed by the EU.

That the Russian-dominated regions of Ukraine might have reasons to be apprehensive rarely forms part of the Western discourse. Under their 'de-Russification' programme, Ukrainians were 'trying to erase Russia – and the Russian language – from their culture and landscape'. This effort to 'decolonize' Ukraine has its roots in the movement to 'de-communize' the country during the so-called Maidan Revolution of 2013–2014 (Mellen et al., 2023).

Despite intense diplomatic pressure from the United States and its Western allies, much of the global South did not isolate Russia diplomatically, especially at the United Nations (UN). India and the United Arab Emirates abstained from crucial votes, and 35 countries – representing almost 50 per cent of the world population – abstained or voted 'no' on resolution to condemn the Russian invasion on 2 March 2022. While Ukrainian President Volodymyr Zelensky received standing ovations wherever he spoke – in Western parliaments, film festivals and security conferences – when he addressed the African Union in June 2022, only four out of 55 invited heads of state attended the virtual session (BBC, 2022c).

The myth of the EU as an autonomous geopolitical actor

When she assumed office, the European Commission President, Ursula von der Leyen, defined it as a 'geopolitical Commission', although the EU's policy in the global arena is often seen outside the Euro-Atlantic space as following dictates from across the ocean. On Ukraine for example, the EU generally supported Washington's agenda of legitimizing the eastward expansion of NATO at considerable social, political and economic cost to itself. When the French-supported regimes in the Sahel region were replaced by Moscow-friendly governments in 2022–2023, the EU was largely absent, as was the case when Azerbaijan took over Nagorno-Karabakh in 2023, expelling more than 100,000 Armenians from the enclave.

At the heart of the EU project is Germany, the powerhouse of the EU, which made itself strong in the post-Cold War period by pursuing three key policies: ensuring a regular supply of cheap gas from Russia; exporting its high-end industrial products to China, one of the world's biggest markets, and importing raw materials for its booming industry from China, and lastly, unlike other Western powers, having a small defence budget. In the past two years, all three policies have been reversed, with the result that Europe's biggest economy is in recession, while it is buying $3 billion worth of high-tech weaponry from Israel – the biggest defence deal for that country. The muted response from the government to the September 2022 destruction of Nordstream 2 (Hersh, 2023) and the enthusiasm with which its 'green' foreign minister is buying liquefied natural gas from the United States, at three times the cost of the Russian gas, indicates the limitations of the EU project. In addition, the Ukraine invasion has contributed to over a million refugees in Germany, fuelling political tensions arising from anti-immigration feeling, benefitting far-right political parties.

Despite claims that the Ukraine crisis is unifying Europe, it has instead shown how the United States has weakened it, especially the 'old' Europe. Poland is being seen by the United States as the leader of what was described by the former US Secretary of Defense Donald Rumsfeld in 2003 as the 'New Europe'. Poland has demanded $1.3 trillion in reparations as compensation for German damages during World War II. The United States, which has its first permanent military installation in Poland in the city of Poznan, is supporting Poland's plans to double the size of its standing army, making it the largest in Europe. A senior US official told the *New York Times* that US thinking on security was shifting eastward: 'we are meshing together with the Poles in a way that is truly historic in this relationship' (quoted in Zerofsky, 2023).

Such realignment reflects what Jack Matlock, the last US ambassador to the Soviet Union, had argued, that 'the end of the Cold War 'diminished rather than enhanced American power': with the removal of the Soviet threat, allies were less willing to accept American protection and leadership (Matlock, 2011). However, the Russian invasion of Ukraine has re-established the US security umbrella, strengthened NATO and 'mercilessly exposed' the EU's lack of 'strategic autonomy', as two commentators wrote in a leading German magazine (Kurbjuweit and Neukirch, 2022). They added that Europe has 'long cowered beneath the protective umbrella of the United States, but that isn't a reliable long-term strategy' (ibid.). It could be argued that the re-establishment of US hegemony in Europe was provoked by Washington's need to challenge the EU's power to restrict its digital empires through their stringent regulations.

The 'Rise of the Rest'

For the last half century, the United States has dominated the global geopolitical scene with its other group of seven partners – Britain, France, Germany, Italy, Canada and Japan. Founded in 1975, the G-7 embodies and sustains historical power relations from a different, colonial era: two were European empires (Britain and France); Germany, Italy and Japan were the losers in World War II, destroyed and rebuilt by the United States and then under the geopolitical influence of

Washington, while Canada, a former dominion of Britain, is now under tutelage of the United States. Soon after the end of the Cold War, Russia joined the G-7, making it the G-8, but it was a short-lived experience.

The claims by the G-7 that it represents the 'most advanced industrial countries,' cannot be sustained in 2023 when many other countries outside this elite grouping are bigger economies – notably China and, to a lesser extent, India. According to the International Monetary Fund (IMF), by 2027, the global South will account for 29 per cent of global GDP surpassing the G7, with China contributing more than 20 per cent. IMF says, in 2020, Britain made up 2.3 per cent of global GDP in purchasing power parity terms, while China represented nearly 19 per cent of global GDP, and it is growing in relative terms, while the United States was at 16 per cent but declining (IMF, 2023).

The main challenger to the G-7 in geopolitical terms is BRICS (Brazil, Russia, India, China and South Africa), in operation as a formal group since 2006 and holding annual summits since 2009. Originally a Russian project to gather the large non-Western nations together in a geopolitical forum, the BRICS was co-opted by China to demonstrate to the world at large that it was not the only economy that was 'rising' to allay Western fears. Despite predictions to the contrary among dominant Western scholarship and elite media, the BRICS grouping of nations is increasing in influence. As the G-7's share of global GDP declines, the BRICS economies continue to grow. The share of BRICS in global GDP grew from 18 per cent in 2010 to 26 per cent in 2021, with China accounting for more than 70 per cent of BRICS GDP in 2021 (UNCTAD, 2023: 5). New members are queuing up: During the 2023 BRICS summit in Johannesburg, six new countries were admitted to the group: Egypt, United Arab Emirates, Saudi Arabia, Iran, Argentina (which later decided not to join) and Ethiopia. Indonesia and Türkiye want to join, too, among other aspirants. Its first expansion in 13 years, engineered mainly by China, was described by a Reuters report as 'push to reshuffle a world order it sees as outdated' (Reuters, 2023a). The expanded BRICS group will contain some of the world's largest oil exporters, namely Saudi Arabia, Russia, United Arab Emirates and Iran, as well as some of its biggest importers, China and India (Daoud and Johnson, 2023).

A Bloomberg report notes that BRICS+ will overtake the G-7, noting that if it 'succeeds in shifting some settlement of oil transactions toward other currencies, that could have a knock-on effect on the share of the dollar in international trade and global foreign exchange reserves'. BRICS members have also been keen to work towards de-dollarization to counter their dependence on the dollar and trade amongst themselves in local currencies, as indicated by an IMF paper (Arslanalp et al., 2022). For example, in 2021, China signed a $400 billion deal involving Chinese investments in Iran over 25 years in exchange for the regular supply of oil. In 2022, BRICS accounted for 36 per cent of the global economy, against 30 per cent for the G-7, forecasting that by 2040, the share of BRICS+ will be 45 per cent compared with 21 per cent for the G-7.

BRICS represents a trend to multi-polarity in global power relations, having a major role in a post-unipolar and 'post-Western' global order, as Brazilian (Stuenkel, 2016 and 2018), Indian (Chaturvedi and Saha, 2021) and South African (Zondi, 2022) accounts suggest. The resulting redistribution of power has been described as a system of 'unbalanced multipolarity', diffusing away from the superpowers toward a variety of capable, dynamic middle powers that will help to shape the international environment in coming decades (Ashford and Cooper, 2023). Putin has suggested that a 'multipolar system of international relations is now being formed. It is an irreversible process; it is happening before our eyes' (TASS, 2022). Even French President Emmanuel Macron has advocated that Europe should 'seek to be a third pole' in an emerging world order (Foroudi and Rose, 2023).

India has been an active promoter of the notion of global multipolarity, although it has a particularly complicated position in this India is aiming to strike a delicate balance in promoting its geopolitical interests by strengthening its close security and economic ties with the United States and retaining traditional relations with Russia and trade connections with China in such multilateral forums as BRICS, of which India was a founding member, and Shanghai Cooperation Organization (SCO), which it joined in 2017.

'The rise of the BRICS countries', notes a think tank report from India, will put 'significant pressure on the existing hegemony in multilateral institutions'. As these countries begin to play a proactive role in global governance, it observed, 'their contributions can be amplified through parallel efforts at supporting the development needs of the Global South' (Chaturvedi and Saha, 2021: 10). Along with its BRICS partners, India has been pushing for reform of the bodies of global governance, such as the WTO, and the expansion of permanent membership of the UN Security Council to reflect contemporary global realities.

India has revitalized its position as a leading voice of the global South, coinciding with a three-year stretch where the G-20 is being led by countries from the global South: Indonesia in 2022, India in 2023 and Brazil in 2024. India has hosted two Voice of the Global South Summits in January and November 2023, aimed at encouraging more effective and sustainable cooperation among the developing countries.

Arguments have been advanced that, in an interdependent world, all should come together to strengthen global multilateral institutions and, since Asians constitute 60 per cent of humanity, they should take leadership in what is described as 'an Asian century'. They should restore the primary role of the UN General Assembly to serve as the global parliament; to strengthen key multilateral organizations, like the WHO by providing them with more resources; and to share with the world one of the best models of regional multilateral cooperation such as ASEAN (Mahbubani, 2022: 10–11).

How global communication is changing

US-based corporations still control large swathes of the global communication infrastructure, owning satellites, telecommunication hubs and cyberspace (Boyd-Barrett, 2014). This hardware enables US-originated or inspired media software to traverse the global digital superhighways, giving the country and the corporations based on their formidable power to shape the media agenda in fields ranging from news (CNN, CNBC, *New York Times*) to documentary (Discovery), and from sport (ESPN) to entertainment (Hollywood), to the streaming universe (Netflix, Amazon Prime), increasingly on an online space colonized and commodified by a few digital conglomerates (Thussu, 2019). According to the International Intellectual Property Alliance, the core copyright industries in the US economy accounted for $1.8 trillion in 2021, while the export of select US copyright products was more than $230 billion (IIPA, 2022). This global presence is supported by well-resourced epistemic communities: specialized NGOs, think tanks, universities and media foundations, with their international partners and affiliates, which provide an intellectual infrastructure within which neo-liberal ideologies are communicated and legitimized.

However, this traditional domination of global communication by the West is being challenged as a result of the transformation of digital technology and globalization of communication systems. Powerful non-Western nations, notably China and Russia and their other BRICS partners, as well as Türkiye and Iran have developed their own communication infrastructure and media to promote their geopolitical interests (see contributions in Nordenstreng and Thussu, 2015; Thussu and Nordenstreng, 2021).

One substantial change in the geopolitics of global communication has been the internationalization of media channels by powerful rivals to the US-dominated system, China (Cook, 2020; Kurlantzick, 2023) and Russia. The most powerful voice of Chinese state media, CGTN, has expanded in recent years to cover the globe, broadcasting, apart from English, in French, Spanish, Russian and Arabic (Varrall, 2020), with a special focus on Africa (Marsh, 2023), while programmes on such networks as the StarTimes, with operations in 30 African countries, promote China's image and worldviews (Lewis, 2024). Disseminating the message of China as a 'responsible power' is supported by other generously state-funded 'central media', notably Xinhua news agency, China Radio International, the English-language publications *China Daily* and more popularly the *Global Times*. With international editions including in the United States and in Europe, *China Daily* was circulated as a supplement with notable global newspapers, including the *Washington Post* and *Wall Street Journal*, while its monthly supplement *China Watch* published supplements in English, French, German and Spanish with newspapers across the world including a Russian edition in partnership with *Rossiyskaya Gazeta*.

China Radio International broadcasts in 61 languages via its six overseas regional hubs and had affiliations with 70 overseas radio stations. Though nominally independent, many of these were operating as mouthpieces for the Chinese government. However, despite this push, the effectiveness of Chinese international media remains untested and, so far, none of them have ever broken a major global news story. Since the Central Propaganda Department sets the 'ideological direction', selecting and monitoring content for state media, it is viewed, accurately outside China, as little more than party propaganda and therefore remains largely ineffective, despite the heavy resources invested in the last two decades to tell 'the China story' to the world. What erodes the international credibility of such media is the 'multilayered political control that results in pre-censored content' (Repnikova, 2022a: 26), as a result of which many Western regulators have revoked the licenses of Chinese international media outlets, notably CGTN.

China continues to invest in promoting its overseas policies through media. Such targeted messaging, notes an Atlantic Council report, helps China to legitimize its 'discourse power', which it sees 'as essential for reshaping the international environment in a way that better facilitates the expression of Chinese power' and, in the long run, 'makes the soil fertile globally for their message to seed' (Thibaut, 2022: 3). Another US think tank report argued that China has used 'America's openness to convey its message both to English- and Chinese-speaking residents' of the United States, where rules 'allow media companies, even ones run by foreign governments, to broadcast freely via American cable and satellite networks' (Hoover Institution, 2018: 95). In 2020, the US House of Representative's China Task Force warned of China's 'global malign behaviour' and recommended 'coordinating a whole-of-government offensive information statecraft campaign to counter' it (China Task Force Report 2020: v). A 2023 report of the US-China Economic and Security Review Commission cautioned that 'China's Party-state aims to bolster its global image by encouraging positive coverage, manipulating local media environments, and silencing critical voices' (US Government, 2023a: 224).

Despite these setbacks, Chinese diplomats have been using Twitter – as part of the strategy of 'talking back' – in what has been termed as 'Wolf Warrior' diplomacy (Martin, 2021; Dai and Luqiu, 2022; Chen, 2023). The propagandists have also used clickbait to enhance the visibility of Chinese discourse, often deploying platforms such as Facebook and Twitter, which are banned in the country (Lu and Pan, 2021). Some have cautioned about the globalization of a 'surveillance state' using its technological prowess to control information and to shape as well as monitor the discourse (Chin and Lin, 2022).

The 'RT effect'

Unlike Chinese overseas media, Russia's RT (formerly Russia Today) has had more impact on the global media sphere, especially in Western Europe, where studies have shown that its Twitter audiences are 'heterogeneous' and not necessarily 'anti-Western and fringe', as claimed by many commentators (Crilley et al., 2022). In operation since 2005 and with its catchy slogan of 'question more', RT has been accused by its distractors of creating dissensions and disruption among liberal democracies, especially in Western Europe, and promoting a right-wing nationalistic agenda (Elswah and Howard 2020). The network – available in Russian and English as well as in German, Spanish, French, Portuguese and Arabic – has created enough disquiet among Western chancelleries, indicating what I have elsewhere described as the 'RT effect' which has provided 'a robust – though unsubtle – counter-narrative on global affairs' (Thussu, 2019: 220). In the Western policy and academic discourse, RT is often categorized as a crude propaganda channel, home to anti-Western conspiracy theories, including those about Covid-19 (Yablokov and Chatterje-Doody, 2021), or demonizing America (Fisher, 2020).

During the Russian military intervention in Syria, RT used its strong presence on YouTube as one of the most watched channels to project it as morally and legally justified (Crilley and Chatterje-Doody, 2022). Beyond the West, RT is expanding its presence in the global South: since September 2022, Twitter RT has been aiming at a Hindi-speaking audience in India, where a Telegram account was also established. However, three days after the Russian invasion of Ukraine, on 27 February 2022, Ursula von der Leyen announced that RT and Sputnik (a Russian video news agency) were banned from European media space, citing the outlets' attempts to 'to spread their lies to justify Putin's war and to sow division in our Union' (European Commission, 2022), while a European Parliament resolution adopted in March 2022 accused Russia of 'engaging in disinformation of an unparalleled malice and magnitude across both traditional media outlets and social media platforms', proving that even 'information can be weaponized' (European Parliament, 2022: 4).

The Russian government itself has banned or blocked almost all independent media or declared them as 'foreign agents' or 'undesirable organizations'. Pro-Western news outlets such as *Moscow Times* and *The Bell* were forced to operate from outside Russia, as were *Meduza*, in operation since 2014, and *Novaya Gazeta*, as well as TV Rain, known as *Dozhd* in Russian, owned by a Dutch entrepreneur (Gessen, 2023). On the other side, in Ukraine, Zelensky had already, in 2021, banned three pro-Russian television networks – the 112, NewsOne and ZIK news (Mirovalev, 2021) – and since the invasion access to Russian social media was restricted, without any concerns for media freedom being voiced in the liberal West.

However, any collaboration between the so-called 'sharp' powers, Russia and China, is immediately labelled as dangerous in the West. Studies have noted this geopolitical cooperation in how RT covers BRI-related stories (van Noort and Chatterje-Doody, 2023). Sputnik has agreements with *Global Times* and Xinhua, including sharing content in Arabic and Spanish, while RT and Xinhua 'have mirrored each other's messages' in blaming the United States for 'fomenting protests in both Hong Kong and Russia' (Rosenberger, 2020: 152). One US commentator has described them as 'malicious actors seek[ing] to turn their businesses into geopolitical battlegrounds' while 'Chinese and Russian state media outlets increasingly work together, echoing each other's narratives' (Rosenberger, 2020: 158).

Unlike China and Russia, the Indian presence in the global news media sphere is negligible and its digital public diplomacy lacks a global push (Thussu, 2013a; Sinha Palit, 2023). However, with the rising international profile of India, tycoons such as Gautam Adani want to build 'a global news brand in a sign of the widening influence and vaulting international ambition'. 'India does not have one single [outlet] to compare to *Financial Times* or Al Jazeera', he told the *Financial Times* in 2022 after acquiring NDTV (New Delhi Television), India's best known and oldest news network (Cornish and Parkin, 2022). Beyond media, the Adani Group is also a leading player in Indian telecommunications, where it shares space with other conglomerates, notably the Reliance Group (also owns TV18), the Tata Group, the Aditya Birla Group and Bharti Telecom, which the government is trying to promote as global brands, following the example of South Korea's *chaebols* (large conglomerate groups such as Hyundai and Samsung). Given India's booming digital services economy and a continuing demographic advantage (nearly 70 per cent of India's 1.4 billion people are below the age of 35), it has the potential to operate at a global level (Acharya, 2023; Nageswaran and Kaur, 2023).

Among the media of the Arab/Muslim world, Al-Jazeera has a global presence in the international 24/7 news arena, gained initially through its coverage of the wars in Iraq, while enhancing the geopolitical interests of Qatar, whose government owns the network. Its coverage of the Arab Spring, especially a pro-Muslim Brotherhood approach in Egypt and a not-so-subtle support for the Islamist (some even extremists) groups in the Syrian civil war, as well as mediation in Taliban's takeover of Afghanistan in 2021, offered a widely accessible, alternative geopolitical and communicative perspective to that offered by Western global media channels.

Iran's Press TV – in operation since 2007 – which has been banned in many Western countries, is an example of using television to promote explicit foreign policy goals, while Türkiye's TRT News (Turkish Radio and Television), which has emerged as a mouthpiece of Turkish President Recep Erdoğan, also promotes the geopolitical interests of a country, which sees itself as a leading power representing the Muslim world (Elswah and Howard, 2022). In addition to the state broadcasters, there are many 'proxy media' outfits, some of which are activist groups. Among those that are funded and supported by Western governments/private foundations, one could include Iran International, an anti-Iranian regime news website based in London, media output from 'the White Helmets' on the Middle East and from Bellingcat on Russia.

Many of the global English-language 24/7 news channels can be seen as a key part of what Monroe Price has defined as the 'new strategic communication' as 'consolidating the relationship between information and power' that is 'heavily subsidized, usually transnational, engineered and often deceptive', part of 'strategic architectures', defined as 'large-scale efforts to fix or stabilize the relationship of states and other major players to information flows' (Price, 2015: 7 and 9).

'Strategic communication' by hostile governments becomes 'disinformation': 'Disseminating disinformation is central to China and Russia fulfilling their geopolitical aspirations', notes the 2022–2026 Strategic Plan of the US government's outfit for global media. Titled 'Truth Over Disinformation: Supporting Freedom and Democracy', the document claims that its adversaries 'Russia, China, Iran, and violent extremists, in particular' use an 'arsenal of spin, obfuscation, hyperbole, concealment, and propaganda to shape their global narratives', and 'collectively', they use these tools 'ultimately to undermine our democratic values and foreign policy interests' (USAGM, 2022: 5). In such ideological framing, the assumptions are that these adversaries work in collusion, and the liberal West counters 'these campaigns by broadcasting accurate, trusted, and reliable news and information' (ibid.).

Such has been the technological transformation of strategic communication that some scholars now suggest developing a new human science of 'quantum international relations', in a world characterized by 'networked simultaneity, AI-generated synthetic media, and endlessly multiplying meta-verses'. The most concrete stimulus for a 'quantized international relations', they suggest, is technological – particularly an 'accelerating global race to build advanced quantum systems for computing, communication, control and artificial intelligence' (Der Derian and Wendt, 2022: 6). It has been pointed out that China's rising digital footprints have an impact on how the future of AI and Blockchain will be shaped (Ma, 2021). In this constantly evolving communication space, the global digital conglomerates are increasingly playing a crucial role. They are not merely 'pawns their government masters can move around on a geopolitical chessboard' but 'increasingly geopolitical actors in and of themselves', as the president of Eurasia Group has argued (Bremmer, 2021: 128).

The US 2023 National Cybersecurity Strategy states that 'cybersecurity is essential to the basic functioning of our economy, the operation of our critical infrastructure, the strength of our democracy and democratic institutions, privacy of our data and communications, and our national defence' (White House, 2023a). Some have highlighted the geopolitical implications of increasing militarization and securitization of space (Doboš, 2019; Bowen, 2020), while the United States notes its loss of monopoly on GPS, as the EU, China and Russia offer alternative global satellite navigation options (Defense Intelligence Agency, 2022: 41).

Concerned that China was aiming to set standards for artificial intelligence and technology education around the world in forums such as UNESCO, the United States decided in 2023 to rejoin the UN body (from which it withdrew in 2017 in protest for membership for Palestine) and pay more than $600 million in back dues.

The digital 'Cold War' with China

China is already a 'leading provider [of] information and telecommunications networks', as well as their supporting hardware, software and the standards, which, according to one commentator, gives it the 'potential to cement its global

TABLE 0.1 Countries with the most cross-border data, 2001–2019

Rank in 2001		Rank in 2019	
1	United States	1	China/Hong Kong
2	United Kingdom	2	United States
3	Germany	3	United Kingdom
4	France	4	India
5	Japan	5	Singapore
6	China/HK	6	Brazil
7	Brazil	7	Vietnam
8	Russia	8	Russia
9	Singapore	9	Germany
10	India	10	France

Source: *Nikkei Asia*, November 25, 2020

dominance' (Markey, 2020: 3–4). In November 2023, the country launched the world's fastest internet, which can transmit the equivalent of 150 films per second (Tong, 2023), with global significance for the speed and rate of data flow. The level of cross-border data flow is a resonant indicator of the scale of digital communication power and the digital economy. In 2001, China was at the sixth place in terms of cross-border data, a list led by the United States and Britain; by 2019, it had moved to the top of the list, while India climbed from the tenth place to fourth, indicating the exponential growth of data and data flows in Asia (see Table 0.1).

A China expert at the Brookings Institution, who previously was China Director at the US National Security Council, has suggested that US global network of alliances and partnerships should be further strengthened to counter China's rise (Hass, 2021). Some scholars have called for 'conditional competitive co-operation' with China to 'decouple the economic issues from the inherently contentious security and values issues' (Bergsten, 2022). However, others question how strong the geopolitical gains from economic statecraft have been, suggesting that China's long-term strategic influence remains limited as 'China cannot count on automatically converting its growing economic clout into a new geopolitical reality' (Wong, 2021: 53).

Many of China's eastern neighbours, especially the countries around the South China Sea, are also concerned about its geopolitical ambitions. Such US-led security partnerships as the QUAD (Quadrilateral Security Dialogue), which includes Australia, India and Japan, as well as the AUKUS (Australia-UK-US), have emerged as anti-China outfits in the Indo-Pacific region. In August 2023, the United States, Japan and South Korea announced a trilateral agreement to deepen economic and military cooperation aimed to check China's 'dangerous and aggressive behavior' (White House, 2023b). On its western horizon – which includes its relations with India – the evolution of China's role will have a direct bearing on 'its geopolitical competition' with the United States, notes one study (Markey, 2020: 9). Almost impervious to this rhetoric, trade between the United States and China reached a record high in 2022, while US FDI into China has increased continuously by almost 20 per cent since 2019 (US Government, 2023b and 2023c).

All digital technologies depend on semi conductors and 75 per cent of the world's microchip manufacturing capacity is concentrated in East Asia, with China projected to command the largest share of global production by 2030. The US share of global semiconductor manufacturing capacity declined from 37 per cent in 1990 to 12 per cent in 2023. In an attempt to reduce this strategic weakness, in 2021, the 'CHIPS for America Act' enabled investment to incentivize US chip manufacturing and research. According to the Semiconductor Industry Association (SIA), global semiconductor sales in 2021 were nearly $556 billion (SAI, 2022). US ally, Taiwan, is home to the Taiwan Semiconductor Manufacturing Company, which makes more than 90 per cent of the most advanced chips, while the American company Nvidia designs graphic processing units, critical for running AI applications (Miller, 2022). As one commentator has noted, 'dominating chip design, manufacture and supply will be at least as significant geopolitically as oil was in the 20th' (Morozov, 2021).

The geopolitics of semiconductors are overly centred on the United States and East Asia, ignoring other nodes in this ecosystem, including Europe and India (Kotasthane and Manchi, 2023). The United States and its European allies now speak of 'friend-shoring' to reduce China's role in strategically important supply chains. In addition, the West's reliance on China's lucrative market forces it to speak of 'de-risking' rather than 'decoupling' from China (Cave, 2023, also see McKinsey Global Institute, 2023). US hawks have advocated 'weaponization' of US 'digital trade relationships to create a system that promotes its preference for internet governance', forcing countries to choose between maintaining access to their markets in what has been described as 'democratic digital supply chain', or embracing China's authoritarian model (Knake, 2020: 1 and 2).

As an intersection between global communication and international relations, this book aims to bridge the gap between traditional 'hard' IR and softer aspects of global interactions, with nation-states as primary definers of discourse, an unfashionable idea in an age of 'a-territorial' sovereignty. The chapters that follow deploy a critical approach, which is historically informed but up to date, drawing on a range of diverse sources: academic, professional and journalistic, synthesising them in a narrative, with the hope of advancing the discourse on the constantly evolving dynamic between global communication and geopolitics. One central theme that emerges is the continuity of asymmetries in power relations that can be traced back to 19th-century European imperialism, manifested in its various incarnations from 'liberal' to 'neo-liberal', to 'digital' imperialism. The ideas and arguments advanced here privilege a reading of geopolitical processes and examples from the perspective of the global South, which has had to operate in a world system that is still deeply structured by those histories.

Chapter 1 provides a historical context for the discussion of geopolitics and communication, identifying the legacies and leverages that the preeminent former colonial powers continue to wield. The chapter examines how the control of undersea cables gave Britain unparalleled power to shape global communications, especially the international news media and commerce as well as assisting in its imperial wars. It then analyses the geopolitics of the Cold War and the competing ideologies of communism and capitalism and how they were communicated to win the hearts and minds of what was then called the Third World. This includes a discussion of the cultural cold war, in which artists, writers and intellectuals were coopted to promote ideological and geopolitical interests. The chapter concludes with the resistance to the Western dominance of communication channels in debates on the New World Information and Communication Order.

Chapter 2 examines the transformation of global communication triggered by the end of the Cold War and the process of globalization. The establishment of a new global communication infrastructure through the processes of liberalization and privatization is discussed, especially focusing on the role of the WTO in effecting these fundamental changes. The chapter then examines the hardware of global communication, which continues to be dominated by the US-led Western bloc of nations, though, as the chapter argues, new entrants notably China have developed their own versions of communications infrastructure, with ambitious programmes such as the creation of a 'digital silk road'. Finally, the chapter discusses a more subtle form of infrastructure: the role of epistemic communities – think tanks, universities and professional organization – in shaping geopolitical debates.

Chapter 3 discusses the potential of the internet for both digital democracy and digital empires. In its geopolitical dimension, the use of digital, particularly social, media by groups and individuals has empowered campaigns, protests and popular uprisings. However, its potential for digital capitalism and trade has grown exponentially, and the chapter shows how digital communication and the data thus transmitted have been harnessed for global capitalism. It examines how data has become the new currency, circulating globally through digital communication channels, in the latest incarnation of capitalism and the apparent dichotomy between the 'democratic' and 'authoritarian' types of an emerging 'soft-touch imperialism'. The final part of the chapter outlines the constraints on digital imperialism – by way of regulation and data localization debates and the geopolitics associated with this.

Chapter 4 examines the geopolitics of how conflicts are covered in the US-dominated international media. With detailed case studies including the invasions of Iraq and the 'forever war' in Afghanistan, the chapter shows how geopolitical considerations dictate the tone, tenor and treatment of the conflict and how image wars are waged in parallel with the actual battlefield. This is then contrasted with the 'invisible wars' that are mostly taking place in Africa. The Ukraine war and its associated propaganda blitz are examined, as is the role of global public relations industries in shaping the narratives of war. Finally, the chapter scrutinizes the growing trend towards the privatization of warfare and its geopolitical implications.

Chapter 5 looks at the weaponization of information for geopolitical purposes, first, at the example presented by the Ukrainian conflict and at how Silicon Valley has been coopted by Western governments into supporting Ukraine's resistance against the Russian invasion. The chapter analyses the nature of the cyber threats to the global information system presented by China and Russia, authoritarian states that are challenging the liberal 'rule-based' information order. It also examines how communication technologies are deployed for surveillance and espionage in the West and in authoritarian states such as China. This is followed by an investigation into the 'infodemic' of dis- and mis-information, looking at the case of Covid-19 and its geopolitical implications. The final part of the chapter is concerned about the contribution of AI to weaponizing information, including deep-fakes and the framing of the debate as a contest between a 'democratic' and 'authoritarian' AI.

The final chapter focuses on the title of the book, enumerating the changes that have occurred in the past two decades with the declining West and the 'rise of the rest', especially the BRICS nations. Such narratives as 'Sino-globalization' and 'de-globalization' are discussed, as are the debates about 'digital for development', contrasting the Chinese model of development with the Western one and including an Indian model 'in the making' to provide a fuller perspective. The chapter ends with a discussion of the need to decolonize the fields of both geopolitics and communication, as a much-overdue corrective to the intellectual and discourse hegemony of the English-language scholarship and perspectives that restrict, even distort the multiplicities of a multipolar world.

A book that aims for a 'composite' account of communication and adopts a holistic approach benefits from the work of scholars and commentators of various academic affiliations and agendas. I owe an enormous intellectual debt to their scholarship. I must also express my profound appreciation of the constant support of my wonderful wife, Liz, to whose invaluable professional help in editing the manuscript are due the strengths of this book, while I have no hesitation in owning its remaining shortcomings, and to whom this book is dedicated. I am also immensely grateful to my brilliant editor at Routledge Natalie Foster for her unending patience with an author trying to make sense of rapidly changing global geopolitics. Finally, I should like to record my deep gratitude to James Curran for including this book in his prestigious Communication and Society series for Routledge.

1
COMMUNICATION, GLOBALIZATION AND EMPIRE

Legacies and leverages

The global communication system of the 21st century cannot be understood without appreciating the historical origins of the global information infrastructure put in place in the 19th century and earlier. Although we are living in the 'first empire-free millennium' in history, the legacies and leverages of empire continue to influence and shape the world, in what one commentator has called a 'great imperial hangover' (Puri, 2020; Stern, 2023). As in other fields, in communication, too, this imperial imprint has profoundly affected the development of a modern global communication system, both hardware and software.

As with all imperial projects, communication was central to the expansion and consolidation of the modern European empires (Innis, 1972), the largest and the most powerful being that of Britain, which, at its height (1880–1914), dominated a quarter of humanity. British control of the sea routes of international trade and commerce, arising from the pre-eminence of its navy and merchant fleet, was inextricably linked to the acquisition and development of its colonies. The technological advances of Britain's earlier Industrial Revolution, such as the steam engine, the iron ship and electric telegraph, all helped to keep it ahead of its rivals. It is not surprising that the means of communication with far-flung territories developed in parallel with the rapid expansion of trade and empire in the second half of the 19th century, bolstered by the new steam ships and the opening of the Suez Canal in 1869 (which only Britain could use) (Daudin et al., 2010). The growth of international commerce and finance required a constant source of reliable data about trade and economic affairs, while the European empires required a consistent supply of information essential for maintaining political alliances and military security.

With the first commercial telegraph link set up in 1838 in Britain, by 1851 a public telegraph service was in operation, including a telegraphic money order system, forming the basis of a unified financial and technological structure for

DOI: 10.4324/9781315271699-2

the British Empire (Winseck and Pike, 2007; Choudhury-Lahiri, 2010). With Samuel Morse's invention of the telegraph in the United States in 1843 and the inauguration of the first commercial telegraph there – between Washington and Baltimore in 1844 – telegraphy initiated a revolution in communication that was as significant as the modern internet (Standage, 1998; Choudhury-Lahiri, 2010). It transformed global communication spaces and actors and contributed significantly to a 19th-century version of globalization (Wenzlhuemer, 2013).

When the first successful commercial undersea telegraph cable was laid under the English Channel in 1851, the London *Morning Herald* predicted 'an electric union of the entire planet'. The first permanent transatlantic cable was laid in 1866, initiating the rapid emergence of a system of global communication, enabling near-instantaneous transmission of information over distance. The laying of undersea telegraph cables connected Britain with Egypt (1869), India (1870), Southeast Asia (1870), from Singapore to Australia and New Zealand by 1873, the Caribbean (1873/1874), Brazil (1874) and South Africa (1879), and other cables extended to Hong Kong, China and Japan (Choudhury-Lahiri, 2010).

By the end of the 19th century, the global telegraph network had connected all continents and brought distant people into direct communication 'at the speed of thought'. 'For the first time in history', writes Headrick, 'the colonial metropolis acquired the means to communicate almost instantly with their remotest colonies' (1981: 129–130). The telegraph allowed the various hubs of imperial communication to communicate directly with London within minutes, when before it had taken months for post to come via sea (Bonea, 2016). Businesses saw the huge potential of using the telegraph to expand their operations overseas for profit and were the first to invest in and adopt it, as it enabled the rapid transmission of information, while ensuring secrecy (Headrick, 1991; Hugill, 1999; Hochfelder, 2012). The speed and reliability of its networks enabled the transmission of the up-to-date financial information by reporting spot prices for commodities such as cotton, benefitting British merchants and leading to the development of international financial markets.

Another key geopolitical advantage for imperial powers was that telegraphy revolutionized military communication. During the Crimean War (1854–1856), the rival imperial powers, Britain and France, trying to prevent Russian westward expansion that threatened overland routes to their colonial territories in Asia, exchanged military intelligence through an underwater cable in the Black Sea laid by the British during the conflict. The first examples of 'breaking news' were the war reports – sent back by telegraph from the Crimea by Irish journalist William Howard Russell for the *Times* in London, heralding the close relationship between communications technologies, conflict and the media. On the other side of the world, the American Civil War (1861–1865) accelerated the cabling of the continent-sized country: more than 24,000 kilometres of cable was laid to send more than 6.5 million telegrams, ensuring that the American Civil War became not only another of the earliest conflicts to be extensively reported but also an example of the early use of photojournalism (Hochfelder, 2012).

Within a quarter of a century, the world's cable networks had more than doubled in length (Hugill, 1999; Winseck and Pike, 2007). By the 1870s, telegraph lines were operating in many parts of the globe and an international communication network, dominated by Britain, was beginning to emerge. The cables were, in the words of Headrick, 'an essential part of the new imperialism' (1981: 163), and in 1865, the International Telegraph Union (ITU) was founded by the colonial powers as 'the first international institution of the modern era and the first organization for the international regulation of a technical network' (Mattelart, 1994: 9).

Control over cables

By the late 19th century, the Anglo-American domination of international communication was emerging, with the two countries owning nearly 75 per cent of the world's cables. Undersea cabling required huge capital investment, which was provided by the colonial authorities and by banks, businessmen and the fast-growing newspaper industry. Of the total cable distance of 167,371 kilometres, less than 10 per cent was government-owned; the cable networks were largely controlled by private companies, with Britain's Eastern Telegraph Company and the US-based Western Union Telegraph Company being the leaders in the industry. The cable companies created their own cartels 'in Euro-American, Euro-Asian, South American, and Indo-European markets in 1869, 1872, 1874 and 1878 respectively. Later, the big four commercial wireless companies – Marconi, Radio Corporation of America (RCA), Compagnie Generale de Telegraphie Sans Fil (TSF), and Telefunken – did the same after the World War I' (Winseck and Pike, 2007: 5).

Britain had privileged access to the raw materials needed to produce cables, owning copper mines in Chile, the world's biggest producer in the 19th century (Read, 1992), and setting the price of copper in the commodity markets in London. In 1904, 22 of the 25 companies that managed international cable networks were affiliates of British firms; Britain deployed 25 ships totalling 70,000 tons, while the six vessels of the French cable fleet, for example, amounted to only 7,000 tons.

British supremacy over the undersea networks was overwhelming: in 1910, the Empire controlled about half the world total, or 260,000 kilometres. France, which, in contrast to the United States and Britain, opted for the state administration of cable, and controlled no more than 44,000 kilometres (Headrick, 1991; Mattelart, 1994). By 1923, private companies had nearly 75 per cent of the global cabling share, with British firms accounting for nearly 43 per cent, followed by American companies, which owned 23 per cent (Headrick, 1991). However, colonial governments gave considerable support to the cable companies, either scientifically through research on cartography and navigation or financially through subsidies.

Military operations – such as the Japanese–Russian war of 1904–1905 – were both assisted and reported by the first transpacific cable completed in 1902, which was the joint property of Britain and its dominions of Australia, New Zealand and Canada. The second transpacific cable was completed in 1903 by US interests, providing a link between San Francisco and Manila, through Honolulu, Midway Island and Guam, and from there to the Asian mainland and Japan by existing British cables. All of these landing points were controlled by the United States: the Hawaiian Islands had been a US territory since 1900, and Midway was claimed by it in 1867, while Guam and the Philippines had become US colonies as a result of the 1898 Spanish–American War (Desmond, 1978; Britton, 2013).

The rapid expansion of communication to meet the needs of world trade and the increasing spread of European empires demanded more capacity. The number of telegraphic transmissions in the world rapidly expanded from 29 million in 1868 to 329 million in 1900, according to the International Telegraph Union (ITU, renamed the International Telecommunication Union in 1932). The US secretary of war, Elihu Root, observed in 1899 that 'trade tends to follow the line of least resistance in communication', and urged that Americans take the lead in exploiting new communications in order 'to secure a large share of the vast trade of the East' (quoted in LaFeber, 2000: 9).

The importance of cables as the arteries of an international network of information, of intelligence services and of propaganda can be gauged from the fact that the day after the World War I broke out, the British cut both German transatlantic cables (Hugill, 1999).

Following the war, radiotelegraphy threatened the dominance of cables (Headrick and Griset, 2001). The new technology of radiotelegraphy (also called 'wireless' telegraphy) was invented by Marconi in 1901 and promised to meet the need for increased capacity not catered for by the cables and filled in the gaps that cable telegraphy could not bridge (Anduaga, 2009; Evans, 2010). The Marconi Wireless Telegraph Company of Great Britain dominated global telegraph traffic and had a virtual monopoly on international telegraph exchanges, as it refused to communicate with any other system other than its own.

After the 1880s, Britain encountered increasing competition in wireless telegraphy from the United States and other European powers, notably Germany (Tworek, 2019). At the turn of the 20th century, sections of the German political, economic and intellectual elites aspired to world-power status for Germany (*Weltmacht*), realizing that 'international powers needed international communications infrastructures' (Tworek, 2019: 6). One manifestation of this was the establishment of the German government-owned news agency Transocean, which rather adroitly used the new wireless telegraphy between 1914 and 1922 to carve out their own sphere of operation for maritime traffic, broadcasting to moving 'target' ships and regions such as East Asia, where German telegraph news had never played a major role (Evans, 2010). For Germany, wireless telegraphy offered a chance to avoid the British-dominated cable routes to German colonies in Africa and Asia and helped to circumvent a communication blockade in World War I, when German cables had been taken over, one by the British and another by the French.

After World War I, the question of who should control Germany's cables dominated discussions at the 1919 peace talks at Versailles and reflected the rivalry between the British cable companies and the growing US radio interests for ownership and control of global communications networks. The United States argued that the cables be held jointly under international control or trusteeship and that a world conference should be convened to consider international aspects of telegraph, cable and radio communication (Luther, 1988). Wireless telegraphy remained one of Germany's only means to disseminate its news outside its territory in the early 1920s. As a news agency outside the cartel agreement (see below), Transocean was free to broadcast in any region and used it to raise Germany's profile abroad and influence East Asia and South America (Evans, 2010).

Communicating the news

The innovation of the news agency was inextricably linked with both geopolitics and developments in communication technology, altering the process of news dissemination internationally (Putnis et al., 2011). British control of international communication via telegraphy made London itself an unrivalled centre for world news, which was further enhanced by Britain's wide-ranging commercial, financial and imperial activities (Read, 1992). Britain's imperial expansion created a pressing need for improved commercial intelligence, reflected in the demand for speedy and accurate news and thus contributed to the commercialization of news and information services. The French Havas Agency (ancestor of AFP [*Agence France-Presse*], founded in 1835), the German agency Wolff (1849) and the British Reuters (1851) were all supported and subsidized by their respective governments. As Boyd-Barrett has noted, the major European agencies were based in imperial capitals, and 'their expansion outside Europe was intimately associated with the territorial colonialism of the late nineteenth century' (Boyd-Barrett, 1980: 23).

In 1870, the three agencies set up the 'Ring Combination', signing an agreement to divide up world news market between them into 'reserved territories' for each agency, a form of cartel. This Ring Combination was used by the respective governments to suit their own geopolitical and economic interests (Boyd-Barrett, 1980; Mattelart, 1994; Silberstein-Loeb, 2014). Reuters was the leading agency in this, specializing in financial and commercial information, with the most staff and stringers throughout the world able to report more original news. Reuters also had the most influence as it operated within the British Empire, which was of greater importance politically and economically and thus also for news (Silberstein-Loeb, 2014). It has been described as 'empire within an empire' (ibid.), given its symbiotic relationship with the British foreign and colonial administrations: as the official historian of the agency has noted, Reuters effectively functioned 'as an institution of the British Empire' (Read, 1992: 40).

The geopolitical role of the news agencies, which were subsidized by their respective governments, can be seen when Reuters attempted to circumvent the cartel to set up a joint venture with Havas in Berlin and buy Wolff's agency. Bernhard Wolff asked King Wilhelm I for help against both Reuters and Havas and underlined the importance of preserving the agency, for 'should Havas succeed, Prussia would become dependent on foreigners for its political intelligence' (quoted in Nalbach, 2003: 109).

The global reach of Reuters was useful for the British colonial authorities, especially after 1910, when Reuters started an imperial news service, which then offered to wire official speeches to every corner of the Empire in return for an annual fee from the Colonial Office. During World War I, Reuters launched a wartime news service by arrangement with the Foreign Office, which by 1917 was circulating about one million words per month throughout the Empire, which had the benefit of circulating apparently objective news but with 'propaganda secretly infused', according to a British official in 1917 (quoted in Read, 1992: 127–128). This arrangement was replaced by an agreement with the Foreign Office that Reuters would be paid to circulate specific messages on its international wires, which lasted until 1939. After World War II, with the decline of the British Empire and the ascendancy of the United States, Reuters had to compete with the American news agencies, especially Associated Press (AP). AP and other US agencies, such as the United Press (founded in 1907 – later called UPI, United Press International), began to encroach on the markets once dominated by the European news cartel (Silberstein-Loeb, 2014).

Radio and the geopolitics of propaganda

Western countries were the first to grasp the strategic implications of radio communication, particularly the United States, as radio could be used to challenge British domination of the cables used for international telegraphy (Luther, 1988). Undersea cables were expensive and vulnerable, requiring bilateral agreements for the construction and operation of landing stations. Radio waves could freely travel anywhere, and radio sets could be produced cheaply on a massive scale. The main issues were vulnerability to interference and the availability of radio frequencies. These were discussed at the 1906 Berlin Conference on Wireless Telegraphy, at which 28 states debated radio equipment standards and procedures and set up the International Radiotelegraph Union (IRU). Having its origins in ship-to-ship communications, the great naval powers were also the major users of radio (Britain, Germany, France, the United States and Russia) and used their power to impose a system of radio frequency allocation by the ITU on a 'first come, first served' basis (Mattelart, 1994). As a result, the companies or states with the necessary capital and technology to operate international radio broadcasting gained control over the limited spectrum space, to the disadvantage of most of the world.

At the World Radio Conference in Washington in 1927, private companies helped to write an agreement that allowed them to continue developing their use of the spectrum, without regard to possible signal interference for other countries. As an international treaty, this became international law and had the result of reinforcing US and European domination of the international radio spectrum (Luther, 1988).

Nevertheless, it was the recently founded Soviet Union that was first to use radio for international broadcasting: the world's first short-wave radio broadcasts were sent out from Moscow in 1925. In the same year the Telegraph Agency of the Soviet Union (TASS) was set up (Potter et al., 2022), and by 1929, the Soviet Union had launched the Radio Moscow World Service (Lovell, 2015). Within a few years, it was regularly broadcasting communist propaganda in German, French, Dutch and English, recognizing the power of radio to reach an international audience in order to influence values, beliefs and attitudes (Taylor, 2003).

The geopolitical significance of radio and its use for propaganda, both at home and abroad was quickly evident in its use during World War I. As the leading writer on propaganda, Harold Lasswell wrote afterwards, the war made it clear that 'the mobilisation of men and means was not sufficient; there must be mobilisation of opinion. Power over opinion, as over life and property, passed into official hands' (Lasswell, 1927: 14).

By 1933, when Hitler came to power in Germany, radio was an essential communication tool for international propaganda and diplomacy. Josef Goebbels, the head of Hitler's Propaganda Ministry, used radio to broadcast the anti-Semitic ideology of the Third Reich worldwide. The Nazi *Reichssender* broadcasts were initially for German emigrants in places such as Argentina and Australia and then extended to short-wave programmes in several languages, including Afrikaans, Arabic and Hindustani: by 1945, German radio was broadcasting in more than 50 languages. Nazi propaganda also found its way into US newspapers, when AP entered a formal cooperation with the Hitler regime in the 1930s, with material directly produced and selected by the Nazi Propaganda Ministry, as a German historian revealed in 2016 (Scharnberg, 2016). AP was the only Anglo-American news agency able to stay open, continuing to operate until the United States entered the war in 1941. The agency ceded control of its output by signing up to the so-called *Schriftleitergesetz* (editor's law), promising not to publish any material 'calculated to weaken the strength of the Reich abroad or at home' (ibid.). In Italy, under Benito Mussolini, the Ministry of Print and Propaganda was created to win over public opinion on Fascist policies and colonial campaigns, such as the invasion of Abyssinia (Ethiopia) in 1935. Mussolini also distributed radio sets to Arabs, tuned to only one station – *Radio Bari* in southern Italy.

Propaganda in 'gentlemanly' tones

From its inception in 1932, overseas radio broadcasting by the BBC became an essential adjunct to British diplomatic and foreign policy objectives. Originally called the 'Empire Service', it was renamed the 'Overseas Service' during World War II and then became the 'World Service' in 1965. Unlike the main BBC, the Empire Service was directly funded by the Foreign Office to connect the scattered parts of the British Empire (Potter, 2012) and to 'educate' its populations in 'British values'. Given the very low levels of literacy among most of the population in the colonies, radio was seen as a crucial medium for dissemination of information and propaganda.

It is not surprising, given the geostrategic and economic interests in oil supplies, that the Arabic Service became the first foreign-language section of the BBC's Empire Service, to be followed by the Persian Service in 1940 (Potter, 2012). At the beginning of World War II, the Empire Service was broadcasting in seven languages apart from English – Afrikaans, Arabic, French, German, Italian, Portuguese and Spanish (Walker, 1992: 36). By the end of the war, the service was being broadcast in more than 40 languages.

The BBC was employed at home and abroad during World War II by the government to further its geopolitical and economic interests. More importantly, given Britain's proximity to the war theatre, the BBC played a key role in the propaganda offensive, and often it was more effective than American propaganda, which, as one British media historian commented, was 'both distant and yet too brash, too unsophisticated and yet too contrived to challenge the propaganda forces already at work on the continent' (Briggs, 1970: 412).

John Reith, the first director general of the BBC, felt obliged to accept an arrangement that, as Potter puts it, 'included agreeing that news editors would accept specific guidance from civil servants as to which items needed to be included in, or omitted from, different foreign-language services. All this was subsequently enshrined in a secret "gentleman's agreement" between the BBC and the government, unwritten and thus eminently deniable by both parties' (Potter, 2022: 66).

Under the direction of the Ministry of Information and the Political Warfare Executive, the Overseas Service broadcast in various European foreign languages directed at occupied, neutral and enemy countries (Ribeiro and Seul, 2018). The Overseas Service also helped the US Army to create the American Forces Network (AFN), which broadcast recordings of American shows for US forces in Britain, Middle East and Africa. In contrast to the Voice of America's (VOA's) state propaganda, the BBC's Overseas Service prided itself on presenting a more mature, balanced view, winning by argument, rather than hammering home a point. This proclaimed policy of 'balance' gave the BBC more international credibility than any other broadcasting organization. In addition, the government exerted indirect influence on the BBC, since the relay stations and overseas transmitters were negotiated through or owned by the Diplomatic Wireless Service.

After the war, the BBC's continuing dependence on the British Government was evident, since the Government even decided which languages were used for programmes and for how long they were broadcast to each audience. For example, during the Berlin blockade of 1948–1949, almost the entire output of the BBC's external services was directed to Eastern bloc countries. The Information Research Department of the British Foreign Office, set up during Clement Attlee's post-war Labour government and dissolved in 1977, also monitored and advised the British media, including the BBC, to toe the official line on foreign policy issues (Webb, 2014). According to a new history to mark the centenary of the founding of the corporation, 'over the last century' the BBC has 'probably been the single most important institution generating British soft power and overseas propaganda' (Potter, 2022: 7).

With the establishment of its Russian language unit in 1946, the BBC played a key part in the Cold War as the primary means of engaging with attitudes and opinions behind the Iron Curtain. It also reached audiences across the world through its strategically located global network of relay stations (Weir, 2020). These included stations in the Ascension Island and in Antigua (to cover the Western hemisphere); in Cyprus (for the Middle East, Europe and northern Africa); in Masirah, leased from Oman (for the Gulf region); in Seychelles (for east Africa); in Kranji in Singapore (for Southeast Asia); and in Hong Kong (for East Asia, especially China). The 'expansion of medium-wave coverage' through these relay stations shows the unique role played by the BBC in the 'information war' against its adversaries, as well as to maintain 'soft' imperial power of radio relations in, 'recently or soon-to-be vacated colonial spaces' (Weir, 2020: 963). Other major broadcasters followed: China Radio International in 1941, VOA in 1942, Deutsche Welle in 1953 and Radio France International in 1975, to name the prominent examples.

The global 'voice' of America during the Cold War

Just as the VOA had been a part of US diplomacy during World War II, propaganda became a crucial component of US foreign broadcasting with the advent of the Cold War (Cull, 2009; Cummings, 2010; Johnson and Parta, 2010). The key instruments of US international broadcasting – VOA, RL (Radio Liberty), RFE (Radio Free Europe) and the American Forces Network – were all state-funded. The VOA was the official mouthpiece of the US Government, the largest single element in the US Information Agency (USIA) and ultimately answerable to the US State Department (Cull, 2009). Unlike the BBC World Service, VOA depended on official comment, as it only used VOA staff for commentaries, thereby restricting the range of opinions expressed by its programmes and thus straining its credibility as an international broadcaster. VOA came to prominence as a source of strident anti-communist propaganda during the Korean War (1950–1953), under President Harry Truman, the first of many proxy conflicts between the superpowers in the developing world during the Cold War.

In addition to VOA, other Cold War US propaganda broadcasts emanated from Radio Free Europe (RFE), which started broadcasting in 1951 and Radio Liberation (RL) in 1953 (renamed Radio Liberty in 1963), both based in Munich and targeting the Soviet Union (Mickelson, 1983). Unlike the VOA, the official broadcaster of the USIA, RFE and RL were covert organizations, funded by the CIA, crusading for 'truth' and 'freedom' (Cummings, 2010; Johnson, 2010; Pomar, 2022). RFE was accused of encouraging the uprising in Hungary in 1956 by broadcasting rumours of the arrival of a 'UN delegation' – a euphemism for US military intervention – which never materialized. The Soviet Union and other members of the Warsaw Pact regularly jammed RFE/RL's signals, denouncing them as a network of 'radio saboteurs' and an integral part of US 'electronic imperialism' (Kashlev, 1984).

In the 1980s RFE played an important role in supporting Poland's Solidarity movement, the first 'independent' trade union in a communist country, with over 60 per cent of the adult population listening to its broadcasts. This was a key reason behind the Soviet-decision not to intervene as it had done in Czechoslovakia (Lord, 1998). From 1988, RFE/RL signals were no longer jammed by Moscow, and RFE/RL's contribution to the end of communism is widely acknowledged (McNamara, 1992; Sosin, 1999). As one broadcaster wrote, 'Well before the Iron Curtain rusted – let alone was dismantled – its metal had been perforated by the sounds on the airwaves' (Partos, 1993: 91).

The expansion of international radio broadcasting during the Cold War meant that access to the high-frequency end of the radio spectrum for communication became a contested area between the two Cold War blocs. The controversy was fuelled by the defence-related space race, which received new momentum in 1957 with the launch of the world's first satellite, Sputnik, by the Soviet Union, which led to a demand for an agreed allocation of space frequencies (Luther, 1988). Two years later, in 1959, the UN set up the Committee on the Peaceful Uses of Outer Space to establish an international regulatory framework with the aim of reducing Cold War tensions, which culminated in the Outer Space Treaty in 1967.

Article I of this treaty, which forms the basis for international law in the field of space, stated that the exploration and use of outer space 'shall be carried out for the benefit and in the interests of all countries, irrespective of their degree of economic and scientific development, and shall be the province of all mankind', while its Article II established that outer space 'is not subject to national appropriation by claim of sovereignty, by means of use of occupation, or by any other means'. Despite this, the controversy over frequency allocation continued to figure prominently in the ITU's World Administrative Radio Conferences all through Cold War years and beyond.

Challenging the Western narrative

By the late 1960s, Radio Moscow was relaying its content in 84 languages, the highest number of languages in the world at that time: between 1950 and 1973, external broadcasting from the Soviet Union grew from 533 hours to around 1,950 hours per week, greater than the entire US external broadcasting, including VOA, RL and RFE (Hale, 1975: 174). Soviet broadcast policies were aimed at countering Western propaganda, such as during the uprisings in Hungary (1956) and Czechoslovakia (1968). During the invasion to suppress the latter, broadcasts rose from 17 hours per week before to 168 at the height of the crisis in August, falling back to 84 by September (Hale, 1975: 24). After the Sino-Soviet split of 1968, it was increasingly important for Moscow to have its voice heard by communist parties across the world. More influenced by geopolitical than ideological differences, the split led to mutual propaganda battles between the communist giants, with Radio Moscow increasing its Chinese-language broadcasts from 77 hours a week in 1967 to 200 hours in 1972, while China, which by the early 1970s had become the world's third-largest international broadcaster, also increased its broadcasts criticizing Soviet 'revisionism' (Thussu, 2019).

Unlike professionally produced Western broadcasts, those from Moscow were not known for their entertainment value, but they nevertheless had an impact on news agendas and how the news media were organized in the communist bloc. However, Radio Moscow was at a disadvantage in relation to the ability to transmit outside the communist world, with only one outlet outside Eastern Europe – Radio Habana in Cuba. Western governments did not have to worry about jamming their broadcasts, as there was scarcely an audience for them (Nelson, 1997).

Communicating a cultural Cold War

Communicating the virtues of free-market capitalism, freedom and liberalism was the main objective of US cultural diplomacy during the Cold War period. This involved a US-led project to create a Cold War cultural front targeting the intellectual elites of ideologically divided Western Europe, a process expanded to the Third World during the 1950s to capture the elites of the newly independent former colonies, which persisted until the 1960s.

The Paris-based Congress for Cultural Freedom (CCF) – an organization of largely centre-left artists and intellectuals – was set up in 1950 by the CIA to counter the influence of the Soviet Union (Scott-Smith, 2002; Saunders, 2013; Miller Harris, 2016). At its peak, the CCF had offices in 35 countries, published more than 20 magazines and journals, owned a news and feature service and organized international conferences and arts events (Saunders, 2013: 1). These transnational and multilingual journals included *Preuves* (French, 1951–1975), *Der Monat* (German, 1948–1971), *Quest* (in English, for the Indian elite, 1955–1976), *Cuadernos* (Spanish, 1956–1965), *Jiyu* (Japanese, 1959–2009), *Hiwar* (Arabic, 1962–1967), *New African* (published in English since 1962, first in Cape Town and then in London) and *Horison* (Bahasa Indonesia, in circulation since 1966) (Scott-Smith and Lerg, 2017: 16). As Saunders has noted, 'Across the years, *Der Monat* was financed through "confidential funds" of the Marshall Plan, then from the coffers of the Central Intelligence Agency, then with Ford Foundation money, and then again with CIA dollars. For its financing alone, the magazine was absolutely a product – and an exemplar of – American Cold War strategies in the cultural field' (Saunders, 2013: 30). The content and management of every journal involved 'a constant negotiation between the (Western) transnational interests of the CCF, its ideal of the global intellectual community, and the national contexts that set the terms for their immediate cultural reception' (Scott-Smith and Lerg, 2017: 18).

One of the most significant journals supported by the CCF was the London-based literary magazine *Encounter*, founded in 1953 and edited by the British poet Stephen Spender and American political essayist and journalist Irving Kristol. The magazine was rarely critical of American foreign policy and generally shaped its content to support the geopolitical interests of the United States. *Encounter* celebrated its greatest years in terms of readership and influence under Melvin Lasky, who succeeded Kristol in 1958 and served as the main editor until the magazine ceased publication in 1991.

After the revelation that the CCF was funded by the CIA until 1973, the Ford Foundation took over funding of the CCF and provided support to its successor organization, the International Association for Cultural Freedom, along with providing grants to Pugwash and American PEN (Saunders, 2013; Wolfe, 2018; White, 2019). Dissenting voices from the global South were muzzled or marginalized: one study outlined cases in which – critical views of the United States were minimized, or made less favourable, and listed the writers who were excluded entirely from translation and global circulation (Rubin, 2012). As Saunders notes, 'drawing on an extensive, highly influential network of intelligence personnel, political strategists, the corporate establishment, and the old school ties of the Ivy League universities', the CIA aimed to build a 'consortium' whose 'double task it was to inoculate the world against the contagion of communism and to ease the passage of American foreign policy interests abroad' (Saunders, 2013: 1).

The intelligence agencies were also influencing journalism. Contrary to the notion that the CIA insidiously infiltrated the journalistic community, there is ample evidence that the leading US publishers and news executives were willing collaborators with the intelligence services. In 1977, the noted American journalist Carl Bernstein wrote that 'the use of journalists has been among the most productive means of intelligence-gathering employed by the CIA'. Among the executives who lent their cooperation to the agency included the Who's Who of American journalism: William Paley (CBS), Henry Luce (*Time*) and Arthur Hays Sulzberger (*New York Times*). Other organizations which cooperated included top broadcasters such as the American Broadcasting Corporation (ABC) and the NBC (National Broadcasting Corporation); leading news agencies such as the AP, the UPI and Reuters; and news magazine *Newsweek* and newspapers like *Miami Herald* and *New York Herald-Tribune* (Bernstein, 1977).

The Agency's special relationships with the major organizations in publishing and broadcasting enabled the CIA in the 1950s and 1960s to post some of its most valuable operatives abroad without exposure. The media organizations provided jobs and credentials – 'journalistic cover' – for CIA operatives, lending the agency the undercover services of reporters, including some of the best-known correspondents in the business (Bernstein, 1977). As one former journalist pithily observed, 'The CIA established its network of informants in the news business with the consent of some editors, publishers and other news executives. In some cases, they specifically condoned the arrangement. In others, they tacitly permitted them' (Loory, 1974: 18).

The CIA was also secretly subsidizing the operations of the US National Student Association 'first through wealthy individuals posing as private donors then more systematically, via fake charitable foundations' created specially to act as funding 'pass-throughs' and part of the money was 'channelled abroad, where friendly foreign students organizations spent it on various activities intended to combat the influence of communist fronts' (Wilford, 2008: 2). Frank Wisner, CIA's first chief of political warfare, was said to have compared the CIA front organizations to a 'Mighty Wurlitzer' organ, 'capable of playing any propaganda tune he desired' (Wilford, 2008: 7).

The contribution of the private and public cultural elites in legitimizing free-market capitalism is well documented (Laville and Wilford, 2006). Scholars have shown how in the 1940s and 1950s US government-funded programmes created 'Cold War modernism', using it 'for pro-Western propaganda as well as the politically driven reinterpretation of the modernist movement that undergirded them' (Barnhisel, 2015: 3). As Saunders has argued, the Cold War produced '"false realities" in which Western, and especially American, intellectuals became embroiled in these counterfeits, and more controversially, enlarged them'. The leading intellectuals of the Cold War, Saunders notes, were writing for 'little magazines' until as 'part of the cultural consortium put together by the CIA (with or without their knowledge), they suddenly acquired an international audience' (Saunders, 2013: xii). Others have argued that intellectuals and artists were happy to team up with the political and economic elites because it 'gave their opinions greater effect' (Scott-Smith, 2002: 5). In the late 1960s, the extent of this infiltration came to light: in an 'exclusive' report in 1967 the *New York Times* noted: 'Disclosures in 1967 of some of the C.I.A.'s financial ties to academic, cultural and publishing organizations resulted in some cutbacks, and more recent disclosures of the agency's employment of American and foreign journalists have led to a phasing out of relationships with many of the individuals and news organizations overseas. A smaller network of foreign journalists remains, and some undercover C.I.A. men may still roam the world, disguised as correspondents for obscure trade journals or business newsletters' (*New York Times*, 1977).

'Foundations' of capitalism

The role of the major US foundations such as Carnegie, Ford and Rockefeller – highly influential but unaccountable bodies – in the production of culture and the creation of public policy globally has also been documented (Arnove, 1982; Berman, 1983; Parmar, 2014). Writing at the height of the Cold War, one noted American historian defined the Rockefeller, Ford and Carnegie Foundations and the Council on Foreign Relations as the 'front organizations' of the American Establishment and the *New York Times* and the journal *Foreign Affairs* as 'its organs' (Schlesinger,

1965: 128). According to Berman, who traced the role of these foundations from the early 20th century to the 1980s, the humanitarian aims of their programmes were designed to support US foreign policy. Their investment in education, cultural programmes, research and knowledge production was done in order 'to train individuals who not only share their perspectives, but who will use their influence to "sell" it to others who are less convinced of its merits' (Berman, 1983: 13). The Ford Foundation had a history of sponsoring artistic programmes and supporting the government's value initiatives: throughout the 1950s, it provided funding for organizations such as New Directions Publishing Corporation, Chekhov Publishing House, the Harvard International Summer School, and the Institute of Contemporary Arts; and the magazines *Der Monat*, *The New Leader* and *Perspectives USA* (Wilford, 2008: 126; Saunders, 2013; Barnhisel, 2015).

Others have examined the contribution of the Rockefeller Foundation to global social sciences and humanities research, shaping it in particular ways that legitimized certain ideological orientations, suggesting that the foundation 'was a key actor both in the Cold War political-academic nexus and in the system of science and scholarship patronage' (Mueller, 2013: 110). It was also instrumental in setting up what morphed into 'Sovietology', as an 'integrated Cold War social science' and other area studies (ibid: 114).

The financial support from the 'Big Three' of professional associations, study programmes and elite exchanges contributed significantly to establishing a global network of American Studies in Europe and Asian and African Studies networks, primarily in the United States. Parmer examined how the foundations promoted 'Americanism' throughout the Cold War by supporting American Studies, challenging anti-Americanism and, most importantly, building elite international networks (Parmar, 2014). He outlines how the Ford Foundation offered education and other incentives to train people who would support the Suharto regime in Indonesia and Augusto Pinochet's rise in Chile. US-led Western influence was also visible in such areas as the internationalization of women's organizations (Laville, 2002) and in scientific research and scholarship (Wolfe, 2018). As discussed in Chapter 2, such foundations continue to exert geopolitical influence in today's digital world.

The Cold War battle for 'hearts and minds' in the 'Third World'

As decolonization gathered pace and millions of people began to emerge from centuries of subjugation under European colonial powers, a communication battle ensued for the hearts and minds of people in the so-called 'Third World' (Parker, 2016). While the Soviet Union actively supported the anti-colonial movements in Asia and Africa, seeing the potential to promote communism, and European powers tried to cling to the vestiges of their colonial empires, the United States was interested in taking their place in geopolitical influence through a hegemonic form of 'cultural and media imperialism' (Schiller, 1992; Boyd-Barrett, 2014; Boyd-Barrett and Mirrlees, 2019). In 1953, the United States Information Agency (USIA) was created to 'tell America's story to the world' (Cull, 2009). The American message being sold to the newly independent countries was of freedom, democracy, equality and upward mobility. As the home of the advertising and public relations industries, the United States was well placed to do this, with these industries' sophisticated means of persuasion deployed with great vigour via the US media (Thussu, 2019).

Radio was seen as a crucial medium for communication to the populations of the developing countries, given their low levels of literacy. In addition, the nascent media of the newly independent countries in Asia and Africa were almost always state-controlled and thus less able to compete with foreign media, which had higher credibility and technological superiority. Given its strategic importance as the source of the world's largest supply of oil, the Middle East was a key target for French, British and American broadcasters, who dominated the airwaves in the Arab world. As noted earlier, the BBC Arabic Service had been created in 1938 as the first foreign-language section of the BBC's Empire Service. Declassified British government documents released in 2022 showed that London secretly funded Reuters in the 1960s and 1970s to expand its coverage of the Middle East at the behest of the Information Research Department of the Foreign Office (with close ties to British intelligence) and concealed the funding by using the BBC to make the payments, a Reuters report admitted (Faulconbridge, 2022).

The Arabic service of *Kol Israel* (the Voice of Israel) also played a propaganda role in the Middle East on behalf of the United States, while Egyptian president Gamal Nasser used the radio to promote the idea of pan-Arabism. The Cairo-based 'Voice of the Arabs' was an international service, which in the 1950s and 1960s became the 'pulpit of revolution', notably in the leftist revolution in Iraq in 1958. Pan-Arab sentiment helped the Palestinian 'liberation radios', which regularly and often clandestinely broadcast from Palestine Liberation Organization offices in Cairo, Beirut, Algiers, Baghdad and Tripoli, moving position to avoid Israeli attacks. These radio channels were critical in keeping the Palestinian struggle alive. In Algeria, the Voice of Algeria, the radio station of the *Front de Libération Nationale* (National Liberation Front), played a significant role in the national war of liberation against the French colonial authorities (Thussu, 2019).

Following the Chinese Revolution in 1949, the United States' priority for Cold War communication was to stop the expansion of communism into other parts of Asia, which was reaching its peak during the Vietnam War (Chandler, 1981; Hallin, 1986). Given the nature of the war, the main communication route was by dropping leaflets and broadcasting from low-flying aircraft, and it is estimated that nearly 50 billion leaflets were dropped – nearly '1,500 for every person in both parts of the country' (Chandler, 1981: 3). Radio also played a crucial role in propaganda (as portrayed in the Hollywood film *Good Morning Vietnam!*), while the CIA's Voice of the Patriotic Militiamen's Front in South Vietnam eulogized American military action in that country.

A progressive, anti-imperialist Sukarno government in Indonesia was also brought down by Western intervention, supported by propaganda. In 1965 specialist propagandists from the British Information Research Department were sent to Singapore to produce black propaganda to incite anti-communists among prominent Indonesians, including army generals, to eliminate the Indonesia Communist Party and 'cut out' the 'communist cancer', the *Observer* reported (Lashmar et al., 2021). The United States also launched two radio channels, the Voice of Free Indonesia and Radio Sulawesi to support its anti-Sukarno operations in Indonesia.

After the communist revolution in Cuba in 1959, led by Fidel Castro, US propaganda intensified. The anti-Castro propaganda campaign launched by President John Kennedy, with his *Alianza para el Progreso* (Alliance for Progress) programme, was one of 'the largest concentrations of propaganda effort unleashed against an individual since Stalin tried to purge Tito in 1948', in the words of the former director of VOA George Allen (quoted in Hale, 1975: 101). Unable to dislodge Castro from power, the US Government set up Radio Marti in 1983 and TV Marti in 1990; though the Cuban president died in 2016, both these official propaganda outfits continue to operate.

As part of the British Empire, the BBC had been broadcasting to African countries since 1940, mainly in English, French, Hausa, Portuguese and Swahili. In the 1970s, VOA broadcast to Africa in English, French and Swahili. Though Radio Moscow broadcast in several African languages – usually a translation of anti-imperialist material – its effectiveness was limited, given the lack of communication infrastructure. The Soviet Union invested in transmitters and training courses in Cameroon, while the Chinese supported broadcasting in Zambia and Tanzania. Under the socialist government of President Julius Nyerere, Radio Tanzania became the nerve centre of the liberation movements in southern Africa and of the anti-apartheid struggle (Power, 2000). However, socialist radio stations were no match for the powerful transmitters of Western broadcasters, such as those for BBC from Ascension Island and for VOA from Monrovia (Thussu, 2019). Some areas were targeted for Cold War propaganda, such as Angola, where the US- and South Africa-backed UNITA (National Union for the Total Independence of Angola) rebels used their own radio station – The Voice of the Resistance of the Black Cockerel – which began broadcasting from South Africa in 1979 and was installed in Angola under the CIA's covert aid programme (Windrich, 1992; Power, 2000).

Although it might have seemed that the role of covert broadcasters, such as RFE and RL, would disappear after the fall of the Berlin Wall and the end of the Cold War, and their disbandment was considered, new geopolitical forces demonstrated a continuing need for such communication resources. Already in 1994, RFE/RL began broadcasts to the former Yugoslavia, and in 1998, it launched its Persian Language Service and Radio Free Iraq. The attacks of 11 September 2001 in New York and Washington revived the need for propaganda and public diplomacy, the main aim being to understand the roots of anti-Americanism and win hearts and minds, especially in Arab and Muslim countries (Lennon, 2003). In 2002, an Arabic language popular music and news radio station, *Radio Sawa* ('Radio Together'), aimed at younger Arab audience, was launched by the Middle East Broadcasting Networks (MBN), and *Radio Farda* ('Radio Tomorrow' in Persian) by RFE/RL began transmitting into Iran. Two years later, *Al-Hurra* (Arabic for 'The Free One') TV, operated by MBN, started broadcasting from Springfield, Virginia, as well as from a bureau in the Middle East, funded by the Broadcasting Board of Governors (BBG), the umbrella organization which oversaw all non-military overseas communication for the US government. Today, the United States Agency for Global Media (USAGM), the successor to the BBG, funds and manages the VOA, the Office of Cuba Broadcasting (Radio Marti and TV Marti), RFE/RL, Radio Free Asia, MBN and the Open Technology Fund. By 2022, RFE/RL, now headquartered in Prague, claimed to be reaching a weekly audience of more than 40 million in 27 languages and in 23 countries, including Afghanistan, Iran, Pakistan, Russia and Ukraine. It had 17 local bureaus (including Moscow, Kabul, Kyiv and Islamabad) and more than 1,000 journalists throughout its broadcast region (see USAGM website).

Geopolitics of cultural propaganda

In the propaganda war between the United States and the Soviet Union, 'cultural diplomacy, or soft power, complemented the armament race' (Kalliney, 2022: 7). Both deployed their cultural strengths, including musicians, dancers, writers and filmmakers, hoping to recruit and nurture 'intellectual allies in the decolonizing world'. This included sponsoring literary conferences and prizes, magazines, book publishing, art centres, drama, music and radio programmes for Southern intellectuals and artists; for example, the Soviet Union sponsored *Lotus* magazine and its prize (Kalliney, 2022). In addition, numerous publications from Moscow's Progress Publishers, notably, English translations of books about Marxism and Leninism, as well as great works of Russian literature, were dispatched to countries around the world and were made available in many major languages, including Mandarin and Hindi, 'while such magazines as *Soviet Union, Soviet Life* and *Soviet Land* – in multiple translations – became ubiquitous propaganda vehicles across the developing world until the disintegration of the USSR' (Gavra and Bykova, 2021: 178).

Although many former colonies in the global South were initially receptive to the Soviet message of freedom from colonialism, in the 1950s and 1960s the economic power of the West and dependency on colonial ties, coupled with the increasing influence of modernizing elites, meant that attraction for communism was waning in many parts of the continent, though in southern Africa it remained a powerful force. As major developing countries, such as India, Indonesia and Egypt, opted for non-alignment – a movement founded in 1961 among developing countries which claimed to eschew Cold War bloc politics, joining neither Western nor Eastern alliance – a new perspective on global communication emerged, and decolonization of news media was part of its ideological framing (Lüthi, 2016). Looking beyond the Cold War bipolarity, the Non-Aligned Movement (NAM) countries demanded that international communication issues be seen in terms of North–South rather than East–West categories (Thussu, 2019).

The South talks back, demanding NWICO

In the 1970s, the NAM began to demand greater equality in international news and information flows. This was articulated through the demand for a New World Information and Communication Order (NWICO), the first global attempt to decolonize news media. It argued that there was a 'flagrant quantitative imbalance between North and South created by the volume of news and information emanating from the developed world and intended for the developing countries and the volume of the flow in the opposite direction' (Masmoudi, 1979: 172–173).

Such an order, it was argued, created 'a de facto hegemony and a will to dominate' – evident in the marked indifference of the media in the West to the problems, concerns and aspirations of the developing countries. 'By transmitting to developing countries only news processed by them, that is, news which they have filtered, cut, and distorted, the transnational media impose their own way of seeing the world upon the developing countries' (ibid). This, they argued, had serious implications for developing countries, which were heavily dependent on former colonial masters for both software and hardware in the information sector, and in addition that through their control of major news networks, the Western media tended to cover Third World issues in an exploitative and distorted manner (Nordenstreng, 1986; Frau-Meigs et al., 2012).

These heated debates dominated UNESCO for nearly a decade and, as a result, in 1979 the International Commission for the Study of Communication Problems (popularly known as the MacBride Commission) was set up. Its final report to UNESCO in 1980 brought information- and communication-related issues onto the global agenda for the first time. Following the UNESCO definition of 'a free flow and a wider and more balanced dissemination of information', the MacBride Commission Report related freedom of the press to freedom of expression, to the rights to communicate and receive information, rights of reply and correction, and to civil, political, economic, social and cultural rights. It was critical of the constraints imposed by commercialization, pressures from advertisers and concentration of media ownership and related the growth of transnational corporations to 'one-way flow', 'market dominance' and 'vertical flow' (MacBride Report, 1980).

While the protagonists of NWICO welcomed the report, the West criticized the report's apparent bias against private ownership of media and communication facilities. At the 21st General Conference Session of UNESCO in 1980, a resolution for the attainment of a NWICO was passed, thereby formally approving the report's demands. The resolution proposed the elimination of the imbalance and inequalities in the global media system, as well as the removal of the internal and external obstacles to a free-flow and wider and better-balanced dissemination of information and ideas; and respect for each people's cultural identity and for the rights of each nation to inform the world public about its interests, its aspirations and its social and cultural values (Nordenstreng, 1986).

In the ideologically charged Cold War politics, the West, led by the United States, saw such demands as fundamentally in conflict with the principle of the 'free flow of information', labelling NWICO as a 'Soviet-inspired' Third World design to control the media through state regulation and stifle freedom of expression by imposing censorship. The end of the Cold War and the disappearance of the 'second' (communist) world transformed global communication and debates such as NWICO were confined to history, as market forces took centre-stage in an age of neo-liberal globalization.

The NWICO movement signified a concerted move towards the decolonization of global news flows and has its roots in anti-colonial communication. It is important to record the geopolitical and communication strategies that were deployed by the national liberation movements across the colonial world. The League Against Imperialism was a nascent anti-colonial institution that brought together activists and intellectuals across geographical and political borders for the goal of eradicating colonial rule worldwide, attracting such leaders as India's Jawaharlal Nehru, Indonesia's Sukarno and Kenya's Jomo Kenyatta (Louro et al., 2020). In Lusophone Africa (Portuguese-speaking African countries), between the 1960s and the 1970s, for example, there were many instances of cultural production, international multilingual communication and transnational intellectual networking being used in furtherance of the aims of NWICO. These scholars and activists operated in the transnational circuits of the CONCP (*Confer ̂encia das Organizações Nacionalistas das Colónias Portuguesas* [translated in English as The Conference of Nationalist Organizations of the Portuguese Colonies]), founded in Casablanca in 1961, which represented the alliance between the major anti-colonialist organizations in so-called Portuguese Africa (Cairo, 2006).

These 'subaltern diplomacies' have not been given the importance they deserve: for example, the most famous figure in Lusophone Africa's liberation movement, Amílcar Cabral (1924–1973), who, like his counterpart in Algeria, Frantz Fanon, deployed political and cultural diplomacy to gain support of intellectuals and public opinion worldwide (Ferretti, 2021). In the war of the African colonies against Portuguese imperialism, both sides fought their battles in the field of cultural production and media, including radio broadcasting (Power, 2000).

For African anti-colonialists, the use of communication for both the external and internal construction of national imageries was understood as one of their main weapons and as part of a specific intellectual diplomacy, which led to what has been defined as 'a subaltern geopolitical strategy'. This strategy entailed building, for the attention of worldwide public opinion, public discourses countering mainstream 'geopolitics of development', that is, according to Power, strategies serving counter-insurgency in the newly decolonized 'Third World' (Power, 2019).

In Asia too, this area remains largely underexplored. As Satia has noted, 'The major forces of that history – imperialism, industrial capitalism, nationalism – were justified by notions of progress and thus liable to rationalizations about noble ends justifying ignoble means' (Satia, 2018: 11). To illustrate her point, Satia cites examples of British violence that resulted in the deaths of millions in Kenya and tens of thousands in Sudan (Satia, 2018). As a new history of British colonialism, privileging the viewpoint of the South, the 'forgotten quarter' of the planet, notes, the rhetoric of the civilizational mission of colonialism was a cloak for 'scientific data-gathering, the use of costly armies, new technology and aristocratic militarism disguised with a language of liberation and free trade' (Sivasundaram, 2020: 243). How this imperial continuity persists to define the geopolitics of communication and how it is serviced are the themes of the next chapter.

2
GLOBALIZATION OF COMMUNICATION – CONSTRUCTING AND SERVICING A NEO-LIBERAL WORLD

The dismantling of the Soviet system after the fall of the Berlin Wall in 1989 and the end of the Cold War saw the victory of the United States and its allies as champions of a liberal global world order and the subsequent transformation of global politics, the global economy and, with that, global communication. The privatization of state entities and deregulation of the global economy enabled the creation of a global market for trade and the globalization of the Western capitalist model. These processes of liberalization, deregulation and privatization also transformed the communications and media industries and, combined with new digital technologies, enabled a quantum leap in global communication, revolutionizing connectivity, commerce, and geopolitics. Before privatization and commercialization, the global communication infrastructure was controlled primarily by the United States, Britain and Europe and, despite liberalization and deregulation, continues to be dominated by Western institutional, commercial and intellectual organizations.

This development was led by a triumvirate of powerful institutions – the World Bank, the International Monetary Fund (IMF) and the World Trade Organization (WTO), which, it could be argued, perpetuated the structures and systems of a neo-imperialist, neo-liberal Western hegemony. This US-led post-war multilateral system reflected the values and ideological orientations of their most powerful sponsors, privileging liberal values of private property and individual rights, despite their appearances of being 'neutral' and 'universalistic' (Chwieroth, 2010; Stone, 2011; Voeten, 2021).

In the 1980s, the World Bank and the IMF, through their 'structural adjustment programmes', had been instrumental in opening up the economies of the global South, as well as the countries of the so-called eastern bloc, to Western corporations. This led to catastrophic results in many countries transitioning from a state-controlled socialist economy to the vagaries of free-market capitalism, most notably Russia, which faced the 'shock therapy' of President Boris Yeltsin and his economic reform czar, Yegor Gaidar. As Adam Curtis showed in his 2022 seven-part series, *Russia 1985–1999: TraumaZone*, the 'withering away' of the Soviet state and the unplanned and immediate switch to a market economy resulted in political chaos and extreme poverty for ordinary Russians, while sections of the party apparatchiks and oligarchs made great fortunes by 'rabidly' privatizing state assets (BBC, 2022b).

The globalization of the deregulated, liberalized and privatized communication model was a major policy goal of the US government, echoing the concerns of US-based corporations. Liberalization of telecommunications became increasingly pronounced after the Reagan administration announced an 'open skies' policy in 1984, allowing private telecommunications networks to compete freely. Britain then followed by privatizing 51 per cent of state-owned British Telecom. In the EU too, 'accelerating liberalization' and 'simplifying regulation' became the hallmark of telecommunication policy (Iosifidis, 2011: 200). The vehicle for these processes was the global free trade negotiations of the WTO, building on the work of its predecessor the General Agreement in Tariffs and Trade (GATT).

Set up in 1995, the WTO was a permanent replacement for the GATT, a process established by the United States after World War II to promote global free trade. The final round of GATT in Uruguay, signed in 1994, had included trade in services, including communication, for the first time. The new WTO saw free trade in information and communication as key to economic growth and their policy of neo-liberal globalization, so the dismantling of barriers to the free flow of information was essential (Thussu, 2019). The importance of a strong communications infrastructure as a foundation for international commerce and economic development was also emphasized by other major international organizations, such as the World Bank (World Bank, 1998), the International Telecommunications Union (ITU, 1999) and the United Nations Development Programme (UNDP, 1999).

The first multilateral, legally enforceable agreement of the WTO, the 1995 General Agreement on Trade in Services (GATS) aimed to provide the infrastructure for trade and investment in the lucrative services sector, including telecommunications and IT (telephone, telegraph, data transmission, computing, radio, TV and news); finance; business and insurance, and PR, advertising and market research. Under the banner of the US-initiated Cold War doctrine of 'free flow of information', the agreement required, through its Annex on Telecommunications, equal treatment of foreign and national suppliers of telecommunication services, so that countries had to open up their public networks and services to foreign companies. It also encouraged the establishment of international standards for global compatibility and interoperability (WTO, 1998).

The GATS Fourth Protocol on Basic Telecommunications Services, also referred to as the Agreement on Basic Telecommunications Services, which came into force in February 1998, obliged the 69 signatories, representing more than 93 per cent of global revenue in telecommunications services, to liberalize telecommunications in their respective countries. Cable, radio and satellites were included in the agreement, though broadcasting of radio and television programmes was excluded. It required the signatories to provide market access and equal treatment to international telecommunication corporations.

The Protocol also endorsed the US position that the distinction between 'domestic' and 'international' satellite systems was no longer valid in a digitally connected world and that satellite transmissions could cross national borders. The developing countries, concerned that technological innovations, such as the integrated services digital networks (ISDNs), would make it possible for a huge amount of data to be instantly transferred in or out of countries, wanted to discuss the implications of this for their sovereignty within the UN. However, at US insistence the debate was moved to the Organization for Economic Co-operation and Development (OECD), in essence shifting the argument from national sovereignty to one about trade in global information through electronic networks (Thussu, 2019).

This shift from a state-centric view to a market-led view of communication was also evident in the decision of the ITU to reallocate radio and satellite frequencies to commercial operators (Hill, 2014). Transnational corporations were keen to use digital technologies to offer new global communication services, including satellite TV, electronic data and mobile telephony. Aware of the commercial potential of mobile telephony, the corporations lobbied for an additional use of the electromagnetic spectrum, and the ITU constitution was amended at the 1998 World Radiocommunication Conference to give greater rights and responsibilities to private sector members. In the area of 'technical recommendation', as one senior ITU official conceded, they 'effectively transferred the power to decide from government to the private sector' (MacLean, 1999: 156).

The ITU began to play a leading role among international organizations in the development of electronic commerce, particularly through standardization activities, with a goal to promote connectivity to what the US government defined as the 'Global Information Infrastructure' (GII), critical for the globalization of electronic commerce. One of its key 'governing principles' stated that governments should avoid undue restrictions on electronic commerce and should merely provide an enabling but minimal legal framework for its operation (US Government, 1997).

US policy of liberalizing the global telecommunication system was boosted by the US Telecommunications Act (1996), which enabled US corporations to operate globally, and by the Federal Communications Commission (FCC), which 'aimed at increasing competition in communications markets around the world' (Freedman, 2008). US influence put pressure on the WTO and the ITU, through its World Radiocommunication Conferences (WRC), to further liberalize global communication, including spectrum harmonization, to enable satellite systems, as well as undersea telecommunication cables, to deliver advanced mobile voice and high-speed broadband services.

Such had been the change in the global communication industry that even inter-governmental organizations (IGOs), such as the London-based Inmarsat (International Maritime Satellite Organization), became increasingly driven by market considerations. Established in 1979 as a cooperative of 86 countries, originally to provide global mobile satellite communications for marine communication and then for commercial applications also in the air and on land, in 1999, it became the world's first international treaty organization to transform itself into a commercial company. With privatization, some of the largest national telecommunication businesses in the world, from among its former member countries, became the main shareholders of the new company which claims to be 'the world leader in global mobile satellite communications'. Its Global Xpress satellite series, launched in 2013, was the world's first high-speed commercial broadband satellite network suited to mobile communications. Following this, in 2000, the world's largest satellite operator, the International Telecommunications Satellite Organization (Intelsat), an intergovernmental treaty organization created at the height of the Cold War in 1964 to operate a global satellite system for telecommunications services, was also privatized. By 2022 it operated 'the world's largest satellite services business, providing a critical layer in the global communications infrastructure' (see Intelsat website).

Infrastructure for the internet: US domination of space and sea

In an age when the internet has become, in the words of Castells, 'the communication fabric' of people's lives (Castells, 2009: 115), a geopolitical understanding of the hardware which enables 24/7 global online connectivity is crucial (DeNardis, 2011; Holt and Vonderau, 2015). The exponential growth in communication infrastructure within just over two decades of privatization and deregulation is inextricably linked to the ever-increasing worldwide use of satellites and cables for internet-enabled communication and commerce, contributing to the global digital supremacy of the United States, the originator of the internet (Aouragh and Chakravartty, 2016).

From outer space to under-sea cables, internet hardware is dominated mainly by US-based 'space barons' (Davenport, 2018). The growing privatization of the global digital infrastructure can be seen in US companies' pre-eminence in the satellite industry: of the nearly 2,000 active satellites orbiting the Earth in 2019, the United States accounted for 849, compared with China at 284, Russia at 152 and India at 57. Similarly, the rapid increase in the laying down of fibre-optic submarine cables carrying 99 per cent of international data also has a strong US imprint on it, a fact resented by countries such as Russia and China (Starosielski, 2015). By 2018, major US digital corporations – notably Microsoft, Google, Facebook (now Meta) and Amazon – owned or leased more than 50 per cent of the undersea bandwidth (Satariano, 2019).

Satellites

US-based corporations are also the leading players in manufacturing satellites and space rocket components, as well as ground services and satellite services, notably Hughes and Loral. American defence corporations such as Boeing, Lockheed Martin, Northrop Grumman and Raytheon also have a significant presence in the satellite industry. Hughes, Lockheed Martin and Loral have between them built the majority of the geostationary communications satellites currently in orbit, followed by a European satellite consortium led by the French Aerospatiale. Many US infrastructure projects, however, also have strong governmental backing, including the US Global Positioning System (GPS), a vital element of the satellite communications infrastructure and a key part of the US government's National Strategy for Space. The GPS system is vital to the operation of communication systems, transport and an extensive range of internet services, so is seen as strategically essential.

The privatization of space has also brought new US-based players into the satellite market, including Elon Musk-owned SpaceX, a leading provider of launch services, whose Starlink claims to be 'the world's first and largest satellite constellation using a low Earth orbit to deliver broadband internet'. Amazon, too, has invested heavily in fast satellite broadband to provide connectivity to underserved places, as has Meta – first through Internet.org, a Facebook-led initiative, launched in 2013 and later renamed Free Basics.

Satellites not only transmit the data to enable commerce but they can also themselves generate data that is of commercial interest. Companies such as DigitalGlobe, a division of Maxar Technologies and Airbus Defence and Space, formerly known as the European Aeronautic Defence and Space Company, provide satellite images using their low-orbit satellite constellations, which, unlike fixed-orbit communication satellites, orbit the earth at much lower altitudes and provide full coverage of the earth's surface. The first publicly available data set originating from the US Air Force's Defense Meteorological Satellite Program and NASA's Landsat system has been used to study deforestation and discoveries in the mining industry. High-resolution satellite imagery from low-orbit satellites has an important role in the financial forecasting industry by providing data to analyse phenomena that might affect trading activity (Donaldson and Storeygard, 2016; Dugast and Foucault, 2018).

In recent years of rising geopolitical tensions with the United States' space rivals, China and Russia, the US administration has emphasized the need to combat competition in the space sector. The *United States Space Priorities Framework*, issued in 2021, was candid: 'The United States will work with allies and partners to combat foreign government non-market practices, protect critical US technologies and intellectual property, and reduce reliance on strategic competitors for key space capabilities' (White House, 2021: 5). Emphasizing that 'space systems are an essential component of US critical infrastructure – by directly providing important services and by enabling other critical infrastructure sectors and industries', the framework urged that, in order 'to create free and fair market competition internationally, the United States will work with allies and partners to update and harmonize space policies, regulations, export controls, and other measures that govern commercial activities worldwide' (White House, 2021: 6).

Morgan Stanley estimates that 'the global space industry could generate revenue of $1 trillion by 2040, up from $350 billion in 2020. The satellite broadband internet access will represent 50 per cent of the projected growth of the global space economy by 2040. Launching satellites that offer broadband internet service will help to drive down the cost of data, just as demand for that data explodes' (Morgan Stanley, 2020).

Cabling the world for the internet age

The phenomenal growth in communication via satellite over the past three decades has been overtaken by the expansion of undersea fibre-optic cables. The telegraph and telephone cables that transformed global communication in the 19th and 20th centuries have been replaced by fibre-optic cables for the digital 21st century, which can carry far more data at far less cost and have in the same way revolutionized global communication.

The first fibre-optic cable, called Tat-8, was laid across the Atlantic in 1988 by a consortium of US, British and French telecommunications firms. By 2022, more than 400 fibre-optic submarine cables, spanning 1.3 million kilometres, were transporting transoceanic digital communications and a further 130 were planned, according to industry data, thus becoming a critical infrastructure for the flow of internet traffic. Writing a paper for a think tank in 2017, Rishi Sunak, who became Britain's first prime minister 'of colour' in 2022, described the tens of thousands of kilometres of undersea cables as 'the arteries of the internet age' and 'one of the world's most indispensable pieces of infrastructure' (Sunak, 2017: 14). This infrastructure is crucial for global electronic commerce, which continues to be dominated by 'the transatlantic theatre', described as 'the fulcrum of global digital connectivity' (ibid.).

The highest densities of the submarine cable network are in the northern transatlantic route and the transpacific routes, between the United States and Europe, and between the United States and Asia, respectively, according to the *Submarine Telecoms Industry Report 2021*, produced for the Submarine Telecom Forum (Submarine Telecoms Forum, 2022). Submarine cables in the Atlantic carry 55 per cent more data than transpacific routes, as the United States and Europe are each other's most important commercial partners: they are the two largest net exporters of digitally enabled services to the world (Hamilton and Quinlan, 2022: viii). In 2020, the United States registered a $213.6 billion trade surplus in digitally enabled services with the world. Its main commercial partner was Europe, to which it exported over $247 billion in digitally enabled services and from which it imported $142 billion, generating a trade surplus with Europe in this area of over $105 billion. US exports of digitally enabled services to Europe were about 2.7 times greater than US digitally enabled services exports to Latin America, and roughly double than those to the entire Asia-Pacific region (ibid.).

US and European cities (Frankfurt, London, Amsterdam, Paris, Stockholm, Miami, Marseille and Los Angeles) are the world's foremost hubs for international communication and data exchange. The US Federal Reserve estimated that in 2021 some $10 trillion were transmitted via undersea cables every day. The Society for Worldwide Interbank Financial Telecommunication (SWIFT), which provides the international framework for some 11,000 financial institutions to conduct an average of 15 million transactions a day, is wholly reliant on undersea cables. 'Undersea internet cables', notes a report from the European Council on Foreign Relations, 'are critical infrastructure as important as gas and oil pipelines, and are becoming a focus of growing geopolitical competition' (ECFR, 2021: 4).

In such a highly interdependent world, the shockwaves resulting from a major cable disruption at a leading financial centre such as London, New York, Hong Kong or Singapore would be catastrophic. Although under the 1982 UN Convention on the Law of the Sea undersea cables are given protection in international waters, it does not, however, prohibit states from treating these as legitimate military targets during wartime. With global commerce and security now nearly entirely dependent upon the security of this physical and logical infrastructure, the consequences of such failure could be devastating. Sunak suggests adoption of a new international treaty that protects submarine cables and pressing 'NATO for more naval exercises and war games to hone potential responses to an attack on undersea cable infrastructure and review whether NATO maritime capabilities are sufficient to protect freedom of the seas and our sea lanes of communication' (Sunak, 2017: 8).

Among the major companies involved in this burgeoning business are two US-based corporations: TE SubCom, one of the largest manufacturers of undersea cables in the world, and Verizon, which owns and operates one of the most 'expansive IP backbone networks in the world', including more than 1.2 million route kilometres of terrestrial and undersea cable, spanning six continents and supporting '99 percent of the Fortune 500' corporations. Other major actors include Alcatel Submarine Networks (France); Cable and Wireless (Britain); NTT and NEC (Japan); Huawei Marine Networks, China Mobile, China Telecom, and China Unicom (China); and Tata Communications and Reliance Globalcom (India).

The main users of international bandwidth are also the ones who are most heavily investing in cables. These include content providers such as Google, Meta, Amazon and Microsoft but also include carriers such as Telxius, China Telecom and Telstra. According to TeleGeography, 'Unlike previous submarine cable construction booms, content providers like Amazon, Google, Facebook, and Microsoft are taking a more active role in this recent surge. These companies alone have such incredible demand for data center traffic that they're driving projects and route prioritization for submarine cables' (Telegeography, 2021). Google,

Meta and Microsoft have joined with others to build international submarine cable systems. The 6,600-kilometre-long Marea cable, a project of Facebook, Microsoft and Telefonica, which connects Virginia Beach, Virginia, with Bilbao, Spain, came online in 2018, while the 9,656-kilometre Ella Link from Sines in Portugal to Fortaleza in Brazil came online in 2021. Two Google-funded subsea cables came online in 2022: Grace Hopper, connecting Spain and Britain to the United States; and Equiano, linking Portugal to South Africa. An 8,700-kilometre-long cable named Medusa will link Lisbon with Port Said in Egypt, with connections in France, Spain, Italy, Morocco, Tunisia, Greece and Cyprus, and a consortium of Meta, Nokia, Alcatel and other telecom operators is constructing 2Africa, the world's longest subsea cable system, extending over 45,000 kilometres to connect 33 countries (Hamilton and Quinlan, 2022: 60).

Google is a major part of the consortium which owns UNITY Cable, linking California to Japan, and has also invested in SJC (South-East Asia Japan Cable System), consisting of a series of spurs from the transpacific cables to Brunei, China, Hong Kong, the Philippines, Japan and Singapore. In collaboration with leading East Asian public telecommunication companies, including China Mobile, Google has also invested in the transpacific FASTER cable system between the United States and Japan, China and South Korea (Winseck, 2017). Meta has also invested heavily in this region, for example, in APG (Asia-Pacific Gateway), a submarine cable system linking eight countries in East and Southeast Asia. Globally, the market for submarine fibre-optic cables is estimated to reach $30.8 billion by 2026, growing at an annual rate of more than 14 per cent. Google and Meta have heavily invested in the Pacific Light Cable Network – a submarine cable system initially designed to connect Hong Kong, Taiwan, the Philippines and the United States – aimed to offer the first direct submarine cable connectivity between Hong Kong and Los Angeles. However, due to geopolitical tensions based on 'national security' concerns, the US government asked Google and Meta in 2022 to exclude the Chinese broadband provider's participation in the project and redirect the cable system to connect the United States to Taiwan and the Philippines without the link to Hong Kong (Hamilton and Quinlan, 2022).

The development of data-related, land-based internet infrastructure is as important for the functioning of the internet as the quality of connectivity and internet coverage, to engage more people and companies in the data-driven digital economy. The potential return on investment in this is huge, with the possibility to improve access to data from an increased number of internet users, and thus generate new revenues. This includes Internet Exchange Points (IXPs), the physical locations where different networks connect to exchange internet traffic via common switching infrastructures. The networks that participate in IXPs can be service providers, content providers, hosting companies or governments. It has been shown that access speeds for local content can improve as much as tenfold with an IXP, as traffic is routed more directly (Internet Society, 2017). There were 556 IXPs in the world in 2021, more than half of these based in the West. In addition, the co-location data centres, so-called hyperscale data centres, are engineered to meet the technical, operational and pricing requirements of 'hyperscale companies' such as Amazon and Google, as they require huge amounts of space and power for cloud, big data analytics or storage tasks. These, too, are highly concentrated in the West: in 2021 of a total of 4,714 co-location data centres, almost 80 per cent were based mainly in the United States and in Europe (UNCTAD, 2021: 39). As the volume and value of global data surge, the storage and processing of digital data become a crucial component of infrastructure.

Policy infrastructure: who controls the internet?

It is not surprising that the US imprint on the internet is profound, with the United States having conceived, developed and globalized this network via its formidable technological and economic resources, enabling Washington to create an internet infrastructure and governance system that suits its economic and geopolitical goals. The United States played a central role in creating the architecture and underlying technical requirements of the internet, with its top universities, defence establishments and corporations setting the standards that have been followed by the rest of the world. US policy in this area, therefore, has global impact and implications – not only in relation to how multilateral institutions such as UNESCO or ITU frame communication policy but also on governments and businesses around the world.

With its origins in 1969 as a project of US Department of Defense, consisting of a few connected computers located in US security and university establishments, the protocols to manage the internet were created by US academics, while those of the World Wide Web were developed at CERN (the European Organization for Nuclear Research) in Geneva. These laid the foundations for a global expansion of the internet during the 1990s, driven primarily by US-based private corporations with active support from the US government.

Critical to this was the establishment in 1998 of the Internet Corporation for Assigned Names and Numbers (ICANN), a California-based not-for-profit organization, to allocate domain names worldwide to countries, companies and organizations, as well as IP (internet protocol) addresses without which the internet could not function (Kruger, 2014). Clearly, whoever allocates domain names is very close to being a global controller of the internet and as 'the ultimate intermediary on which everyone depends' (Goldsmith and Wu, 2006: 168): some domain names are worth millions of dollars – and the 'domain name system itself underlies billions in electronic commerce' (Dourish, 2015).

Concerns were raised by many countries about the effective 'unilateral control' by the US government via ICANN of this 'internet backbone' and the high distribution of costs that internet service providers (ISPs) based in the global South had to pay for access (Thussu, 2019). The international network of private companies and ISPs are mostly based in the United States as the 'centre of the network', with

American corporations accounting for the majority of international links (Ruiz and Barnett, 2015). While the system contributed significantly to the smooth running of the internet, it was privileging private corporate interest rather than public interest, which generated criticism, especially among many developing and emerging nations. As Castells noted, 'The internet is a global network, so its regulation could not be left to the US Department of Commerce, even in the form of an ICANN board elected by internet users' (Castells, 2009: 113). For example, Russia has criticized the fact that out of the 13 root servers essential to the functioning of the global internet, ten are located in the United States and the other three are 'on the territory of US allies' (Japan, the Netherlands and Sweden) (Nocetti, 2015: 121).

The US internet giants also dominate the 'code' and 'content layers' of the internet: that is, the operating systems (iOS, Windows, Android), search engine (Google), social media (Meta) and online retailing (Amazon), as well as over-the-top (OTT) TV services (Netflix). The 'core' internet platforms – Google (Alphabet), Amazon, Facebook (Meta), Apple and Microsoft – differ not only quantitatively but also qualitatively from other platforms in that 'their power is not only economic but social, cultural and political. In all of these respects, their power is fundamentally *infrastructural*: it entails the concentrated private control over digital infrastructures that have become or are becoming indispensable for economic, social, cultural and political life' (Brubaker, 2023: 107, emphasis in the original). Brubaker goes on to argue that, as a result, they are 'part of our cognitive, cultural, and social infrastructure: everyday life as we know it has come to depend massively on search engines, video and music streaming services, and social media and messaging platforms' (ibid.).

Challenges to the US-led communication infrastructure

The 'multi-stakeholder model' promoted by ICANN for the governance of the internet, in which governments share policy debates with private sector and civil society groups, has strong supporters in the West and among many developing countries, including India and Brazil, while Russia and China have argued for a UN-approved and UN-managed governance structure, with the ITU undertaking a primary role in defining and implementing governance, and a reduced role for ICANN. Such demands are likely to become more vocal as global power equations alter in the digital age.

Two competing views dominate the debate about how the internet should be governed: a 'sovereignist' view where national governments are final arbiters of cyber policy, and a market-led corporatized governance structure, championed by the US.

Writing in *Foreign Affairs*, Laura Rosenberger, formerly of the US State Department and director of the Alliance for Securing Democracy and a senior fellow at the German Marshall Fund of the United States, said that 'continuing to support a free and open internet is important in opposing the control that authoritarian regimes seek through the spread of "sovereign internets"' (Rosenberger, 2020: 156). She also criticized the 'new path', enunciated by the French president Emmanuel Macron to protect European cyber 'sovereignty', as a substitute to the 'Californian form of internet'. 'Most troubling for US officials', Rosenberger asserted, is 'that European officials are seeking a new model to distance their countries from the US, rather than working to build a broader democratic framework' (Rosenberger, 2020: 155–156).

The EU has the ambition and potential to become a sovereign digital power, but it lacks an all-encompassing strategy for the sector, in which individual governments are still the key players. Since 2019, the European Commission has explicitly stated its aim to be a 'geopolitical commission'. In line with this, the concept of 'digital sovereignty' has become increasingly important as the Commission deals with the new challenges facing Europe. According to a report by the European Council on Foreign Relations (ECFR), the EU should set its own industry standards, help European telecommunications companies win business abroad and protect internet infrastructure against hostile powers. Without its own digital capacities and autonomy, Europe will not be able to 'fully contend with other actors in the tech space, and will find itself caught up in rising US-China competition for technological supremacy' (ECFR, 2021: 4). China and the United States differ in their approaches, but both are racing ahead of the EU in their influence over internet infrastructure and the states that depend on it.

Some BRICS nations have supplemented, if not replaced, US hardware for digital communication with their own infrastructure. Russia, India and China have developed their own satellite navigation systems (GLONASS, NAVIC and BeiDou, respectively). China's Hongyun satellite project, started in 2016, aims to build a space-based communications network to provide broadband internet connectivity to users around the world, especially in developing countries. India has also established itself as a key player in the budget satellite business: in 2014, it launched *Mangalyaan*, a probe into orbit around Mars, at a cost of merely $73 million (see essays in Pillai and Prasad, 2017). In 2023, India became the first country to land a lunar cruiser, *Chandrayaan-3*, on the far side of the moon.

Apart from the long-established Indo-Russian collaboration in space technology and the more recent Sino-Russian collaboration in this field, the intra-BRICS infrastructure exchanges and cooperation had limited success. The 2012 plan to create a 34,000-kilometre-long 'BRICS undersea cable' network, which would have linked the member countries, did not get beyond the planning stages (Zhao, 2015). The failure of this ambitious project demonstrated intra-BRICS geopolitical tensions, especially between China and India, which have increased, especially in relation to the Belt and Road Initiative (BRI), as indicated by a report by a leading defence-related think tank in India which viewed BRI as a project to realize the 'geopolitical, geo-economic and geostrategic ambitions' of China (Lele and Roy, 2019: 56).

Since its accession in 2001 to the WTO, China has evolved from a 'rule taker' that 'passively accepts existing rules imposed by other countries' to a 'rule shaker' that 'tries to exploit the existing rules to its advantage', and to a 'rule maker' that 'is making new rules that reflects its own interests' (Gao, 2012: 76). As a new study notes, for the WTO to accommodate China's unique geopolitical position, it should insist that the country's state-owned enterprises do not benefit from unfair trade advantages, but China is not 'willing to reform its one-party political system and everything it entails in terms of state participation in the working of the economy' (Mavroidis and Sapir, 2021: 7).

China's idea of 'internet sovereignty', as articulated in a 2010 government White Paper, *The Internet in China*, requires that China should be given full scope in international internet administration and for the establishment of an 'authoritative and just international internet administration organization under the UN system through democratic procedures on a worldwide scale. All countries have equal rights in participating in the administration of the fundamental international resources of the internet' (Government of China, 2010).

In the policy arena, too, China has been pushing for its own version of how the internet should be governed. Since 2014, the Cyberspace Administration of China, the agency that controls China's internet, annually organizes the World Internet Conference to debate internet governance and cyber sovereignty and, since 2016, China has also been organizing annual BRICS Media Summits for selected news organizations from the five members, demanding that the imbalance in global news flows should be redressed. Writing in the *Wall Street Journal*, Li Congjun, former head of Xinhua, a major force behind BRICS media summits, advocated the creation of a 'new world media order' since, in his view, 'global opinions are still dominated by Western media outlets', and China's ability to make its own voice heard 'fails to match its international standing' (Li, 2011).

The US-dominated global communication infrastructure is being challenged, most notably, by China, a country that in the past two decades has expanded phenomenally in almost all domains of communication – land, maritime and space. China is ahead of almost every other nation in terms of infrastructure for 5G and 6G technology, giving it mastery of its own industrial future and that of countries using its mobile services for the Internet of Things (IoT) (DeNardis, 2020). With the world's largest smartphone market and internet population, 5G mobile network investments in China are projected to reach $405 billion by 2030. Privately owned Huawei, the world's largest telecoms equipment supplier, with an estimated 40 per cent global market share, is pushing for global 5G projects in 170 countries.

China successfully landed an exploratory rover on the moon and one on Mars in 2020, and by 2022, China was the world's second largest satellite owner after the United States. According to China's 2016 document *'State Plan for Informationization in the Period of the 13th Five Year Plan'*, the country will develop a space-based infrastructure to provide seamless internet and other information services anywhere on the earth's surface, using a dispersed array of floating platforms high in the atmosphere, communications satellites and networked space capabilities in higher orbits.

The plan calls for China to integrate remote-sensing and telemetry systems associated with the BeiDou Global Navigation Satellite System, other satellites, near-space flight vehicles and crewed aircraft, while 'coordinating the construction of ground-based infrastructure and the development of military-civil fusion, in order to obtain global service capabilities as fast as possible'. The document states that China will accelerate the deployment of broadband satellites in highearth orbit, as well as low-earth orbit, and improve its use of the frequency spectrum to 'satisfy the needs of the state's major strategies' (cited in Defense Intelligence Agency, 2022: iv).

China is collaborating with Russia in its space efforts, including in the establishment of the International Lunar Research Station, as a rival to the US-led Artemis programme for lunar exploration. In 2021, Russia's Roscosmos signed an agreement with China's National Space Administration to build the station (Jones, 2021). In 2022 a US government report warned that 'Beijing and Moscow seek to position themselves as leading space powers, intent on creating new global space norms. Through the use of space and counterspace capabilities, they aspire to undercut US global leadership' (Defense Intelligence Agency, 2022: iv). This challenge to US hegemony is most clearly seen in the digital communication dimension of China's Belt and Road Initiative (BRI).

The Digital Silk Road

Since China extended the BRI to the virtual frontier by announcing a Digital Silk Road (DSR) in 2015, there is growing concern about how vital technological infrastructure is to China's geopolitical vision. Given China's technological ambitions, the DSR provides an important pathway for expanding China's global influence in the digital realm and if substantively realized could enable China's goal of becoming a global cyber super power. Huawei and ZTE are spearheading projects focused on basic ICT infrastructure, building fibre-optic cables and smart-cities that are the foundation for enhanced digital connectivity. State-owned telecommunication companies, such as China Mobile, China Telecom and CITIC Telecom, are primarily responsible for DSR projects related to carrier services, which allow for improved telecom coverage and broadband availability. Finally, private companies including Alibaba, Tencent and JD have been involved in the development of over-the-counter services, leveraging their respective specialties to build data and cloud centres and promote e-commerce models in recipient countries.

In its 2018 document 'Implementation Opinions on Standardisation Work in Industrial Sector and Communications Industry Serving Belt and Road Initiative', China's Ministry of Industry and Information Technology defined six areas of focus for the DSR, including 5G, smart cities, the BeiDou satellite and telecommunications projects. The DSR could enable China to become the world's leading supplier of the physical infrastructure for next-generation digital networks. China has devoted significant resources to building 5G technology, fibre-optic cables and data centres in collaboration with DSR recipient countries (Gordon et al., 2020: 20). The DSR encompasses undersea cables, data centres, 5G systems and a 'space information corridor' to supplant GPS as the world's most advanced satellite navigation technology. More than 100 countries have agreed to participate as part of BRI, but not all have accepted Chinese investment into their critical infrastructure. It represents an emerging architecture for a Chinese-led bloc of countries where the United States has minimal access and influence (Freymann, 2020).

Concerns about the DSR typically emanate from the West, and particularly the United States, where Chinese infrastructural projects are seen part of a geopolitical contest and increasingly viewed through 'the security and strategic lenses'. A report from a leading US think tank warned that DSR might enable China 'access to critical information; to carry out disruptive cyberattacks' through 'manipulating digital infrastructures that China would help construct' (Gordon et al., 2020: 21).

Already, by 2019 China's BeiDou was equipped with more active satellites than those that support the GPS. Such a 'competitive positioning service system heralds the end of the GPS's monopoly as the dominant provider of real-time location information around the world', as well as concerns that under the DSR umbrella, Beijing might create a 'cascade of China-driven 5G standards' for adoption by BRI countries (Gordon et al., 2020: 22).

In the maritime domain, Chinese telecommunications firms such as China Mobile, China Telecom and China Unicom have invested heavily in undersea cables across the world, especially focusing on the global South. Hengtong Group and its subsidiaries, Huawei Marine and Hengtong Marine, led the construction of the PEACE (Pakistan East Africa Cable Express) cable, a DSR project that starts in Gwadar and Karachi in Pakistan, connecting South Asia with East Africa, aiming to land in Marseille, France. In 2019, Hengtong signed an agreement with Telecom Egypt to open a landing point in Egypt, 'securing for China a crucial strategic player in the PEACE cable project', as an EU think tank commented (ECFR, 2021: 12). Huawei's construction of the South Atlantic Inter Link (SAIL), linking Kribi, Cameroon, with Fortaleza, Brazil, and the PEACE cable has enabled Chinese telecom companies to expand their reach in the global South.

Epistemic communities: providing the software for the global communication system

Apart from the 'hardware' of the global communication infrastructure discussed earlier, there is also a form of 'software' provided by the 'epistemic community', encompassing the intellectual and cultural infrastructure provided by think tanks, the non-governmental sector and universities (Haas, 2016), which helps to shape the interplay of geopolitics and global communication. As with the technological infrastructure, in this domain, too, a clear US–UK predominance is evident, demonstrating the imperial continuities discussed in Chapter 1. These communities participate in a 'soft' imperialism predicated on an intellectual and professional hegemony, in which geopolitics influences the discourses of the global media and communication field. One of the prerequisites for this is the hegemony of English as the language of global communication.

In the 18th and 19th centuries English was the language of Britain as the leading economic power globally; in the late 19th century, this role transferred to the United States. With the United States developing the new media and communication technologies in the 20th century, English was the default language for innovation, from the press, to advertising, broadcasting, film, sound recording and communications (Crystal, 2003: 120–121). In 2023, English still topped the hierarchy of international languages, being the main language of multinational interactions and the UN system, transnational corporations and international media, including the internet and scientific and technological publishing. As Svartvik and Leech note, although many more people speak Mandarin as their first language than there are native English speakers, the language of what has elsewhere been described as a 'small foggy island at the edge of Europe' (Thussu, 1998), has retained an 'unrivaled position as a means of international communication' (Svartvik and Leech, 2016: 1). English also remains a major presence in corporate communication and in international business, as more than 52 per cent of transnational corporations use English in their everyday transactions (Neeley, 2017).

English continues to have a disproportionate influence among the former British colonial territories – the Commonwealth countries – especially in education and literature, even though it is used by a small minority of the powerful political and cultural elite. Only those authors who can write in English or whose works are translated into English are considered 'international'. Many in the former colonies see English as a manifestation of 'linguistic imperialism', which interlocks with an inherited structure of imperialism in culture, education, the media, communication, the economy, politics and military activities (Phillipson, 1992, 2009). The dominance of English creates a hierarchy of inequality and injustice that privileges those able to use the dominant language. Phillipson has argued that it is not only structural but 'ideological: beliefs, attitudes, and imagery glorify the dominant language, stigmatize others, and rationalize the linguistic hierarchy. The dominance is hegemonic: It is internalized and naturalized as being "normal"' (Phillipson, 1992). The use of English as a lingua franca underpins the global 'epistemic community', which privileges the knowledge and expertise of the English-speaking intellectual elites and reflects a shared system of values and worldviews.

Think tanks: how the fifth estate influences the fourth

At the heart of the epistemic community are think tanks, described as the 'fifth estate' in a 2016 report published by one of the world's leading think tanks, the Washington-based Brookings Institution (McGann, 2016), itself assessed as the

TABLE 2.1 Number of think tanks by country, 2020

Country	Think Tanks
United States	2,200
China	1,413
India	612
Britain	515
South Korea	412
France	275
Germany	266
Brazil	190
Russia	143
Japan	137
South Africa	102

Source: *2020 Global Go To Think Tank Index Report*, cited in McGann, 2021.

top foreign policy and international affairs think tank in 2020 (McGann, 2021). The United States is considered the home of modern think tanks and leads the world in their number, with more than 2,200 in 2020, double than that of 1980. There are 2,932 think tanks in Europe (see Table 2.1). Globally, the growth in think tanks has been remarkable, from about a hundred in the 1950s to 7,800 in 2020 (McGann, 2021).

The 'market leader' in this marketplace of ideas remains the United States: of the top ten foreign policy and international affairs think tanks in 2020, six were based in that country (Brookings Institution, Carnegie Endowment for International Peace, Center for Strategic and International Studies, Woodrow Wilson International Center for Scholars, RAND Corporation and Atlantic Council), with think tanks based in Britain, France, Japan and France filling the other four places (McGann, 2021: 167).

The first think tank in the modern sense was the Royal United Services Institute (RUSI), founded by the first Duke of Wellington in London as far back as 1831, which continues to be an influential voice in 2023. In the United States, which professionalized and propagated the idea of the think tank, the earliest were the Carnegie Endowment for International Peace, founded in 1910, and the Brookings Institution, established in 1916, with the Council on Foreign Relations being established in 1921. Its flagship journal *Foreign Affairs*, launched in 1922, is still arguably the most influential policy journal in international relations. These institutions were set up by business leaders and academics with their belief that 'introducing an objective, "scientific" approach to the development of policy would help avoid repetition of past mistakes and lead to better policy decisions in the future' (Niblett, 2018: 1410).

In Britain, the Royal Institute of International Affairs (also known as Chatham House) was founded in 1920; its mission is driven, in the words of its head, Robin Niblett, by 'liberal imperialism', bringing together 'academic experts and government officials to discuss a particular policy issue, generally within a confidential setting', from which the 'Chatham House Rule' formally evolved in 1927. Chatham House's journal *International Affairs*, established in 1922, continues to be a major voice in global geopolitics, despite Britain's diminished status (ibid.: 1411). The driving force behind the establishment of institutions such as the Council of Foreign Relations and Chatham House was a convergence of views among the Anglo-American elite with their use of 'a rifle not a shotgun approach' to influencing policy (Parmar, 2002: 57). British colonial connections helped popularize the idea of think tanks and local versions were set up in the 'white colonies', notably the Australian Institute of International Affairs (1924), the Canadian Institute of International Affairs (1928) and the South African Institute of International Affairs (1934).

In operation since 1958, another British think tank, the International Institute for Strategic Studies, also remains influential in geopolitical space. Other leading British think tanks and advocacy groups include the Overseas Development Institute (sustainable development), in operation since 1960, and Oxfam, perhaps the world's best-known charity (in operation since 1942), whose reports on global poverty receive much media coverage, not surprising given the geostrategic importance of London as a global 'hub' for international financial networks, NGOs and news organizations.

As the United States ascended the global power league in the post-World War II period, many new think tanks emerged, including the RAND Corporation, founded in 1948, the Atlantic Council and Hudson Institute, both in 1961, and the Center for Strategic and International Studies, in 1962. In the Allied-occupied zones, think tanks for the new democratic West Germany were set up: *Deutsche Gesellschaft für Auswärtige Politik* (the German Council on Foreign Relations), in 1955, and the *Stiftung Wissenschaft und Politik* (German Institute for International and Security Affairs), in 1962. These are well resourced but hardly make an independent impact on global communication space outside the Anglo-American umbrella. The Stockholm International Peace Research Institute, established in 1966, was and remains an exception as an authoritative voice on global arms trade and defence-related information.

The European Council on Foreign Relations (ECFR), which aims to conduct 'cutting-edge independent research on European foreign and security policy and to provide a safe meeting space for decision-makers, activists and influencers to share ideas', has a pan-European footprint, with offices in Berlin, London, Madrid, Paris, Rome, Sofia and Warsaw, and a presence in Brussels. Its Africa programme analyses the geopolitics of the Africa–Europe relationship, while the Asia programme seeks to help Europe recalibrate its relationship with China and foster Europe's relationships with India and Japan. The Uppsala-based Nordic Africa Institute

(Nordiska Afrikainstitutet), a government agency, funded jointly by Sweden, Finland and Iceland, prides itself for 'research, knowledge, policy advice and information on Africa'. In Sub-Saharan Africa, the Berlin-based Konrad Adenauer Foundation supports 'two networks of think tanks who have joined forces in order to strengthen their voice in the political discourse by developing and promoting common positions'. Al Jazeera's Center for Studies is a prominent think tank pertaining to the Middle East.

Seeking to expand their impact, networks and funding sources, many American think tanks have 'gone global', opening offices in key capitals around the world, as part of their development strategy to diversify staff by employing researchers with linguistic and cultural capital and promoting international exchanges and collaboration. Notable examples include Carnegie, with offices in Moscow, Beirut, Brussels, Beijing and New Delhi, and Brookings, with branches in the latter two Asian capitals, in addition to Doha. Britain's International Institute of Strategic Studies has offices in Singapore, Washington and Bahrain. As crusaders for the free market, entities such as the Atlas Network, founded in 1981, connect more than 500 think tanks in nearly 100 countries and, through its Leadership Academy, the Atlas Network runs a Think Tank MBA and Think Tank Leadership Training programmes 'to help create the climate of opinion in which the ideas of a free society can succeed' (see Atlas Network's website).

Other notable free marketeers include the Hinrich Foundation, an Asia-based organization, working to advance 'mutually beneficial and sustainable global trade' and supporting 'research and education programmes that build understanding and leadership in global trade' (see Hinrich Foundation's website). While several European think tanks produce much policy-based research material, their presence in the global media sphere is relatively limited. Even the newer ones, such as the Netherlands-based Bruegel, founded in 2005, and the ECFR, in operation since 2007, have scant media visibility, though both use English for communication.

In the global arena, think tanks face competition from other influential institutions. Transnational NGOs, transnational corporations and global media groups are channelling their ideas directly into policy debates. NGOs have their own policy units; corporations organize themselves into policy-focused associations, bringing the collective weight of their ideas to bear on specific topics, such as standards for environmental sustainability and transparency for extractive industries. Some companies have their own in-house think tanks, such as the McKinsey Global Institute, which offer insights into global trends that are central to policy.

Leading financial media organizations such as Bloomberg, *The Economist* and the *Financial Times* create their own content by hosting numerous policy-related conferences, as well as developing their own platforms for 'thought leadership' (Niblett, 2018: 1417–1418). For-profit think tanks such as Boston Consulting Group, PricewaterhouseCoopers, Eurasia Group and Oxford Analytica – all four US-based – and the Economist Intelligence Unit in London also provide 'financial intelligence' to the global business and political elites (Stone, 2013).

Since the 1990s, some 20 years after its founding, the World Economic Forum (WEF) has led the way in hosting what it terms 'multi-stakeholder dialogues', with an annual gathering of politicians, business executives, experts and policymakers in Davos, Switzerland. Without any formal authority, it has become a major forum for political and business elites to discuss policy ideas to 'improve the state of the world' (according to its motto). It serves as 'a boundary-spanning think tank involved in the brokerage of transnational knowledge domains, contributing in the long run to developing new, transnational forms of power, authority, and legitimacy' (Garsten and Sorbom, 2018).

Representing the interests of the global corporate elite, the WEF has a role in setting the global policy agenda; its annual conference attended by leading politicians, corporate leaders and intellectuals receives more media coverage than the summits of G-7 or G-20 countries. A survey that McGann conducted among leading think tanks in the United States demonstrates the symbiotic relationship between governments and think tanks through the phenomenon known as 'the revolving door', where think tanks provide former government officials an opportunity to share insights from their public-service experience (McGann, 2021).

Forging and legitimizing geopolitical agendas?

While the think tanks profess that their main purpose is 'to infuse political debate with analysis based on facts and expertise, not on opinions or bias, and that their 'one core principle of their own . . . is their intellectual independence (Niblett, 2018: 1428), it is not difficult to detect that they have a clear bias towards legitimizing the Western geopolitical and economic agenda. Many think tanks have explicit political or ideological agendas: the Alliance for Securing Democracy, housed at the German Marshall Fund of the United States, develops 'strategies to deter, defend against, and raise the costs on authoritarian efforts to undermine and interfere in democratic institutions'.

A UN report noted: 'Several think tanks – such as the European Centre for International Political Economy, the Information Technology and Innovation Foundation and the Hinrich Foundation, among others – strongly support free flows of data, predominantly motivated by economic and trade arguments' (UNCTAD, 2021: 55). In Britain, the mission of the Institute of Economic Affairs – 'to shrink the state, lower taxes and deregulate business' – has been crucial in the Tory party domination of the polity and the economy. US think tanks and their affiliates, which are largely funded by right-wing American billionaires and corporate donations, have teamed up with British politicians and London-based counterparts to help write detailed proposals for Britain's departure from the EU and its future relationships with both the EU and the United States. A leading conservative US think tank, the Heritage Foundation, instrumental in its support for Trump (Mahler, 2018), also had a clear agenda on Brexit, believing that the EU's relationship with Britain had weakened the transatlantic alliance and was '100% in favour of Britain leaving the

EU, with or without a deal', as one of its senior functionaries told *The Guardian*, 'We believe Britain will be an even stronger partner for the US outside of the EU, which is increasingly anti-American' (Lawrence et al., 2019). How corporate interests influence the functioning of the think tanks was exposed by a *New York Times* investigation, which noted,

> in the chase for funds, think tanks are pushing agendas important to corporate donors, at times blurring the line between researchers and lobbyists. And they are doing so while reaping the benefits of their tax-exempt status, sometimes without disclosing their connections to corporate interests.
> *(Lipton and Williams, 2016)*

Such networks have a strong communicative dimension attached to them. The close professional and personal connections between those working in global elite journalism, international public relations companies and think tanks help to orient the media debate and discourse in particular ways often supporting the geopolitical positions of the dominant West while undermining those of the adversaries. One of the key functions of think tanks is 'interpreting policies for electronic and print media, thus facilitating public understanding of and support for policy initiatives' (McGann and Shull, 2018: 8).

'It is now a completely regular occurrence to see an expert from one think tank or another being quoted in top-tier media on major issues of international policy'. They provide 'much more than media quotes' and have become an 'important part of the policy making process across the world' (McGann and Shull, 2018: 9). According to the 2020 indexing of think tanks report, the top ten think tanks were Western in terms of 'best use of media (print and electronic)' – six were American, with Peterson Institute for International Economics leading the pack, followed by Chatham House (McGann, 2021). The policy space has also become increasingly conflated with lobbying, argues Roland Schmidt, director of the Bonn-based Friedrich-Ebert-Stiftung (Friedrich Ebert Foundation). He advises that think tanks would be well advised to embrace a binary role as 'Think and Do Tanks', combining rigorous academic analysis with strategic communication and professional campaigning.

Intellectual infrastructure: universities and publishing

Universities have also moved into the think-tank space for a number of interlinked reasons, including the quality of their resident expertise; the increasing demand from university boards and research funding bodies that academic studies should have real-life impacts, especially in the social sciences; the opportunity for faculty to gain additional recognition and visibility from contributing to policy projects, and the potential for this recognition to help attract more students and more public and private funding (Eaton, 2021). Examples include the Belfer Center at the Kennedy School of Government, Harvard University; the Hoover Institution at

Stanford University; LSE Ideas at the London School of Economics and Political Science, and IRIS at the Sorbonne University.

Often-cited programmes of soft power in higher education include the Ford Foundation, the Fulbright Programme, British Council activities, German Academic Exchange Service initiatives and the EU's Erasmus Mundus projects (Knight, 2022: 48). More recently, the International Committee of the Red Cross and Centre for Research in the Arts, Social Sciences and Humanities at the University of Cambridge agreed to cooperate on research and share knowledge and experience in 'digital and cyber security regulation, policy, and ethics'. The Ford Foundation, for example, by the late 1970s invested $450 million (approximately $1.7 billion in today's dollars) to train a generation of civil servants, diplomats and leaders around the world. In 2001, Ford invested $280 million – its largest single grant ever – to create the International Fellowships Programme, which funded the education of foreign scholars around the world and sought to build the capacity of universities outside the United States. By 2013, when the programme ended, it had paid for more than 4,300 fellows from 22 developing countries (Walker, 2018).

With the commercialization and globalization of higher education in recent decades, Western universities have expanded their operations across the world: 250 'satellite campuses located in a different country than the home university' – primarily in Asia and the Middle East, were in operation in 2020. Another way of extending their reach is to establish international joint universities – 'independent institutions located in the host country and are co-governed and co-managed by the foreign partner country and host country institutions' – whose numbers have grown from four in 2004 to 22 in 2022. Germany has established seven, while China hosts universities from the United States, Britain and Russia (Knight, 2022: 40–41).

US and British/European universities and research organizations still dominate the production of academic research globally, assisted by the hegemony of the English language, the gatekeeping of the process of academic publication and the ranking system, which is largely based on it. The Western system of global ranking of universities and academics creates an infrastructure and hierarchy to knowledge production. A clear Anglo-American domination is evident: according to the *2022 QS (Quacquarelli Symonds) World University Rankings Yearbook*, in the ranking of the top ten universities in 2021, five were American (with the Massachusetts Institute of Technology at the top), four British and a token European presence (ETH Zurich – Swiss Federal Institute of Technology). Such figures reflect the trends over the past two decades.

In relation to academic, scientific and professional knowledge production, the global publishing industry is also predominantly Western, led by publishers such as Pearson, Reed Elsevier, Wolters Kluwer and Thomson Reuters. In the field of scientific, technical and medical publications, Reed Elsevier is one of the largest in the world, covering 170 countries with branches in the United States, the Netherlands, Britain, Spain, Germany and France, as well as in Japan, China, India, Brazil and Singapore. Elsevier's journals are on the ScienceDirect platform, the world's largest database of scientific and medical research, hosting over 13 million pieces of content and 30,000 e-books (Thussu, 2019).

Another key global player in specialist areas such as legal, financial, tax and healthcare publishing and distribution is the Netherlands-based Wolters Kluwer, with customers all over the world, including a million healthcare professionals in 180 countries, 210,000 accounting firms and 90 per cent of top banks. Other academic publishers with a worldwide presence include the Taylor & Francis Group (part of Informa business), publishing more than 1,000 journals and around 1,800 new books each year.

The top global universities also have world-leading academic publishing operations: for example, in the United States, Yale University Press, Princeton University Press and Harvard University Press, and in Britain, Cambridge University Press and Oxford University Press, the world's largest university press and one of its oldest. The ranking of such academic book and journal publishers determines the ranking of publications on which individual researchers' careers can depend. These metrics and ranking systems in academia, combined with the predominance of English language, effectively create a monopoly governing the global knowledge economy, which feeds into a one-way flow of academic and professional communication.

Ranking takes place in all aspects of knowledge production and reinforces global privilege and inequities in terms of who is ranking whom. These global hierarchy makers are mainly based in the United States and Britain, such as the annual Times Higher Education World University Rankings (in partnership with QS). In the field of 'scorecard diplomacy', the London-based Portland Soft Power 30 Index measures the soft power of selected countries on an annual basis to reveal how scorecard diplomacy works through the ranking dashboard (Grincheva, 2022). The *World Press Freedom Index* has been published annually since 2002, compiled by the Paris-based Reporters sans frontières (Reporters Without Borders). The Varieties of Democracy (V-Dem) Institute at the University of Gothenburg, Sweden, publishes state of democracy annual reports. PEN International on the Freedom to Write Index and Médecins Sans Frontières (Doctors Without Borders) in health and development are other prominent rankings of global activity. In addition, in the field of public opinion research and surveys, notably, Edelman Trust Barometer, which produces an annual report about trust in society, Pew Research Center and the Washington-based Gallup are internationally known and cited widely in the media across the world.

Western-based private regulators and technical experts such as the International Accounting Standards Board, which develops financial reporting rules for global corporations, and the International Organization for Standardization and the International Electrotechnical Commission, which account for 85 per cent of all international product standards, are highly political institutions that act as a form of 'global private governance' (Büthe and Mattli, 2011). The cumulative impact of their policy input and coverage in the elite media remains substantial in terms of how global issues are framed. They help provide the intellectual and professional credibility to the dominant Western discourse on contemporary global geopolitics (Freeman, 2020).

Funding media development

As part of the 'epistemic community', charitable foundations based in the West contribute to the intellectual infrastructure of global communication and media by supporting media capacity building and journalism for specific kinds of social change (Rosenstiel et al., 2016). Organizations such as the Knight Foundation – supporter of the International Centre for Journalism – the MacArthur Foundation and Open Society Foundation fund media development projects across the world. The Bill and Melinda Gates Foundation, which has a specific Global Media Partnerships portfolio, aims to support the media coverage of global health and international development issues. In addition to small, specialized media outfits, among its beneficiaries are mainstream publications such as *The Guardian*'s Global Development site, which produces news, features, debate, multimedia and photography on issues related to global development. In the past two decades a variety of news organizations – largely based in the West – have received grants of at least $1 million from the foundation to support international public service journalism: ABC News, AllAfrica.com, Al Jazeera, *El País*, *The Guardian*, National Public Radio, PBS' NewsHour; Public Radio International and *Der Spiegel*'s Global Societies project.

Another major presence in this arena is the MacArthur Foundation, which, in 2016, awarded $25 million in grants to 12 different news organizations to support accountability and explanatory reporting, including the Pulitzer Center on Crisis Reporting ($2.5 million) and Public Radio International – $1.75 million for its news programme *The World*. The UN Foundation supported the establishment of the Sustainable Development Goals news aggregator site – *Global Daily* – and the Global Development Watch section of the *Los Angeles Times*. Other active foundations include the Ford Foundation and the Rockefeller Foundation, as well as, and more controversially, the Open Society Foundation established by the financier George Soros, which funds many media outlets and activist media groups worldwide to the tune of more than $130 million (Open Society Foundation, 2023).

In 1992, Soros made a $1 billion bet against the British pound, a trade that famously earned him the nickname 'the man who broke the Bank of England' when his aggressive selling of the currency pushed the government to devalue the pound (Weisman and Shorey, 2022). However, his goal was 'to become the conscience of the world', he told the *New York Times* reporter who wrote his biography (Kaufman, 2002). Soros-funded Human Rights Watch has received more than $32 million from Soros's groups between 2000 and 2014. The Soros Economic Development Fund of the Open Society Foundation (OSF) by 2022 had contributed $400 million to 54 countries in 'private-sector investments to advance OSF's progressive agenda, of which $9.3 million went toward "independent media"'. These include openDemocracy, which 'attracts more than 11 million visits per year' and has projects published 'in Russian, Spanish and Portuguese as well as English'; and Project Syndicate, the 'World's Opinion Page' which claims that its commentaries are published across the world in 156 countries in 66 languages.

The Soros foundation has also supported Wikipedia, Vice Media and the left-leaning Free Press, as well as the Media Democracy Fund and its 'Disinfo Defense League', which urges governments to fund journalism to 'combat the problems of disinformation, hate and other malign practices online'. It also funds the Poynter Institute's International Fact-Checking Network, encompassing global fact-checking for 100 organizations. In 2020, Soros committed a combined sum of more than $2.3 billion to create a global university network – The Open Society University Network – of which the Central European University, founded by Soros, is part. His approach, he claims, has been to use his media power to promote liberal democracy and check authoritarian tendencies, especially in Europe (Tamkin, 2020).

Such agenda-driven narratives are also promoted by many other powerful international advocacy campaign groups, for example, for transparency and good governance, including the Brookings Institution, Freedom House, Carnegie Endowment for International Peace, National Endowment for Democracy, Heritage Foundation, Cato Institute, and Human Rights Watch (all based in the United States); Amnesty International (Britain); Transparency International (Germany), and the Belgium-based International Crisis Group. In operation since 2005, the New York-based Human Rights Foundation, a non-profit organization, 'promotes and protects human rights globally' and hosts the Oslo Freedom Forum – held annually in the Norwegian capital – and other international conference series that bring 'dissidents, activists, and journalists together with industry leaders to help make the world more peaceful, prosperous, and free'.

Media corporations also have charitable offshoots to promote media development and literacy globally. The BBC's international development charity BBC Media Action commissioned a study in 2020 for the feasibility of establishing a new International Fund for Public Interest Media, and the Center for International Media Assistance at the National Endowment for Democracy proposed that a target of 1% of development assistance be devoted to international media assistance (BBC, 2020b). Before it closed in 2018, the International Reporting Project had supported over 650 journalists to travel to 115 countries.

Charitable support for thematic international news is increasingly being provided directly to news organizations. For example, *The Guardian*, the *Los Angeles Times*, *El País* and the National Public Radio have specific sections or blogs, supported by foundations, which focus on global development. Launched in 2013 by eBay founder and philanthropist Pierre Omidyar, First Look Media has invested in both for-profit and non-profit media, including First Look Entertainment, which is a for-profit organization, and non-profit entities such as *The Intercept* an online news organization for adversarial journalism; the documentary unit Field of Vision; and The Press Freedom Defense Fund for supporting journalists, news organizations and whistle-blowers. When foundations do provide support for international news, it is often channelled via intermediaries such as the Pulitzer Center on Crisis Reporting and GroundTruth.

The question arises whether donors exert their own forms of political and economic influence by encouraging journalists to 'channel . . . their energies into safe, legalistic, bureaucratic activities and mild reformism' (Feldman, 2007: 427). Within the Gates-funded 'Living Proof' campaign, 'the privileging of individual empowerment as an approach to social change . . . serves the agenda of privatized development within a neoliberal project', argue Wilkins and Enghel (2013: 166). In the case of humanitarian news, philanthro-journalism may adopt an elitist, technocratic approach to social change that legitimizes 'ameliorative' rather than 'transformative forms of humanitarian action' and fails to challenge power structures (Scott et al., 2023). The notion of the broker fits this form of neo-liberalism in which 'brokers of capitalism' are an important link in the development industry where brokers channel resources between the state, NGOs and local communities and as a mode of governance and service distribution within states. This 'NGOization' – the professionalization and institutionalization of social action – has long been a hotly contested issue in grassroots social movements and communities of resistance (see essays in Choudry and Kapoor, 2013; Freeman, 2020).

Within conventional news coverage of humanitarian crises, there is an especially heavy reliance on a narrow range of institutional sources, such as the UN and large international NGOs. This reliance on a 'hierarchy of trustworthy sources' (Lawson, 2021: 1), it is claimed, enables journalists to maintain the credibility of their work without the need to verify, contest and/or challenge the official information they cite. However, it also means that the international institutions they 'hide behind' routinely become the 'primary definers' of a crisis – that is, experts who have the power to frame and interpret events for the audience.

Challenges to the US model: 'think tanks with Chinese characteristics'

In 2020, after the United States, China had the largest number of think tanks, recognizing the value of 'thought leadership' to influence the global discourse. With its size, growing global engagement and competitive growth model, China has led the way in the establishment of new think tanks (Zhu, 2013; Zhou, 2023). In his report at the 19th National Congress of the Communist Party of China (CPC), President Xi emphasized 'strengthening the development of new types of think tanks with distinctive Chinese characteristics', elevating it to a national strategy. The Center for China and Globalization, the Chinese Academy of Social Sciences and the China Institute of Contemporary International Relations are major actors in this arena. To legitimize and intellectually justify the global ascent of China, the Chinese government has released such documents as the 'Plan to Promote the Development of New Types of Think Tanks with Chinese Characteristics' and the 'Opinions on Strengthening the Development of New Types of Think Tanks with Chinese Characteristics' (Xinhua, 2015).

In this context, 'national high-end think tanks' (*guojia gaoduan zhiku*) are leading the development of China's think tanks, many of which are affiliated to universities in addition to corporate, media and social think tanks. According to the Chinese Think Tank Index, there were 341 university-affiliated think tanks in China, far outnumbering the government-affiliated ones, with an international focus. According to the Chinese Think Tank Report, released by the Shanghai Academy of Social Sciences, from 2013 to 2018, think tanks affiliated with top universities such as Peking, Tsinghua, Renmin and Fudan are in the top ten list of best think tanks in China, along with government-affiliated think tanks, as measured by the criteria of comprehensive influence (Zhou, 2023).

For nearly two decades now, the Confucius Institutes (CI), established by the Chinese Ministry of Education, have been contributing to the country's public diplomacy by disseminating Chinese language and culture to different nationalities. By 2019, there were more than 530 institutes operating across the globe, though since then their numbers have declined, especially in the West, where they have been seen as instruments not just for promoting Chinese language and heritage but also for realizing Beijing's geopolitical projects. To address this, since 2020, the Chinese International Education Foundation, a non-governmental organization, has taken over their running, though the effective decision-making power remains with the government (Li, 2022).

Despite a concerted effort to develop its think tanks, China's challenge to the US-dominated Western epistemic communities is still in early stages as the professional and intellectual hegemony remains well entrenched. Other major non-Western powers – Russia, Japan, India, Iran and Türkiye – have still a lot of catching up to do in this arena, though the trends towards developing an indigenous geopolitical discourse are beginning to emerge. India's Observer Research Foundation is one such example which has created a niche for voicing the concerns of the global South.

Over the past two decades, the Chinese government has had a concerted programme of investment in developing the quantity and quality of its higher education provision, to develop its knowledge and human resources and to increase its global intellectual standing via international rankings. In this it has been very successful: in 2004 Chinese universities were represented by only four in the top 200 in the *Times Higher Education World University Rankings* – by 2023 there were 13, of which six were in the top 60, with Tsinghua reaching the 12th position and Peking too being very close to breaking into the top ten (THES, 2023). This has been achieved by sending out its students and staff to study in leading Western universities, as well as developing its domestic academic and research capacity often in collaboration with the latter. However, the golden age of academic collaboration and partnership seems to be over, with a combination of President Xi's move away from reliance on the West, discouraging the study of English and Western thought, as well as the West's suspicion of intellectual property theft and spying, part of the 'new Cold War' mentality.

3
DIGITAL DEMOCRACY VS. DIGITAL IMPERIALISM

Having examined the hard and software of global communication in the previous chapter, the focus here is on analysing how this globalized connectivity has impacted on international and transnational communication. The rapid globalization of the internet was initially hailed as a democratizing force in global geopolitics, contributing to the creation of a 'global public sphere', where competing ideas would flourish in alternative forums, with space even for subversive public and private communication alongside governmental, corporate and commercial information.

There has been much written about the empowering potential of digitization, bringing communities and cultures closer at a transnational level and contributing to a more plural global commons (Negroponte, 1995; Cairncross, 1997; Benkler, 2006; Shirky, 2010, 2011; Volkmer, 2014). Seen as a profoundly democratic mass medium, whose fundamental principles were based on access to free information and a decentralized information network, internet-enabled communication opened up possibilities for transnational 'many-to-many' digital dialogues across cultures and communities, where active consumers created their own content – ranging from the mundane and the banal to the perceptive and profound – and distributed it to a 'networked public sphere'. According to Castells, in a 'global network society', interpersonal, mass communication and mass self-communication 'co-exist, interact and complement each other' (Castells, 2009: 54). A recent study found that activists tend to receive their news from 'search engines, social media, and other platform products' and the 'automated serendipity' produced by search engines and social media leads online audiences to gain exposure to more sources of news (Nielsen and Fletcher, 2020).

One early example of digital empowerment using the World Wide Web was the 1994 Zapatista National Liberation Army fighting for self-rule in Mexico's Chiapas state and whose leader Commandante Marcos became something of a celebrity, using the then new technology of email to communicate and campaign to talk to journalists internationally, with the US media christening it as the world's 'first informational guerrilla movement' (Golden, 1994). The 'anti-globalization movements' of the 1990s skilfully used online mobilization against the growing corporate control of global trade, contributing to the scuppering of the WTO's ministerial meeting in Seattle in 1999 and other gatherings of the World Bank, the IMF and the WTO, as well as annual summits of the G7.

Proponents of 'alter-globalization', including civil society groups such as the World Social Forum, Global Social Justice Movement, Change.org and Avaaz, have been almost exclusively based in the West, shaping the empowerment discourses (Castells, 2000; Atton, 2004; Wolfson, 2014; Tufekci, 2017). As Article 19, the freedom of expression advocacy group, proclaims, 'Control the information space. Build your own truth. Use it to consolidate power. This is the playbook we see repeated over and over again across the world'...'The suppression of freedom of expression is not just a symptom of autocracy: it creates the environment for autocracy to flourish' (Article 19, 2022: ii). Such communication strategies have galvanized links between non-governmental organizations (NGOs), community groups and political activists in different parts of the world, including Europe (Bennett and Segerberg, 2013), the Middle East (Howard and Hussain, 2013), Asia (Shah et al., 2015), Africa (Mutsvairo, 2016) and Latin America (Segura and Waisbord, 2016).

In many countries where media and communication systems are state-controlled, the role of internet bloggers has been crucial to enable dissenting voices to be heard in political communication: notable examples include Iran (Sreberny and Khiabany, 2010; Akhavan, 2013), China (Yang, 2016) and Egypt (Kraidy, 2016). Digital platforms have also been used by extremist outfits – from supremacist groups circulating Nazi merchandizing and hate propaganda to militant Islamic cells broadcasting videos of beheadings on their websites (Archetti, 2013; Simpson and Duxies, 2015; Aly et al., 2016).

The suggestion that the new, digital 'liberation technology' of internet and social media would help free people living under repressive regimes such as Iran may not be tenable (Morozov, 2011). Western media outlets dubbed the 2009 Green Movement in Iran as a 'Twitter revolution', holding a cyber-utopian view that digital technologies provided 'the consciousness, knowledge, and mobilizational capacity that will eventually bring down autocracy in Iran' (Diamond, 2010, 80). Iran had been facing extensive US sanctions since the 1979 Islamic revolution, including technology-related sanctions encompassing 'everything developed in the computer age' (ibid.).

The US government changed its policy to coincide with the Green Movement when in 2010 it authorized the export to Iran of 'no-cost services' enabling the 'exchange of personal communications over the internet and no-cost software necessary to enable such services' (Katzman, 2021). The goal was to provide a free flow of information, including services such as blogging, email and instant messaging, photo and movie sharing, social media and web browsing, which were extended before the June 2013 Iranian presidential election, to include antivirus software, cell phones, computers and website hosting (Mehta, 2016: 175).

As protests spread in Iran and the authorities responded by blocking internet access, the US tech entrepreneur Elon Musk tweeted 'Activating Starlink', the satellite network part of his rocket company, Space X. The United States lifted some sanctions to ensure Starlink offered the potential to bypass the government's blockade of land-based internet connections (Metz et al., 2022). While these US efforts at intervention via digital communications were clearly unsuccessful, it resulted in Iran viewing Western digital media platforms as a national security threat, as an Article 19 report noted: 'This seminal event realigned much of Iran's national security forces and resources towards internet governance, policies, and laws' (Article 19, 2020: 13).

Similarly, the 2011 so-called 'Arab Spring' demonstrated further examples of the Western promotion of digital communications as an enabler for 'democratization' by challenging autocratic regimes, leading to coups and wars across the Middle East. These popular uprisings were projected in Western media as the harbinger of democratization in a region traditionally governed by authoritarian regimes (Howard and Hussain, 2013). Such endeavours were part of US policy, supported by the willing and knowing cooperation of hacker groups like Anonymous, digital corporations and mainstream media outlets. However, the use of social media as a force for democracy was highly exaggerated by the West: the number of people using Twitter and Facebook in Egypt, a country with the largest population in the Arab world and arguably the most important regional geopolitical power, was extremely low; in March 2011 when the anti-government protests gained ground, barely 0.001 per cent of the Egyptian population were using Twitter.

Despite celebrating the triumph of the people's will in the Arab Spring, the grim reality of the elections which followed the ousting of President Hosni Mubarak demonstrated double standards in Western attitudes towards democracy. The election of Mohamed Morsi, Egypt's first democratically elected civilian president, serving as president from 30 June 2012 to 3 July 2013, was not acceptable to the United States. He was removed from power by General Abdel Fattah el-Sisi in a military coup in July 2013; put in detention for months, along with key members of the Muslim Brotherhood and his Freedom and Justice Party, and died in prison. While the West and the Westernized sections of the Egyptian elite vehemently opposed 'the Brotherhoodization of the state', which portrayed the country's growing concern with members of the Muslim Brotherhood taking over most of the vital positions in government (Abdullah, 2014) and supported the coup, in 2013 the African Union voted to suspend Egypt under what was described as 'the AU doctrine on unconstitutional changes of government'.

It is important to emphasise the role of the epistemic community in promoting the discourse of democracy: much online activism, especially in the global South, is supported by Western NGOs operating globally. As discussed in Chapter 2, these have become increasingly important in international interactions, influencing policy and affecting media discourses (Willetts, 2011). Despite their claims to being international, many represent and reflect Western thinking on global issues, some even steeped in a colonial mindset: a study of British international NGOs found that their messages projected 'many colonial discourses' (Dogra, 2012). The National Endowment for Democracy, Freedom House, the United States Agency for International Development and the George Soros's Open Society Institute were key inspirations for the Arab Spring. Many of these had been active in supporting dissidents in the name of promoting democracy during the 'Colour Revolutions', orchestrating 'regime change' in Serbia (2000), Georgia (2003), Ukraine (2004) and Kyrgyzstan (2005), among others (see Stewart, 2012).

Twitter has become an important medium in geopolitical communication, with politicians, corporates, celebrities and other interest groups using it to communicate. Its hashtags have been effectively used in social movements and anti-government campaigns, enhancing 'digitally networked *connective action* that uses broadly inclusive, easily personalized action frames as a basis for technology assisted networking' (Bennett and Segerber, 2013: 6, italics in original). Movements such as the 2013 '#BlackLivesMatter', which prompted conversations about race and racism, and the 2017 gender justice hashtag #MeToo were able to 'go viral' through digital media across the United States and beyond and 'not just online but offline', resulting in 'measurable backlash and change' (Jackson et al., 2020: 186 and 187).

Scholars and activists have claimed these 'networked protests' as examples of 'globalization from below', which rely 'heavily on online platforms and digital tools for organizing and publicity' and are adept at using giant software platforms like Facebook, Twitter and Google that have 'become central to social movement organizing around the world' (Tufekci, 2017: xxiii and xxix). However, the question arises whether 'hashtag activism' has been hyped up to conceal a form of 'slacktivism', requiring little effort to engage and settling for signing online petitions or joining a social media discussion. Sceptics such as Morozov see the power of empowerment often exaggerated, arguing that successful activism organized online is often 'accidental, a statistical certainty rather than a genuine achievement' (Morozov, 2011: 180).

Those countries critical of the US-dominated digital media platforms have not hesitated in deploying these themselves to promote or protect their own geopolitical interests and visions. The Chinese government, for example, uses Twitter, Facebook and YouTube for such purposes, although these platforms are banned in their country. In 2008, China set up a website 'anti-cnn.com' in response to what was perceived by Chinese authorities as biased CNN coverage of the unrest in Tibet (Jiang, 2012). Most high-ranking Iranian officials have social media accounts typically on Instagram, but often on Twitter or both – despite the ban on the latter. Former president Mahmoud Ahmadinejad – under whose administration Facebook, Twitter and YouTube were blocked – regularly tweeted political commentary in

English. All seven qualified candidates in the 2021 presidential election had Twitter accounts (Dagres, 2022: 16).

During the 2016 coup attempt against Türkiye's president Recep Tayyip Erdoğan, which was blamed on the Gülenist movement – whose leader, Turkish cleric Fethullah Gülen, lives in the United States as a permanent resident – the president used digital media to galvanize the people against the perpetrators (Tufekci, 2017). While the plotters took over TRT, the state-run television channel, Erdoğan connected to CNN-Turk over FaceTime – in what was later dubbed as 'the victory of the digital age over an analogue coup', Erdoğan was saved by the very social media outlets he had been trying to ban (Unver and Alassaad 2016; Dogan, 2021).

In democracies too, politicians have deployed social media outfits to communicate to millions of followers: the Indian prime minister Narendra Modi had the world's highest following on Twitter in 2022, with 126 million regular followers, while the former US president Donald Trump's use of his Twitter account is a case of a new form of 'digital demagogy' (Fuchs, 2018).

However, beyond the dominant narratives of digital empowerment, some of which were outlined before, the ground reality of digital democracy rests awkwardly with the unmistakable trend towards digital consolidation and domination by a small number of hugely powerful, mainly US-based corporations, defining the age of digital capitalism.

Digital capitalism

Defined as 'capitalism with digital technologies' (Sadowski, 2020: 49), digital capitalism has grown phenomenally over the past two decades and has transformed the way trade in both goods and services is conducted around the world. The developments in digital infrastructure discussed in Chapter 2 have enabled the rapid expansion of global digital trade, defined as 'digitally enabled transactions in goods and services, whether digitally or physically delivered' (OECD, 2019: 136). In 2017, for the first time, global digital advertising spend (at $200 billion) overtook TV advertising. The economic geography of the digital economy, notes UNCTAD's (United Nations Conference on Trade and Development) *Digital Economy Report 2019*, is consistently led by the United States and China, which 'account for 90 per cent of the market capitalization value of the world's 70 largest digital platforms' (UNCTAD, 2019: xvi).

These platforms are increasingly important in the world economy: in 2017 the combined value of platform companies with a market capitalization of more than $100 billion was estimated at more than $7 trillion. The seven 'super platforms' – Microsoft, Apple, Amazon, Google, Facebook, Tencent and Alibaba – 'account for two thirds of the total market value' (ibid.). Google had 90 per cent of the market for internet searches; Facebook accounted for two-thirds of the global social media market and was the top social media platform in more than 90 per cent of the world's economies. Amazon boasts almost 40 per cent share of the world's online retail activity, and its Amazon Web Services accounts for a similar share of the global cloud infrastructure services market (UNCTAD, 2019: xvii).

The United States leads the world in international trade in products delivered through data flows, followed by Britain, France, Germany, India, Ireland, the Netherlands and Switzerland (Hamilton and Quinlan, 2022: ix). In 2020, the United States was the largest global exporter and importer of what UNCTAD calls 'digitally deliverable services', exporting $533 billion and importing $317.6 billion, registering a $215.4 billion trade surplus. Its Western allies were among the other top ten exporters and importers, while India, China and Singapore were also top digital services traders. As mentioned in Chapter 2, the main commercial partner of the United States in this area is Europe, to which it exported in 2021 nearly double than to the entire Asia-Pacific region, according to the US government data.

Another key hub in this digital capitalism is the increasing delivery of digital services by US 'foreign affiliates': in 2021, half of all services supplied by US affiliates abroad – worth $1.8 trillion, roughly 2.5 times the US global services exports of $705.6 billion – were digitally enabled. Europe – which in the past decade has received more than half of total US FDI (foreign direct investment) outflows globally – accounted for nearly 50 per cent of the 'foreign affiliates', which are 'key export platform and pan-regional distribution hub for US firms', with Ireland emerging as the 'number one platform in the world from which their affiliates can reach foreign customers'.

US capital stock in Britain ($890 billion in 2020) was more than triple its combined investment in South America, the Middle East and Africa ($278 billion). US investment presence in China and India ($124 billion and $42 billion, respectively in 2020) was 19 per cent of total US investment in Britain. In 2020, Europe accounted for roughly 63 per cent – $17.6 trillion – of corporate America's total foreign assets globally, with Britain having the largest share, accounting for 20 per cent, worth $5.5 trillion in 2019, while US asset base in Germany ($960 billion in 2019) was more than double its assets in China (Hamilton and Quinlan, 2022: vi).

Digitally enabled capitalism

Not unlike the news cartels of the 19th century, referred to in Chapter 1, in the age of digital capitalism, 'data cartels', run by a few corporations operating as 'data analytics' or 'business solutions', harvest, commodify and sell data and informational resources at a global scale and scope. Like their predecessors, they, too, are engaging in anticompetitive, cartel-like behaviour to maintain and expand their control of data and information markets. They supply the digital lifeblood that flows through the 'circulatory system of the internet', characterized by a two-tiered information system where premium financial intelligence is paywalled, while the public receives minimal financial information (Lamdan, 2022).

In digitally enabled capitalism, markets can be distorted by high-speed supercomputing, replacing traditional floor trading and human market makers with algorithms, while centralized exchanges have fragmented into competing exchanges and trading platforms with 'shady trading schemes' and 'dark' markets, some of which are deliberately designed to enable the transfer of wealth from the weak to the powerful (Mattli, 2019). Others warn of the criminogenic nature of digital capitalism, with its 'shadow trades', characterized by illegal markets, fraud and manipulation, human trafficking, money laundering and arms trade (Thomas, 2021).

Speedy and regular transmission of accurate financial intelligence is crucial for the news organizations and their clients that undergird digital capitalism. The blurring of boundaries between financial news and financial data has transformed financial journalism, a field traditionally shaped by Western news conglomerates. Reuters remains a leading international player in financial news and data and prioritizes its operations as an international electronic data company rather than being merely a news agency. Since its merger with Thomson Financial in 2008, this financial role has become even more prominent.

Other global key players in financial journalism include the Murdoch-owned Dow Jones ('market-moving, trusted news, exclusive insights and rich data sets for financial firms, professionals and investors') and Bloomberg, which claims to connecting 'decision makers to a dynamic network of information, people and ideas, "quickly and accurately" delivering business and financial information, news and insight around the world', distributed through its more than 1,600 partners, to media outlets and corporations across 130 countries. Bloomberg TV is a ubiquitous presence on the floors of banks and financial institutions across the world, as is CNBC with its many regional services catering to different geo-economic constituencies. The *Financial Times* (now owned by Japan's Nikkei) and the Murdoch-owned *Wall Street Journal* continue to be the 'bible' of financial news and analysis.

Many financial news and information services generate extra income from large-scale trading in shares and currencies, and a fluid and insecure financial market can be good news for them since they take commission from billions of dollars' worth of weekly currency trading. This raises questions about their role as objective data providers and commentators on global trading, as they may themselves have corporate interests in the volatility and instability associated with currency fluctuation, commodity prices and trading in 'futures'.

With increasing corporate control of the channels of communication, the financial media can become the mouthpiece of global corporations and their supporters in governments. An indictment of limitations of such journalism was the skewed coverage in the mainstream financial media of the 2001 Enron scandal, when the US-based energy company Enron Corporation, a darling of Wall Street investors with $63.4 billion in assets, went bankrupt in what was described as the biggest fraud in US corporate history. The 2008 bankruptcy of the investment bank Lehman Brothers was the largest in US history, triggering a global financial crisis (McDonald, 2015). The world's leading financial media, as well as geopolitical and economic experts and specialists, failed to predict either of these financial crises (Schiffrin, 2011; Davis, 2011; Starkman, 2014; Stiglitz, 2017).

Scholars have argued that financial journalism has been 'captured' by corporate and pro-business agendas (Davis, 2002). Writing in the context of the 2008 financial crisis, the Nobel laureate Joseph Stiglitz spoke of 'cognitive capture' by media, which can lead to 'cognitive capture by society', since the media 'can become part of the echo chamber that amplifies and solidifies conventional wisdom' (Stiglitz, 2017: 15). In 24/7 digital capitalism, media stories help drive economic events, and financial panics can spread like epidemic viruses through what has been called 'narrative economics' (Shiller, 2019: 3).

As an international elite, financiers have intimate ties arising from their shared experience at prestigious universities, from which they gain credentials, connections and social status. Among the 400 wealthiest billionaires in the United States, 65 per cent of private equity and hedge fund managers have bachelor's degrees from America's top 30 private universities (Eaton, 2021). The mechanisms of influence at work in the 'transnational power elite', are evident in the highly discreet Bilderberg Group, which has been organizing an annual conference since 1954, attended by leaders from political, financial and intellectual spheres with the aim of fostering global free market capitalism and to strengthen Western unity (Richardson et al., 2011). Another such influential institution is the 'secretive' Trilateral Commission, an NGO that seeks to 'deepen understanding between the US, Europe and Asia'. Established by philanthropist David Rockefeller in 1973, to bring Japan firmly into the Western camp, the commission has since expanded to include members from South Korea, India and Southeast Asia (The Trilateral Commission, 2022; Moriyasu and Okumura, 2023).

Less opaque but equally influential are other such Western institutions as the Canada-based Fraser Institute, which since 1996 has been publishing an annual report on the *Economic Freedom of the World* that aims to examine the impact of economic freedom on investment, economic growth, income levels and poverty rates. Not surprisingly, these widely cited reports have found that countries which tend to have institutions and policies more consistent with 'economic freedom', that is, deregulation and privatization, have higher investment, more rapid economic growth, higher income levels and a more rapid reduction in poverty rates. In their 2021 report, Hong Kong remained in the top position, followed by Singapore. The next highest-scoring nations were Switzerland, New Zealand, Denmark, Australia, United States, Estonia, Mauritius and Ireland. The rankings of some other major countries were Japan (12th), Canada (14th), Germany (24th), Italy (43rd), France (54th), Mexico (65th), India (90th), Russia (94th), Brazil (114th) and China (116th). The ten lowest-rated countries were Democratic Republic of Congo, Algeria, Republic of Congo, Iran, Libya, Argentina, Syria, Zimbabwe, Sudan, and lastly, Venezuela.

The 2021 'Network Readiness Index' by the Washington-based Portulans Institute (a think tank which devised and defined the criteria) ranks countries in relation to their capacity for global digital capitalism. Unsurprisingly, Western nations represent nine of the top ten countries, with Singapore being the only

Asian country in the top ten, while China ranked 29th on the basis of 'the state of technology infrastructure, the ability of individuals, businesses and governments to use ICT productively, how conducive the national environment is for a country's participation in the network economy, and the economic, social, and human impact of a country's participation in the network economy' (Dutta and Lanvin, 2021). Such ideologically driven categorizations and rankings have geoeconomic and geopolitical connotations. These champions of the digital economy are counting on the burgeoning growth in global data creation, projected to grow to more than two billion times the internet's size in 1997, while the monthly global data traffic is expected to surge to more than three times the data usage rates in 2020, according to UNCTAD's *Digital Economy Report 2021* (UNCTAD, 2021). Former Cisco chairman and CEO John Chambers called this phenomenon 'the Internet of Everything': 'pervasive connections among people, things, data, and processes like social networking, machine learning and artificial intelligence' (Chambers, 2012).

As more and more people go online at an astonishing pace – a million users a day joined social media in 2021 – they are being 'converted' into data, as their activities and events become digitalized in what has come to be called the 'surveillance economy' (Clarke, 2019), where people themselves become the product. As a global commodity and the transnational currency of the digital age, data has become 'a new economic resource for creating and capturing value', a UN report noted (UNCTAD, 2019: xvii). Global digital platforms are playing a key role in this 'platform capitalism', thanks to their ability to collect massive amounts of data from the consumers of digital media. 'Clicks', 'likes' and 'tweets', as well as geolocation, traffic information, food preferences and all other activities and behaviours that leave digital traces (including body data from wearable devices) are routinely gathered and monetized by platforms, prompting scholars to speak of the 'like economy' (Gerlitz and Helmond, 2013).

User-generated data, either as a by-product of transactions or as metadata produced within platforms online, are very valuable for data brokers, data analytics industries, advertisement companies and artificial intelligence (AI) developers, as well as for intelligence agencies. The digital advertising market, comprising thousands of interconnected platforms, is projected to be worth over $300 billion (van der Vlist and Helmond, 2021), which suggests that the integration of trackers has the potential to be used as part of the 'digital influence machine'. 'The world is moving from "a market economy", a UN report has suggested, to a "market society", as it allows the market to extend to more and more aspects of life' (UNCTAD, 2021: 69).

In such a society, the right to access, control and use the data becomes paramount as data is directly related to human rights and security. It can be abused or misused in ways that can affect political systems, especially in democratic societies. Analysts have warned against the dangers of 'data trafficking', by which the commercial extraction of consumer data is used 'to support a government outside the legal system users consented to have protect them' (Kokas, 2022: 2).

Others have challenged the concept of 'digital universalism', considering digital platforms as 'models' devised in 'technological centres' that would 'simply come to be adapted and copied' in the global South (Chan, 2014). Rather than being a neutral and natural development of technological entrepreneurism, it could instead be argued that the global digital platforms constitute agents of US-led 'imperialism' (Jin, 2015) or of 'colonialism' (Kwet, 2019), within the context of the transnational capitalist system. The growth in mining, trading and manipulation of data in the data-driven economy and data-dependent society has provided extraordinary power to the largely US-based digital giants, who deal with an enormous amount of private data and public information (Mayer-Schönberger and Ramge, 2018), prompting concerns about 'digital colonization' (Couldry and Mejías, 2019). Jin sees this as a new form of capitalism which in turn is shaping a new version of imperialism and labels the phenomenon 'platform imperialism' (Jin, 2015: 11).

Platforms for digital imperialism?

The globalized commodification of information within digital capitalism (Schiller, 2011) has strengthened the position of digital corporations making billions of dollars in profit as 'the result of monopoly privileges, network effects, commercialism, exploited labour, and a number of government policies and subsidies', as McChesney has argued (McChesney, 2013: 223). In the context of data-driven economies, digital colonialism is understood to have a broader reach than the historical colonialism of countries over countries: colonialism in the digital context is related to the exploitation of human beings through their data by companies or by governments, and it can happen in all countries (Couldry and Mejias, 2018; Mejias and Couldry, 2024).

As noted in Chapter 2, US digital conglomerates have been investing in digital infrastructure in the global South to ensure an outflow of domestically generated data to companies in the United States, affecting the global South nations' capacities to innovate and capture value by processing them, seen by some as a new form of 'colonialism' through data privacy, disinformation and reinforcing market concentration and inequalities (Pisa and Polcari, 2019). Elmi has defined data extraction, monopolization and monetization as 'data colonialism's core tenets' (Elmi, 2020). These corporations have also expanded their operations worldwide by acquiring successful digital start-ups and potential competitors, affecting the ability of domestically grown companies to contribute to long-term development.

The EU export of its General Data Protection Regulation (GDPR), considered one of the most comprehensive frameworks for data protection, may also be construed as a mechanism for extracting data from the global South to create value from their processing, not dissimilar to the exploitative and extractive import of natural resources by global corporations. Their raw data can be value added and converted into digital intelligence in what might be termed as 'soft touch' imperialism.

While the unelected corporations mine, collate and trade enormous amounts of private data, governments also regularly and systematically monitor public information (Mayer-Schoenberger and Cukier, 2013) that are increasingly stored in clouds, while the 'Internet of Things' has established a 'pax-technica ... a political, economic and cultural arrangement of institutions and networked devices in which government and industry are tightly bound in mutual defence pacts, design collaborations, standard settings, and data mining' (Howard, 2015: xx). The platforms offer a new business model: they 'enrol people in the production process and provide a variety of services or commodities on a peer-to-peer level' (Srnicek, 2017: 5).

Not only are the platforms a key part of the commercial infrastructure, 'they have also become part of our *cognitive, cultural, and social infrastructure*, as everyday life as we know it has come to depend massively on search engines, video and music streaming services, and social media and messaging platforms' (Brubaker, 2023: 108, emphasis in the original). Platforms have undergone infrastructural evolution and increasingly taken on the features of scale and ubiquity, and embeddedness in everyday life. The rise of digital technologies has 'made possible a "platformization" of infrastructure and an "infrastructuralization" of platforms' (Plantin et al., 2018: 295).

This 'platformization' shows that platform corporations integrate diverse businesses, 'hosting and curating media content and functioning as advertising networks, data intermediaries, social networking and identity services, content production companies, and software and hardware manufacturers' (Poell, 2020: 651). Despite repeated claims of platform neutrality, platform owners can reflect ideological preferences in terms of content they allow and services they provide or restrict.

Demanding a 'postcolonial data politics' as a distinct domain of analysis, some scholars have argued that colonial dominions and possessions are now being 'reconfigured as objects of knowledge' (Isin and Ruppert, 2019: 209). They refer to 'data's empire' as an emergent form of power that involves new as well as existing mechanisms of domination between the former colonizer and post-colony. In their view, the new 'data's empire' combines the logic of government from Euro-American imperialism with new mechanisms of power and principles of knowledge arising from and enabled by the digital technologies (ibid.: 224).

As was argued by the West in the discussions of the New World Information and Communication Order in the 1970s (see Chapter 1, p. 45), the 'free flow of data' is central for the success of imperialism, and this is no less true in the digital world. Predictably, Western and Western-dominated institutions such as the OECD, the World Bank and the World Economic Forum, as well as think tanks such as the European Centre for International Political Economy, the Information Technology and Innovation Foundation and the Hinrich Foundation, 'strongly support free flows of data' (UNCTAD, 2021: 55). Business associations, such as the Global Data Alliance, created in 2020, and the International Chamber of Commerce, a cross-industry global coalition, also advocate free, cross-border data flows, as does the London-based GSMA (Global System for Mobile Communication), the association of mobile network providers.

Lobbying on this issue is important for digital corporations and conforms to trends around the world (McKay, 2012; Chari et al., 2019). The digital platforms are highly active dealing with the US Congress, spending large amounts of money on lobbying and hiring people with political connections. In 2020, Facebook and Amazon ended up in the top ten spenders on lobbying. Alphabet, Amazon, Apple, Facebook and Microsoft increased their spend on this from $16 million in 2010 to over $63 million in 2020. Google and Microsoft spent the most on lobbying in the early 2010s, but Amazon and Facebook also increased their spending on this between 2010 and 2020, with the latter's spend rising from $0.35 million in 2010 to almost $20 million in 2020 (Centre for Responsive Politics, 2021b).

Alibaba has also been an active lobbyist to the US Congress. Not surprisingly, increased spending was reflected in the increase in the number of those hired to engage in lobbying (UNCTAD, 2021: 27). Google, Facebook and Microsoft – in that order – were also the top three lobbying spenders in the EU in 2021; their influence enhanced by funding think tanks to favourably 'influence new regulations by publishing studies and position papers and organizing discussion forums' (Corporate Europe Observatory, 2020).

Digital empires and democracy?

Like the imperialists of yore, the corporate digital empires, too, compete and complement each other in creating a new world order, predicated on the supremacy of the United States. The MAAAMT grouping – comprising six discipline-defining mega corporations: Microsoft, Apple, Amazon, Alphabet, Meta and Twitter – represents the heart of digital imperialism (Lee and Jin, 2018; Moore and Tambini, 2018; Brubaker, 2023). All of these are essentially US-based entities with global operations and subsidiaries and affiliates, as noted earlier, and power is increasingly concentrated in fewer and fewer hands (Schiller, 2011; McChesney, 2013; Mosco, 2014; UNCTAD, 2019).

The computational and algorithmic organization of narratives and discourses gives these digital superpowers exceptional ability to set the global agenda. They have been described as 'behemoths' that 'dominate the dissemination of information and the coordination of political mobilization' (Fukuyama and Goel, 2021: 98). Even though they all operate in a democratic space and are eloquent supporters of an open internet, it is argued that they pose a 'unique threat to a well-functioning democracy'. Their political biases – preference for a 'socially progressive' agenda, even as they are 'driven primarily by commercial self-interest' – lead to complaints from conservative elements (ibid.: 102). The relationship that Trump had with social media is a case in point. The platforms have the power to de-platform a user, as Facebook and Twitter did to Trump in January 2020, but only after they knew that he had lost the election and, therefore, power.

Elon Musk, the co-founder and CEO of Tesla and owner of Twitter, has more than 88 million followers on the platform which he bought for $44 billion in 2022 to strengthen his global technology empire, with operations running from under the ground to space, led by the world's wealthiest private citizen. According to the *Bloomberg Billionaires Index*, in 2022, eight of the world's 12 richest individuals were technology entrepreneurs, including Amazon founder Jeff Bezos, Google co-founders Larry Page and Sergey Brin, Microsoft co-founder Bill Gates and former CEO Steve Ballmer and Facebook/Meta co-founder Mark Zuckerberg.

They publicly exhort their commitment to free speech, gender and ethnic equality and political pluralism. When Musk purchased Twitter, his statement read: 'Twitter is the digital town square where matters vital to the future of humanity are debated'. Such grandiose statements are routinely made by other Silicon Valley tzars too and distributed instantly through their formidable control of the hardware and software of global digital superhighways. 'Meta's rampant user data gathering, Google's vast data monetization and other such practices' have all 'established the global identity of US tech sector as one defined by exploitative practices', observes one study (Kokas, 2022: 3).

Google has emerged in the past two decades as the undisputed leader of internet-based communication and leads the way in the global commodification of increasingly individualized and personalized communication – the 'Googlization of everything' (Vaidhyanathan, 2011). A pioneer of 'big data', the company can harvest data from billions of its users with its intimate access to the search history, documents and videos on Google Drive, and email traffic via Gmail, as well as geolocation through Google Maps and mobile movements, courtesy of the Google Android operating system. Thus YouTube, Android, Chrome and Google Maps – each with more than a billion users – give Google unprecedented power in shaping global digital life. A global single-app marketplace has been created by Google Play and Apple's App Store, the world's two largest digital distributors.

Though these services are supposed to be free, they are paid for by advertising by so-called sponsored links using 'advermovies, advergames and other forms of advertainment', as well as animation, memes, auto-play and GIFs to routinize digital capitalism: by 2022 global online advertising had crossed $600 billion, according to eMarketer. Deploying 'predictive algorithms', Google and Facebook work closely with companies such as Taboola and Outbrain that specialize in 'promoted stories' or 'around the web' links – which are advertisements dressed up to look like news – to benefit from a global market for such 'native advertising' of more than $60 billion. This kind of 'soft news', I have argued elsewhere, 'is masking the hard realities of neo-liberal imperialism' (Thussu, 2007: 155).

Vaidhyanathan speaks of a 'global system' that 'develops algorithms that favour highly charged content and is dependent on self-service advertising system that precisely targets ads using massive surveillance and elaborate personal dossiers' (Vaidhyanathan, 2018: 9). Integrated mobile apps, multi-platforms and multi-screens and the resultant experience of 'connected viewing' is commodified by what has been described as the 'attention merchants' of digital capitalism, who specialize in 'harvesting' consumer time (Wu, 2016). The 'influencers' use various types of clickbaits, including eye-catching TikTok clips to promote a product, an ideology or a conflict. This 'targeted personalization' of information can contribute to ideologically constructed 'filter bubbles' (Pariser, 2011). These networks expose the way in which governments, businesses and individuals can steer 'the global conversations toward their ends, to mould public opinion, and ultimately to change what we do' (Aral, 2020: 12–13).

With over three billion users (if it were a country, it would have the world's biggest population), Facebook has enormous global reach and influence, with access to a vast reservoir of real-time data, which it can personalize and use to monopolize user attention, making their lucrative platforms extremely attractive to advertisers as well as governments and politicians to control and command global communication. As Vaidhyanathan has noted, 'No company better represents the drama of a fully connected planet "sharing" words, ideas, images, and plans. No company has better leveraged those ideas into wealth and influence. No company has contributed more to the paradoxical collapse of basic tenets of deliberation and democracy' (Vaidhyanathan, 2018: 4). Such platforms can also be used to manage or manipulate geopolitics. One prominent example was the 2018 Cambridge Analytica scandal when Facebook was forced to suspend its dealings with this London-based data analytics company, which had 'harvested' millions of Facebook profiles of voters and used the data to build a software programme to 'predict and influence choices at the ballot box' during the elections in the United States, India, Kenya, Malaysia and Nigeria (Cadwalladr and Graham-Harrison, 2018; Rosenberg et al., 2018). In 2021, The *Wall Street Journal* published a series of articles under the heading of 'Facebook Files', while The *Washington Post* reported the 'Facebook Papers' to highlight the manipulative practices including exempting high-profile users from its rules under a programme called 'cross check' or 'Xcheck', despite overt and regular contestation of any irregularity in relation to content moderation and privacy issues (Horwitz, 2021; Lima, 2021).

The 'authoritarian' BATS: digital capitalism with Chinese characteristics

If the MAAAMT combination represents a new version of imperialism, are the Chinese digital conglomerates different? Will they bring an 'authoritarian' character to their form of digital capitalism, as they increasingly go global? Unlike US-based digital corporations, the Chinese companies Baidu, Alibaba, Tencent and Sina (referred to by the BATS acronym) are routinely described as representing authoritarian or state-centric digital capitalism. Given concerns about cyber censorship in what remains as a one-party state with its increasingly sophisticated 'Great Firewall', China has developed its own version of the internet, with its equivalent versions of Google (Baidu), Facebook (Renren), Amazon (Alibaba),

Twitter (Weibo), WhatsApp (WeChat) and other US-based digital properties (Tang, 2019; Wong, 2022; Chen, 2023).

Although such connectivity is creating new social formations among the Chinese citizens based on shared interests in entertainment, it has also been used by government authorities to monitor and censor information and discourse (Harwit, 2016). Under Xi's leadership, censorship regimes have become more pervasive and rely on covert methods (Yang, 2016). China has one of the world's most advanced censorship regimes of the internet for 'information management', but this censorship is deliberately 'porous' and frequently 'circumvented by savvy internet users'. Most censorship methods implemented by the Chinese government, a study notes, 'act not as a ban but as a tax on information, forcing users to pay money or spend more time if they want to access the censored material' (Roberts, 2018: 2).

International debates about the Chinese internet tend to focus on these censorship-related issues. At the same time, however, the Chinese government and its cyber corporations have strengthened their digital imprint globally in the context of 'cyber capitalism with Chinese characteristics'. These can be defined as 'giving high priority to cyber sovereignty, creating and sustaining the world's largest online market for a global Sino-sphere, establishing domestic cyber properties and protecting them from competition from global digital giants by introducing and implementing strict regulatory regimes, and the globalization of Chinese digital corporations' (Thussu, 2018: 26).

It has been argued that like their US counterparts, the BATS, too, follow the logic of 'mercantile capitalism, expansionism and data accumulation', both driven by profit and shaped by surveillance-industrial complexes that combine capitalist and state control (Fuchs, 2016). They are integrated into the global digital economy in terms of the structure of capital, ownership and control, helped by their government's 'protective policies in information industry development and push to develop the country's digital economy', which have 'propelled these enterprises to embrace innovation, international finance capital and the global market' (Jia and Winseck, 2018: 34). Alibaba Cloud, ranked fifth in the world in an arena dominated by Microsoft and Amazon, for example, has many data centres outside China, including in the United States, Japan, Australia, Germany and Dubai. *Chuhai* (going overseas) is part of their global expansion, 'a business decision, driven by platform capitalism; at the same time, it is underpinned by a political imperative, particularly in the context of what appears to be a cosy state-business relationship' (Keane et al., 2021: 75).

This global expansion is predicated on a massive domestic digital market, with a huge data resource: according to a White Paper released by the Chinese Academy of Information and Communication Technology, a government think tank, the 'market scale of China's digital economy reached $7.2 billion in 2022'.

In 2012, Tencent launched an English version of its Weixin messenger application, as WeChat, to promote the brand internationally. A decade later, the app is being used by a billion people globally and is also accessible in translated versions in Spanish, Russian, Portuguese, Turkish, Japanese, Korean and Polish. In 2017, the market value of the company had reached nearly $535 billion, making it the first Asian corporation to break into the $500 billion league. Unlike its Western counterparts such as WhatsApp, WeChat allows its users not only to make calls and send messages but also to pay bills and for shopping (including in many overseas stores), order goods and services and transfer money. Chinese corporations such as Vivo, Lenovo, Xiaomi and Oppo account for nearly half the smartphones in India, which is part of Chinese media's efforts in 'actively brand-building China for securing the state's economic goals of business' (Lashinsky, 2017: 17).

Dealing with such large-scale data also raises questions about privacy and commodification of information, since organizations such as Alibaba and Tencent have extraordinary access – Alipay introduced a facial recognition payment service in 2017. As a typical example of what has been described as 'surveillance capitalism', (Zuboff, 2019), ByteDance-owned TikTok relies on AI for user profiling and targeted advertising and has the power to mould public opinion and promote particular narratives, especially aimed at a younger demographic.

In the Chinese version of digital capitalism, one major characteristic is the rapid growth of digital finance, ranging from mobile payments to online investment, from Big Tech lending to digital insurance and from open banking to central bank digital currency (see essays in Dollar and Huang, 2022). China's mobile payment apps – notably Alibaba's Alipay and Tencent's TenPay – represent most of China's mobile payment system, one of the world's largest in terms of volume. As more Chinese tourists, students and business people travelled abroad, such services were being increasingly globalized (Erisman, 2015). Alibaba even suggested an electronic World Trade Platform (e-WTP) as a 'counterhegemonic discourse', which, using the economic and technological power of Alibaba and its support of the BRI, could promote a global digital trade order led by China and its private corporations (Vila Seoane, 2020).

However, such projects have been curtailed, as an increasingly assertive Xi administration tries to control the innovative and competitive strengths of such privately owned internet giants as Alibaba, whose access to data and their reach 'across all aspects of Chinese life' is seen as a national security issue. Xi scrapped Alibaba's Ant Group's initial public offering, as the company's cofounder Jack Ma had criticized the government for limiting financial risk, in an October 2020 speech. The Cyberspace Administration of China said: Alibaba had used its capital 'to manipulate public opinion'. Ma gradually reduced his stakes in Alibaba and retired as Alibaba's chairman in 2019 (Zhai and Wei, 2021). By 2023, the company had been divided into six separate, specialist segments.

Some of these companies have collaborated with major Western corporations to assist their globalization process. The Chinese telecommunications giant Huawei, a privately owned company, worked with European telecom companies to create a global presence and influence (Tao et al., 2016), investing heavily in 5G mobile systems, with more than a billion dollars in 5G research, and has tested its equipment with leading European telecom operators. In this endeavour, it had the support of the Chinese government (Wen, 2020). However, due to increasing security concerns, Western governments, as well as many others, including that of India, have demanded that Huawei technology be removed from state-sensitive communication systems (see Chapter 5).

A 2023 report by the China Academy of Information and Communication Technology predicted that 5G will drive $946.8 billion of economic output in the country by 2030. China Mobile Communications Corp., the world's largest telecoms carrier by subscribers, said it aims to deploy more than 10,000 5G base stations. The Chinese government and corporations are heavily investing in 5G networks, IPv6 protocols, virtual reality (VR), the Internet of Things (IoT) and AI, as evidenced by the number of patent applications filed by China with the World Intellectual Property Organization. Some have warned that the scale and pace of Chinese innovation might lead to an AI arms race with the United States (Ma, 2021).

However, the 'financial cold war' set off by the 2008 global financial crisis and aggravated by the Trump administration's imposition of new tariffs on Chinese imports in 2016 thwarted such ambitions. The growing risks of dependence on the US dollar and the debates about the need for 'de-dollarization' (discussed in Chapter 6) and the challenges posed by China's influence in global financial markets have contributed to this new geopolitics (Fok, 2021).

Since then, Western commentators have increasingly warned about the consequences of the global presence and influence of Chinese digital and technology companies, regarding them as 'Trojan horses that enable and export China's digital authoritarianism and surveillance capitalism' (Cave et al., 2019). A project undertaken by an Australian think tank – 'Mapping China's Technology Giants' – analysed the Chinese Communist Party's 'global data ecosystem', looking at the interactions between political agenda-setting, active shaping of international technical standards, technical capabilities and data as a strategic resource: 'For the Chinese party-state, data and the information derived from it contribute to everything. . . . Globally, it ranges from expanding the PRC's role in the global economy to understanding how to shape and control its global operating environment' (Hoffman and Attrill, 2021: 6).

Checking digital imperialism? Cyber sovereignty vs free data flows

Whether democratic or authoritarian, how should the digital empires be regulated and by whom? How important is the notion of cyber sovereignty and need for data localization? What role do the states play in protecting their territorial cyberspace when the digital does not respect traditional territoriality, given its 'a-territorial' nature? Geopolitics is central to the governance and regulation of cyberspace, especially since new issues about cybersecurity and digital property rights have gained salience in a networked, globalized and mobile electronic marketplace (Brousseau et al., 2012; Negroponte and Palmisano, 2013; Radu, 2019).

Since the 1990s, the US government and the corporations based there have argued that the digital realm is qualitatively distinctive from the analogue world and that digital spaces therefore need to be treated differently from all previous technological innovations. This 'cyber exceptionalism' of course benefits the cyber empires, as it undermines state sovereignty in a 'borderless' world. Such 'cyber libertarianism' was the formative ideology in the early days of the internet, with a strong cultural and economic backing from Silicon Valley (Couture and Toupin, 2019).

The US government has always given full support to data liberalization and strongly resists attempts at data localization, which is seen as a threat to 'a free and open global internet'. A 2013 task force report by the US Council on Foreign Relations recommended that all trade agreements between the United States and its trading partners should contain 'a goal of fostering the free flow of information and data across national borders while protecting intellectual property and individual privacy' (Negroponte and Palmisano, 2013: x).

At the UN-sponsored ITU World Conference on International Telecommunication held in Dubai in 2012, Russia and China introduced a proposal for equal rights among nation states 'to manage the internet', which was rejected by the United States and its Western and other allies, forcing it subsequently to be withdrawn and the ITU to adopt a non-binding resolution. 'A truly global platform is being undermined by a collection of narrow national internets' is how a task force report from the US Council on Foreign Relations described the proposal (Negroponte and Palmisano, 2013: 4). Of the 144 members of the ITU, 89 nations signed the resolution, while 55, including the United States, either chose not to sign or abstained.

After the 2013 disclosures by Edward Snowden of the extensive surveillance programme and worldwide mobile phone tracking by the US National Security Agency (Greenwald, 2014; *Washington Post*, 2014), digital sovereignty and state security have become the focus of internet governance debates. President Putin demanded that Russian internet firms move their servers to Russia and the Kremlin launched a group of 'cyber guards' to search for 'prohibited content'. In 2019, the Russian Duma approved a law on 'digital sovereignty', which tried to 'separate Russia's internet from the global one' (*Economist*, 2019: 43).

Nevertheless, the National Cyber Strategy of the United States maintains that its key objective is to 'promote the free flow of data across borders' (US Government, 2018: 15). The document is explicit in its strategy, urging that the United States 'will continue to work with like-minded countries, industry, civil society, and other stakeholders to advance human rights and internet freedom globally and to counter authoritarian efforts to censor and influence internet development' (US Government, 2018: 25). The policy against digital and data protectionism and unambiguous support for free flow of data has been reiterated in Congressional Research Service reports (CRS, 2020a, 2020b). This approach enables data to flow back to the United States when users around the world engage with firms headquartered in the country. Despite that, the United States has adopted strict localization policies for defence-related data, requiring that any company supplying cloud services to its Department of Defense must store its data only domestically.

In 2020, the United States adopted the Clean Network Programme to protect critical assets from foreign interference and to guard individual privacy by restricting untrusted telecommunications carriers, applications and cloud services, especially from China. The 2019 Clarifying Overseas Use of Data (CLOUD) Act allows its law enforcement authorities to require US-based companies to provide user data stored abroad, and it established a procedure by which the United States can enter into executive agreements with foreign countries. One of the first countries to enter an executive agreement was Britain, demonstrating the US–UK axis in the digital domain (US Department of Justice, 2019).

The US-based Internet Society's 2022 report warned of the dangers of 'splinternets' for global prosperity, suggesting that 'digital sovereignty policies may move us from an internet that benefits everyone toward a series of fragmented, closed-off networks where the opportunities that arise from global connection are lost' (Internet Society, 2022: 2). Such warnings have been reiterated by the Internet Association, 'the voice of the world's leading internet companies', another formidable lobbying group advocating, since its inception in 2012, for a 'free and open' internet, echoing the interests of its members, which include the giants of digital capitalism – Google, Microsoft, Amazon, Meta, Twitter, Netflix and eBay. In relation to digital trade, it says policymakers 'should advocate for the adoption of America's digital framework across the world – including in our trade deals – and defend against unwarranted attacks on US technology leadership' (Internet Association, 2023).

Data as a global public good

While the powerful global corporations are lobbying to preserve their access to the free flow of data, multilateral organizations are seeking to ensure that these digital resources work to the benefit of the global public good. As UNCTAD argues in its 2021 report, global data-sharing can help address major global development challenges such as poverty, health, hunger and climate change. The needs for and benefits of global data and information-sharing were evident during the Covid-19 pandemic. Thus, according to UNCTAD, some data should be considered as 'global public goods' (UNCTAD, 2021: 175) and 'an international governance framework should seek to enable gains from data flows to be equitably distributed within and between countries, indicating the 'need for the creation of a new international body that focuses on data-related governance' (ibid.: 191–192).

UNESCO's work on cross-border data flows is based on 'FAIR (findability, accessibility, interoperability and reusability) data principles', advocating the use of information and communication technologies (ICTs), open educational resources, open access to scientific information, open data and broadband-enhanced ICTs. The agency has also been leading UN inter-agency work, with ITU, for recommendations on the ethics of AI, in which data play a key role (UNESCO, 2022).

The ITU's Global Initiative on AI and Data Commons is working to establish 'a framework and collaborative platform that supports the implementation of beneficial AI-based solutions to accelerate progress towards the UN's Sustainable Development Goals (SDG)' (https://digitalregulation.org).

Issues around the governance of cross-border data flows are also prominent in the work of the OECD, as part of its integrated Going Digital project, while the World Economic Forum regularly provides commentaries on this topic, which are widely distributed globally by the US-dominated global media. The German-based Internet and Jurisdiction Policy Network also aims to facilitate 'a global policy process, engaging over 400 key entities from governments, the world's largest internet companies, technical operators, civil society groups, academia and international organizations, from over 70 countries'. Its 2021 study concluded that addressing the challenges related to the governance of the growing 'datasphere' requires a global multi-stakeholder debate across sectors and exploring and fostering innovative approaches in tools, frameworks and concepts (De La Chapelle and Porciuncula, 2021). In contrast to this predominantly Western discourse, in many regions of the global South, data-related governance is in its early stages, for example, in Africa, where the African Union has issued a 'digital transformation strategy' for the continent for the next decade (African Union, 2020).

As mentioned in Chapter 2, over the past decade, two competing views have emerged: the 'sovereigntist' in which national governments take the major decisions about governance and regulation, vocally championed by China and Russia, and the US-led, market-oriented privatized network model that promotes a 'multi-stakeholders' approach (Ebert and Maurer, 2013; DeNardis, 2014; Mueller, 2017, 2020). The latter reflects, says OECD, the 'Internet's own DNA: open, distributed, borderless, multi-stakeholder and global' (OECD, 2019: 152).

The US position has consistently been anchored in the principles of what has been called 'commercial non-regulation' and 'anti-censorship' (Goldsmith, 2018). In April 2022, the United States and 60 other countries launched 'the Declaration for the Future of the Internet – Digital Freedom Initiative, bringing together a broad, diverse collation of partners – the largest of its kind – around a common, democratic vision for an open, free, global, interoperable, reliable and secure digital future' (White House, 2023a: 29). The 'multi-stakeholder model' has supporters in the global South, including India and Brazil; Russia and China have argued for an UN-approved and managed governance structure, with the ITU undertaking a primary role in defining and implementing governance (Negro, 2020).

UNCTAD notes five distinct approaches to the issue of data localization and cyber governance in the five major economies that have a global influence on the regulation of cross-border data flows: the United States, China, the EU, Russia and India. It defines their approaches as a market-oriented approach (United States), a complex mixture of security-oriented and digital development-oriented approaches (China), a rights-oriented approach (EU), a security-oriented approach (Russia) and a domestic development-oriented approach (India) (UNCTAD, 2021: 99).

In their 2013 book, Eric Schmidt, the executive chairman of Google, and Jared Cohen, director of Google Ideas, predicted that the internet would 'fracture and fragment', leading to its 'Balkanization', with 'co-existing and sometimes overlapping but in important ways, separate national systems' (Schmidt and Cohen, 2013: 85). It can be argued that China and Russia have contributed significantly to this 'fragmentation', which they may not define as 'Balkanization' but as claiming their cyber sovereignty, as one commentator has noted, 'to align the internet with their jurisdictional boundaries', adding that the fragmentation debate is 'really a power struggle over the future of national sovereignty in the digital world. It's not just about the Internet. It's about geopolitics, national power, and the future of global governance' (Mueller, 2017: 3).

China and Russia also oppose US control of the internet via its digital powerhouses compromising their security, resulting in them imposing strict censorship regimes, particularly strong in China (Yang, 2016; Roberts, 2018; Griffiths, 2019) but also in Russia (Oates, 2013; Soldatov and Borogan, 2017; Nocetti, 2015), where it has become more pervasive since the 2022 invasion of Ukraine, prompting one AP report to describe the country as 'cyber gulag' (AP, 2023).

Rifts in the transatlantic digital alliance

Despite its close links with the United States, the EU has been following a data localization policy at variance with the principle of free flow, thus asserting a greater role for the state in protecting digital space (Shapiro, 2020; Pohle and Thiel, 2020; European Commission, 2021; Monsees and Lambach, 2022). In 2017, the European Commission fined Google $2.7 billion, the largest such penalty in the Commission's history, for favouring its own comparison shopping service. In 2020, the German government, in its official programme for its presidency of the European Council, announced its intention 'to establish digital sovereignty as a leitmotiv of European digital policy' (German Presidency of the European Council, 2020: 8). Europe's comparatively weak digital industries are considered a security issue as China and, to a lesser degree, the United States are seen as economic rivals and potential security threats in relation to data protection and espionage (Monsees and Lambach, 2022).

However, the EU's proposed data localization initiative – Schengen Routing – to avoid routing EU data flows via exchange points and routes outside the continent, proposed by Deutsche Telekom, has so far failed to materialize. Similarly, the EU's cloud service, Gaia-X, a European alternative to the US-based service providers conforming to the continent's data protection standards, announced jointly by France and Germany in 2019, aims to

> create a federated open data infrastructure based on European values regarding data and cloud sovereignty. The mission of Gaia-X is to design and implement a data sharing architecture that consists of common standards for data sharing, best practices, tools, and governance mechanisms.
>
> *(GAIA-X, 2022: 5)*

According to an UNCTAD report, these measures are aimed at creating 'a secure and robust infrastructure and ecosystem' in the EU 'to facilitate data exchange across European industries and thereby support the growth of data-driven sectors within Europe by enabling AI, IoT and Big Data analytics' (UNCTAD, 2021: 106).

Since digital platforms based in the EU only play a marginal role in a global context, regulation of cross-border data flows focuses on protecting the privacy of 'personal data', which is defined as 'any information relating to an identified or identifiable natural person'. The EU's GDPR, a comprehensive framework for data protection in operation since 2018, contains extensive controls in relation to the transfer of personal data outside the region. No explicit restriction exists, however, for cross-border transfers of non-personal data within the EU, since it aims to build a single digital market, where digital products, as well as data are 'free to flow' (UNCTAD, 2021: 104).

The EU's emphasis on 'digital sovereignty' is partly a response to the predominance of US and Chinese companies in the digital technology sector and also to the need to reduce dependence on external technologies in the absence of successful European technology companies. The inability of EU countries to develop indigenous contact-tracing apps during the Covid-19 pandemic and their dependence on technologies designed by Google and Apple were seen as major constraints on their digital sovereignty. As the European Commission noted, 'The Commission will work towards ensuring that its businesses can benefit from the international free flow of data in full compliance with EU data protection rules and other public policy objectives, including public security and public order' (European Commission, 2021: 15).

The authoritarian challenge

According to the *Digital Trade Restrictiveness Index* produced by the Brussels-based European Centre for International Political Economy, China, Russia and India were the three countries with the 'most restrictive policy environment for digital trade' (Ferracane et al., 2018: 8). China's internet is an example of cyber sovereignty in practice, with the 'party-state' controlling both the infrastructure and software of Sino-cyberspace (Cheung, 2018; Hong, and Goodnight, 2020). In a 2018 essay, written soon after taking over as chief of the Cyberspace Administration of China, Zhuang Rongwen outlined his country's plan to 'exert full control over the information flowing over China's portion of the internet', adding that 'whoever masters the internet holds the initiative of the era, and whoever does not take the internet seriously will be cast aside by the times' (cited in Creemers et al., 2018).

China has always had control over its data, so localization issues there have had a different trajectory and are more concerned with what happens when Chinese internet providers access and trade in data in other countries, such as data harvested from global consumers of apps like TikTok. Given that China already leads the world in such areas as AI and digital mobile payments and is exporting its model globally through the BRI, it will also resist attempts at data localization.

China was the first country to propagate its idea of digital sovereignty – mostly framed as cyber sovereignty – a concept which 'is nearly universally accepted as a foundation for engagement with global cyber affairs as a matter of principle' (Creemers, 2020: 129). The country is emerging as the global leader in internet governance and policy, and thus of the data that defines our public and private lives, 'it has devised interactions between the digital products of US techno-liberalism and China's state-directed social order' (Kokas, 2022). The notion of 'cyber sovereignty' is different from the US-centric, market-oriented internet governance scheme and covers a combination of the Chinese government as well as its internet-based corporations, which increasingly operate at a transnational level (Shen, 2016). Lu Wei, China's internet chief, has suggested that China wants to follow a path of 'cyber-governance with Chinese characteristics' (cited in Denyer, 2016). Since 2021, China's Data Security Law includes new guidelines for handling data, updated enforcement measures and additional restrictions on the transfer of data outside China. It expands the extraterritorial reach of China's existing data rules, creating a critical new set of guidelines for companies doing business with Chinese citizens, both within and outside the country's borders.

Since countries must choose between US and China's digital infrastructure, products and services, Kokas argues, 'China's role as a global data extractor is a Chinese government process grounded in the exploitative data-gathering practices that built Silicon Valley' (Kokas, 2022: 2). Such data extraction is likely to grow, as China expands its digital footprints via BRI and Digital Silk Road telecommunications infrastructure projects, especially in the global South. It is feared that the increasing adoption of Chinese data-driven technologies and services in BRI countries and interconnectivity across China and BRI countries might support new global surveillance regimes predicated on Chinese technologies.

Officially though, the Chinese position remains benign, as it launched the 'Global Data Security Initiative to provide a blueprint for developing global data security rules'. A White Paper titled 'China's Law-Based Cyberspace Governance in the New Era', issued in March 2023 by China's State Council Information Office states: 'China supports the UN's role as the main channel in international cyberspace governance'. It concludes: 'Based on its own realities, and learning from other countries' experience, China has created a cyberspace governance model with distinct Chinese characteristics' (quoted in *China Daily*, 2023a).

In Russian cyberspace, despite the popularity and availability of US-based digital platforms, Russian companies continue to hold sway. Vkontakte (Vk.com), a home-grown social media network; Yandex (the search engine), and Mail.ru (with 100 million users across its social media, messaging, email and online gaming platforms) are widely used in Russia and by the Russian-speaking global diaspora. The Russian-language RuNet is the predominant internet provider (Davydov, 2020: v). The evolution of RuNet in Russia is another interesting case of resisting digital imperialism. The country's 2019 law on 'sovereign internet' was changed to 'sustainable internet', in response to criticism from Western-oriented and

Western-supported civil society groups, which termed it as 'online Iron Curtain'. The Russian regulatory model on cross-border data flows is premised on the centrality of network and data security as a political and national security issue. Russia considers cybersecurity to be a purely sovereign prerogative (Nocetti, 2015).

However, unlike China, it has not put such a strong focus on the economic agenda for digital development and has been relatively less successful in boosting the domestic digital sector, with some notable exceptions, such as Yandex (an internet services provider) and Kaspersky (a cybersecurity services and antivirus software provider). Russia has imposed a series of restrictions on cross-border data flows. The most significant is a blanket data localization requirement for personal data, requiring all companies operating in the country to 'record, systematize, accumulate, store, amend, update and retrieve personal data of all Russian nationals, using Russian servers' (Russian Federation, 2014).

In 2015, Russia implemented a new law that demanded companies store data about Russian citizens on Russian territory. According to the law, foreign companies which operate within Russian cyberspace must notify the national internet watchdog Roskomnadzor (Federal Service for Supervision of Communications, Information Technology and Mass Media) about their data location. In 2019, Yandex set up a 'public interest fund' that could provide the Russian government power over key governance decisions to ensure that Russian data remains within the country.

Russia has also amended its federal laws 'On Communication' and 'On Information, Information Technologies, and Information Protection' (often referred as the 'Sovereign Internet Law'), requiring Russian internet providers to install equipment to route all domestic internet traffic through servers located within the country. Additionally, these amendments allow for the implementation of a Russian domain name system that would enable the domestic internet to function, even when disconnected from the global network, a move which perhaps foresaw the Western digital boycott triggered by the Russian invasion of Ukraine in 2022 (Epifanova, 2020).

The third way?

Much of the debate around data sovereignty in relation to developing countries focuses on India, which has an extensive digital services industry and strong links abroad. It also has the world's third most productive ecosystem for start-ups worldwide, after the United States and China. With more than 900 million users, India is home to the world's second largest internet after China, and it is the biggest 'open' internet. As broadband penetration grows, Indian presence in cyberspace is bound to become more prominent. India is the second largest market for smartphones in the world after China and has the highest number of registered users of both Facebook/Meta and WhatsApp. Unlike China, India has a huge demographic dividend by being home to the world's largest population of young people – 700 million – with an increasingly active digital presence (Agrawal, 2018; Arora, 2019). India's Jio Platform, part of Reliance, the country's leading conglomerate, with interests in energy, retail, e-commerce and media, has transformed digital life for most Indians. Since its launch in 2016, Jio's cheap mobile internet services, including free calls and affordable data, has won it 500 million users, helping to open up India's largely untapped digital markets (see Chapter 6).

This data abundance – largely circulating on US-owned digital platforms – has raised concerns about data localization, though the government's position on this is influenced by India's role as a major player in global business process outsourcing, which is largely dependent on Western, and particularly US, customers, and their international data.

Indian cyberspace is dominated by the US giants (Meta, Google and Amazon and their affiliates), and the government has largely supported the US multi-stakeholder approach to internet regulation. However, in recent years, Indian internet companies, with support from the government, have begun to demand the localization of Indian data. Reliance Industries chairman Mukesh Ambani, one of India's most influential businessmen, told a high-profile conference in 2019 that India needed a new movement against 'data colonization . . . [as] data is the new wealth', invoking the movement against British colonialism (quoted in Langa, 2019).

Yet India has a complicated digital path to traverse. As the world's largest democracy, it instinctively supports an open internet. Ambani's Jio has close connections with both Meta and Google, the dominant players in Indian cyberspace. While India has yet to develop its indigenous digital platforms and is heavily dependent on US digital conglomerates, apart for devising a public digital payment system (discussed in Chapter 6), it simultaneously admires and is envious of Chinese success in this arena. The Competition Commission of India, which is supposed to implement antitrust regulations and prioritize the rights of users, has not been very effective in breaking up monopolistic platforms. In 2023, India introduced its Digital India Act to regulate the country's online environment and digital data protection policies, replacing the 2000 Information Technology Act (amended in 2008 and 2011). The aim was to formulate policy to set digital standards and laws to address new digital issues, including AI, 5G, IoT devices, cloud computing, metaverse and cryptocurrency.

Data localization and demands for cyber sovereignty within a democratic system are an integral part of the official discourse in India, which other countries of the global South might emulate, though many of these have smaller digital markets (World Bank, 2021). As a major global services industry powerhouse, India has benefitted from free transnational data flows, drawing on its large, well-educated and English-speaking middle class, something which might be difficult to replicate in other developing countries.

Nevertheless, data localization has become a focus of attention to counterbalance US hegemony of the internet, and countries such as Russia, China and India provide an alternative discourse on data sovereignty that could be a model for the 'majority world'. This might also influence the development of global internet governance, as digital empires extend their reach across all sectors of life – social, political and economic. In her study of global internet governance (IG), Radu raises a pertinent question: 'In light of more influential roles played by the business sector in IG, be it at the level of infrastructure or content, and the stronger national approaches adopted recently, will the internet move closer to or further away from being understood as a global commons?' (Radu, 2019: 197).

4
GEOPOLITICS OF COMMUNICATING CONFLICT

Wars and image wars

As discussed in Chapter 1, propaganda and strategic communication are central to the geopolitics of global communication and this chapter examines how, in the post-Cold War period, military conflict has been framed in the mainstream Western media to serve geopolitical interests. From the US 'Operation Just Cause' in 1989 in Panama to the Russian invasion of Ukraine in 2022, the communication of conflict has been shaped by geopolitical forces, through political institutions, think tanks, the military-industrial complex and transnational media corporations. Despite occasional challenges by the media to the dominant framing of Western wars, there is little doubt that the majority of the US-led Western media have tended to operate within the basic terms of a well-honed narrative.

While the media in Western democracies operate free from direct government control and profess high professional standards of accuracy and accountability, they nevertheless act as instruments to legitimize the interests of their governments, especially in times of war and conflict. In their study of the mainstream US media in the pre-internet age, Edward Herman and Noam Chomsky described the 'propaganda model' of the US media system, in which coverage was passed through several 'filters', including the ownership and orientation of media firms, and their dependence on advertising and on business and governmental sources, as well as the overall dominant ideology ([1988] 1994, p. 2). Given the historic and contemporary domination by the West of global news and information space, certain wars receive extensive coverage, especially where it has clearly defined geopolitical or economic interests, while others are largely ignored or marginalized: the most mortal war is the least reported – more than five million have died since the mid-1990s in the conflict in the Democratic Republic of Congo – called 'Africa's world war' (Stearns, 2022).

War reporting is good for the business of media corporations, as it offers dramatic visual spectacles of violence, death and destruction, providing compelling material for networks to feed the 24/7 news channels. Given the political economy of news organizations, there is an economic imperative to keep the audience engaged, using entertainment formats, including video/computer-game-style images of 'surgical strikes' by 'intelligent' weaponry, arresting graphics and satellite pictures, contributing to the desensitization of the horrors of war (Thussu, 2007). However, covering conflict is also a complex and expensive operation for international media organizations in the age of global 24/7 news and the digital communication environment, with the proliferation of universal access to mis- and disinformation, as well as dependence on often vulnerable local journalists and 'fixers' (Murrell, 2015; Palmer, 2019).

It was the live broadcasting of the US bombing of Iraq in 1991 – 'Operation Desert Storm' – that catapulted a little-known cable TV channel, CNN (Cable News Network) into a global television icon. A decade after the first Gulf War and during another US invasion – this time in Afghanistan – the first pan-Arabic news network Al-Jazeera became a global broadcaster, its position strengthened with the coverage of the 2003 invasion of Iraq and subsequent conflicts in one of the world's most geo-politically sensitive region, including wars in Libya, Syria and Yemen (Abdul-Nabi, 2022).

Growth in global conflict

According to the 2023 Stockholm International Peace Research Institute (SIPRI) Year Book, there were 56 conflicts raging in different locations around the world in 2022 – almost all in the global South (SIPRI, 2023). In 2019, the Uppsala Conflict Data Program (UCDP) recorded the highest frequency of internal armed conflicts with foreign troop involvement since World War II. In the period 1975–2017, the main supporter of these insurgencies across all decades was the United States (Meier et al., 2022: 5). That conflict is central to geopolitics may sound like a truism, but 'militarization and militarism' are increasingly 'integral to global society', as a recent study notes, 'in the growth of standing armies, paramilitaries, and military contractors; the stockpiling of weaponry; burgeoning state surveillance programs; the colonization of research by the national security state; and the circulation of militarized imagery in popular culture' (González and Gusterson, 2019: 6).

As the world's most powerful military-security state, with a global imprint in all domains of warfare, the United States remains the prominent player in the geopolitics of militarism. In 2022, the US military budget was almost $800 billion, a world record for military expenditure and production of new weapon types. Both real and manufactured threats to US national security – from adversaries such as China and Russia – are constantly advanced by the security establishment and dutifully legitimized by the elite media to justify further militarization. The Pentagon's 2018 National Defense Strategy, which targeted 'great power rivalry' as the greatest threat to US security and global influence, was followed in 2019 by the National Defense Strategy Commission, which proposed up to 5 per cent annual growth in the Pentagon budget: 'Nine of the 12 members of the commission', notes one observer, 'had direct or indirect ties to the arms industry, a reality that no doubt had some influence over their deliberations and conclusions' (Hartung, 2021: 19).

Given US military presence and engagements across the world, with more than 800 declared overseas military bases, as well as its primacy as the largest weapons exporter, the US military-industrial complex thrives on the nexus between the political and security establishments. Since 2001, the US defence industry has contributed $285 million to political campaigns, with a special focus on presidential candidates, Congressional leadership and members of the armed services and appropriations committees in the House and Senate. In addition, it has spent $2.5 billion on lobbying over the past two decades, employing, on average, over 700 lobbyists per year over the past five years, according to the Center for Responsive Politics. These lobbyists have been extremely successful as four of the past five US Secretaries of Defense came from the top five arms contractors: in the former Trump administration, James Mattis (board member at General Dynamics), Patrick Shanahan (executive at Boeing), Mark Esper (head of government relations at Raytheon); and in the Biden administration, Lloyd Austin (board member of Raytheon Technologies) (Center for Responsive Politics, 2021a).

During the war in Afghanistan, Pentagon's spending totalled over $14 trillion, one third to one half of which went to defence contractors: the figure is even higher if US and NATO troop support costs are considered (SIGAR, 2021; also see Costs of War Project, 2022). According to one study, 'the benefits of the post-9/11 surge in Pentagon spending have been highly concentrated. One-quarter to one-third of all Pentagon contracts in recent years have gone to 'just five major weapons contractors: Lockheed Martin, Boeing, General Dynamics, Raytheon, and Northrop Grumman' (Hartung, 2021: 4).

The defence industry also gives funding to the think tanks that provide them with the intellectual justification for such expenditure, to support their advocacy for higher Pentagon budgets. A report by the Center for International Policy found that, between 2014 to 2019, the top 50 think tanks in the United States – including internationally influential ones like the Center for Strategic and International Studies, the Heritage Foundation and the Center for a New American Security – received one billion dollars from weapons firms and the US government (Freeman, 2020).

This military expenditure is undertaken ostensibly with the aim, not only of defending US interests but also of providing 'security assistance' to the rest of the world. However, it is questionable how effective or even plausible this intention is. For example, the RAND Corporation found no evidence that security assistance over several decades contributed to greater peace or stability in Africa (Watts et al., 2018). The massive infusion of resources in Iraq, which received about $30 billion in security assistance from 2003 to 2013, did not prevent the Iraqi Security Forces' being defeated by the Islamic State (Gaub, 2016). Despite two decades and nearly $90 billion of security sector support in Afghanistan, their security forces collapsed in a matter of weeks when the Taliban took back control in August 2021 (SIGAR, 2022).

Assessing the impact of militarism across the world, the Costs of War project of Brown University in the United States estimates that the total death toll in 'the post-9/11 war zones' of Afghanistan, Pakistan, Iraq, Syria and Yemen could be at least 4.5 million, victims of 'the reverberating effects of war', including the spread of disease and the 'destruction of economies, public services and infrastructure and the environmental contamination, and reverberating trauma and violence' (Savell, 2023: 2; 38–39).

Exporting democracy by war and peace

Under the banner of promoting peace, stability and democracy across the world, the United States aims to advance its geo-strategic and economic interests. As Robert Kaplan proclaimed in 2003, 'It is a cliché these days to observe that the United States now possesses a global empire. . . . It is time to move beyond a statement of the obvious' (Kaplan, 2003). Instead of colonies, a global network of military bases provides evidence of imperial might, with one recent analysis concluding, 'Although few US citizens realize it, we probably have more bases in other people's lands than any other people, nation, or empire in world history' (Vine, 2015: 3). The global reach of security and economic hierarchies controlled by the United States is 'the most striking fact about the pattern of authority in the modern world system' (Lake, 2009: 82). And this authority is dependent on the new 'strategic communication' in a globalized era where the 'capacity of the state to exercise authority in a world in which large-scale strategic communication of others (including other states) becomes a defining factor in establishing a state's legitimacy' (Price, 2015: 19).

'Promoting democracy' has been a staple claim of US foreign policy since the days of the Cold War, and using force to bring democracy to the world has been a tried-and-tested strategy of the US establishment, with strong support from its epistemic communities, NGOs and the media (see Chapter 2). Waging 'just wars' to bring freedom to the world can be achieved by both overt and covert means: Congress can be persuaded that a threat exists to US interests and therefore the president should be authorized to recommend military action. A more insidious intervention revolves around a narrative for 'regime change' by engineering social anarchy to achieve a geopolitical goal, supported and legitimized by the supposedly 'independent' think tanks, NGOs and the elite media.

The US State Department and associated NGOs receive state support for foreign operations through its State, Foreign Operations, and Related Programs, with the United States Agency for International Development (USAID) receiving the largest portion – its 2022 budgetary resources was $47.79 billion – followed by the National Endowment for Democracy (NED), with $2.6 billion for 'democracy programme fund' for 2022. NED's Center for International Media Assistance, set up in 2006 to 'support independent media in developing countries', is described as 'a global thought leader on media development, the digital sphere, and their connection to democracy' (see NED website). The International Fact-Checking Network, a subsidiary of the 'journalism research organization' the Poynter Institute, is also funded by the NED, as well as other foundations and information NGOs.

Despite such lofty ideals, evidence of the United States exporting democracy to the global South is mixed, with numerous examples of how the US-led West has thwarted, rather than protected, democracy. During the Cold War, despite its adopted role as the 'leader of the free world', the United States on many occasions deliberately acted to undermine democratically elected governments. Notable among these are the 1953 Iranian coup d'état against the democratically elected Prime Minister Mohammad Mosaddegh in favour of the monarchical rule of Shah Mohammad Reza Pahlavi (Abrahamian, 2013); the assassination of Patrice Lumumba, a pan-Africanist leader and the first prime minister of Congo after its independence from Belgium in 1961, in collaboration with the Belgian government and the CIA (De Witte, 2003; Gerard and Kuklick, 2015); the military takeover of Indonesia by overthrowing the nationalist leader Sukarno in 1967 (Roosa, 2022); and the 1973 CIA-led coup against Chile's elected President Salvador Allende (Haslam, 2005).

Another manifestation of double standards in promoting democracy in the so-called Third World was the treatment that was meted out to India, the only democracy in the post-colonial world, by the West, which favoured Pakistan, which was under a military dictatorship at that time and a member of the now defunct SEATO (Southeast Asia Treaty Organization, 1954–1977) and CENTO (Central Treaty Organization, 1955–1979), receiving defence supplies and diplomatic support from the West. A brutal example of this was the not-so-subtle backing of Pakistan when it committed atrocities in its eastern part in what became Bangladesh in 1972, as Bass has documented (Bass, 2013). As many as 10 million Bangladeshis came to India within a span of six months in 1971 – the biggest such movement of population fleeing atrocities and fearing worse. Estimates of those killed vary from 100,000 to 3 million, and yet in the international media, this genocide does not figure prominently.

A similar situation can be seen in the 'genocide' in oil-rich southern Sudan, which had its roots in the Cold War-related 20-year civil war in neighbouring Chad, creating a confrontation between Libya (with Soviet support) and the Reagan administration (allied with France and Israel), which then spilled over into Darfur. By 2003, the West presented the conflict as part of the 'War on Terror' and called for a military invasion dressed up as 'humanitarian intervention', as Mamdani has argued, stripping Darfur and the violence there of any 'context' and presenting it in the Western media as 'racially motivated, perpetrated by "light-skinned Arabs" on "Black Africans"' – a kind of 'framing of the violence continues the error that came out of the colonial tradition of racializing the people of Sudan' (Mamdani, 2010: 6 and 7).

The conflict in Iraq, which, in the past four decades, has reshaped the geopolitical map of the post-Cold War Middle East, is perhaps the most salient example of how strategic communication masks geopolitical considerations, using the narrative of promoting democracy and freedom. For example, the 1991 Iraqi invasion could be seen as one of the Middle East's 'energy conflicts', bringing together the geopolitical and economic interests of a 'Weapondollar-Petrodollar coalition' of the US government, large defence contractors and oil companies (Bichler and Nitzan, 1996).

The invasions of Iraq and strategic communication

The so-called first Gulf War of 1991, which should be more accurately described as the US-led invasion of Iraq, heralded what was then described as 'a new world order', with the United States as the sole remaining superpower, having won the Cold War against the Soviet Union. The original epithet of 'Gulf War', though, belongs more properly to the nearly decade-long Iran–Iraq war of the 1980s, a proxy war by the then US ally the Iraqi dictator Saddam Hussein, supported by Saudi petrodollars to check the growing regional influence of Iran after the Islamic revolution of 1979. That war claimed more than a million lives and many more millions were injured on both sides.

For the 1991 'Operation Desert Storm', the US military organized a 'pool' system to coordinate the media coverage of its invasion, which also became the first conflict to be covered instantaneously through live feeds from CNN. This channel made its name by bringing Pentagon-supplied cockpit videos of 'precision bombings' of Iraqi targets into living rooms across the globe, 'as a painless Nintendo exercise, and the image of Americans as virtuous, clean warriors' (Said, 1993: 365). Another important source of visuals for reporting conflicts was satellite imagery, often used to illustrate the successes of aerial bombings. As a report from the US Defense Intelligence Agency acknowledged, 'The 1991 Gulf War and subsequent U.S. military operations illustrated the value of the US GPS satellite navigation system for troop movement, force tracking, and precision munition delivery' (Defense Intelligence Agency, 2022: 41).

In such a high-tech and 'virtual' presentation of the invasion, described by Baudrillard as the 'War that didn't happen' (Baudrillard, 1994), the geopolitical significance of the first major post-Cold War conflict, heralding a new 'pax-Americana,' was lost. A veteran BBC reporter pointed out a few months after the invasion that 'not many people seem interested in finding out what really happened' (Simpson, 1991: xiv).

Just over a decade later, on March 20, 2003, the United States officially launched its illegal invasion of Iraq, despite widespread demonstrations against this action across the world – the biggest since the Vietnam war (Friel and Falk, 2004). For 'Operation Iraqi Freedom' the United States introduced an 'embedded' reporter system to broadcast their so-called Shock and Awe campaign, enabling 'direct use of Pentagon's PR material' and 'feeding the news channels' insatiable demand for footage' (Lewis and Brookes, 2004: 298–299). Again, the story was all about 'winning and losing, rather than a consideration of context in which the war was fought' (ibid.). The rationale promoted by the media was based on Saddam Hussein's alleged links to Al Qaeda and intelligence regarding the presence of weapons of mass destruction in Iraq, both claims later turned out to be false.

The more substantial geopolitical reasons behind the invasion of Iraq included a desire for control over oil fields, the idea of creating a 'showcase of democracy' in the Middle East, and a demonstration of the 'fight against terrorism' in response to 9/11 attacks on the United States. On 30 January 2002, the then-president George W. Bush first used the expression 'axis of evil' in his State of the Union address when referring to North Korea, Iran and Iraq.

A major reason for the military action against Iraq was its alleged support for Al Qaeda post 9/11. In September 2002, Secretary of State Condoleezza Rice told the PBS Newshour with Jim Lehrer, 'We clearly know that there were in the past and have been contacts between senior Iraqi officials and members of Al Qaeda going back for actually quite a long time' (cited in CNN, 2002). This information was apparently based on an 'intelligence dossier' compiled by the British government, which plagiarized a section of an Oxford PhD dissertation by Ibrahim al-Marashi and shared it with the American intelligence community. The British government had changed the key words in the 'intelligence dossier' to suggest that Iraq had supported Al Qaeda and then 'padded the plagiarised material with their own pages' that argued for military action, wrote al-Marashi, now working at the California State University, adding 'Iraq remains a republic of anarchy' (al-Marashi, 2023).

The mainstream media in the United States and among its allies toed this line, diligently, consistently and without any restraint. The 'influence campaign' was aimed at projecting the invasion as a 'just war', according to the US National Security Archive, available at the George Washington University (National Security Archive, 2022). However, the 2006 Senate Intelligence Committee was unambiguous in its conclusion that 'according to debriefs of multiple detainees – including Saddam Hussein and former Deputy Prime Minister Tariq Aziz – and captured documents, Saddam did not trust Al Qaeda or any other radical Islamist group and did not want to cooperate with them' (ibid.).

The other main reason for the invasion was the allegation that Iraq was developing weapons of mass destruction. In early February 2003, the US secretary of state Colin Powell publicly discussed a potential change of regime in Baghdad and, at a meeting of the UN Security Council on 5 February 2003, he showed a test tube with white powder that he claimed contained samples of chemical weapons found in the country – a lie, later admitted as such even by the US government. The consistent line leading up to the invasion was that Saddam Hussein had broken his promises to the UN that he would destroy and cease further development of weapons of mass destruction and long-range missiles and submit to unrestricted inspections. However, the Senate Intelligence Committee report in 2006 again found no evidence connecting Iraq to weapons of mass destruction: 'Post-war findings do not support the 2002 National Intelligence Estimate assessment that "Iraq has biological weapons" and all key aspects of Iraq's offensive biological weapons program are larger and more advanced than before the Gulf War' (cited in Miller, 2006).

The demonization of Saddam Hussein was also integral to the media coverage justifying the invasion. President Bush frequently referred to the Iraqi dictator as 'evil incarnate', copiously repeated by media columnists, in editorials and radio and TV studio discussions: 'There's no question that the leader of Iraq is an evil man. After all, he gassed his own people. And we know he's been working on weapons of mass destruction', said the president. John Burns, the *New York Times* foreign correspondent compared Saddam to Stalin and denounced him for plunging Iraq into a 'bloodbath of medieval proportions' (Burns, 2003). No wonder then that exterminating such a threat was almost an official policy with the US military, which was attempting to execute the 'decapitation of government', by destroying communication networks and targeting Saddam Hussein.

Toppling Saddam

The televised toppling of a statue of Saddam Hussein on 9 April 2003 in Firdos Square in central Baghdad, next to the hotel where most of the world's media were staying, was staged at the most crucial time of the invasion to indicate a quick, righteous victory and a revolt against the hated dictator. What turned out to be an example of what American historian Daniel Boorstin identified as 'pseudo-events' was a well-orchestrated media event and public relations exercise, highly symbolic in its significance, not just for Iraqis but for the wider Arab world, as the impression was given that US troops were removing the statue at the behest of crowds of cheering Iraqis. In a geopolitically highly figurative gesture, a US flag was wrapped over the head of the statue as 'a symbol of occupation' – being filmed live for a global audience – and then was promptly replaced with the Iraqi national flag (Maass, 2011).

The then US defence secretary Donald Rumsfeld called the spectacle 'breathtaking', while television commentators compared the toppling to the fall of the Berlin Wall and the collapse of the Iron Curtain. Fox News replayed the footage of the statue's fall every 4.4 minutes on the day of the staged event, while CNN was close behind at 7.5 minutes. An analysis of the US broadcast news coverage of the toppling showed that it employed a 'victory' frame that replaced the gruesome stories about heavy fighting continuing in Iraq. 'Whereas battle stories imply a war is going on, statues falling – especially when placed in the context of truly climactic images from recent history – imply the war is over', the study noted (Aday et al.,

2005). Such images were being consumed by television viewers around the world, given the reach and influence of networks such as CNN.

After having destroyed the country in a short and brutal bombardment, Bush's declaration of 'mission accomplished' and an 'end to hostility' on 1 May 2003 was shown on television in a Hollywood-style military setting as a '*Top Gun* act'. Bush co-piloted a navy jet on to the deck of the *USS Abraham Lincoln*, reported to be in the Persian Gulf to cheering troops and television crew; live visuals beamed around the world, but, as was reported much later after the spectacle was already beamed around the world by AP, the ship was nowhere in the vicinity of the Persian Gulf but close to the San Diego coastline (Krugman, 2003: 31).

Such framing is part of what has been defined as the 'military-industrial-media-entertainment network' (Der Derian, 2009), in which popular culture becomes part of the geopolitical dynamics. Hollywood blockbusters such as *Platoon* and *Full Metal Jacket* (on the Vietnam war), *Black Hawk Dawn* (on Somalia), *American Sniper* (on Iraq) and *The Covenant* (on Afghanistan), among many others, have provided the popular cultural context within which US military interventions are represented as virtuous endeavours (Weber, 2006).

With the US military occupation of Iraq after the end of the war on 25 May 2003, the US-led Coalition Provisional Authority, relying on the advice of many exiled Shia leaders, launched an extensive 'de-Baathification' process aimed at eliminating the former ruling Baath party's influence in Iraq, which effectively meant the end of the civil service, disbanding of the military and security services, and thus creating chaos, sectarian conflict and political instability.

The United States then installed a provisional Iraqi government with a viceroy: this de facto occupation, which lasted from 2004 to 2011, was a blatant violation of Iraqi sovereignty and an illegal act under international law, but it rarely received any criticism in the mainstream media, or from Western NGOs and think tanks (Friel and Falk, 2004). Numerous war crimes committed by the invading forces in Fallujah and elsewhere were filtered out of media coverage and political discourse and, if mentioned, were projected as an outcome of sectarian conflict between Arab Sunnis and Shiites. In a 14,000-word piece published in the left liberal journal *Current Affairs*, to mark the 20 years of the invasion, Noam Chomsky and the magazine's editor Nathan Robinson presented a trenchant criticism of the US policy and its impact not just on Iraq but also on the wider region (Robinson and Chomsky, 2023).

The US invasion of Iraq had deep geopolitical impacts across the Arab world and beyond. The ensuing chaos caused by the destruction of existing civil, military and political structures and the resultant vicious sectarianism contributed to the emergence of non-state actors such as the militant Sunni revivalist group Islamic State (The Islamic State of Iraq and al-Sham [ISIS], also called Daesh). This increase in instability and violence was compounded by NATO's involvement in the overthrowing of Muammar Gaddafi in Libya and the civil war in Syria. In contrast to Al Qaeda, ISIS initially focused on what it described as the 'near enemy' – Shia; the Iraqi and Syrian regimes; and secular, pro-Western states in the Middle East – before targeting the 'far enemy' in Europe and other places beyond the Middle East (Gerges, 2017).

The violent radicalism of Al Qaeda and ISIS, financially supported by conservative Gulf states promoting *da'wa* (propagation of Islam) activities around the world, as well as Iran's outreach in countries with significant populations of Shia, notably in Iraq, Syria, Lebanon and Palestine, continues to exacerbate the political instability in the region (Gerges, 2017; Hamid, 2017; Mandaville, 2020, among others). For its part, ISIS produced professional-level propaganda, using violent videos, memes and social media postings, offering a voyeuristic involvement in a 'theatre of violence' (Griffin, 2010: 8). ISIS's English-language magazine *Dabiq* (which ran between 2014 and 2016) and its Arabic-language weekly *al-Naba'* (set up in 2015) were established to recruit new members and propagate their ideology, showing 'death and about to die images' as part of their media campaign and information warfare (Gambhir, 2016; Kraidy, 2017; Winkler et al., 2019). As one US think tank report warned, the 'information operations' campaign of ISIS was supporting multiple objectives, including 'control over territory, coercion of populations, and recruitment', as well as 'execution of international terror attacks'; the campaign, the report warned, may 'ultimately usher in a "Virtual Caliphate" – a radicalized community organized online – that empowers the global Salafi-jihadi movement and that could operate independently of ISIS' (Gambhir, 2016: 7).

The United States continued to launch counter-terrorism actions such as pre-emptive decapitation strikes by drone and aircraft (Byman, 2021: 38), as well as raids by special operations forces, notably killing leading jihadists such as bin Laden (in 2011 in his hideout in Pakistan), and propagandists Anwar al-Awlaki (an English-speaking jihadist, the first American citizen to be targeted and killed, in 2011 in Yemen, by a US drone strike) and Abu Bakr al Baghdadi, the self-proclaimed caliph of ISIS (killed in 2019). These attacks were reported in the mainstream media as though they were a natural and legitimate continuation of US security strategy to protect democracy and freedom. In addition, 'the US military and intelligence agencies now often resort to training and equipping local forces that can act as the tip of the counterterrorism spear' (ibid.: 41). This counterterrorism action has more to do with the West's geopolitical and economic interests than combating extremism, as the cases of Libya and Syria demonstrate.

Libya

One often ignored aspect of the reason for the US invasion of Iraq was President Saddam's wish to sell the country's oil in euros, replacing the US dollar. Energy politics was also at the heart of the US-led NATO bombing of Libya in March 2011: Libyan dictator Gaddafi's apparent plan to start selling oil in dinars (a new gold-backed pan-African currency) instead of US dollars or euros was considered unacceptable, and humanitarian causes were constructed, and invasion was planned and mediatized. Gaddafi was overthrown and one of the richest and most stable countries in Africa became a failed and lawless state controlled by a mishmash of rebel groups, some affiliated or sympathetic to Al Qaeda. Libya's destruction triggered a war in neighbouring Mali and helped strengthen Al Qaeda and ISIS in North Africa, some elements from which got involved in the Syrian civil war.

The NATO-led invasion of Libya was ostensibly undertaken within the Western-sponsored framework of 'Responsibility to Protect (R2P)', to provide a legal fig leaf to cover another example of imperial warfare, legitimized by the mainstream media, Western NGOs and think tanks, with their passionate denunciations of the maverick dictatorship of one of the longest serving leader of Africa who was attacking 'his own people'. One commentator in the *Washington Post*, approving of the intervention, reported that 'a massacre of civilians, amounting to crimes against humanity', would likely have transpired had NATO forces not invaded (Abramowitz, 2011), while a prominent *New York Times* columnist praised the attack as 'the beau ideal of a liberal internationalist intervention', claiming that its 'humanitarian purpose' was plain for all to see (Douthat, 2011).

Such media facilitators as the US-based campaigning group *Avaaz* (Voice), in operation since 2007, played a crucial role in justifying the invasion. Claiming to be free of political bias, the group, with a global membership of more than 69 million in 2023, undertook a PR campaign on mainstream and social media to generate support for a 'no-fly zone' in Libya and delivered a petition with over a million signatures to the UN. It was also allegedly involved in training and giving communication equipment to anti-Gaddafi rebels. In the past, too, the group had provided proxy servers to anti-Iranian government supporters during the country's 2009 general elections and facilitating Western journalists to Syria to cover the war, without authorization from the Syrian government.

No one from the liberal media, NGOs or epistemic community expressed any horror in seeing the pictures and videos of Gaddafi being sexually assaulted and beaten to death in the road by a mob, which was presented as a deeply disturbing and even macabre form of infotainment. The precedent for such visual cruelty was established by the global circulation of the one-minute video of the last moments of Saddam Hussien on 30 December 2006, aired without sound by Arabic satellite channel *Al-Arabiya* and later with sound (from a mobile phone recording), showing the Iraqi president being taunted by his executioners. These videos were repeatedly shown on news networks across the world.

The destruction of the Gaddafi regime inevitably led to chaos – not dissimilar to what had happened in Iraq – as an assortment of militias, with allegiance to various outside powers, including Qatar, United Arab Emirates (UAE), Russia, France and the United States, as well as sections of the Islamic State, filled the political and security void. More than a decade after the violent ousting of Gaddafi, the country remains deeply divided. A Government of National Accord (GNA) – viewed by the UN as the legitimate government – was formed in the aftermath of the 'regime change'. The government was later under attack by forces belonging to the Libyan

National Army, led by a former general in Gaddafi's army, with support from Egypt, the UAE and Russia. Türkiye intervened in Libya in 2019 on behalf of GNA to secure its stakes in the control of the development of energy resources in the eastern Mediterranean.

The chemical attack in the Syrian civil war

External forces were also central to the war in Syria: the geopolitical interests of Iran and Russia on the side of the Syrian president Bashar al-Assad and the Gulf monarchies, Türkiye and US-led Western alliance supporting the rebels of various political ideological orientation. As with Libya, discussions of the violation of human rights in Syria by the Assad government were the pretext for military action. As the anti-Assad movement gained ground, the then US president Barrack Obama proclaimed that the Syrian president should go (Wilson and Warrick, 2011), while a 2012 *New York Times* report was headlined as 'State Department and Pentagon Plan for Post-Assad Syria' (Lee Myers and Shanker, 2012).

The military operation against Syria in 2014 was christened *Operation Inherent Resolve* and involved a large variety of proxy wars – including supporting Islamist groups. The alleged use of chemical weapons – especially in Douma – became the most controversial aspect of the Syrian conflict. The Western media followed an old script that Assad was a dictator 'gassing his own people' and therefore military action was necessary to save lives. A *New York Times* multimedia feature was explicit in blaming Assad (Browne et al., 2018). Even the Hague-based watchdog Organization for the Prohibition of Chemical Weapons (OPCW) was politicized, as two of its former employees were accused of altering its original findings to make them sound more convincing, and its final report even concluded that 'the Syrian Arab Air Forces are the perpetrators of this attack' (Boyd-Barrett, 2022). Damascus denied the use of chemical weapons and insisted that it had handed over its stockpiles under a 2013 agreement, prompted by a suspected sarin gas attack that killed 1,400 in the Damascus suburb of Ghouta. Syria's voting rights at the OPCW were suspended in 2021 for its refusal to cooperate after being accused of more chemical attacks.

A study of the coverage of Al-Jazeera's Arabic and English channels of the Al-Ghouta chemical weapons attack showed that Syrian opposition sources were given more space (more than 45 per cent) than the regime sources (25 per cent) (Abdul-Nabi, 2022). More than 80 per cent of the news and features from both channels were dominated by pro-Qatar framing, attributing the responsibility of committing the attack to the Assad regime and legitimizing a military strike in Syria (ibid.). The Saudi-owned *Al Arabiya* network, established in 2003, covered the wars in Syria and Libya from an almost exclusive anti-regime perspective, reflecting the geopolitical interests of Riyadh. Similarly, the Russian coverage was almost entirely pro-Assad, while Türkiye, another key geopolitical player, was supporting anti-regime rebels, some with dubious association with extremist Islamist groups (Tol, 2023).

While the Assad regime's atrocities were highly publicized in the media, the violence committed by the Salafist militia was largely ignored (Boyd-Barrett, 2022). The Russian military response, which began in 2015, made the Western-led 'regime change' project difficult to execute. Nevertheless, in the vicious conflict, as many as half a million people were killed, while millions more were displaced – about half of the country's pre-war population. According to the 2023 *World Development Report*, 5.5 million refugees had fled Syria and were living as refugees mostly in Türkiye, Lebanon, Jordan, Iraq and Egypt (World Bank, 2023).

Public relations and image wars

The Syrian conflict made the White Helmets group (officially called the Syria Civil Defence) a very visible entity in the Western media narratives, especially through the extensive coverage of their operations to save lives in Syria's rebel-held territories during the conflict. Set up by former British army officer James Le Mesurier, the group's principal financial support came from USAID's Office of Transitional Initiatives. In July 2012, a year after the Syrian conflict began, USAID began to lay the groundwork for its Syria Regional Option. With American analysts proclaiming the imminent downfall of the Assad government, USAID rushed to 'provide support to emerging civil authorities to build the foundation for a peaceful and democratic Syria', according to a USAID executive report from that year. Beginning 2013, the aid was to the tune of $23 million, part of the $339.6 million budgeted by USAID for 'supporting activities that pursue a peaceful transition to a democratic and stable Syria', diplomaticspeak for regime change. The British government as well as the Qatari government also helped the organization by way of funding.

Why did an obscure civil defence group operating in Syria receive international recognition? The role of the appropriately titled *The Syria Campaign* is crucial in this regard. Run by London- and New York-based international public relations companies and a British-registered private company (the Voices Project) and mostly funded by the Asfari Foundation (owned by the London-based Syrian billionaire Ayman Asfari), the 'campaign' contributed to the White Helmets becoming an internationally visible entity. The group was awarded the 'alternative Nobel Prize', known as the Right Livelihood Award, and was even nominated for the Nobel Peace Prize. The 2016 Netflix documentary *The White Helmets* with its tagline, 'To save one life is to save all of humanity', received extensive promotion in Western news and entertainment media and endorsements from Hollywood celebrities. Asfari has strong links to the epistemic community: in 2015, he was invited to speak at a Carnegie Endowment for International Peace conference, while the Centre for Syrian Studies at Britain's St Andrews University was partly funded by Asfari's foundation (Abu-Nasr and Pendleton, 2016). On the other hand, the Russian media conducted a 'sustained campaign to discredit' the White Helmets, as the group highlighted the human rights violations of the Assad regime.

Other highly successful global public relations exercises used the media to exploit the genuine victimhood of two young girls, strategically chosen for geopolitical and propaganda points. The 16-year-old Pakistan-born Malala Yousafzai was shot in the head by the Taliban in October 2012 for attending school. Projected as a campaigner for girls' education, she received the 2014 Nobel Prize for Peace, addressed the UN and won the EU's prestigious Sakharov Human Rights prize. The 'Malala machine' grew in November 2012 when the PR agency Edelman started working for her family, as *The Dawn*, Pakistan's leading newspaper, reported (The Dawn, 2013).

Her 2013 book *I am Malala* received glowing endorsements in liberal newspapers: 'Ms. Yousafzai's stature as a symbol of peace and bravery has been established across the world', said The *New York Times*; 'Ms. Yousafzai has single-handedly turned the issue of the right of girls – and all children – to be educated into headline news', the *Financial Times* reported. Translated into more than 40 languages, the international bestseller catapulted a young woman into global fame, though in her native Pakistan, the country's Private Schools Federation announced an 'I Am Not Malala' day in 2014 and called for her memoir to be banned (Kugelman, 2017). Her co-recipient of the Noble Peace Prize Kailash Satyarthi, a former policeman who has spent the past four decades of his life to campaign against child labour in India, did not have any recognition even within India, let alone globally.

Another example is that of eight-year-old Bana al-Abed who barely spoke English but was sending tweets in perfect English during the siege of the Syrian city of Aleppo in 2016. Her tweets, 'I'm very afraid I will die tonight', 2 October 2016; 'Stop killing us', 6 October 2016; and 'I just want to live without fear', 12 October 2016, were widely circulated in Western media and helped her to become a minor celebrity, as she was attending galas, meeting the Turkish president (after her family was evacuated to Türkiye in December 2016) and receiving a 'Freedom Award' from the influential think tank the Atlantic Council. Her 2017 book, *Dear World: A Syrian Girl's Story of War and Plea for Peace*, published by a major New York publishing house with endorsements from best-selling author J. K. Rowling (Al-Abed, 2017) received rave reviews. In a 2018 apparently rehearsed interview with Bellingcat, the British-based 'alternative' web portal with strong ties to the Western discourse building, she broke into singing 'We shall overcome' (www.youtube.com/watch?v=oOLMFtlBc-g).

In the cases of Iraq, Libya and Syria, there is a consistency of media narrative: regime change is a clearly defined geopolitical aim, and every weapon in the communication arsenal is deployed to achieve this. The inevitable disruption caused by such invasions has contributed to the expansion of radicalism of all descriptions, especially the Islamic varieties, which, as in the case of Taliban, have been supported or at the very least facilitated by Western military interventions. The inadvertent or organized arming of rebel groups to engineer regime change is well articulated in case of Syria (Mazzetti and Younes, 2016) – a Brookings Institution piece suggested ways in which the anti-Assad forces could be converted into a 'real fighting force' (Pollack, 2014) – as is the arming of Al Qaeda and the Islamic State, in Syria and Iraq (O'Connor, 2017), despite apparent scrutiny by the CIA (Stein, 2014; O'Connor, 2017). The United States ended up relying largely on Türkiye, Qatar and Saudi Arabia – states known to support Sunni Islamist factions – to run US-supplied armaments to the rebels (Mazzetti and Younes, 2016).

According to a 2017 report published by Conflict Armament Research, an EU-funded group, international weapon supplies to factions in the Syrian conflict 'significantly augmented the quantity and quality of weapons available to [ISIS] forces' (Conflict Armament Research, 2017: 5). By the time the United States finally ended its official project of arming and training Syrian rebels, about one billion dollars had been spent in what had been one of the costliest such projects until then in the history of the CIA (Hanania, 2020). Russian support for the Assad regime – as part of its own geopolitical interests in Syria – the only country in the region where Russian military has bases, ensured that the 'regime change' was unsuccessful, at a very grim human cost, and Assad remains in de facto control of the majority of the country, while rebel forces are dissipated, despite billions of dollars of military support and media legitimization not only from the United States and its Western allies but also from Saudi Arabia, UAE and, perhaps most significantly, Türkiye. As Syria was readmitted to the Arab League in 2023, Assad warned his Arab compatriots of the 'danger of expansionist Ottoman thought'.

Another consistent aspect of such coverage is to project the adversary as irrational, following the 'madman theory' of international relations. Soon after Iraq invaded Kuwait in August 1990, a *Washington Post* report began with the words: 'Madman, crazy, insane and maniac are the adjectives of choice to describe Iraq President Saddam Hussein' (Anderson and Van Atta, 1990). The apparently irrational geopolitical behaviour of adversaries – Saddam, Assad, Gaddafi and Putin – to name the most prominent ones – fits into a discourse where the rational West is taking action to deal with the chaos unleashed by an unreasonable – not to say – fanatical leader, who is threatening the status quo and needs to be removed in regime change.

Often, fake discourses are constructed to promote geopolitical positions that favour the United States and its allies. The role of epistemic communities in such a narrative construction is crucial, as noted in Chapter 3. Which arguments are given prominence and which are marginalized can often depend on what kind of 'expert' opinion journalists prefer to use. During the '9–11 wars', the mainstream media were saturated with pro-war voices, while dissent was largely marginalized. A 2021 survey conducted by the US-based Fairness and Accuracy in Reporting (FAIR) to find out which epistemic experts were quoted by the *New York Times* since 2016 discovered that US pro-peace think tanks, such as the Institute for Policy Studies and the Center for Economic and Policy Research, elicited 86 and 53 mentions, respectively. In stark contrast, the newspaper carried opinions from hawkish think tanks such as the Center for American Progress, which was featured in 432 articles in the *New York Times* since 2016, while conservative think tank the Heritage Foundation appeared in 529 articles over the same period (Macleod, 2021).

Such framing legitimizes the 'force of freedom' as a central tenet to US foreign policy rhetoric, impelling Washington to transplant freedom and liberty to 'outposts of tyranny', anchored as it is within the ideological tropes of a 21st-century version of imperialism. The dominant media discourse deliberately skirts around the deeper analysis of geo-political issues. Instead, in what amounts to an extremely skilful and generally successful diversion, wars are presented as undertaken for just and moral causes and as high-tech infotainment spectacles, thus helping to create a 'feel-good factor' among Western publics: 'the world's superpower is literally being shown doing something to make the world safer for them' (Thussu, 2007: 132). It also feeds into another prominent discourse, that of Islamophobia: Kumar sees 'anti-Muslim racism as a product of empire – not just empire in crisis but as a normal modality of imperial domination from the early modern era all the way up to the twenty first century' (Kumar, 2021: 10).

Afghanistan: the geopolitics of 'the forever war'

In August 2021, the US-funded government of Afghanistan collapsed and the Taliban took over in a bloodless change of regime, almost 20 years after the United States had 'liberated' the country from them in 'Operation Enduring Freedom' in November 2001, pursuing Osama bin Laden, Al Qaeda's leader, which had claimed responsibility for the 9/11 terrorist attacks. In the ensuing two decades, the United States has spent $83 billion on 'building, training, equipping, and developing Afghanistan National Security Forces (ANSF)', though the 300,000-strong ANSF, equipped with some of the best American weaponry, simply melted away in the face of the Taliban advance.

A report from the US government's Special Inspector General for Afghan Reconstruction noted that, from 2001, the US government spent $145 billion 'trying to rebuild Afghanistan, its security forces, civilian government institutions, economy, and civil society', while the Department of Defense spent $837 billion 'on warfighting', during which 2,443 American and 1,144 allied troops were killed. The reported death tolls of both the Afghan troops (66,000) and civilians (48,000) were 'likely significant underestimations' (SIGAR, 2021: vii). The reasons for the US failure to bring democracy to Afghanistan were thus articulated in the report:

> The US government 'clumsily forced Western technocratic models onto Afghan economic institutions; trained security forces in advanced weapon systems they could not understand, much less maintain; imposed formal rule of law on a country that addressed 80 to 90 percent of its disputes through informal means; and often struggled to understand or mitigate the cultural and social barriers to supporting women and girls'.
>
> Without this background knowledge, US officials often empowered power-brokers who preyed on the population or diverted US assistance away from its intended recipients to enrich and empower themselves and their allies. Lack of knowledge at the local level meant projects intended to mitigate conflict often exacerbated it, and even inadvertently funded insurgents.
>
> *(SIGAR, 2021: xi)*

As a recent history of the conflict has argued, despite their medieval ideology and brutal misogyny, the Taliban were able to project themselves as authentically Afghan and resisting foreign occupation, whereas the government forces lacked conviction and were seen as pawns of the West and on their payrolls (Malkasian, 2021). The account of a *Washington Post* journalist showed that some US officials questioned the futility of having spent billions of dollars to turn Afghanistan into a modern country and to curb corruption and the drug trade (Whitlock, 2021). Katherine Brown, president and executive director of the US Advisory Commission on Public Diplomacy, noted that, in Afghanistan, the US news media 'largely amplified' US power and 'an American worldview' (Brown, 2019).

After the 'fall' of the government, a *New Yorker* report, based on unreleased documents, 'showed a dispiriting record of misjudgment, hubris, and delusion' (Coll and Entous, 2021). This sentiment was echoed by *The New York Review of Books*, which noted, 'Spending so much time in Kabul, journalists lost sight of what was happening outside it. Viewing the Taliban as a terrorist group alien to Afghan society, they neglected exploring the sources of the fighters' support' (Massing, 2021). The Taliban used their own propaganda outlet, *Voice of Jihad*, to disseminate an extremely conservative interpretation of Islam in Arabic and English, nationalism in Dari (a form of Persian spoken in Afghanistan) and regionalism in Urdu texts. The Taliban categorized all Muslims as members of the *ummah* and all non-Muslims as outsiders and convinced the Muslims of the need for violence (Aggarwal, 2016).

Although much of the coverage of Afghanistan in the Western media gave the rationale for Western involvement as the promotion of democracy and humanitarian assistance, the fact that the country was well endowed with mineral resources was hardly mentioned in mainstream discourses. The US Geological Survey carried out a series of aerial surveys of Afghanistan in 2006 and 2007, and the US government in 2010 estimated that $1 trillion worth of untapped mineral deposits, which include copper, iron and rare earth elements (including chromite, the only commercially extractable source of chrome). Apart from significant oil and gas reserves, the country has precious gemstones, as well as gold and silver (Byrd and Noorani, 2017). Speaking to employees of the CIA in 2027, Trump said the United States had erred in withdrawing troops from Iraq without holding on to its oil: 'The old expression, "To the victor belong the spoils" – you remember', he declared (cited in Lander and Risen, 2017).

War on terror – part of the 'forever war'

The 'forever war' in Afghanistan was central to the US-led 'war on terror' and, 'thanks to a successful narrative project', Al Qaeda's terrorism came to be seen as a 'security threat' not just to the United States but to the world at large (Krebs, 2015: 25). As the leader of Al Qaeda, bin Laden had been funded and trained by the CIA through the conduits of Pakistan's Inter-Services Intelligence (ISI) to fight 'godless' communism in Afghanistan. In the post-9/11 era he had become 'enemy number one' of the United States and entered a strategic alliance with the Taliban, thus gaining, notes one observer, 'an entire country as a base for operations. He was able to gather around thousands of Islamic extremists and extend his operations around the world. His main logical support came from Pakistani extremist groups – suppliers and means of communication' (Rashid, 2008: 15).

The arsenal for fighting terrorism included dropping the 'mother of all bombs' on Islamic State fighters in eastern Afghanistan in 2017; the first time the Massive Ordnance Air Blast weapon, to give its technical name, was dropped. As the *New York Times* helpfully reported, it was 'the most powerful bomb in America's non-nuclear inventory, weighing about 22,000 pounds' (Cooper and Mashal, 2017). Yet after more than two decades of fighting terrorism – at the cost of billions of dollars and hundreds of thousands of deaths – in 2023, the Taliban were again entrenched in Kabul, and Islamic terrorist organizations, notably Al Qaeda and Daesh Khorasan (ISIS-K), remain active. Indeed, the Taliban's takeover in August 2021, without firing a shot, could not have been possible without covert US support: it may be significant that the United States left $40 billion worth of arms and ammunitions on their chaotic departure.

The mainstream US media covered the withdrawal as premature and presented the situation of Afghans controlling their own country as an unacceptable outcome. The *New York Times* asserted that the illegal invasion had evolved into a humanitarian mission, via a counterterrorism mission, to one devoted to nation-building, democratization and securing rights for women. The 'paper of record' drew parallels with the failures of previous imperial interventions in the country: the 'same long, bloody, unpopular slog that forced the British to withdraw from Afghanistan in the 19th century and the Soviet Union to retreat in the 20th', it averred (Cho, 2021). The Western media also gave much space to Tolo News ('Tolo' meaning 'dawn' in Dari), Afghanistan's largest broadcaster set up by Said Mohseni, an Australian–Afghan former investment banker, with $2.2 million from USAID, part of Washington's $166 million to support independent media in Afghanistan. Tolo News also ran, from 2007, a Persian-language satellite TV channel *Farsi1*, which was beamed from Dubai to Iran, in collaboration with Rupert Murdoch, as part of the information war against the Iranian regime (Bowley, 2013).

At the time of forming a provisional government in August 2021, the Taliban organized their first press conference, which was streamed live on Al Jazeera, a network with ties to Islamist groups in the region, including in Egypt, Libya and Syria. Qatar played an important mediator's role in negotiating Taliban deal with the United States in several rounds of talks held in Doha, where President Ashraf Ghani and the former president Hamid Karzai were not even part of the negotiations; their governments were considered to be deeply corrupt, as one US observer with close proximity to the Afghan leadership noted, describing it 'not as a government at all but as a vertically integrated criminal organization whose core activity was not in fact exercising the functions of a state but rather extracting resources for personal gain' (Chayes, 2015).

Like the cases discussed above, the conflicts in Africa, too, are essentially about control of resources, but the true geopolitical interests are not communicated, instead there is a consistent narrative of anarchy and corruption, where the West is projected as still exercising the 'White man's burden' to bring order and stability to a 'violent' continent.

Africa's invisible wars

Ever since the now infamous 1884 Berlin conference when the major European powers, meeting to carve up Africa, grabbed the best land for plantations and for mineral and other natural resources to be processed in Europe, its exploitation has continued in some shape or form to contemporary times. The allocation and exploitation of resources lies at the heart of conflict there, as do the colonial borders drawn with scant consideration of ethnic or cultural affinities, a scourge which continues to bedevil relations in much of the global South, but particularly on the African continent. Although contemporary conflicts in Africa are inevitably framed within the colonial vocabulary of 'tribal,' or more recently, 'ethnic' or 'religious' fault lines, the ground reality is that beneath the surface of this vast continent lies a wealth of mineral resources of enormous value. In 2019, Africa produced almost 1 billion tonnes of minerals worth $406 billion, according to the UN. It is also home to about 30 per cent mineral reserves, 12 per cent of the oil reserves and 8 per cent of the natural gas reserves of the planet.

The conflict in the Democratic Republic of Congo, one of the world's deadliest, having claimed millions of lives, is rooted in the country's rich resource base: it produces two-thirds of the world's supply of cobalt, a key component for batteries in mobile phones and computers. According to an investigation by the *New York Times* in 2020, 15 of the 19 cobalt-producing mines in Congo were owned or financed by Chinese companies, with government-supported banks giving credit to the tune of $124 billion. In Southern Sudan, too, the conflict is not necessarily about ethnic violence but resources, a major reason for supporting the independence of the oil-rich Darfur region, which received support from Hollywood celebrities, including George Clooney (Vertin, 2019), as well as evangelical Christians, while the Chinese oil companies had the biggest investment in the newly formed country (Searcey et al., 2021).

The bloodiest war of 2022 was not the Russian invasion of Ukraine but between the Ethiopian government (led by Prime Minister Abiy Ahmed, the recipient of the 2019 Nobel Peace Prize) and the Tigrayan People's Liberation Front, in which more than half a million lost their lives between 2020 and 2022 (Schaap, 2023). Though the Russian invasion received almost blanket coverage in the global media, there was scarcely any coverage of the Tigrayan conflict. The WHO director-general, Tedros Adhanom Ghebreyesus, labelled it as the 'worst humanitarian crisis in the world' and contrasted the lack of international attention with Ukraine invasion as a signal of inherent racism. 'Maybe the reason is the colour of the skin of the people',

Ghebreyesus, who is from Tigray, told journalists in 2022, having previously questioned whether 'black and white lives' in emergencies worldwide are given equal attention (quoted in Reuters, 2022). This demonstrates how 'the global racial imaginary' (Barder, 2021) operates in a world saturated by visual geopolitics. The Ugandan scholar Mamdani asks a pertinent question: 'Why do we call Darfur a "genocide" and the Iraq violence not – when more people have died in Iraq' (Mamdani, 2010: 6).

As elsewhere, in Africa, too, the United States remains the most powerful geopolitical player, despite the recent increase in Chinese investment and engagement. As decolonization took roots in Africa after the independence of Ghana in 1957 (then called Gold Coast), the United States was engaged in the continent to check the perceived spread of communism, a hallmark of the Cold War. While the Soviet Union was directly involved in arming anti-colonial liberation movements – most notably in Angola, the US-led Western alliance was supporting the apartheid regime in South Africa, as well as some of the most ruthless dictatorships, including the three-decades-long misrule of Mobutu Sese Seko in the Congo (which was later renamed as Zaire and now called the Democratic Republic of the Congo). Since the disintegration of the Soviet Union in 1991, Russian involvement dwindled as the West consolidated its presence.

Quoting from the International Military Training Activities Database-USA (IMTAD-USA), researchers found that between 1999 and 2016, across 34 different programmes, the United States trained nearly 2.4 million personnel from virtually every country in the world, spending more than $14.8 billion worldwide on its training efforts, and sold training worth another $4.9 billion, working through private military companies (McLauchlin et al., 2022). It could be argued that these training relationships reinforce a US-centric military system (Martinez Machain, 2021) and contribute to promoting US geopolitical interests. Since 2008, US-trained officers have succeeded in at least eight coups across five West African countries, including Burkina Faso (three times), Guinea, Mali (three times), Mauritania and Gambia.

Decades after the 1992 US military intervention in Somalia, called 'Restore Hope' and timed to coincide with the evening news bulletins in the United States, and the formal withdrawal from the country after the 'Black Hawk Down' episode of 1993, US military presence in the country remains pronounced through US Africa Command (AFRICOM). This has been in operation since 2007, fighting Islamic terrorism, including the targeted killings of the leaders of terrorist groups al-Shabab, Al Qaeda in East Africa and the Islamic State. Over the past 15 years, the United States has conducted more than 260 airstrikes and ground raids in Somalia (see Air War website). Under the auspices of the secretive '127e authority', which allows US Special Operations forces to train, arm and direct local 'surrogates' to carry out missions, the United States has employed dozens of proxy forces in the global South (Turse and Speri, 2022). Though other powers such as Russia and China are also actively engaged in the security of the continent, as are Türkiye and some Gulf states, they pale into insignificance when compared to the Western presence, and especially that of the United States.

Despite its unrelenting exhortation of protecting and promoting human rights, the United States was remarkably absent during the 1994 Rwandan genocide. President Bill Clinton told CNBC in 2013: 'If we'd gone in sooner, I believe we could have saved at least a third of the lives that were lost' (CNBC, 2013). Instead, Europeans and Americans extracted their own citizens, and the UN peacekeepers quietly withdrew, leaving millions to a sure death (Epstein, 2017). France was also accused of not doing enough to halt the genocide. A 600-page report, *A Foreseeable Genocide: The Role of the French Government in Connection with the Genocide Against the Tutsi in Rwanda*, by the US law firm Levy Firestone Muse, commissioned by the Rwandan government and released in 2021, labels France a 'collaborator' of the extremist Hutu regime that orchestrated what the report called 'as one of the darkest and most horrific chapters of the 20th century' (Muse Report, 2021: 1). The France-led 'Operation Turquoise', a military-humanitarian intervention launched under a UN mandate between June and August 1994, was in reality 'aimed at supporting the genocidal Hutu government', the report noted, concluding, 'the genocide was foreseeable. From its knowledge of massacres of civilians conducted by the government and its allies, to the daily dehumanization of the Tutsi, to the cables and other data arriving from Rwanda, the French government could see that a genocide was coming' (ibid.: 2).

The French presence across the Francophone Africa has been considerable – in its economic, political and security manifestations. In the Central African Republic it supported the megalomaniac Jean-Bédel Bokassa and was involved in the assassination of Burkina Faso's left-leaning nationalist leader Thomas Sankara in 1987. Between 1950 and 2020, according to French government sources, France undertook more than 50 military interventions into Africa to prop up dictatorships (www.assemblee-nationale.fr/14/rap-info/i2777.asp). Since the 1960s, notes one commentator, France 'played a disproportionate role in propping up the African theatre of the Cold War conflict. With or without US help, France had been playing policeman at the four corners of the continent, taking the protection of its economic interests as a reward for its violent involvement' (Prunier, 2009: xxxiv).

Even decades after independence, the French-run oil industry continues to be a dominant player in the region and, until recently, the economies in West and Central Africa were tied to the CFA franc, the currency of more than a dozen African nations, in a form of monetary colonialism (Pigeaud and Sylla Samba, 2021). The French Foreign Legion has been involved in providing 'security' to various African nations: its main military operations in recent years include Rwanda (1990–1993), Central African Republic (1996 and 2013–2016), Ivory Coast (2002–2015) and Mali (2013–2023), as part of *Operation Barkhane*, the longest war in France's recent history and largest deployment of troops in the region to fight Islamist threat in the Sahel region. After its withdrawal from Afghanistan, Mali was the largest foreign deployment of the *Bundeswehr*, Germany's armed forces, where they were also training Malian soldiers on behalf of the EU. The Western powers are finding a fierce competition of power with growing Chinese, Russian and Turkish involvement in France's 'backyard', forcing France to close its military bases in Mali.

The French have utilized their experience in Southeast Asia in counterinsurgency operations when in 1951 France created a special unit in Indochina, the Groupement de Commandos Mixtes Aéroportés (Mixed Airborne Commando Group), to infiltrate the population, gather intelligence and establish guerrilla bands to subvert the rural base of the Vietminh (Pottier, 2005). In Algeria, where the anti-colonial conflict was very intense, the French deployed the Foreign Legion to suppress the nationalist movement (Michels, 2002). Unlike the French, the British Army generally conducted counterinsurgencies in a less coercive and more political fashion, working on winning the 'hearts and minds' of populations (Dixon, 2009; Porch, 2013).

The Russian invasion of Ukraine – covering the 'white man's war'?

The cases in Africa discussed above contrast starkly with the interest shown by the US-led Western media in the Russian invasion of Ukraine and the suffering of the Ukrainian people. Unlike other wars, the Russian invasion is presented unambiguously as an unprovoked act of aggression rather than a more generic 'conflict'. The Russian invasion of Ukraine, therefore, offers interesting insights into the double standards in the mainstream Western media in covering international conflict (Zollmann, 2019). This is a war of the West against a formidable adversary with strong reverberations of the ideological and geopolitical rivalry of the Cold War. When Russia launched its invasion of Ukraine (described in official Kremlin speak as a 'special military operation') on 24 February 2022, the United States and other leading European nations labelled it as 'Putin's war', thus drawing a distinction between the actions of the Kremlin and ordinary Russians. The conflict was framed as one between democracy and authoritarianism, between European integration and Russian imperialism (Diesen, 2022).

In the Kremlin-controlled Russian media, the overwhelming framing is that the war is an existential one to protect Russian geopolitical and even civilizational interests and is a 'pre-emptive' action in defence against NATO's expansion to the borders of Russia. Echoes of the initial reasons for the military action – protecting the Russian-speaking population of Ukraine's Donbas region and the 'de-Nazification' of Ukraine – shaped the official narrative emanating from Moscow also through its formidable cyberpresence. Russian information warfare has long depicted Ukraine as a country where Nazi putschists came to power during the 2013–2014 Euromaidan Revolution and have since ruled the country on behalf of Washington, and Ukraine's re-absorption into the 'Russian World' is considered 'unfinished business' (Rumer and Weiss, 2021; Kuzio, 2022). Anti-Ukrainian diatribe and symbols, including 'Z', the Kremlin's symbol of war, clutter the Runet, as Soviet-era slogans such as *borba za mir* ('battle for peace' in English) resonate in Russian cyberspace (Garner, 2023). Research tracking the anti-Ukraine discourse and disinformation visible in online and off-line Russian media found that out of 13,000 examples of Kremlin disinformation in the 'EuvsDisinfo' database, 5,000 target Ukraine (see https://euvsdisinfo.eu/).

Under Putin's increasingly authoritarian tendencies, Russian media freedoms have been progressively curtailed, and many journalists who had been critical of the regime have been forced to leave their media organizations, after the annexation of Crimea in 2014 (Soldatov and Borogan, 2015; Paul and Matthews, 2016). The news network NTV was put under state control. Kremlin propagandists paid bloggers and hired commenters, using anonymous Telegram channels and YouTube videos, to promote their narratives. The law on foreign agents was extended in 2019 to include media organizations, as well as individual journalists: any media content, also on social media, should be labelled to say it was produced by a 'foreign agent', making it almost impossible for Western or Western-oriented journalists and media organizations to freely operate in Russia. As the Russian forces invaded Ukraine, a law against discrediting the Russian army in effect made independent journalism illegal in Russia, as only official information about the special military operation could be used, forcing the closure of well-established independent media outlets such as *Novaya Gazeta* and *Echo Moscow* (Gessen, 2022). Journalists were forced to either comply with military censorship – which included banning the use of the terms like 'war' or 'invasion' – or leave Russia and work in exile in the West, using platforms such as Telegram and YouTube to continue critical reporting. Vassily Nebenzia, Russia's permanent representative to the UN, said in November 2022: 'It's no secret that the West has launched a real information war against us, which affects not only the residents of Russia and Ukraine but also people around the world'.

The Ukraine invasion also starkly demonstrated Western double standards in representing the victims of war and conflict. Coverage in the mainstream Western media was saturated with reports about the white-skinned, blue-eyed refugees who were being allowed immediately into the EU, with Poland and Germany each receiving more than one million Ukrainians in 2022. Germany had a policy of granting Ukrainian refugees a stay permit, without needing to go through the elaborate and highly bureaucratic asylum request processing; they were paid higher allowances and given an immediate work permit. In contrast, refugees who were not white received very different treatment. At the time of the Russian invasion of Ukraine, the largest number of foreign students studying in that country was from India, and they had extreme difficulties trying to leave Ukraine, until the Indian Air Force evacuated them; African students had even worse experiences. The Indian news networks were covering the exodus of the students, and at least two national networks – India Today TV and CNN/IBN – had their crew in Ukraine during this period. Interestingly, those Indian reporters were escorted by their Russian minders to the eastern part of Ukraine to cover the atrocities being committed by Ukrainian forces – both official and quasi-official military and paramilitary units – on Russian-speaking populations. Scarcely, if ever, did the Western mainstream news organizations cover this part of the conflict – though it is inconceivable that the Russian media managers would not have liked them to go to the other frontline to cover not only the atrocities but also the exodus of Russian-speaking populations in eastern Ukraine to Russia.

Western support for media

Soon after the Russian invasion, the US Defense Department created a 'Ukraine Defense Contact Group', a coalition of 40 countries 'to address Ukraine's needs and requests' and, what a *New York Times* report called a 'little-known group', the International Donor Coordination Center, along with officers from more than two dozen countries were 'playing a pivotal role in supporting Ukraine's military' (Schmitt, 2022). In an opinion piece for the US military blog 19fortyfive.com, John Bolton, former advisor to Donald Trump, wrote a provocative heading 'Putin must go: Now is the time for regime change in Russia'. The blog, published on 4 October 2022, was explicit in its recommendation for regime change, almost a staple of the State Department in the post-Cold War world. Weeks after the invasion, a report by the London-based Henry Jackson Society recommended that 'a campaign must be established to increase information being shared with the Russian public through Russian independent media outlets, through Western radio stations, and through operations conducted by Anonymous on the impact of Western sanctions on the Russian economy and finances and the high number of casualties of Russian soldiers' (Chkhaidze et al., 2022: 23).

Ukraine's propaganda blitz

Unlike the Kremlin, Ukraine has the formidable support, advice and resources of Western, or more specifically, Anglo-American political public relations and media managers. Ukraine's Ministry of Foreign Affairs has a strong strategic communications unit, with advice 'from the UK and the US' (Taylor, 2022). An indicative example of this media-savvy approach was in evidence in October 2022, when the Ukrainian blast on the Crimean Bridge was projected as a major propaganda victory. Ukraine's domestic intelligence agency the 'Security Service of Ukraine' (Ukrainian acronym SBU) posted on Twitter, rephrasing part of a poem by Ukraine's national poet: 'Dawn, the bridge is burning beautifully; A nightingale in Crimea meets the S.B.U', while in his nightly address, President Volodymyr Zelensky remarked that it 'was a good and mostly sunny' day in Ukrainian territory, adding, 'unfortunately, it was cloudy in Crimea' (cited in Schwirtz and Kramer, 2022). During the same month, on October 13, the Parliamentary Assembly of the Council of Europe, where Zelensky also spoke during a session, branded Russia as a 'terrorist regime'. Zelensky closed three pro-Russian television channels expressing the views of the Opposition Platform, headed by pro-Russian oligarch Viktor Medvedchuk, whose unabashedly pro-Russian message was widely viewed by many as propaganda.

Before he was elected as president of Ukraine in 2019, Zelensky was a comedian and a political novice but nevertheless won 73 per cent of the vote, defeating the incumbent president Petro Poroshenko, a veteran politician and businessman. Zelensky's popularity was based on political comedy sketches and his star role in the TV sitcom *Sluga Narodu* (*Servant of the People*), in which he played a schoolteacher who became president after a secret video recording of his tirade against corrupt Ukrainian politicians went viral. Produced by Kvartal 95, a company co-founded by Zelensky, which also produced a variety show by the same name (Jacobsen, 2016), the sitcom depicts the fictional president as a principled leader fighting corrupt oligarchs, living a modest life and helping ordinary citizens (Roman et al., 2022). Zelensky announced his candidacy just three months before the elections, naming his new political party as *Servant of the People* party and appearing in the final episodes of the sitcom, which was broadcast days before the first round of elections. During the actual presidential campaign, Zelensky encashed his popular image as a complete outsider (Karatnycky, 2019).

The Ukrainian president's persona is a great example of how media and public relations experts can construct the image of a leader, one who demonstrates 'tremendous courage' by remaining in Kyiv during the initial attack in February 2022, projecting an air of defiance to promote cohesion at home and support internationally. Two days into the invasion, the AP reported that Zelensky had rejected a US offer to evacuate him from Kyiv, saying, 'I need ammunition, not a ride'. A senior US official told the *New Yorker*: 'To the best of my knowledge, that never happened. But hats off to Zelensky and the people around him. It was a great line' (quoted in Yaffa, 2022). Days after the invasion, Zelensky filmed video messages of himself speaking in front of monuments or other recognizable buildings, but his speech to the European Parliament was given via video feed from a nondescript room decorated only with the Ukrainian flag. The invasion and its mediatization made Zelensky the global icon No. 1 on the *Jerusalem Post*'s Top 50 Most Influential Jews of 2022 (Harkov, 2022), while he was also named by *Time* magazine as '2022 person of the year', a decision 'the most clear-cut in memory', wrote the magazine's editor-in-chief Edward Felsenthal, adding that the Ukrainian president's 'information offensive shifted the geopolitical weather system, setting off a wave of action that swept the globe' (*Time*, 2022).

Part of this information campaign is the fact that the Ukrainian government provides extensive and professionally produced publicity material in English – in terms of memes, short videos and other information (see https://war.ukraine.ua/for-media/). Its innovative propaganda repertoire includes online jokes, effective for the digital age. Ukraine's Defence Ministry shared a doctored photograph of a 'Shiba Inu' dog wearing a military uniform, gushing over the site of a missile launch. 'Today we want to give a shout-out to a unique entity', the tweet read, before pointing to the North Atlantic Fellas Organization (NAFO). The NAFO group's propaganda, littered with references to American popular culture, is widely shared on Telegram, Twitter and other social media platforms 'resonating' with 'a global English-speaking audience', reported the *Washington Post*. 'Ukrainian Memes Forces' – a supposedly independent group – has been deployed to 'create a further reservoir of caustic content that is disseminated widely'. The largely English-language memes have 'kept Western attention on Ukraine's war – attention that is vital given the importance of Western arms to Ukrainian forces' (Matloff, 2022). Such humorous propaganda contrasts with Russian digital messaging which focuses on threats such as a nuclear war (Taylor, 2022).

In addition to media and propaganda support, the Biden Administration has provided valuable intelligence and increasingly powerful weaponry, which has been widely covered in the Western media. However, less widely reported has been the fact that many of these weapons have failed to reach the frontline. In November 2022, the *Washington Post* stated that US monitors have inspected just 10 per cent of high-risk weapons sent to Ukraine, even as the Biden administration launched new measures to stop arms smuggling (Ryan, 2022).

Another popular media subject has been the thousands of volunteers that have travelled from Western countries, including the United States and Britain, to join the International Legion, which has been recognized by the Ukrainian government. Ukraine's then defence minister Oleksii Reznikov said there were ideological and political benefits to having foreign soldiers fighting alongside Ukrainians to defend 'European values' (Gall, 2023). The media coverage of such military groups was bordering on the euphoric, with excited journalists and commentators fighting a narrative war for the Ukrainian underdog against the Russian imperial invasion. A notable example was a report published in the *Washington Post* in December 2022, which eulogized 'how deepening cooperation with NATO powers, especially the US, enabled Ukrainian forces – backed with weapons, intelligence and advice – to seize the initiative on the battlefield, expose Putin's annexation claims as a fantasy, and build faith at home and abroad that Russia could be defeated' (Khurshudyan et al., 2022).

Managing expectations and shaping perceptions were integral to developing the anti-Russian narrative. The US-generated 'Resistance Operating Concept', described by CNN as 'an innovative and unconventional approach to warfare and total defense', called for a major public relations campaign to control the narrative of the conflict, preventing the dissemination of the other side's message and keeping the population united. Video footage, edited to catchy tunes, showing destroyed Russian hardware forms part of the strategy, along with clips of Ukrainian troops rescuing stray animals, and the daily addresses by Zelensky (Liebermann, 2022).

Hollywood, too, got into the act: Sean Penn, who made a documentary about the war, handed his Oscar to Zelensky as a symbol of faith in Ukraine's victory. From Ben Stiller to Jessica Chastain, celebrities embraced Ukraine's president and offered support to the country's war effort. In 2022, Zelensky's address at Cannes film festival received a standing ovation. One journalist extolled Zelensky's ability to 'command the 24-hour news cycle using social media and video addresses', which generated 'major respect and props in Hollywood, rather than fleeting fame', while his former press secretary Iuliia Mendel credited this to the fact that 'as a former actor, Zelenskiy appreciates the power of actors, especially from Hollywood' (cited in Koshiw, 2023). Mendel, who helped organize channels of communication with celebrities, also wrote a glowing account of the President, which received extensive and very positive coverage in Western media (Mendel, 2022). Academics now speak of the 'Zelensky effect', that is, how a non-political ordinary individual came to symbolize the aspiration and spirits of a nation (Onuch and Hale, 2023). Reports of large-scale corruption in the Zelensky regime are often overlooked in the Western media: when Biden was vice president in 2015, he told the Ukrainian parliament to stamp out 'the pervasive poison of cronyism, corruption, and kleptocracy', but as president his tone has changed (Lutsevych, 2023). The *New York Times* framed the story about the leaked official documents exposing corruption in food procurement contract signed by the Ministry of Defence as saying that Zelensky was 'committed to fighting corruption' (cited in Crowley and Wong, 2023). The alleged smuggling of Western arms destined for battlefield and circulating them in other conflict zones are reported, if at all, as a matter of fact, and without criticism or concern (Ryan, 2022), as is the use of cluster bombs, banned in many countries, against the Russian forces (Hudson and Khurshudyan, 2023).

Privatization of conflict management

An important component of contemporary conflicts is the growing privatization of mercenary-led wars, especially in the global South (Brayton, 2002; Singer, 2008). As Singer notes, in the post-Cold War era, the 'cross of the corporate form with military functionality has become a reality', and a global industry – 'both in its scope and activity' – has emerged. 'It is outsourcing and privatization of a twenty-first century variety, and it changes many of the old rules of international politics and warfare' (Singer, 2008: 9).

The UN Working Group on the Use of Mercenaries claimed in 2011 that private military and security contracting had become a global phenomenon and estimated that the market turned about $100 billion in yearly profits. One important aspect of this phenomenon is the outsourcing of logistics to private companies that hire labour from poorer countries at bases located in warzones in the global South. The 'US military empire is profoundly dependent upon a global army of labor', notes a new study, adding that the increasing 'reliance on private companies and foreign labor to provide logistics support for operations around the world is as significant as the various technological innovations toward network-centric warfare over the past two decades' (Moore, 2019: 1 and 4). Even humanitarianism and UN peacekeeping operations have been 'privatized and securitized' through the 'profit-driven Private Military Security Companies', which, because of their inherent commercial interest in selling security services and equipment and their militaristic approach to security problems, are likely to 'undermine peacebuilding effectiveness' (de Groot and Regilme, 2022).

The public–private nexus is best illustrated by the security, reconstruction and logistics company Halliburton, which operated in Iraq and Afghanistan and whose CEO was Dick Cheney until he became the vice president in the George W. Bush administration in 2001. Cheney had stock holdings in the company worth $46 million, and until 2002 he received $162,000 in deferred compensation from the company, reported a former *Los Angeles Times* journalist in Iraq (Miller, 2006: 77–79). Halliburton's Pentagon contracts grew more than tenfold from 2002 to 2006 on the strength of its contracts to rebuild Iraq's oil infrastructure and provide logistical support for US troops in that country and in Afghanistan. By 2008, the company had received over $30 billion for work under the Pentagon's Logistics Civil Augmentation Programme contract, an open-ended arrangement that involved coordinating a wide array of support functions for troops in the field, from setting up military bases, to maintaining equipment, to providing food and laundry services (US Congressional Research Service, 2021).

The private security company Blackwater, founded by Erik Prince and operating in Iraq post-2003 invasion, is another prominent example of privatization of warfare. The 2007 Nisour Square massacre in Baghdad forced Blackwater to change its name to XE Services and then as Academii, and the firm eventually merged with Triple Canopy, another private contracting firm. Erik Prince was operating in Afghanistan (Copp, 2018) and subsequently involved in recruiting mercenaries on behalf of the UAE for deployment to the civil war in Libya. Another private firm, DynCorp International, owned by the US billionaire Stephen Feinberg, was awarded, in 2004, a $2.5 billion contract from the State Department's Bureau of International Narcotics and Law Enforcement Affairs to develop and train a new Iraqi police force and, by 2009, over half of DynCorp's revenues were coming from the Iraq and Afghan wars. In Afghanistan, DynCorp was seen as playing a role in guarding mines, a major concern, given that some of the country's richest deposits were in areas controlled by the Taliban' (Lander and Risen, 2017), and the firm was a primary contractor on a $20 billion State Department programme to train and develop the Afghan police force between 2002 and 2017 (Hartung, 2021).

A sympathetic profile in the *New York Times* described the mercenary Andrew Milburn, founder of the Mozart Group, as an 'unconventional former Marine colonel', for whom 'Ukraine represents the morally just war'. Set up within weeks of the Russian invasion and supported by 'hedge fund managers from New York' with 'Ukrainian roots' and humanitarian organizations, the Mozart group was 'one of the biggest private military companies in Ukraine' (Gettleman, 2022). A *New York Times* report valourized the volunteers – the International Legion – 'who rushed to Ukraine by the thousands, to bring military experience, money or supplies to the battleground of a righteous war', noting that some have tried to 'profit off the war' while others fought alongside 'Da Vinci's Wolves', a neo-fascist group; a few with military experience were covering the invasion as regular commentators on major networks such as MSNBC (Scheck and Gibbons-Neff, 2023).

Wagner and the Russian wars

Unlike their Western counterparts, the Russian private security groups, notably Wagner, receive a very different kind of treatment in the Western media: their ruthlessness and atrocities are constantly emphasized, in contrast to the nobler motives of Western private military companies (Munshi and Seddon, 2021; Burke and Akinwotu, 2022; Ling, 2023). A 2021 investigation by CNN and The Sentry ('an independent investigative group co-founded by George Clooney and John Prendergast that follows the money connected to mass atrocities') reported serious human rights abuses and atrocities by Wagner group in the Central African Republic, quoting confidential UN documents (Lister et al., 2021).

Led by Yevgeny Prigozhin, a Putin ally, Wagner gained strategic footholds in at least eight African countries, among 13 nations where the mercenary group has been operating. 'The Wagner group is moving aggressively to establish a "confederation" of anti-Western states in Africa as the Russian mercenaries foment instability while using their paramilitary and disinformation capabilities to bolster Moscow's allies', according to leaked secret US intelligence documents, the *Washington Post* reported (Miller and Dixon, 2023). Operating in the Central African Republic, Libya, Burkina Faso, Mali, Sudan, Chad and Eritrea, the group's tasks included extracting natural resources, conducting offensive combat operations, providing personal or regime security and training to counter US and French influence in parts of sub-Saharan Africa (Ling, 2023). Russia's return to Africa has revived the competition for military and political influence that recalls the colonial scramble for African resources (Munshi and Seddon, 2021; Ramani, 2023). In 2018, the United States charged Prigozhin for his suspected role in funding the Internet Research Agency, a St Petersburg-based 'troll farm' that sought to create digital disruption in the West. In January 2023, the US State Department designated Wagner as a 'transnational criminal organization', while the CIA director William Burns described the group as 'a particularly creepy Russian organization' (quoted in Miller and Dixon, 2023).

While the Western media demonized the Wagner Group, Russian media such as RT gave prominent coverage to the 'valour' and 'vanquishing' powers of the group. From a communication perspective, Wagner seemed to have a highly developed strategy. The group helped finance the 2021 Russian feature film *Tourist* about mercenaries in Africa. Prigozhin featured regularly on the group's Telegram channel, where he posted short videos, dressed in military gear, sometimes on the navigator's seat of a Sukhoi Su-24, presenting himself as a patriot of the 'fatherland' (Meek, 2023). Prigozhin's death in a plane crash in Russia in August 2023, following an attempted 'coup' in June of that year, put paid to its future as a powerful mercenary army, though its presence in conflict situations in resource-rich countries in Africa forms part of Russian geopolitical engagement with the continent (Bergengruen, 2023).

However, the 'image wars', to a large extent, have been shaped by Western-originated narratives and representations by dominant Western news and communication networks which the United States, especially, has been very successful in deploying in its image diplomacy. Despite overwhelming evidence to the contrary, as discussed above, Washington is able to retain the moral high ground in conflicts which benefit its geopolitical and economic priorities. A striking case in point is the 'post-9/11 wars'; the ostensible and official reasons for such conflicts was to bring democracy and freedom among the 'outposts of tyranny'. If one were to contrast the scale and continuing duration of the suffering in these Muslim-majority nations with the violence and displacement emanating from the Russian invasion of Ukraine, the double standards of the US-led mass media are clearly revealed.

5
WEAPONIZING GLOBAL COMMUNICATION

Cyberwars, surveillance and spying

Control of the message and the medium has always been key to geopolitical power but the latest communication technologies have intensified this exponentially. These technologies have the ability to weaponize information for geopolitical purposes and exert control over what is perceived to be 'reality' (Woolley, 2020: 9). The weaponization of information has been clearly demonstrated in the Ukrainian conflict, particularly the co-option of Silicon Valley by Western governments into supporting Ukraine's war against Russia. From cyberwarfare to spying and surveillance, communication technologies are being used both by the 'democratic' West and the authoritarian states but the discourse focuses on threats to the global information system presented by China and Russia as challenging the liberal 'rule-based' information order. The 'infodemic' of dis-and misinformation reached a peak during the global pandemic of Covid-19, with significant geopolitical implications, which will only be intensified by the growing role of artificial intelligence (AI) in weaponizing information and the framing of the debate as a contest between a 'democratic' vs. 'authoritarian' global communication order.

Digital warfare: the weaponization of information in the Ukraine war

The war in the Ukraine has become a crucible for innovation in communications and information warfare, driving the development and adoption of new concepts and technologies such as AI (Parker, 2022) and the deployment of social media in spreading mis- and disinformation. When Ukrainian President Volodymyr Zelensky said, 'The weapon of information is very important', he added, 'it's also important to point this weapon not at one's own head, but in the direction of the enemy' (quoted in Shuster, 2023).

New information and communication technologies are accelerating warfare by enabling forces to analyse the field of battle using drones, sensors and targeting aids, which compresses the decision-making process, making survival on the battlefield even more challenging. For example, drones are not only vital to collect and transmit data as the military's 'eyes and ears' but are also weapons. In July 2022, Zelensky launched an 'Army of Drones' appeal to countries worldwide for funds to buy a fleet of military-grade lethal autonomous weapons – unmanned aerial vehicles (UAVs) – according to Mykhailo Fedorov, Ukraine's Minister of Digital Transformation. The near-constant wartime footage from such drones was shared on messaging apps and social media platforms and was circulated on Telegram by official military and civilian channels on both sides of the conflict.

Even before the Russian invasion, Ukraine had set in place, with US support, a mechanism for information warfare and digital propaganda, in order to counter the Russian information assault and generate support across the West. Since 2017, the United States had invested $40 million in helping Ukraine buttress its information technology sector and, according to the then US Deputy Secretary of State Wendy Sherman, the investments helped Ukrainians 'keep their internet on and information flowing, even in the midst of a brutal Russian invasion' (quoted in Kagubare, 2022b). In May 2022, the then NSA Director and US Cyber Command chief, General Paul Nakasone, revealed that US Cyber Command had undertaken offensive Information Operations in support of Ukraine, 'a series of operations across the full spectrum: offensive, defensive, [and] information operations' (Kagubare, 2022a).

The Ukraine conflict is also an effective case study of how the epistemic community, discussed in Chapter 2, is drawn into the information/propaganda war. A National Endowment for Democracy report attributed Ukraine's propaganda victory in the West to what it called 'deep preparation' and 'open networks of cooperation', noting that 'civil society organizations have leveraged common values and diverse skill sets to form cooperative networks that have the sophistication and speed necessary to combat the scale of the Kremlin's propaganda machine' (Fivenson, et al, 2023:1). 'In the run-up to the Ukraine war, all across Central and Eastern Europe', wrote the *Washington Post* in an editorial, 'civil society groups were sharpening techniques for spotting and countering Russian disinformation'. It added that more than 20 organizations, along with the National Democratic Institute in Washington, had created a 'disinformation debunking hub in 2019' that played a key role in 'the battle against the onslaught of lies' (Washington Post, 2023).

These collaborative networks of governmental, nongovernmental and private sector organizations, as well as citizen-driven initiatives, were used to identify and analyse disinformation narratives to 'illuminate their underlying messages and target audiences, and design timely, effective responses' (Fivenson et al., 2023: 1–2, 9). NGOs became the first and most frequent contributors to the European External Action Service's 'EUvsDisinfo' database, helping the EU to collect examples of Russian disinformation (ibid.: 21).

Silicon Valley support

The corporate communications community also collaborate with government in weaponizing information. Just as the Ford Motor Company converted automobile production lines to manufacture tanks in World War II, even before the Russian invasion, Microsoft launched new teams to work 'around the clock' to defend Ukrainian organizations and government agencies from 'an onslaught of cyberwarfare'. The company also took technical measures to remove internet launching points used by the Russians for their attacks. Brad Smith, Microsoft's president, noted in a blog post that his company was not 'neutral' in the conflict, being in 'constant and close coordination' with the Ukrainian government, as well as US officials, the NATO and the EU (Sanger et al., 2022). Their executives joined secure calls to hear briefings organized by the National Security Agency (NSA) and US Cyber Command, along with British authorities. Much of 'the actionable intelligence is being found by companies like Microsoft and Google, who can see what is flowing across their vast networks' (Sanger et al., 2022).

Satellite companies like Planet, Capella Space and Maxar supplied strategically significant imagery to the Ukrainian military, which 'has done everything from inform ground operations to mobilize global opinion, thanks to the publicity garnered on Twitter and prominent news outlets' (Fox and Probasco, 2022). Maxar's imagery was provided free to international news agencies as part of its 'data philanthropy' effort. Support was also provided by Silicon Valley entrepreneurs such as Andrey Liscovich, who established the Ukraine Defense Fund in the United States to supply equipment to Ukrainian defense forces and convinced Germany to provide drones and also brokered deals to make commercial satellite imagery available to the Ukrainian army, Chinese batteries for Western-donated armoured personnel vehicles and German-made radio-frequency sensors that can track the electronic signatures of Russian drones (Boot, 2023). Elon Musk's Starlink became an essential tool of the Ukrainian army, and in October 2020, Musk tweeted a 'peace plan' for Ukraine to end the conflict (Metz et al., 2022).

Other US-based start-up companies were key players, including Capella Space (which produces small satellites that track troop movements at night or under cloud cover), Fortem Technologies (unmanned aircraft that can disable drones) and HawkEye 360 (satellites that use radio waves emitted by communications equipment and other electronic devices to detect troop concentrations). As the *New York Times* reported, 'When it comes to drones, satellites, artificial intelligence and other fields, start-up companies frequently offer the Pentagon cheaper, faster and more flexible options than the weapons systems produced by the handful of giant contractors the Pentagon normally relies on' (Lipton, 2023). One important component of this strategy was the Ukrainian military investigations company called Molfar, partly funded by the Civilian Research and Development Foundation, an NGO whose backers include the US State and Defense Departments.

The Ukraine conflict also witnessed the expansion of threat intelligence companies such as Recorded Future and Janes, event detection platform Dataminr and commercial satellite imagery providers Orbital Insight and Planet Labs. These and other such organizations were crucial in the creation of new investigatory groups such as the Ukraine Digital Verification Lab, OSINT for Ukraine and initiatives such as Ukrainian Weapons Tracker (Hewson, 2023).

PrimerAI helped analyse news and social media, as well as decode unencrypted Russian military leaders' voice communications, while Clearview AI provided facial recognition services to aid Ukrainian officials in countering disinformation and to help identify victims and war criminals. These companies used their formidable communication power to publicize their work, aided by the Western media with online posts about their involvement and activities, as well as reports about Russian cyber-activities. Sections of the US intelligence were directly involved: 'The Ukrainians would outline the types of high-value targets they were looking for in an area, and the US would use its vast geospatial intelligence apparatus to respond with precise locations' (Khurshudyan et al., 2022).

The Ukraine war has also reopened debates about the role of machine-generated propaganda. During the first two weeks of the Russian invasion, 'bot armies' put out 5.2 million tweets, between 60 and 80 per cent of which were shared by fake accounts, and 90 per cent of those posts were pro-Ukraine, promoting hashtags such as #IStandWithUkraine, #IStandWithZelenskyy and #ISupportUkraine, according to researchers at the University of Adelaide. That more than 3.5 million tweets, or 67 per cent, were in English, with barely two per cent in Russian and Ukrainian, indicated their origin and supposed audience. On 5 March, after the #IStandWithPutin hashtag had trended on Twitter, the company banned over 100 accounts using the hashtag for violating its 'platform manipulation and spam policy' and participating in 'coordinated inauthentic behaviour'.

The National Security Correspondent of *Yahoo News*, in an exclusive report in March 2022, spoke of how a secret CIA training programme in Ukraine helped the country prepare for Russian invasion. CIA's secret US-based training initiative for Ukrainian special operations forces and other intelligence personnel, which began in 2015, included topics such as 'how to use covert communications tools'. The report quoted a senior intelligence official who said that the purpose of the training was to assist 'in the collection of intelligence' (Dorfman, 2022).

The *New York Times* was explicit about US intelligence support: 'Throughout the war, the US has provided Ukraine with information on command posts, ammunition depots and other key nodes in the Russian military lines. Such real-time intelligence has allowed the Ukrainians to target Russian forces, kill senior generals and force ammunition supplies to be moved farther from the Russian front lines' (Cooper and Schmitt, 2023). The German foreign intelligence service *Bundesnachrichtendienst* (BND) forwarded satellite imagery, radio and phone intercept data to Kiev, helping the Ukrainian war effort, even though Berlin officially maintained it was not party to the conflict, as revealed by *Zeit* magazine in September 2022.

US-based think tanks and information activists have also contributed to this digital warfare. The Atlantic Council (of which Meta is a funder, as is the US State

Department), established its Digital Forensic Research Lab to 'operationalize the study of disinformation by exposing falsehoods and fake news', while Graphika, which claims to be 'the best in the world at analysing how online social networks form, evolve, and are manipulated', has also been instrumental in exposing Russian disinformation and has even, on very rare occasions, investigated Western-led digital assaults, which receive minimum coverage in the mainstream media in the West.

One such example was the little-reported Graphika/Stanford University report *Unheard Voice: Evaluating Five Years of Pro-Western Covert Influence Operations*, which examined nearly 300,000 tweets from 146 Twitter accounts and found an interconnected web of accounts on Twitter, Facebook, Instagram and five other social media platforms that used deceptive tactics to promote pro-Western narratives in the Middle East and Central Asia. Calling these campaigns 'the most extensive case of covert pro-Western Information Operation on social media', the researchers noted that over a period of almost five years, the platforms consistently advanced narratives promoting the interests of the United States and its allies, while opposing countries including Russia, China and Iran (Graphika and Stanford Internet Observatory, 2022: 3).

They highlighted the Pentagon's clandestine information warfare after Twitter and Facebook identified and took offline 150 personas and media sites created under some fake US military accounts in violation of the platforms' rules. Another was linked to a Twitter handle of Centcom, which has purview over military operations across 21 countries in the Middle East, North Africa and Central and South Asia. The accounts heavily criticized Russia for the deaths of innocent civilians and other atrocities its soldiers committed in pursuit of the Kremlin's 'imperial ambitions' following its invasion of Ukraine (ibid.).

Reviving their Cold War expertise, Radio Free Europe/Radio Liberty (RFE/RL) used their Russian-language news site and a 24-hour Russian-language television network, *Current Time*, as well as websites aimed at regional audiences in a wide range of languages to broadcast deeper into Russia. The accounts included a constructed Persian-language media site that shared content reposted from the Voice of America Farsi and RFE. The number of video views on RFE/RL YouTube channels more than tripled in the first three weeks of the war, to 237.6 million (Barnes and Wong, 2022). Its Russian-language articles are published on copies of its websites called 'mirrors', which are set up by the US government-run Open Technology Fund, which constantly create new ones to stay a step ahead of Russian government censors. It also enables sites to be hosted by Tor, a digital communications network that helps shield ordinary internet users from surveillance. Such digital warfare involving numerous small units, in constant communication with one another, overwhelming targets in swarms, represents a form of warfare that has been called *Bitskrieg* (Arquilla, 2021).

On the very rare occasions that Western media reported stories portraying Ukraine in a negative light, they had to backtrack. Two examples illustrate this:

first, in August 2022, Amnesty International reported on Ukrainian troops basing their forces and weaponry in residential areas, including schools and hospitals; second, during the same month, a CBS documentary suggested that merely 30 per cent of the Western arms sent to Kiev reached the frontline, the rest disappearing or being sold on the black market. Such was the outrage in digital media – orchestrated by the North Atlantic Fellas Organization (NAFO), a Twitter-based anti-Russian 'counter-disinformation group that trolls the Russian government' and the broader network of pro-Russian accounts (an operation which has been positively profiled by the *Economist* and the *Washington Post*, among others) – that Amnesty had to tender apologies for any 'anger and distress' caused by its disclosures, while CBS pulled its documentary from the web (Cronau, 2022). NAFO is more widely known for 'using provocative and sometimes absurd memes' to highlight and expose the 'falsehood of many Russian narratives' (Fivenson et al., 2023: 9).

Russian disinformation receives a disproportionate amount of coverage and commentary in Western media, in contrast to the similar or even more sophisticated operations undertaken by the West itself. For example, Kremlin propagandists tried to discredit the United States and its European allies by suggesting that one of the threats that forced Russia to invade was the existence of a 'network of Western bio-weapons labs' in Ukraine (Myers, 2022). The EU's European External Action Service reported this as part of a Russian campaign of 'information manipulation and disinformation targeting international audiences' using the official social media accounts of Russia's diplomats (EEAS, 2022: 5).

Another example of this was the tweet of the Russian embassy in London in response to a report in July 2022 of an attack on a prison near Donetsk in eastern Ukraine that killed more than 50 Ukrainian prisoners of war, which said: 'Azov militants deserve execution, . . . not by firing squad but by hanging, because they're not real soldiers' (ibid.). The tweet reflected the Russian view of Ukrainians as Nazis, with a link to a YouTube video from the embassy and ending with the hashtag #StopNaziUkraine. The Russian Embassy account's tweets were being liked or retweeted about 279 times on average, and there was a jump on Facebook, where the average number of reactions, comments or shares on the Embassy account's post rose 108 per cent after the invasion.

About 26 channels affiliated with Russian embassies were operating on Telegram, more than 80 per cent of which were created after the invasion. Facebook and YouTube banned Russian state media globally, and yet many of the restrictions were not extended to Russian Embassy accounts (Oremus and Zakrzewski, 2022). The presence of neo-Nazis was not just highlighted by the Russian side, Ukrainian intelligence also posted videos on social media of anti-Kremlin Russian militia such as the 'Legion of Free Russia' and 'Russian Volunteer Corps' (whose leader Denis Kapustin has 'links with neo-Fascist groups throughout Europe', the *Washington Post* reported) (Koshiw, 2023).

Cyberwars

The disinformation campaign by Russia in the war in Ukraine should be seen in the context of ongoing cyberattacks on the West allegedly sponsored by the Kremlin. Trump's 2016 US election victory was attributed to St Petersburg's Internet Research Agency (aka 'The Russian IRA') which reportedly corralled online networks of bots and trolls that perpetuated pro-Trump propaganda in a bid to get the outsider elected at the Kremlin's request. This narrative quickly became widely accepted among US liberals and remains entrenched today. However, a study, published in *Nature* about the exposure of Twitter users to alleged activity on the social media platform by the IRA during the campaign and its relationship to attitudes and voting behaviour found that 70 per cent of so-called IRA-connected posts during that campaign were seen by just one per cent of the network's users, 'who strongly identified as Republicans'. The study concluded that 'the relationship between the number of posts from Russian foreign influence accounts that users are exposed to and voting for Donald Trump is near zero' (Eady et al., 2023).

The #TwitterFiles exposures, ignored by the mainstream Western media but fully covered by RT, showed how Twitter was pressured by US intelligence services and lawmakers into extensively investigating alleged Russian disinformation on its platform, following the 2016 election. As Levin has shown, although the alleged Russian intervention in the 2016 US elections received saturation media coverage, such meddling is not uncommon: the United States and the Soviet Union/Russia intervened in one out of every nine national-level executive elections between 1946 and 2000 – the United States interfered in foreign political elections 81 times, while Russia did so 36 times (Levin, 2020).

The Guardian, in collaboration with the Munich-based investigative start-up Paper Trail Media and other leading Western newspapers, reported Russian cyberoperations, based on secret documents linked to the Russian hacking group 'Sandworm' – which was allegedly responsible for disabling Ukraine's power grid in 2015 and behind NotPetya, the 'most economically destructive malware'. The engineers operating these systems were employees of Vulkan which worked for Russian military and intelligence agencies, including the SVR, Russia's foreign intelligence organization, to spread disinformation and support hacking operations. The 'Vulkan files', which date from 2016 to 2021, were leaked by an anonymous whistle-blower angered by the invasion of Ukraine, the paper claimed, adding that five Western intelligence agencies confirmed that the files 'appear to be authentic' (Harding et al., 2023).

In a 7,000-word long piece, *Spiegel* reported in August 2022 that Russian secret service agencies were 'waging a shadow war against the West'. These intelligence services were influencing political parties, manipulating elections, controlling Telegram channels and fomenting protests in the West using disinformation, with the goal 'to demoralize, divide and unsettle Russia's adversaries'. *Spiegel* listed a range of Russian subversive activities, including the 2006 poisoning of Alexander Litvinenko in Britain; the attack on the digital infrastructure of Estonia in 2007;

the theft of sensitive data from the Bundestag in 2015; the use of social media to influence the 2017 Catalonian independence referendum and, in the same year, the theft of data from President Macron's election campaign team; and in 2021 the purchase of information about Ariane 6 rocket from Italy and of classified NATO documents in Poland, as well as the purchase of classified information from an employee of the British Embassy in Berlin (Baumgartner et al., 2022).

Russia's alleged involvement in the 2016 US presidential election and the hacking operations, mentioned earlier, demonstrate the disruptive potential of the web and interference in democratic processes in the West (Soldatov and Borogan, 2017). Several other cases of cybersabotage have been reported in the Western media involving countries including China, Iran and North Korea.

Cyberthreats from the digital dragon

China's growing assertiveness in reshaping the cyber domain challenges Western domination of this arena. The Chinese term for cyber-enabled warfare is 'war under conditions of informatization', in which the People's Liberation Army (PLA) and the 'broader security establishment' must be prepared for 'informationized warfare' (Cheng, 2016: 2). Penetration into US government's computer systems by Chinese hackers, allegedly sponsored by the Chinese government, has led to accusations of illegally procuring intellectual property from industrial manufacturers and military contractors in the United States (Singer and Friedman, 2014). In 2015, China conducted 'distributed denial of service attack' against certain US websites.

In his 2023 National Cybersecurity Strategy document, Biden summarized cybersecurity 'as essential to the basic functioning of our economy, the operation of our critical infrastructure, the strength of our democracy and democratic institutions, privacy of our data and communications, and our national defence' (White House, 2023a). The US government's Annual Threat Assessment of the US Intelligence Community, issued in February 2023, says that China currently represents 'the broadest, most active, and persistent cyber espionage threat to US Government and private-sector networks' and is 'the only country with both the intent to reshape the international order and, increasingly, the economic, diplomatic, military, and technological power to do so' (US Government 2023a).

China's cyberpursuits and its export of related technologies increase the threats of 'suppression of the free flow of information in cyberspace – such as US web content – that Beijing views as threatening', and the expansion of technology-driven authoritarianism globally (US Government, 2023a: 10). The perception of threat is mutual: after Twitter CEO Elon Musk told Fox News in an interview in April 2023 that 'the degree to which government agencies effectively had full access to everything that was going on Twitter blew my mind', a *China Daily* editorial, provocatively titled 'USA Is Universal Spying Agency', noted that the United States wants to be 'all-seeing, all-hearing and all-knowing, so it can reinforce, maintain and perpetuate its hegemony' (*China Daily*, 2023c: 9).

There is evidence to suggest that China has used various instruments in its global cyber communication strategy. Analysing a decade of posts on Weibo, *Nikkei Asia* found the use of *ruhua* or 'insulting China', a powerful feature of the country's internet which social media users invoke to attack perceived cultural slights and defend the Chinese regime. The newspaper examined incidents that led to surges in the use of *ruhua*, the web users responsible for this and who amplified those posts on 'Weibo hot searches', or trending topics, which works to promote themes if Chinese authorities deem them to have 'positive energy' – and play down or remove if they are considered negative. This so-called 'Weibo effect' is an integral part of China's rising online nationalism and its geopolitics (Asada et al., 2022).

The recognition of China as the primary strategic intelligence threat is echoed across many branches of US government, including the Pentagon. US and British domestic intelligence chiefs – the FBI director, Christopher Wray, and the MI5 director general, Ken McCallum – signalled rising concern over this with an unprecedented joint news conference in July 2022 to warn of a 'breathtaking' Chinese effort to steal technology and economic intelligence and to influence foreign politics in Beijing's favour. Addressing a House Appropriations Committee hearing in April 2023, Wray claimed that Chinese hackers outnumber US cybersecurity agents by at least '50 to 1', alleging that China 'operates a larger cyber programme than all other world powers combined', and it has 'stolen more of our personal and corporate data than all other nations, big or small, combined'. China denied such allegations, suggesting instead that the United States was the 'biggest threat to global cybersecurity' and seeks to 'maintain its hegemony in cyberspace', thus urging the United States to cease its 'global hacking operations'.

Intelligence operatives are present in state-owned enterprises and state media organizations and embassies and consulates, the United States claims, as if this were not the case with American embassies, or for that matter, any other major country with global geopolitical and economic interests. The Chinese consulate in Houston was closed by the Trump administration in 2020 after it allegedly served as a national hub for collecting high-tech intelligence. China's Intelligence Law, in operation since 2017, requires its citizens to assist intelligence agencies. The wider China challenge comes from organizations and actors engaged in activities that may not conform to normal concepts of espionage. Much of this is organized by the United Front Work Department, a party organization that seeks to co-opt well-placed members of the Chinese diaspora. One aspect of such efforts is 'elite capture', in which influential Western corporate or government figures are offered 'lucrative sinecures or business opportunities in return for advocating policies that jibe with Chinese interests', according to Inkster, a former director of operations and intelligence for Britain's Secret Intelligence Service and currently the senior adviser for cybersecurity and China at Britain's International Institute for Strategic Studies (Inkster, 2022).

In May 2023, Microsoft claimed that the Chinese hacker group, which has been dubbed 'Volt Typhoon', had been monitoring US infrastructure organizations, including in the telecommunications sector, since 2021. China has also conducted operations to spy on US defence facilities in Guam in the Pacific Ocean: the Five Eyes intelligence network, comprised of agencies in the United States, Britain, Canada, Australia and New Zealand, highlighted a 'recently discovered cluster of activity of interest' from what it said was the state-sponsored Volt Typhoon cyber actor in China. Beijing's foreign ministry spokesperson described the claims as a 'collective disinformation campaign' that proved Washington was expanding its spread of disinformation outside of government agencies (Reuters, 2023b).

In 2022, Al Jazeera reported that a US-based cybersecurity firm Recorded Future, alleged that a hacking group, RedAlpha, linked to the Chinese government, carried out an espionage campaign against governments, NGOs, think tanks and news agencies. Those targeted for 'credential phishing' since 2019 included the International Federation for Human Rights, Amnesty International, Germany's Mercator Institute for China Studies, Radio Free Asia, Taiwan's ruling Democratic Progressive Party and India's National Informatics Centre (Gibson, 2022). Some see such 'cognitive warfare' as the sixth domain of warfare and include in this China's influence campaigns on TikTok (Farahany, 2023).

For its part, quoting a Beijing-based cybersecurity lab, the Chinese newspaper *Global Times* reported in an exclusive piece in 2022 that an elite hacking group, Equation, affiliated with the NSA, was involved for over a decade in 'advanced and covert operations' to monitor developments in more than 40 countries including China, Russia, Japan, Germany, Spain and Italy, and involving 287 important institutional targets. The mouthpiece of the Chinese Communist Party described the United States as 'the world's largest cyber attacker, secrets stealer and the veritable "matrix", like in the movies' (Siqi, 2022). In March 2022, calling the United States a 'hacking empire' of the world, the Chinese Foreign Ministry urged Washington to stop 'malicious' cyber activities following reports that American hackers subverted a network in China to launch attacks on Russia and Belarus. 'China is gravely concerned about cyberattacks against other countries that originate from the US and use China as a springboard', Foreign Ministry spokesperson Zhao Lijian told reporters.

China's information operations are closely linked with those of its ally North Korea, whose cyber offensive tactics have evolved from basic distributed denial of service (DDoS) attacks to sophisticated use of malware. Pyongyang uses cyber tools to support 'active measures' and spread disinformation to sow division in South Korean society and to undermine its government. The heavily sanctioned and cash-strapped country also uses cyberattacks to generate illicit funds from ransom payments, cryptocurrency exchange hacks and fraudulent inter-bank transfer orders (Ha and Maxwell, 2018). In 2016 military coders from Pyongyang stole more than 200 gigabytes of South Korean Army data (Caesar, 2021). According to the UN, many of the funds stolen by North Korean hackers are spent on the weapons programmes, including the development of nuclear missiles (Panda, 2020).

Although North Korea remains a relatively small player in the geopolitical game, it receives a disproportionate amount of coverage as a global threat in the Western media, emanating from South Korea (Moon, 2020). Se-Woong Koo, co-founder and publisher of *Korea Expose*, an online magazine noted: 'In my five years on the English-language media scene, I have met not one Western reporter covering the Korean Peninsula who could speak Korean fluently. . . . Not speaking Korean means sidelining from the global conversation qualified experts who do not speak English – of whom there are many in South Korea' (Koo, 2020).

One of the key strategic objectives of the United States is to build coalitions with the tech corporations to counter these threats to its 'digital ecosystem', given their mutual interest in protecting the internet and its infrastructure of data centres, servers and devices, as well as customer data. In 2017, Microsoft called for the establishment of a Digital Geneva Convention, as a direct response to the expansion of state-sponsored cyberattacks. According to the company's president, Brad Smith, such a commitment should be of utmost importance for maintaining peace and stability in cyberspace, given that 'nation-state hacking has evolved into attacks on civilians in times of peace' (Smith, 2017).

While the Digital Geneva Convention was met with different degrees of enthusiasm and scepticism by diplomats, scholars and governments alike, other Microsoft initiatives, such as the Cybersecurity Tech Accord, launched in 2018 to promote collaborative development of sector norms (Tech Accord, 2019) the Paris Call for Trust and Security; and the CyberPeace Institute 'suggest that, at least, when it comes to cyberspace, companies have devised distinct regulatory and organizational strategies to build their legitimacy to negotiate with states' (Barrinha and Renard, 2018).

In doing this, Microsoft explicitly positioned itself as a 'quasi-diplomatic actor', establishing a Global Security Strategy and Diplomacy Team, which then became the Digital Diplomacy Team (Hurel and Lobato, 2018, 2020). The Global Internet Forum to Counter Terrorism (GIF-CT) was established in 2017 by Twitter, Facebook, Microsoft and YouTube to combat terrorist abuse of platforms (Hurel and Lobato, 2020: 301). With an issue so fundamental to national security, the technology sector has been '[propelled] even more squarely into the world of international diplomacy' (Smith and Browne 2019: 110). These and other dynamics have raised important questions as to what kind of role the private sector plays in global cybersecurity governance. Some commentators have referred to these continuous efforts as 'tech diplomacy' or 'corporate foreign policy' (Economist, 2019). However, despite the rhetoric of a cyberwar or a terrorist attack on electrical grids and communications networks – a 'cyber 9/11' – it has been argued that the real threat is espionage, sabotage and subversion (Rid, 2013).

Global covert spying and overt surveillance

The demonization of hacking operations by or on behalf of authoritarian governments masks the fact that the West, led by the United States, has been at the forefront of global spying and surveillance since the end of World War II. There is naturally a symbiotic relationship between intelligence agencies and communication technologies, which are a key component of the US-led global spying and surveillance systems. The CIA pioneered the use of aerial reconnaissance when, in 1954, President Dwight Eisenhower authorized the agency to develop a top-secret spy plane, the U-2, which was crucial in procuring intelligence to the United States about the Soviet Union, as a new history of spying recounts (Walton, 2023). Despite claims to the contrary, the US government has a long record of keeping secrets and its 'secrecy system', a creation of the Cold War, successfully hid an unsavoury record of US interventions, as Columbia University historian Matthew Connelly details in *The Declassification Engine* (Connelly, 2023).

More than 70 per cent of satellites launched during the Cold War years were used to spy on the protagonists' defence and nuclear capabilities, a crucial part of geopolitics. In 1948 an extensive international surveillance operation called Echelon was established by a secret pact between the Anglo-Saxon countries – the United States, Britain, Australia, Canada and New Zealand, led by the US National Geospatial-Intelligence Agency (NGA). A combination of spy satellites and digital surveillance devices at bases in these countries intercept mobile phone calls, and sensitive listening stations eavesdrop on international electronic communication – phones, telexes, emails and all radio signals, including airline and maritime frequencies. These nations, which formed the 'Five Eyes' in 1956, run the global spying system in secrecy (Kerbaj, 2022).

In the post-Cold War era, the US military used the communications technologies for 'Psychological Operations (PSYOPS)' (Taylor, 1997: 148), increasingly carried out electronically in cyberwarfare. Advanced spy satellites provide intelligence about 'information battlespace', while unmanned electronic war planes jam enemy radar or feed it false images, as well as block or intercept digital transmissions. The enemy's computer systems, especially those running a country's financial networks, could be disabled. By the end of the 20th century, the US Army had already developed an electronic 'Land Warrior', while during the 1999 NATO bombing of Yugoslavia – termed as the first war on the internet – hackers from both sides disrupted Serb and NATO websites, while American 'Information Operations' disabled the Yugoslav government's email system.

The CIA has been eavesdropping on global communication since the 1960s. An investigation in 2020 by the *Washington Post*, conducted jointly with the German public broadcaster ZDF, revealed that the Swiss company Crypto AG, which for over half a century had a near-monopoly of making encryption devices used by governments in more than 120 countries, was secretly owned by the CIA in a highly classified partnership with the BND, the West German intelligence agency. These spy agencies rigged the company's devices so they could easily break the codes that countries used to send encrypted messages. It describes how the United States and its allies exploited other nations' gullibility for years, taking their money and stealing their secrets. The operation, known first by the code name 'Thesaurus' and later 'Rubicon', ranks among the most audacious in CIA history. Though the BND left the operation after the end of the Cold War, the CIA bought the Germans' stake and kept 'wringing Crypto for all its espionage worth until 2018' (Miller, 2020).

The satellite imagery industry collaborates extensively with the defence forces, which use satellite intelligence from commercial companies such as Space Imaging (a company formed in 1994, by Lockheed Martin and Raytheon) and Google Earth, which hugely benefit from this highly lucrative global satellite imaging market. US satellite and internet operators have the pre-eminent position in reconnaissance, surveillance and imaging systems and in integrated space, air and terrestrial information and communications systems, ensuring US control – 'full spectrum dominance' – over global communications. Commercial cyberspace companies have been engaging with the US government since the establishment of Information Sharing and Analysis Centers in 2003, wrote Christine Fox, formerly of the Department of Defense, in *Foreign Affairs* (Fox and Probasco, 2022). The Maxar satellite company, mentioned earlier, is a member of the US Space Command's 'commercial integration cells', operational since 2015, which harness the 'commercial space industry to military space domain awareness and intelligence, surveillance, and reconnaissance operations'.

US global technology corporations are also involved in supporting the state in relation to surveillance. A version of Google Maps was sold to the Pentagon and associated federal and state agencies on multimillion-dollar contracts. Google also provides the NSA with search tools and, in 2008, it helped launch an NGA spy satellite, the GeoEye-1, into space. Google shares the photographs from the satellite with the US military and intelligence communities. In 2010, NGA awarded Google a $27 million contract for 'geospatial visualization services' and, after the Chinese government was accused of hacking Google in the same year, the company entered into a 'formal information-sharing' relationship with the NSA, which was said to allow NSA analysts to 'evaluate vulnerabilities' in Google's hardware and software (Nakashima, 2010).

Companies such as Google, Meta and Apple facilitate spying on non-US citizens located overseas as Section 702 of the Foreign Intelligence Surveillance Act, renewed twice since its original passage in 2008 with large votes, in 2012 and 2018, allows US intelligence agencies to carry out warrantless spying on foreigners' email, phone and other online communications. In 2021, the United States targeted 232,432 'non-US persons' for surveillance, according to government data. The American Civil Liberties Union estimates that the US government has collected more than one billion communications per year since 2011.

Meta produced a report in 2021 on what it labelled as 'the global surveillance-for-hire industry' which targets people in order to collect intelligence, manipulate and compromise their devices and accounts across the internet. While these 'cyber mercenaries' often claim that their services target only criminals and terrorists, 'targeting is indiscriminate and includes journalists, dissidents, critics of authoritarian regimes, families of opposition members and human rights activists'.

It said that the company had disabled seven entities who targeted people across the internet in over 100 countries (Meta, 2021).

The 'full-spectrum surveillance and information disruption' that the internet offers provides the United States with an upper hand in any cyberwar (Singer and Friedman, 2014). Ostensibly fighting Islamist terrorists in sub-Saharan Africa, the CIA has been conducting surveillance flights from a base in Niger, while the Pentagon's Africa Command operates MQ-9 Reaper drones from Niamey, Niger's capital. This adds to the agency's covert missions in eastern Afghanistan for strikes in Pakistan and in southern Saudi Arabia for attacks in Yemen.

The United States' close ally Israel has been a leading exporter of surveillance software, which it has successfully translated into geopolitical gains. Israel's NSO Group, the world's most 'notorious maker of spyware', has been selling its Pegasus surveillance software to law-enforcement and intelligence agencies around the world for nearly a decade, promising that it could consistently and reliably crack the encrypted communications of any iPhone or Android smartphone. Since 2018, the cyberespionage firm has worked closely with Israel's foreign office, whose practice of 'spyware diplomacy' contributes to the export of the spyware across the world. The Israeli intelligence company Cellebrite pioneered technology that could break into locked iPhones for the Israeli police and has now exported its data-scraping technology to law enforcement agencies across the United States (Goodfriend, 2022).

Israel's ability to approve or deny access to NSO's cyberweapons has become part of its diplomacy. Pegasus played an 'unseen but critical role' in securing the support of Arab nations in Israel's campaign against Iran and in negotiating the Abraham Accords, the 2020 diplomatic agreements that normalized relations between Israel and some of its long-time Arab adversaries. One former military aide to the then prime minister Benjamin Netanyahu, told the *New York Times*: 'With our Defence Ministry sitting at the controls of how these systems move around, we will be able to exploit them and reap diplomatic profits' (Bergman and Mazzetti, 2022).

China spying

Unlike the structural and near-global surveillance and spying operations that the US-led West undertakes to 'promote and protect democracy and human rights' across the world, espionage by authoritarian regimes receives much harsher criticism. 'Beijing's formidable intelligence apparatus' and the Chinese state's capacity for 'industrial espionage' receive a robust and regular criticism in the Western media, thinks tanks and policy discourses. One recent example is a three-part series published in the journal *Foreign Policy* in 2020, written by a commentator associated with a leading American think tank: covering intelligence wars between the United States and China (Dorfman, 2020a), hacking (Dorfman, 2020b) and economic espionage (Dorfman, 2020c).

Within China, the sophisticated surveillance system has come in for scrutiny – in journalistic accounts (Mozur et al., 2022) and academic works (Chin and Lin, 2022), as well as think tanks and policy briefs (Jili, 2022).

The United States sees the 'digital silk road' as a force multiplier for Beijing's espionage capabilities and that it enables the Chinese government to seize an enormous amount of personal data, business information and both government and military intelligence and exploit it for geopolitical ends. In June 2021, President Biden signed an Executive Order to prohibit US investment in China's 'military-industrial complex' – the use of Chinese surveillance technology outside China, as well as the development or use of Chinese surveillance technology, to facilitate repression or serious human rights abuses constitute unusual and extraordinary threats.

The BeiDou Navigation Satellite System, China's version of the Global Positioning System, aims to build a web of commercial products across the BRI: by 2019, the BeiDou system had been equipped with 35 active satellites, as against the 31 active satellites that support the GPS, indicating the end of the GPS monopoly as the dominant provider of real-time location information around the world (Gordon et al., 2020). A 2022 EU report emphasizes the need for 'strengthening our early warning, intelligence picture and secure communications', and coordinating the EU Single Intelligence Analysis Capacity, as well as the EU Satellite Centre, which will contribute to the EU's credibility as 'a strategic actor' (EU, 2022: 33). Such concerns emanate from a sense of being dependent on American intelligence systems, including GPS, which the EU has countered by developing its own Galileo navigation satellites, the first of which was launched in 2005.

Britain's 2021 'integrated military review' echoes similar concerns: 'Long established techniques of influence and leverage, such as economic coercion, propaganda, intellectual property theft and espionage, have been supercharged by ubiquitous information and technological transformation. . . . As we become increasingly challenged below the threshold of open warfare, the battle of the narratives and use of non-lethal means to influence and secure objectives will characterise the future operating environment' (Ministry of Defence, 2021: 5).

A 2019 report from the US-China Economic and Security Review Commission, a congressional committee, lists the myriad ways in which Chinese companies, often backed by their government, help transfer strategic know-how from the United States to China. The Chinese government relies not only on its intelligence services but also on businesses, institutions and individuals to gather proprietary information. The Ministry of State Security, along with other Chinese government-backed organizations, spends considerable effort recruiting spies from the Chinese diaspora (Bhattacharjee, 2023). A *Forbes* investigation into TikTok and ByteDance revealed that a ByteDance tool, run by staff in China, is tracking mentions of what it considers 'sensitive words' across the company's products, enabling them 'to monitor who was saying them, when and how often', William Evanina, the former head of counterintelligence for the US government, told *Forbes* (Levine, 2023). New rules for data that is transferred abroad, requiring that it be assessed by the agency for its 'degree of sensitivity' and possible risks to 'national security', were introduced by the Cyberspace Administration of China in 2022. The country has also approved changes in Counterespionage Law, widening the already broad definition of spying to include providing 'documents, data, materials or objects bearing on national security and interests'.

In a 2023 report, China's National Computer Virus Emergency Response Center noted that the CIA has overturned or attempted to overturn at least 50 legitimate governments and created disturbances in other countries over the decades (even though it has admitted only 7 of them):'the secret operations' led to the disintegration of the socialist camp in the 1980s, to Green Revolution' in Iran in 2009, the 'Arab Spring' in 2011 and 'Colour Revolution' in Ukraine in 2014. The report highlighted the critical role of communication technologies, including the internet 'providing unprecedented technological possibilities for the US intelligence agencies' to launch such operations (National Computer Virus Emergency Response Center, 2023).

A report from the International Cyber Policy Centre of the Australian Strategic Policy Institute issued during the 2019 anti-China protests in Hong Kong noted that Twitter had recoded a network of accounts that it identified as being involved in an 'information operation' directed against the protesters by the Chinese communist party. The unsophisticated nature of the campaign suggested a crude understanding of information operations, reflecting a lack of familiarity on the part of Chinese state-backed actors of social media platforms such as Twitter, as opposed to the highly proficient levels of control demonstrated by the Chinese government over heavily censored platforms such as WeChat or Weibo (Uren et al., 2019: 4).

A Graphika report suggested that a cross-platform spam network – which it labelled 'Spamouflage Dragon' – boosted attacks on the Hong Kong protesters by using hijacked or fake accounts on YouTube, Twitter and Facebook. Using spam posts to avoid social media platforms' detection systems, its political posts were interspersed with high volumes of spam-like content, including TikTok videos, designed as camouflage, diluting the political content with more human-interest posts (Nimmo et al., 2019).

The 5G war

Another battlefield for surveillance supremacy is the arena of 5th generation mobile telephony. A 2020 article in *Party & Government Forum*, a journal run by the Party School of the Chinese Communist Party noted: 'Before the internet era, European and American countries had played a leading role in forming the new world economic order, political order, and legal order' but 'in the era of the internet, especially in the new era of informatization pioneered by 5G, it is entirely possible for China to go ahead and make greater contributions'. 'In the internet era, whoever has the discourse power and rule-making power has the power to lead the future order', it said. From this perspective, 5G offers a 'historic opportunity' for leadership in more than just technology and a chance to 'enhance China's international competitiveness' – despite having missed out on past, similar revolutionary shifts' (quoted in Doshi et al., 2021: 6–7).

In 2012, the Obama administration banned Huawei and another Chinese firm, ZTE, from bidding for US government contracts. Based in Shenzhen, Huawei is the world's largest provider of 5G networks and a leader in sales of telecommunications equipment. For many countries the main concern is that, though it is a private company, the Chinese government could force Huawei to hand over data to the Chinese government. According to the 2017 National Intelligence Law, Chinese companies must 'support, assist, and cooperate with' China's intelligence-gathering authorities. There are also concerns that Huawei's 5G infrastructure could allow the Chinese government to collect and centralize massive quantities of data and give Beijing the necessary access to attack communications networks and public utilities. Huawei has distanced itself from the Chinese Communist Party (CCP), repeatedly asserting that its equipment has never been used, and will never be used, to spy.

However, US intelligence agencies lobbied members of the 'Five Eyes' to ban Huawei from its 5G infrastructure on national security grounds and with success: New Zealand and Australia banned it in 2018, followed by Canada in 2022. The former US secretary of state, Mike Pompeo – CIA director during the early days of the Trump administration – warned Britain in February 2019 that countries using Huawei equipment were a risk to the United States and were jeopardizing their place in the 'Five Eyes' should Britain decide to approve Huawei. Britain decided to phase out the Chinese company by 2027 (Kerbaj, 2022). Huawei's chief financial officer Meng Wanzhou, who is also the daughter of Ren Zhengfei, the founder of the company, was arrested in Canada at the behest of the United States, and two Canadian diplomats, Michael Spavor and Michael Kovrig, were imprisoned in China in retaliation, in a case of 'hostage diplomacy'. Meng was finally returned to China in a diplomatic war that lasted for more than three years (Blanchfield and Hampson, 2021).

In 2020, Taiwan Semiconductor Manufacturing Company (TSMC), the world's largest chip supplier and which had supplied more than 90 per cent of Huawei's smartphone chips, ceased business with Huawei, citing US export controls. In 2021, Biden signed a bill aimed at preventing Huawei and ZTE from receiving equipment-making licenses from US regulators, and in January 2023, stopped providing licenses for US companies to export goods to Huawei and also signed legislation that precludes any Chinese manufacturer from obtaining chips or chip-making equipment made with US parts anywhere in the world. Despite the restrictions, the Commerce Department has allowed some business activities: between 2017 and 2021, it allowed more than $60 billion in transactions between Huawei and US firms (Congressional Research Service, 2022).

Huawei has been made an example of in Washington's new 'technology cold war' against China, as such companies are 'reshaping the distribution of profits along the global value chain' which has traditionally and primarily 'controlled by Western multinationals', notes a recent study (Wen, 2020). The increasing influence that Chinese ICT firms have gained in global markets has also 'endowed them with growing bargaining power vis-à-vis transnational capital and Western governments' (ibid.: 187). The company is 'in direct competition with American giants in multiple ICT business domains' and has challenged Cisco's dominant position in the business networking market and in consumer electronics markets and 'increasingly encroached on Apple's turf with an unprecedented rate of market expansion' (ibid.: 191).

For its part, China is expanding its imprint in the telecom space as 5G networks are expected to form the foundation of a smarter, connected economy linking countless devices and sensors together. Eager to build these networks worldwide, China has subsidized its 5G champion companies and projects around the world as part of a 'Digital Silk Road' initiative. Many countries, especially those participating in China's BRI, are already using Huawei's equipment to build 5G networks, attracted by the company's ability to provide high-quality networks for low prices. Huawei is helping Malaysia and Russia build their 5G networks, and it has signed contracts to build the same for countries in Latin America.

Huawei is investing heavily in order to be a leader in the emerging 6G technology so that other companies are dependent on its patents, rather than relying on imports from the United States. The main software-driven business Huawei is building is cloud services, since some of the functions in a telecom network traditionally performed by base stations can be transferred to software processes in the cloud (Hille et al., 2021: 5). A report by the Australian Strategic Policy Institute and its *Critical Technology Tracker* showed that China is the leading country in 37 of the 44 technologies evaluated, often producing more than five times as much high-impact research as its closest competitor (Gaida et al., 2023).

This means that the United States is currently leading in only seven of the 44 technologies analysed, maintaining its strengths in the design and development of advanced semiconductor devices and in the research fields of high-performance computing and advanced integrated circuit design and fabrication. It also leads in the crucial areas of quantum computing. The next most important technological powerhouses are India and Britain, both in the top five countries in 29 of the 44 technologies. South Korea and Germany follow closely behind, appearing in the top five countries in 20 and 17 technologies, respectively. Such observations are echoed by research done at European think tanks, notably at the Merics (Shi-Kupfer and Ohlberg, 2019).

In April 2020, the US Senate passed the bipartisan legislation Utilizing Strategic Allied (USA) Telecommunications Act, which requires the FCC to create a $750 million grant scheme to create a research and development fund dedicated to an 'open' Radio Access Network (RAN), The RAN as a communication architecture is at the centre of US strategy to exclude competitors such as Huawei from its network. Promoting an 'open RAN' model – based on open and modular interfaces – is supposed to guarantee 'trust' in network management and to replace 'untrustworthy' foreign manufacturers in favour of US-based tech giants – such as Meta,

Google, Amazon or Microsoft – to increase their control over network infrastructure through their cloud capacities. This kind of technology is positioned as promoting 'openness' that is equated with 'democracy' (Plantin, 2021: 405). A month later, the Center for Strategic and International Studies published 'The Criteria for Security and Trust in Telecommunications Networks and Services', as part of the 'Clean Network' initiative. It defines 'Opaqueness [as] indicated by unusual ownership arrangements that disguise who owns, controls, or influences the supplier company or use any other mechanisms to conceal dependencies between the supplier and a foreign state' (CSIS, 2020: 16). As opposed to 'transparent' networks, 'opaque' technology would allow access by the Chinese government to the 5G infrastructure once installed in foreign countries.

More than 50 nations, representing over two-thirds of the world's economy, and 180 telecom companies, joined the 'Clean Network', including 26 of the 27 EU members, Australia, Canada, New Zealand, as well as Japan, Israel, India and Singapore.

Concerns are also being voiced about protecting critical public and private intellectual property on quantum-enabling technologies from 'theft and abuse by the US' adversaries' (Wadhwa and Kop, 2022). The right-leaning Henry Jackson Society, has been very critical of data theft by Huawei (Seely et al., 2019), while its 2020 report highlights the 'strategic dependency', of the five 'Anglo-Saxon powers' – the United States, Britain, Canada, New Zealand and Australia – on China. Strategic dependency is identified when a country is a net importer of and imports more than 50 per cent of its supplies from China, and China controls more than 30 per cent of the global market of that particular good (Rogers et al., 2020).

Disinformation dilemmas

While there is much coverage in the West of the threats posed by mis- and disinformation operations from hostile countries such as Russia and China, the US government and the Pentagon's Special Operations Command are keen to deploy advanced technologies for its global misinformation campaign. Labelled 'Military Information Support Operations', these include 'influence operations, digital deception (such as deepfakes), communication disruption, and disinformation campaigns at the tactical edge and operational levels' (Biddle, 2023). Disinformation is part and parcel of what is described as 'perception management', official propaganda policy since the time of the Reagan presidency. Following the 9/11 attacks, the Bush administration launched what it called the Office of Strategic Influence to 'counter the enemy's perception management' in the 'war on terror', managing those perceptions with its own disinformation, including providing 'news items, possibly including false ones, to foreign journalists in an effort to influence overseas opinion' (Shanker and Schmitt, 2004). While perception management involves denying, or blocking, propaganda, it can also entail advancing the United States' own narrative.

The Defense Department defines perception management as actions 'to convey and/or deny selected information and indicators to foreign audiences to influence their emotions, motives, and objective reasoning' (Department of Defense, 2009). Such activities have been enhanced after the US Congress passed in 2019 a law – known as 'Section 1631' – affirming that the military could conduct operations in the 'information environment' to 'push back against foreign disinformation aimed at undermining US interests'. It allows the US military to undertake clandestine psychological operations in cyberspace without crossing the CIA's covert authority.

In 2022, the Pentagon established a new entity called the 'Influence and Perception Management Office', whose responsibilities include overseeing and coordinating the various counter-disinformation efforts being conducted by the military, including the United States' own propaganda abroad, as well as the 'Defense Military Deception Program Office', tasked with 'sensitive messaging, deception, influence and other operations in the information environment'. As noted in Chapter 1, psychological operations to promote US narratives overseas have a long history. What is new, however, is the ubiquity and global popularity of US social media platforms, necessitating 'an expansion of tactics, including the use of artificial personas and images, the logic is that views expressed by what appears to be, say, an Afghan woman or an Iranian student might be more persuasive than if they were openly pushed by the US government', said the *Washington Post* (Nakashima, 2022).

Jared Cohen, a former Director of Google Ideas, who previously worked at the US State Department's Policy Planning Unit, is a keen advocate of deploying digital tools to achieve foreign policy goals. He is reported to have contacted Twitter CEO Jack Dorsey to delay scheduled maintenance to assist activists in Iran, during the protests that followed the Islamic republic's 2009 elections (Donnan, 2011). With Google CEO Schmidt, he advocated using digital technologies as a foreign policy tool creating what they termed as the 'coalitions of the connected' (Schmidt and Cohen, 2010).

Disinformation – including conspiracy theories – are an integral and growing component of such a media ecosystem and particularly pronounced in US political history, as a recent study documents (Konda, 2019). Systematic and sophisticated disinformation are legion in political and strategic public relations: from the 1968 My Lai massacre during the Vietnam war, to manufactured stories about newborn babies being pulled out of incubators by invading Iraqi forces in occupied Kuwait in 1990.

The truth will out?

The other side of the coin to the use of information technologies for propaganda and deception is the rise in using the same to expose disinformation and reveal the truth. The convergence between whistle-blowers, hackers, activists and journalists is evidenced most prominently in the cases of WikiLeaks and the Snowden affair. The founder of WikiLeaks, Julian Assange, is in prison for publishing almost 400,000 classified diplomatic cables – the 'largest leak of classified documents in American history' (McCurdy, 2013: 123), which are said to endanger US national security. In April 2010, WikiLeaks published a shocking video filmed from a US helicopter showing the killing of civilians in Baghdad. In October of that year, WikiLeaks became international news when the raw data were edited and transformed into journalistic stories in a project supported and funded by major international newspapers – the *New York Times*, *The Guardian*, *El País*, *Le Monde* and *Der Spiegel* (Berkhoff, 2012). After spending nearly seven years in the Ecuadorian Embassy in London, Assange has been in a British prison since 2019, awaiting extradition to the United States. Although the liberal media initially hailed him as a brave investigator – he was named *Time* magazine's 'Person of the Year' in 2010 – Assange has since been subject to a media campaign of denigration.

The scale of mass surveillance within a democratic and free internet was revealed by the Snowden affair in 2014 (Greenwald, 2014). A series of special investigations by the *Washington Post* (later published as an e-book) revealed the extensive surveillance programme and worldwide mobile phone tracking of the US National Security Agency (NSA) (*Washington Post*, 2014). Particularly controversial was the NSA's PRISM programme, which allowed US intelligence agencies to access information from companies such as Google, Facebook and Apple. It was also revealed that, under its Foreign Intelligence Surveillance Act, the US government collected 'the contents of electronic communications, including telephone calls and emails' of 'non-US persons located outside the US', according to a US government report (NSA, 2014).

Human Rights Watch noted that such surveillance of personal communications on an unprecedented scale damaged 'US credibility in advocating internationally for Internet freedom, which the US has listed as an important foreign policy objective since at least 2010' (Human Rights Watch, 2014: 3). That Snowden is ensconced in Moscow and Assange did a series of programmes for RT show the geopolitical underpinnings of such sensitive 'leaks'. The Snowden disclosures of US government surveillance practices, including the monitoring of foreign leaders, reignited an international debate over internet governance (Greenwald, 2014; Lyon, 2015).

The 2016 Panama Papers scandal exposed an international network of offshore bank accounts and tax havens used by the world's financial and political elite to avoid taxes. The internal documents of the Panama-based law firm Mossack Fonseca were gathered by the German daily *Süddeutsche Zeitung* and then distributed throughout the world by the International Consortium of Investigative Journalists. A more recent case of the political nature of intelligence leaks was the April 2023 Pentagon leak – the largest leak of classified Pentagon documents since Snowden – on the popular free chat platform Discord, allegedly by Jack Teixeira, the 21-year-old American airman, sharing hundreds of classified military documents, several including links to CIA briefings.

As a *Guardian* report noted, the leaks might be 'significantly overwrought', and they were 'rather more damaging to Russia than to any Western power. Consider the extent of information revealed about Russia's internal confusion, with the security services arguing with the defence ministry over proper death counts, for instance' (Ledwidge, 2023). Russian propaganda networks such as RT ran an extensive interview with Sarah Bils, a former US Navy enlisted aviation electronics technician and the face of the pro-Russian social media team that helped to spread leaked Pentagon data. Bils was revealed to be behind Donbass Devushka ('Donbass Girl') – a team running several pro-Russian social media channels that was among the first to spread the Pentagon leak (RT, 2023).

A more recent example of such an investigation in Israel exposed the working of a 'Team Jorge', which had been involved in planting material in compromised accounts, leaking of real or forged material through an army of online avatars (fake accounts) for social media manipulation, voter suppression and election disruptions. Part of a global journalistic consortium which included 30 media outlets, including *Haaretz*, *Le Monde*, *Radio France*, *Der Spiegel*, *Die Zeit*, and *The Guardian*, the investigation showed that the company, an example of 'disinformation-for-hire industry', had meddled in '33 presidential-level election campaigns' around the world, 'in 27 of them successfully' (Kirchgaessner et al., 2023).

The company claimed it disseminated false information against former president Hugo Chavez to influence the 2012 Venezuelan elections (Megiddo and Benjakob, 2022). As *The Guardian* reported, one of Team Jorge's key services was a sophisticated software package, Advanced Impact Media Solutions, which coordinated thousands of fake social media profiles on Twitter, LinkedIn, Facebook, Telegram, Gmail, Instagram and YouTube and controlled a multinational army of more than 30,000 avatars, complete with digital backstories that stretch back years (ibid.).

That US journalists work in conjunction with intelligence services was evident in September 2022 when the *New York Times* published 'Visual Investigations', sharing private phone calls from Russian soldiers to friends and relatives at home, where they were giving 'damning insider accounts of battlefield failures and civilian executions, excoriating their leaders'; the newspaper admitted that it had 'exclusively obtained more than 4,000 recordings of calls', 'intercepted by Ukrainian law enforcement agencies' (Al-Hlou et al., 2023).

Countering disinformation – fact-checking

To mitigate such digital disruption, it is mainly Western-based organizations who are involved in fact-checking, establishing the so-called 'truth'. The leading Western news organizations – ranging from news agencies (AP, AFP and Reuters) to broadcasters, such as BBC and CNN, and newspapers like the *New York Times* and *Washington Post* all have fact-checking units. In 2020–2021, the *New York Times* ran a series of extensive stories about 'viral misinformation', including on China and Russia, to 'chronicle and debunk false and misleading information that is going viral online' (New York Times, 2020). In India, DisInfo Lab, claiming to be Asia's first DisInfo Lab, has been set up for 'unveiling fake news and propaganda that intend to create turmoil among people' (https://thedisinfolab.org/). The International Fact-Checking Network, part of the Poynter Institute has, since 2015, brought together fact-checkers worldwide to support 'best practices and exchanges in this field'. The network 'monitors trends, formats and policy-making about fact-checking worldwide', creating common standards and principles and providing training and grants to fact-checkers.

The growing availability of open-source intelligence (OSINT) from social networks and internet-connected devices has enabled the development of more sophisticated fact-checking processes, especially in the Western world. Drawing on the vast amounts of publicly available online information, OSINT can use intelligence-gathering techniques and technologies including satellite imagery, social media posts and user-generated content to go beyond the surface of a news picture or a video and determine how it has been produced and its validity. The data analysis can discern patterns, trends and anomalies that may be useful in interpreting information. Defined by Mark Lowenthal, a US-based intelligence expert, as 'any and all information that can be obtained from the overt collection: all media types, government reports, and other files, scientific research and reports, business information providers, the Internet, etc.', OSINT has been used by investigative journalists mainly in the West to expose corruption, war crimes and financial and trade irregularities, with the focus on the global South (Lowenthal, 2005).

Doing a reverse image search using TinEye or Google Images allows journalists to upload an image and immediately see when and where the image was first used across the web. Other platforms like WeVerify help to fact-check videos and images online. Similarly, determining the geographic position of a particular event or incident can be done with increasing accuracy, using tools such as Google Maps or Google Earth. It is then possible to match the geographical features seen in the footage and cross-reference stills from the footage to satellite imagery to confirm whether or not a video was indeed taken from a particular location. In some cases, it is possible to identify the approximate time the footage was captured: using SunCalc, for example, it is possible to analyse the position of shadows and the sun at any given time and date, at any given location.

Malicious deepfakes and synthetic media are further blurring the lines between what is a real and fake image, and new technologies are being developed to detect these, such as the test provided by the MIT Media Lab. The 'Crisis Evidence Lab' at Amnesty International uses digital 3D models to analyse these media and then communicate their findings. Exposing organized crime and corruption around the world, the Offshore Leaks Database, developed by the International Consortium of Investigative Journalists (ICIJ), contains leaked documents about nearly 785,000 offshore companies and trusts.

Subscription based companies such as Maxar and Planet Labs publish very high-resolution, up-to-date satellite images on image wire services and provide image archives to the media, while the Open Source Intelligence Framework has a detailed and ever-growing list of digital investigative tools. Most of the organizations which use OSINT are essentially Western-based and funded: notably, Global Investigative Journalism Network (GIJN), Organised Crime and Corruption Reporting Project (OCCRP), ICIJ and C4ADS, a non-profit organization dedicated to data-driven analysis and evidence-based reporting of conflict and security issues worldwide.

Some of the major activists using OSINT which have been widely publicized in the mainstream media include the British-based investigative journalism group, Bellingcat, which gained prominence during the Syrian conflict, exposing the abuse of power and human rights violations with the goal of using it to contribute to investigations, court cases and other accountability mechanisms. Its investigation of al-Assad's usage of chemical weapons in Syria and its exposure of the Russia-backed separatists that shot down Malaysia Airlines Flight MH17, among others, have established OSINT as a potent journalistic tool (Higgins, 2021). That both the US and British government support Bellingcat might be one of the reasons it receives prominent coverage in the mainstream Anglo-American media. The process for archiving and investigating open-source evidence to be used for prosecution by such organizations as the Global Legal Action Network and the Syrian Archive, among others, can be used to promote geopolitical agendas. However, OSINT is also a resource for governments in their intelligence gathering and will provide more data than any group of analysts can process, which will need the power of AI (Mattis, 2023).

Synergies of authoritarian disinformation

Unlike the Western dissemination of disinformation, which receives relatively limited coverage in the media, the weaponization of information from authoritarian countries such as Russia and China is given extensive coverage and criticism. The alleged interference in the 2016 US and the 2020 Taiwanese presidential elections, it has been suggested, indicates that Russia and China are using digital interference to shape the contest between democracies and autocracies. A 2020 report by the Center for a New American Security argued that this is aimed to undermine liberal democratic norms and institutions and cautioned about the 'growing synergy between the two authoritarian powers in the information environment' and 'a growing convergence in their digital influence efforts' (Center for New American Security, 2020).

According to the report, Chinese and Russian narratives overlap: Russia propagates narratives designed to undermine trust in Western institutions and governments, creating a fertile ground for Chinese narratives about the superiority of authoritarian systems to take root. The media and diplomatic institutions of the two countries have 'forged symbiotic relationships' that support the creation of an 'entirely alternative information ecosystem' in which truth is called into question. They are jointly chipping away 'at norms and standards governing the free flow of information', and they 'seek to bend the arc of the global information architecture to their advantage by legitimizing high-tech illiberalism at home while continuing to exploit the relative openness of the digital environment in the United States and other democracies. The report warns that the two authoritarian states could leverage their comparative strengths 'to pollute the global information environment', promoting alternative platforms by which information can be disseminated. While Russian efforts remain focused on weakening and dividing democratic societies in Europe and the United States, China is 'spreading the tentacles of its online influence campaigns in strategically positioned developing countries' (Kliman et al., 2020).

Such arguments are strengthened by a litany of reports, journalistic accounts and academic research about the weaponization of information by authoritarian states, largely emanating from the world of think tanks. A 2018 report by the Netherlands Institute of International Relations, 'Clingendael' suggested that Russia was spreading disinformation, interfering in political processes, cyber-attacks and leveraging economic influence for political means as part of its 'hybrid' warfare to weaken the influence of the EU, the NATO and the United States by destabilizing democratic processes and institutions in Europe. China's version of hybrid conflict, it averred, was visible mainly in East Asia, notably in the South China Sea (van der Putten et al., 2018).

The US-based 'cyber threat analysis and research company' Miburo, whose mission is to 'protect democracies, secure the free information environment, and ensure the integrity of the free Internet', ran a six-part series in 2021, exploring the disinformation campaigns of the pro-Chinese propaganda network 'Spamouflage'. Miburo suggested that Spamouflage has consistently amplified the arguments of the Chinese government – its disinformation campaigns; denying atrocities in Xinjiang, providing false information about the origins of Covid-19 virus, spreading propaganda and stoking tensions in Taiwan; and attacking democracy and journalists. It claimed to have detected more than 2,000 accounts spreading disinformation and propaganda aligned with the CCP on Facebook, Twitter and YouTube, though it also added that 'no hard digital signals have definitively tied Spamouflage to the Chinese government', and yet Miburo finds honourable mention in mainstream media including the *New York Times* (Monaco, 2021).

Since 2022, Miburo has been owned by Microsoft, part of the Digital Threat Analysis Center which 'analyses and reports on nation-state threats, including both cyberattacks and influence operations' with its mission being 'to detect, assess, and disrupt threats to Microsoft, its customers, and democracies worldwide' (Microsoft Threat Analysis Center (formerly Miburo) https://miburo.substack.com/about). The Centre focuses on Russian and Chinese propaganda and largely ignores the much more widespread and sophisticated propaganda of the West. Other activist/ NGO sources help legitimize the discourse on authoritarian threat to democracy. One example was the study conducted by Avaaz showing how Russian-generated fake news surrounding the French 'Yellow Vests' movement reached 105 million views in a country with just over 35 million Facebook monthly active users. It argued that RT France used these to fuel the protests (Avaaz, 2019).

Covid-19 as a global 'infodemic'

Mis- and disinformation received an added dimension with the outbreak of the Covid-19 pandemic in December 2019: the WHO 'situation report', issued in February 2020, stated that the 'outbreak and response has been accompanied by a massive "infodemic" – an over-abundance of information – some accurate and some not – that makes it hard for people to find trustworthy sources and reliable guidance when they need it' (WHO, 2020). 'Infodemic' has since become a 'popular catch-all metaphor', being used uncritically in academic, policy and journalistic writing, which is misleading 'as information does not spread like a virus' (Simon and Camargo, 2021). Nevertheless, there was much speculation about the origins of Covid-19 – from the habit among some Chinese of eating wild animals, possibly infected by bats, to a secret biological warfare programme being carried at the Wuhan Institute of Virology, to a bioweapon developed in the United States and smuggled to China during the 2019 Wuhan Military Games, to a population control scheme of Bill & Melinda Gates Foundation and even to the supposedly dangerous effects on the immune system of 5G mobile communication systems (Himelboim et al., 2023).

'Most of these dubious concoctions circulated via social media, in a frenzied global ping-pong via Twitter, Facebook groups, WhatsApp chats, right-wing telegram groups and other platforms and outlets' (Cosentino, 2023: 11). In 2020, Facebook disabled fictitious personas created by CentCom (US Central Command) to counter disinformation spread allegedly by China suggesting that the coronavirus responsible for Covid-19 was created at a US Army lab in Fort Detrick. The pseudo profiles – active in Facebook groups that conversed in Arabic, Farsi and Urdu – were used to amplify truthful information from the US Centers for Disease Control and Prevention about the virus's origination in China (Graphika and Stanford Internet Observatory, 2022; Nakashima, 2022).

The US-based Center for Countering Digital Hate that 'seeks to disrupt the architecture of online hate and misinformation', along with Anti-Vax Watch, an alliance seeking to educate the American public about the dangers of 'the anti-vax industry', are at the forefront of confronting misinformation in the United States. According to their research, 'the anti-vaccine activists' spread 'conspiracies and lies' about the safety of Covid vaccines' on Facebook, YouTube, Instagram and Twitter. They singled out what they called the 'disinformation dozen', 12 anti-vaxxers who play 'leading roles in spreading digital misinformation about Covid vaccines' (CCDH, 2021: 4 and 5).

The academic community also contributed to the effort, for example, through the 'virality project' led by Stanford Internet Observatory with support from New York University and the Atlantic Council's Digital Forensic Research Lab and Graphika. Anti-vaccine narratives in the US included 'long-standing anti-vaccine influencers and activists, wellness and lifestyle influencers, pseudo-medical influencers, conspiracy theory influencers, right-leaning political influencers, and medical freedom influencers' (The Virality Project, 2022). Foreign actors in China, Russia and Iran took 'a full-spectrum propaganda approach', spanning both media and social media, to influence vaccine conversations in the United States and around the world (ibid). Other studies highlighted the role of such organization as QAnon who focused on the conspirators behind the pandemic (Himelboim et al., 2023; also see the 2022 Special Issue of the journal *Convergence*).

A review of the global circulation of such conspiracy theories online revealed that the content was focused on Anglophone Western democracies, neglecting non-Western countries (Mahl et al., 2023; Cosentino, 2023). Distortions in the public discourse about Covid-19 and how to treat it were also reflected in the way whole communities were targeted as 'super-spreaders' in India (Kumar, 2023) where vaccine hesitancy on religious grounds was emphasized in fake news produced in other South Asian countries (Kanozia and Arya, 2021). The use of what has been termed 'dark platforms', such as 8kun and Gab, as well as search engines like DuckDuckGo, also contributed to spreading Covid-19-related conspiracy theories, with results that deepened the conspiracy, rather than relying on mainstream news outlets or government sources (Zeng and Schäfer, 2021). Platforms such as Telegram and VKontakte were also widely used for this purpose, especially in Russia.

The Harvard Kennedy School launched a *Misinformation Review* in 2020 to map the phenomenon and provide a platform for fresh research, including trawling web archives to dig out 'harmful health misinformation linked to the coronavirus pandemic'. The researchers argued that old resources from the Internet Archive's Wayback Machine and subsequent screenshots were contributing to the Covid-19 'misinfodemic' on social media platforms (Acker and Chaiet, 2020). Another report by Stanford University researchers analysed the Chinese government's English-language presence on Facebook, sharing positive stories about the Communist Party's pandemic response, rewriting recent history in a manner favourable to the CCP as the coronavirus pandemic evolved and using targeted ads to spread preferred messages.

Li-Meng Yan, a Hong Kong-based researcher, appeared in the United States on Fox News making the unsubstantiated claim that the coronavirus was a bio-weapon manufactured by China and deliberately released by the Chinese Communist Party. This story was crafted by Guo Wengui, a fugitive Chinese billionaire, and Stephen Bannon, a former adviser to Trump. Yan's interview on Tucker Carlson's show in September 2020 gained at least 8.8 million views online. Bannon based his podcast to the coronavirus, calling it 'the CCP virus' long before Trump started using the term for the pandemic. Guo circulated the same claims on his media outlets, which included GTV, a video platform, and GNews, a site that features glowing coverage of Guo and his associates (Qin et al., 2020). A Graphika report noted multiple instances of efforts to amplify such content on social media as the network acted as a 'prolific producer and amplifier of mis- and disinformation' about Covid-19 and QAnon narratives (Graphika, 2021).

For its part, the Chinese government co-opted fact-checking as a way to propagate official discourses and censor unwanted information. Analyses of two prominent fact-checking sites – the official, 'The Joint', and the commercial, 'Jiao Zhen' – show that although they had a similar interface and even similar article structure as other international professional fact-checkers, their content overwhelmingly relied on single government sources and strictly followed official lines. Official documents and policy directives further illustrate that the Chinese government considered it as important to battle rumours that threatened social and regime stability as the pandemic itself. Social media platforms and portal websites were used to discount such information and promote official messages. The propaganda apparatus also worked with the police to punish thousands of individuals involved in creating and spreading the 'rumours' (Fang, 2022).

A 2021 Chinese think tank report by the Chongyang Institute for Financial Studies, Renmin University, Taihe Think Tank and Intellisia Institute, entitled *The Truth about America's Fight against Covid-19*, claimed that Trump was 'probably the biggest promotor of Covid-19 misinformation'. It referred to unanswered questions about the outbreak of a 'respiratory, white lung disease' of unknown cause in the United States in the second half of 2019 and the research going on at Fort Detrick and other biological laboratories. According to the Xinhua news agency, the United States was the world's No. 1 'disinformation country' (Xinhua, 2021). Despite such efforts, the Chinese reaction to misinformation was largely ineffective: surveys, as one conducted by CGTN Think Tank in July 2021, were largely unreported internationally, though available in six languages (CGTN, 2021).

The crisis of credibility in global communication has prompted US-based think tanks to suggest remedies. A December 2022 report from the Carnegie Endowment for International Peace suggested ways to bridge the divide between researchers within major social media companies and those in academia and other research professions (Green et al., 2022). It noted that the public needed to be provided with 'more skills, context, and tools to evaluate the information they encounter online' (ibid: 19). Meta organized the US 2020 Facebook & Instagram Election Study, a first-of-its-kind collaborative research effort between a team of over 15 external academics with internal Meta researchers, engineers, and project managers, and in December 2021, Twitter announced a new consortium of external researchers to which it plans to disclose data about content moderation and platform governance issues, with the stated goals of providing 'data-driven transparency' and encouraging public-interest research.

Information weaponization on steroids – AI

In their 2021 book *The Age of A.I. and Our Human Future*, Henry Kissinger and his co-authors – Eric Schmidt, a former chief executive and chairman of Google, and Daniel Huttenlocher, the inaugural dean of the MIT Schwarzman College of Computing – suggest that 'the A.I. era risks complicating the riddles of modern strategy further beyond human intention – or perhaps complete human comprehension' (Kissinger et al., 2021). Many others have echoed similar concerns, the biggest being that this transformational revolution has been largely created by the Silicon Valley elites, who have also funded research and innovation in this field. This contrasts strikingly with the development of nuclear technology in the 20th century, which evolved largely under state control and thus was subject to global regulations developed within the UN system.

The US-led militarization and weaponization of communication in the era of 'emerging and disruptive technologies' – AI and robotics, 5G telecommunication networks and the Internet of Things – represent a transformation of both the global economy and global security. In the military domain, countries are developing AI for cyber defence, intelligence, surveillance and logistics. Three centres of AI leadership have emerged across the global security landscape: China, Russia and the United States. Industry estimates suggest that annual global investments in AI are expected to jump from $85 billion in 2021 to more than $204 billion by 2025. Building on satellite applications, 5G telecommunications and cloud computing, information systems can easily and efficiently collect and transmit massive amounts of data, which can now be processed using AI at great speed, providing real-time analytics in support of military operations. The robotics revolution in military evidence by the growing use of drones (mentioned earlier) demonstrates how machine learning is enabling the application of what is called 'lethal autonomous weapons systems' (LAWS) (Bergen et al., 2020).

In 2019, the US Government's Strategic Plan to Advance Cloud Computing in the Intelligence Community noted that the future 'intelligence community cloud environment' will effectively function as a 'force multiplier to enhance our effectiveness' and 'expand flexibility and improve our ability to leverage data', using 'multiple commercial cloud vendors' which promote 'greater innovation and rapid deployment of new capabilities' (Office of the Director of National Intelligence, 2019: 11). Think tanks such as CSIS clearly lay out the benefits of incorporating unclassified, cloud-based, open-source intelligence (Katz et al., 2021),

The Department of Defense has begun the 'comprehensive process of integrating the US military across a commercial cloud platform', working with largest cloud service providers, including Amazon, Microsoft and Google in its 'Joint Warfighting Cloud Capability', a multi-cloud architecture supporting the entire US military to analyse and share data in real time from a command centre to the theatre of operations, accelerating the decision cycle. NATO has selected the French multinational Thales to provide its first defence cloud infrastructure. Networked platforms are now critical to multi-domain operations across NATO countries.

The globalization of AI and machine-learning capabilities has speeded up global communication and the acceleration in the deployment of AI technologies in surveillance, political propaganda and media manipulation is influencing geopolitics. A 2018 report, *The Malicious Use of Artificial Intelligence: Forecasting, Prevention and Mitigation*, written by experts from leading Western universities, think tanks and NGOs, including the Electronic Frontier Foundation, examined three 'domains' of security (digital, physical and political). It investigated how AI could be used to compromise or manipulate political communication by doctoring visual content. 'The use of AI to automate tasks involved in surveillance (e.g., analysing mass-collected data), persuasion (e.g., creating targeted propaganda) and deception (e.g., manipulating videos) may expand threats associated with privacy invasion and social manipulation', notes the report (Electronic Frontier Foundation, 2018: 6).

Innovations in AI-powered biometric and digital surveillance, from facial recognition cameras and cyberespionage weapons to license-plate scanners, have bought more intrusive but softer version of surveillance around the world. In 2021, UN experts called for a moratorium on the sale and transfer of AI-powered surveillance technology, urging 'the international community to develop a robust regulatory framework to prevent, mitigate and redress the negative human rights impact of surveillance technology and pending that, to adopt a moratorium on its sale and transfer' (UN Human Rights Commission, 2021). The Israeli authorities use a facial recognition system known as Red Wolf to track Palestinians and automate harsh restrictions on their freedom of movement, Amnesty International documented in a 2023 report called *Automated Apartheid*.

Authoritarian AI – China

Like the debate about disinformation, the emergence of AI on global communication is also being viewed through the lens of geopolitics: a contest between democratic West, led by the United States, and authoritarian China. Putin has declared that 'whoever controls AI will be the ruler of the world'. AI is transforming warfare, global security and the future of human freedom, argues a commentator associated with the Center for a New American Security, and therefore democracies must protect their values which are being threatened by authoritarian and automated information warfare (Scharre, 2023). One of India's leading defence analysts has warned that in any future conflict with China the 'primary battleground will be in cyberspace and the electromagnetic spectrum' (Sawhney, 2022). AI will contribute to this form of warfare through increased information processing, accelerated decision-making, swarm attacks and cognitive warfare (Takagi, 2022).

Unlike the United States, the Chinese government directly controls its information and telecommunications networks and their supporting hardware, software and standards – as 'potent sources of power', and in 'much of the world, China is already a leading provider of these technologies and has the potential to cement its global dominance' (Markey, 2020: 3–4). Its exports of tools that enable censorship and surveillance offer the country new opportunities to influence other states and 'gain access to their information' (ibid.: 4). China's *Next Generation Artificial Intelligence Development Plan* (AIDP), released by the State Council in 2017, provides a detailed road map for developing an increasingly integrated AI ecosystem under a $150 billion centralized programme to enable China to become the world's leader in AI by 2030 (AIDP, 2017).

An essential part of the Made in China 2025 plan, it seeks to use AI to upgrade China's manufacturing and service industries in order to catch up with the United States, where the plan is viewed as a threat to US domination of this emerging sector (National Security Commission on Artificial Intelligence, 2021). Considering itself as a 'cyber great power', Qin An, director of the China Institute of Cyberspace Strategy, argued in 2016 that 'due to the highly monopolistic nature of information technology systems, it is unlikely that there will be two different systems for military and civilian use. . . . It is particularly necessary [for China] to integrate military and civilian resources through a military-civil fusion system' (cited in Doshi et al., 2021: 4). Xi has consistently emphasized China's commitment to AI development and 'intelligent warfare', most recently at the 20th Party Congress in 2022. The newly established PLA Strategic Support Force has been charged with a mandate to innovate and tasked with integrating numerous 'strategic functions'. To achieve this ambition, the Chinese government is working with its leading private corporations to create its AI 'national team' (Jing and Dai, 2017). Digital entrepreneurs speak of China as an 'AI Superpower' (Lee, 2018).

The US government had already in 2019 issued an Executive Order emphasizing the need to 'maintain American leadership in Artificial Intelligence' (White House, 2019), recognizing that in many IT related fields China was a 'full-spectrum peer competitor' to the United States, laying the intellectual groundwork for a generational advantage in AI, according to 2021 report *The Great Rivalry: China vs. the US in the 21st Century*, from the Harvard Kennedy School (Allison et al., 2021). China also figures prominently as an adversary 'determined to surpass us in AI leadership' in the 756-page, 2021 report of the American National Security Commission on Artificial Intelligence, led by Eric Schmidt, the former CEO of Alphabet, with former US secretary of defense Robert Work as vice chair.

The tone and tenor of the report was termed by one commentator as a case of 'hegemonic anxiety' – the fear of losing global dominance (Naughton, 2021). 'For the first time since World War II, America's technological predominance – the backbone of its economic and military power – is under threat', the report says. 'China possesses the might, talent, and ambition to surpass' the United States as the 'world's leader in AI in the next decade'. 'AI is deepening the threat posed by cyberattacks and disinformation campaigns that Russia, China and others are using to infiltrate our society, steal our data, and interfere in our democracy' (US Government, 2021: 7).

Of the 15 members of the group which wrote the report, eight were from the technology industry including incoming Amazon CEO Andy Jassy, Oracle CEO Safra Catz, Microsoft chief scientific officer Eric Horvitz, former FCC commissioner

Mignon Clyburn and head of Google Cloud AI Andrew Moore. Unsurprisingly, therefore, the recommendations of the report advised minimum regulation on US tech giants, which, unlike their Chinese counterparts 'are not instruments of state power' and thus able to compete and conquer the AI battlefield in which 'America must lead the charge', and that the government should let AI flourish unhindered by bureaucratic hurdles.

The US Department of Defense's report *Military and Security Developments Involving the People's Republic of China 2022* noted that a 'core component of China's strategy is to integrate by 2027 the 'mechanization, informatization, and intelligentization' of its armed forces. The report suggests that the People's Liberation Army (PLA) has been honing the concept of 'Cognitive Domain Operations', an improvisation on concepts such as public opinion and psychological warfare to the modern information environment through the aid of AI with the goal of achieving 'mind dominance', defined as the use of propaganda as a weapon to influence public opinion to effect change in a nation's social system (Department of Defense, 2022: 161).

According to the 2023 report *Private Eyes: China's Embrace of Open-Source Military Intelligence*, published by the US security company Recorded Futures (which claims to be the 'world's largest intelligence company'), China's defence industry takes advantage of other countries' open information environments to extract open source intelligence (OSINT) from foreign governments, militaries, universities, defence industry companies, scientific research organizations, think tanks, news media outlets, social media platforms, forums and commercial data providers. The Chinese military, the report noted, tries to 'learn from other countries' OSINT programmes while also seeking to prevent foreign countries from collecting military OSINT from Chinese sources, which very likely helps preserve the PLA's advantage over the West in OSINT' (Recorded Future, 2023: 1).

There are concerns that AI will further exacerbate the menace of misinformation, particularly in authoritarian societies where there are no democratic mechanisms to rein in government excesses and where such technology can be used to further strengthen surveillance systems and tighten greater control over discourse (Farrell et al., 2022). It is claimed that AI is being used in the surveillance of the Uyghur population in Xinjiang in what one Western advocacy group described as 'Algorithmic oppression with Chinese characteristics' by using AI-enabled facial recognition templates distinguishing 'Uyghur' features (Dely, 2019). However, in democratic societies, too, AI could be used on a massive scale to manipulate information and control narratives, with the potential to subvert democracy.

Wider dangers of AI

There also the danger that AI-infused systems will further accelerate the tempo of battlefield decisions to such a degree that they create entirely new risks of accidental strikes, or decisions made on misleading or deliberately false alerts of incoming attacks (Coy, 2023). As the international race in militarized AI intensifies, systems reading each other's moves could accelerate the danger of actual war since AI can calculate a million times faster than people. Geoffrey Hinton, who worked for Google for many years until 2023, is deeply opposed to the use of AI on the battlefield, what he calls 'robot soldiers' (Metz, 2023). However, sceptics suggest that the data-saturated 'warbots', would be tactically brilliant, though not 'as good as strategists' (Payne, 2021). The Campaign to Stop Killer Robots, an international coalition, has suggested a moratorium on the development of militarized AI, arguing 'Life and death decisions should not be delegated to a machine. It's time for new international law to regulate these technologies'.

A study published in the journal *Scientific American* warned about the consequences of machines taking control, noting that people are being 'remotely controlled ever more successfully', and the trend is moving 'from programming computers to programming people' that allows one to govern the masses 'efficiently without having to involve citizens in democratic processes'. Connecting people and things to 'the Internet of Everything' is a perfect way to obtain the required data as input of cybernetic control strategies (Helbing et al., 2017).

Artificial intelligence tools are now being used to populate 'content farms', referring to low-quality websites around the world that churn out vast amounts of clickbait articles to optimize advertising revenue. NewsGuard, a New York-based organization, identified 49 websites in seven languages – Chinese, Czech, English, French, Portuguese, Tagalog and Thai – generated by AI language models designed to mimic human communication in the form of a typical news website and saturated with advertisements (Sadeghi and Arvanitis, 2023).

Digital deepfakes – realistic and often indistinguishable artificial images, audio, and videos – created by AI can be used to manipulate public opinion and disrupt political and social cohesion in many countries. Deepfake videos of President Zelensky appearing to surrender to invading Russian forces were widely circulated on social media during the initial stages of the Russian invasion. They can also be used to disrupt digital capitalism. One striking example was the circulation of a fake image purporting to show an explosion near the Pentagon, which was shared by multiple verified Twitter accounts with blue check marks, including one that falsely claimed it was associated with Bloomberg News, in May 2023, leading to a brief dip in the stock market. In the moments after the image began circulating on Twitter, the Dow Jones Industrial Average fell about 80 points between 10:06 am and 10:10 am, fully recovering by 10:13 am, CNN reported (O'Sullivan and Passantino, 2023).

In many countries, governments have invested in AI research. In the United States, the Defense Department has traditionally funded most AI research, but now the digital empires are taking control. As major digital platforms enjoy a data advantage, they are also increasingly investing in AI-related research and development, which is deemed key to reaping future benefits from processing and analysing data. AI research takes place mainly in universities, research institutions and private companies. The private tech firms constantly increased their participation in major

AI conferences in the period 2000–2019 (Zhang et al., 2021) and, for the most prestigious ones, they even dominate in the number of submitted papers. Google is by far the leading institution among the top-tier AI research institutions, while Microsoft and Facebook also feature among the top ten (UNCTAD, 2021: 30).

The 2023 AI Index Report, released by the Stanford Institute for Human-Centered Artificial Intelligence, notes that AI investment has significantly increased. In 2022 the amount of private investment in AI was 18 times greater than it was in 2013 (HAI, 2023). According to market research company Verified Market Research, the big five US intelligence conglomerates (Booz Allen Hamilton, CSRA, Leidos, SAIC and CACI International) are making significant commitments to open-source intelligence. As a result, the OSINT industry, valued at $5.1 billion in 2021, is projected to reach $34.9 billion by 2030 (www.verifiedmarketresearch.com/product/open-source-intelligence-osint-market/). The overall generative AI market is expected to exceed $109 billion by 2030, according to the market research firm Grand View Research.

Since ChatGPT, the AI language developed by OpenAI – with its ability to respond to complex questions, generate code and translate languages – was released in November 2022, a new anxiety, in addition to excitement, has emerged across the world. This was rapidly followed by GPT-4, introduced in March 2023 by OpenAI, then part of Microsoft, who added a chatbot, capable of having open-ended text conversations on virtually any topic to its Bing search engine. Google's chatbot Bard (later renamed Gemini) and Baidu's chatbot Ernie, China's first major rival to ChatGPT, were also released.

Some see enormous potential for human well-being: quantum computing and AI could offer new tools in medicine and health care and for peace-making. The use of automated language processing could smooth negotiations, reducing the time spent on consecutive interpretation, thus speeding up negotiations. Some tools will better inform diplomats ahead of talks. IBM's Cognitive Trade Advisor has already assisted negotiators by responding to questions about trade treaties that might otherwise require days or weeks to answer. Intelligent systems can also help negotiators test various positions and scenarios in a matter of minutes (Moore, 2023).

However, many critics are concerned that AI could reduce the role of human judgement, empathy and creativity, arguing that the AI revolution was ultimately a political phenomenon (Simons, 2023). AI could operate as what one commentator has called a 'weapon of math destruction', arguing that data is not neutral and models reflect goals and ideologies – they are 'opinions embedded in mathematics' (O'Neil, 2016) – as well as the biases of its designers, which could be misused, for example, in facial recognition software used for surveillance (Russell, 2019).

In an essay for the *New York Times*, Noam Chomsky, along with Ian Roberts, professor of linguistics at the University of Cambridge, and Jeffrey Watumull, director of AI at Oceanit, a science and technology company, argued that the human mind is not like 'ChatGPT and its ilk' but 'a surprisingly efficient and even elegant system that operates with small amounts of information; it seeks not to infer brute correlations among data points but to create explanations'. 'ChatGPT and its brethren . . . either overgenerate (producing both truths and falsehoods, endorsing ethical and unethical decisions alike) or undergenerate (exhibiting noncommitment to any decisions and indifference to consequences). Given the amorality, faux science and linguistic incompetence of these systems, we can only laugh or cry at their popularity' (Chomsky et al., 2023).

More than 1,300 technology leaders and researchers, including Elon Musk and Apple co-founder Steve Wozniak, signed an open letter released by the US-based Future of Life Institute (which received its biggest donation from Musk), saying that the current rate of AI progress was becoming a 'dangerous race to ever-larger unpredictable black-box models'. The 'emergent capabilities' of these models, the letter said, should be 'refocused on making today's powerful, state-of-the-art systems more accurate, safe, interpretable, transparent, robust, aligned, trustworthy and loyal'.

The letter called for a six-month moratorium on the development of new systems because AI technologies pose 'profound risks to society and humanity', as 'powerful AI systems should be developed only once we are confident that their effects will be positive and their risks will be manageable'. This was followed by a letter from the Association for the Advancement of Artificial Intelligence, a 40-year-old academic society, also warning of the risks of AI. In a survey highlighted in the 2023 AI Index Report released by the Stanford Institute for Human-Centered Artificial Intelligence, 36 per cent of researchers said AI-made decisions could lead to a 'nuclear-level catastrophe', while 73 per cent said they could soon lead to 'revolutionary societal change' (HAI, 2023).

Regulating AI

As a way to address the threats from AI-generated or manipulated media, there is a growing movement pointing towards the need for disclosure when synthetic media has been created or shared (e.g., the EU Code of Practice on Disinformation or Partnership on AI's Synthetic Media Code of Conduct). 'Disclosure' can take the form of labelling, or of other less visible techniques such as inserting forensic trace that are machine-readable, or metadata that contains information about its provenance. Who would formulate such laws? Will AI be another US-originated communication system whose protocols the rest of the world will have to follow? The United States has announced a National Standards Strategy for Critical and Emerging Technology, which includes sections on the topic of AI. Washington and Brussels are trying to lay the groundwork for global governance of AI through the bilateral Trade and Technology Council, while the digital ministers of the G-7 group of countries speak of 'responsible AI and global AI governance'.

The OECD recommends that governments should foster a 'digital ecosystem' for 'trustworthy AI', which includes 'digital technologies and infrastructure' and mechanisms for sharing AI knowledge'. It also recommends promoting mechanisms, such as 'data trusts', to support the 'safe, fair, legal and ethical sharing of data' (OECD, 2020: 324). Governments should 'promote the development of multi-stakeholder, consensus-driven global technical standards for interoperable and trustworthy AI' (ibid.: 328). The World Economy Forum Insight Report in November 2022, written in collaboration with Accenture, KPMG and PwC, proposed a framework for 'digital trust': 'Digital trust is individuals' expectation that digital technologies and services – and the organizations providing them – will protect all stakeholders' interests and uphold societal expectations and values'. . . . Between states (and private enterprises), questions of digital sovereignty, data trade and other issues will significantly impact digital trust in the coming years' (World Economic Forum, 2022: 34).

As with the governance of the internet, the subtext again is that authoritarian AI is not trustworthy. The 'OECD/G20 (read Western) AI Principles' are framing the global debate over AI policy, as more than 50 countries have endorsed these. India, for example, had indicated it would take a more independent line on AI policies and practices but is now seeking to harmonize its approach to AI with the OECD countries. The security aspect of AI also reflects current geopolitical shifts as India appears to be increasingly aligned with the US position – notably at the Quadrilateral Security Dialogue which links it with the United States, Australia and Japan.

In a networked world, it has been argued, 'The state with the most connections will be the central player, able to set the global agenda and unlock innovation and sustainable growth. Here, the United States has a clear and sustainable edge' (Slaughter, 2009: 95). Countries such as the United States can 'weaponize networks – to gather information or choke off economic and information flows, discover and exploit vulnerabilities, compel policy change, and deter unwanted actions' (Farrell and Newman, 2019: 45). In this the United States can deploy its 'structural power over financial and cyber networks' (Drezner et al., 2021: 4). In a 2020 special issue of the journal *Security Dialogue*, Der Derian and Wendt expressed the fear that, with the transformations in the nature, production and distribution of power and knowledge caused by quantum computing, there will be a new division into 'quantum haves' and 'quantum have-nots'. As with every powerful new technology, 'the effort to weaponize quantum has already begun' (Der Derian and Wendt, 2020: 401).

Tech giants such as Meta have provided free access to the AI technology with a view to generate new ideas. In 2023, Meta, which had created an AI technology called LLaMA (Large Language Model Meta AI), decided to give it away as open-source software – computer code that can be freely copied, modified and reused – providing outsiders with everything they needed to quickly build chatbots of their own. At the same time, they stated: 'We believe that the entire AI community – academic researchers, civil society, policymakers, and industry – must work together to develop clear guidelines around responsible AI in general and responsible large language models in particular' (Meta, 2023). Microsoft, while lobbying to limit regulation, also admits: 'Overall, elucidating the nature and mechanisms of AI systems such as GPT-4 is a formidable challenge that has suddenly become important and urgent' (Microsoft Research, 2023: 95).

There has been a concerted effort by what we have described as digital empires with support from their respective governments to globalize AI and to ensure that this happens with limited public scrutiny. As the Brussels-based Corporate Europe Observatory has reported, the EU has faced intense corporate lobbying, mainly from the US tech giants, to moderate the proposed EU legal framework on AI, introduced in 2021. The EU Commission proposed a risk-based approach to regulating AI, meaning that as the risk increases, AI systems have to conform to stricter rules. Tech companies sought to reduce requirements for high-risk AI systems and limit the scope of the regulation. The Software Alliance argued for rejecting strong regulation as it would 'impact' AI development in Europe and 'hamper innovation'. The 'balance between voluntary and regulatory approaches' refers to the EU's approach of regulation versus the United States' voluntary frameworks and self-assessment tools.

Another argument the US government and tech firms deployed in their lobbying blitz was that the EU's strict regulation on AI would stifle innovation, which in turn would benefit competitors like China. Over recent years, the use of ethical guidelines has become a powerful tool in Big Tech's lobbying toolbox. It allowed tech companies to argue they're on the right side of history. Days after the Commission launched its proposal, Microsoft asked for a meeting to discuss 'the right balance on the regulatory front' and where the AI Act 'put Europe in the global scheme of things between the US and especially China, where AI is less regulated and where investments are spiralling?' Google topped the list of the number of MEP meetings attended by lobbyists, at 28. Its CEO in a meeting with Commission president argued that 'the transatlantic relationship . . . on responsible AI [is] even more important since [Russian] aggression against [Ukraine]'. Such think tanks as Centre for European Policy Studies, funded by big tech, had a crucial role in diluting the regulation on AI (Schyns, 2023).

The presence of digital superstars Elon Mask was striking at the first global 'summit' on AI held in 2023, symbolically at Britain's Bletchley Park, the site for communication 'codebreakers' during World War II, and an 'international declaration' it produced suggested a light-touch regulation for the rapidly developing industry.

6
EMERGING CONTOURS OF A NEW GLOBAL COMMUNICATION ORDER

The 'unipolar moment' that defined the post-Cold War world seems to be ending: in 1990, the US's mission, as one leading commentator wrote in *Foreign Affairs*, was to use 'American strength and will . . . to lead a unipolar world, unashamedly laying down the rules of world order and being prepared to enforce them' (Krauthammer, 1990). This global order, with its Western imprint, is being challenged in a growing geopolitical and geo-economic competition between the United States and its European and other allies, on the one hand, and Russia and China, on the other. Many commentators fear the decline of the 'rules-based' and 'liberal' international order and the triumph of populist authoritarian values and norms in a 'clash of civilizations' (Huntington, 1996). According to two leading scholars of international relations, 'The international system is at a historical inflection point. As Asia continues its economic ascent, two centuries of Western domination of the world, first under Pax Britannica and then under Pax Americana, are coming to an end' (Haass and Kupchan, 2021).

The *Munich Security Report* 2020 noted a widespread feeling of uneasiness and restlessness in the face of increasing uncertainty about the enduring purpose of the West, which it refers to as 'Westlessness'. What does it mean for the world if the West leaves the stage to others? A multitude of security challenges seem to have become inseparable from what some describe as the decay of the Western project (Munich Security Conference, 2020). According to the report, 'Western societies and governments appear to have lost a common understanding of what it even means to be part of the West. Although perhaps the most important strategic challenge for the transatlantic partners, it appears uncertain whether the West can come up with a joint strategy for a new era of great-power competition' (ibid.).

Although the Russian invasion of Ukraine in 2022 brought the West closer in geopolitical terms, the effects, particularly on Germany, have made an increasingly vulnerable EU even more dependent on and subservient to the United States. The feeling of Europe under threat was indicated in October 2022 by Europe's senior most diplomat, Josep Borrell, at the inauguration of the new European Diplomatic Academy in Bruges. He compared Europe to a garden and the world to a jungle: 'The gardeners have to go to the jungle. Europeans have to be much more engaged with the rest of the world. Otherwise, the rest of the world will invade us, by different ways and means'. Despite regular exhortations about protecting freedom, democracy and the liberal world order, the Western ability to set and communicate the global narrative seems to be being eroded.

However, others point out the danger of 'the America trap' – the tendency among enemies and rivals of the United States to underestimate what the country can accomplish (Kagan, 2023) – and argue that US hegemony will continue because it has the largest population among the developed countries: 'If the United States can begin to repair its human capital base and forge new alliances for the twenty-first century, it can strengthen – with the aid of demographics – Pax Americana for generations to come' (Eberstadt, 2019: 157).

Yet Pax Americana is facing real challenges, especially in the geopolitics of the global South, notably in Africa where in the past two decades Chinese investment – with all its associated interests and influence – has soared, although the biggest sources of foreign direct investment in the continent are still the corporations based in France, the United States and Britain. More than one million Chinese speakers now live in Africa. Other nations including Türkiye, India, Brazil, Israel, Saudi Arabia and the United Arab Emirates have also deepened diplomatic and commercial ties with Africa to challenge Western domination. Russia has been reenergizing its Cold War-era ties with many African nations where the Soviet Union supported anti-colonial liberation movements, for example, in Angola (1975–1992), Mozambique (1977–1992) and the Ogaden conflict between Ethiopia and Somalia (1977–1978). In an age of market-driven politics, today's Russia is extracting natural resources in many African countries in return for security assistance.

The Russian security presence in Africa – including in the digital domain – has increased in recent years, with states in the Sahel region expelling French military advisors, with six coups in the past 18 months. These military ties were strengthened by the 2019 Russia-Africa Summit, where the Kremlin signed deals worth an estimated $12.2 billion, with more than 30 African countries to supply military equipment and 50 contracts, agreements and Memoranda of Understanding covering economic, military, environmental and nuclear sectors. In addition, Russia has signed at least 16 contracts for nuclear cooperation agreements with African states (IISS, 2018) and, during the pandemic, it donated more than 300 million doses of Sputnik V Covid-19 vaccine direct to the African Union (Reuters, 2021).

In the Middle East too, 'the rest' is gaining new ground as US dominance wanes and the strategic rivalry with China and Russia provides opportunities for regional powers to balance their security and economic ties with both power centres. The announcement of normalized diplomatic relations in 2020 between Israel and UAE, marking the first new regional partnership for Israel since Jordan in 1994, was hailed in the US media as a 'geopolitical earthquake' (Friedman, 2020). As the region's largest trading partner, China played a crucial role in its 2022 mediation between Saudi Arabia and Iran, which led to the resumption of diplomatic ties between the two main regional arch-rivals. Russia's relationships with countries in the region – especially Iran – remain strong, while it is also promoting its defence deals with countries such as UAE. India and Türkiye, too, have increased their footprint in the region, complementing, if not, challenging Western influence. The members of the Gulf Cooperation Council are also boosting their security and economic development through ties with Russia, China, and India, while maintaining their strategic autonomy.

Is BRICS building an alternative geopolitical order?

As the West recedes, groupings such as BRICS have increased their global imprint. As noted in the Introduction, BRICS was originally a Russian project, which was co-opted by China to demonstrate it was not the only 'rising' power, so as not to alarm the West. However, China remains the leading member of the group. Such groupings as the BRICS and the Shanghai Cooperation Organisation (SCO) are offering alternative geopolitical and financial perspectives to counter the Western hegemony embedded in the international financial system through institutions like the IMF and the World Bank. The creation in 2014 of the BRICS's New Development Bank (NDB) as an alternative to the Bretton Woods institutions has sparked the interest of many countries in the global South. Some have made a case for setting up a New Bretton Woods to address the economic fallout from the Covid-19 pandemic and develop an alternative and sustainable post-Covid world economic order (Gallagher and Kozul-Wright, 2021). During the 2023 BRICS summit in Johannesburg, six new countries were admitted: Egypt, UAE, Saudi Arabia, Iran, Argentina (though Argentina later decided not to join) and Ethiopia. Indonesia and Türkiye, too, want to join. Joining the BRICS might allow members to trade in their own currencies and reduce, if not end, their dollar dependence (see below).

BRICS and multilateral institutions

BRICS countries endorse multipolarity and have demanded a greater voice in international institutions. As a veto-wielding permanent member of the UN Security Council since 1979, China already had a say at the highest table of global governance but, in recent decades, its influence within the UN system has grown. After the United States (which accounts for 22 per cent of the UN's budget, though the country is the top debtor to the UN being $1 billion in arrears), China is the second largest contributor, at 12 per cent. In 2020, out of the UN's 15 specialized agencies, four – the Food and Agriculture Organization (FAO), the International

Civil Aviation Organization (ICAO), the ITU and the UN Industrial Development Organization (UNIDO) – were headed by Chinese nationals. However, to put it in perspective, in the same year, among senior positions at the UN at assistant secretary general level and higher, there were 26 US nationals compared to three Chinese (United Nations, 2020).

The Rand report, part of a project entitled *A China-Russia Axis: Making Mischief Together?*, sponsored by the US Army, notes that 'China and Russia could collaborate more in the United Nations, in regional crises, or in influence operations' (Radin et al., 2021: xviii). The most 'significant logic driving Chinese and Russian alignment', the report suggested, 'is balancing against US hard and soft power' and the 'impetus behind closer cooperation across political, military, and economic spheres is the common perception in Moscow and Beijing that Washington had become more hostile and threatening to the two Eurasian capitals in recent years' (Radin et al., 2021: 267). Sino-Russian collaboration has many dimensions: in 2023 Russia's National Research University, Moscow Power Engineering Institute, announced the establishment of a Chinese campus in Wenchang county, home to China's fourth spaceport, which will specialize in 'aviation and aerospace teaching and research' (Wong, 2023).

From 2001, Russia, India and China were involved in a trilateral engagement forum (RIC), before becoming part of the BRICS grouping. In 2017 India also became a full member of the Shanghai Cooperation Organization (SCO) and, when China proposed the formation of the Asia Infrastructure Investment Bank (AIIB), India signed up as a founding member, with the highest voting power after China, and remains one of the main recipients of AIIB funding. Nevertheless, the two countries espouse different political values: one being a one-party authoritarian state and the other a multi-party democracy.

As the world's most populous country and its largest democracy, India claims greater geopolitical heft than before: under Modi's government India now describes itself as the 'mother of democracy' (Tanwar and Kadam, 2022). India seeks the support of the other BRICS partners with a greater degree of democratic polity. Brazilian president Lula da Silva has developed stronger ties with China and Russia, while maintaining partnerships with the West: as his finance minister stated, Brazil is 'too big to be choosing partners' (Harris and Leahy, 2023). South Africa, too, has demonstrated a careful balancing act in dealing with this conundrum, at one level aware of being a dynamic democracy with free and fair elections, a vibrant press and an independent judiciary, despite apartheid's brutal legacy and the need for investment from an undemocratic China (Lieberman, 2022).

However, although a founding member of BRICS, India is seen with some suspicion by its fellow BRICS partners, Russia and China, as being a close ally of the United States. China has opposed India's membership on the Nuclear Suppliers Group and is the only country among the permanent five members of the UN Security Council to consistently oppose India's long-held demand to be a member of the Council. During the Cold War, the US nuclear industry supported

Indian reactors and 'non-proliferation was swept aside for business interests and Cold War geopolitics' (Sarkar, 2022: 195), the argument being that a democratic non-communist India could function as a geopolitical counterweight to authoritarian communist China. In the current geopolitical environment, when the United States wants to 'de-risk' its dependence on Chinese delivery chains, India is seen as an alternative site for developing superconductors and other high-end products with interesting parallels to the Cold War.

In addition, China sees India as a potential threat to its claim to be the leader of the global South. India's presidency of the G-20 in 2023 was an opportunity that it used to the fullest to re-establish its credentials as an articulate voice for the global South, with its long tradition of Non-Alignment. A virtual summit, the 'Voice of the Global South', was held in New Delhi in January 2023, attended by representatives from 125 countries. During the inaugural address, Modi called for a global agenda of the 4Rs 'respond, recognize, respect and reform' to re-energize the world, arguing that 'this meant responding to the priorities of the Global South, recognizing the principle of 'Common but Differentiated Responsibilities', respecting the sovereignty of all nations, and reforming international institutions to make them more relevant'. Providing further impetus to these key processes of amplifying the voice of the Global South, India ensured that the African Union was given full membership of the G-20 at the summit in September 2023 in New Delhi.

Although India cooperates with China at a multilateral level in such areas as expanding economic globalization within WTO, international institutional reform and tackling climate change, it was the only major economy from the global South not to join the BRI. Instead, it became part of QUAD to deter Chinese expansion in the South China Sea and the Indian Ocean (Pardesi, 2022). However, unlike its Western allies, India avoids raising such contentious issues for China as Tibet, Taiwan and Xinjiang, while India's official reaction and criticism on the passage of the new national security law in Hong Kong was muted.

Given China's economic and military power and India's rising global profile, the dynamics of China-India relations will have a profound effect on the shape of the international order. In 2016, former State Department official in the Obama administration argued that 'China and India will increasingly dictate the terms of global governance. Along with the United States and Europe, they will become the new indispensable powers – whether they rise peacefully or not' (Manuel, 2016: 2–3, also see essays in Bajpai et al., 2020).

Some analysts argued that increasing economic co-operation between the two nations, despite political differences, will lead to an era of 'Chindia' (Ramesh, 2005; Thussu, 2013b), while others point to the entrenched rivalry, especially at the regional level (Pant, 2016). Bajpai has suggested that 'negative mutual perceptions, unresolved and stalemated conflict over territory, rival strategic partnerships, and power asymmetry' as four factors accounting for why China and India 'are not friends' (Bajpai, 2021). The border dispute – which led to a fatal confrontation between the two armies in Galwan in 2020 – has brought the relationship to its lowest point in recent decades. However, one area that brings together the mutual interests of the BRICS countries and aspiring members of the group is the move to de-dollarization, which is of high strategic significance in determining the foundations/shape of the future global order.

BRICS and de-dollarization

It is no coincidence that the BRICS emerged in the wake of the 2007–2008 financial crisis, a largely Western problem since the European and American financial systems are so deeply intertwined (Tooze, 2018). Russia was already selling gas supplies to China in yuan and roubles; the dollar and euro are used in less than half of Russia's export settlements, while India, the world's third largest importer of oil, paid for most Russian oil in non-dollar currencies, including the UAE's dirham and rouble, according to Reuters. Another BRICS member Brazil was also using the yuan in its financial transactions and trade settlements, reflecting China's increasing regional presence through expanding trade, investments, development and infrastructure projects.

Being aware that dependence on the dollar – and the dollar-based global financial system – is a strategic vulnerability that stands in the way of China's geopolitical ambitions, China has been trying for more than a decade to carve out a bigger global role for the yuan and insulate China from the potential weaponization of the dollar. The United States has been increasingly willing to sanction foreign individuals and institutions by denying them access to US financial markets and dollar payments networks, the fulcrum of the international financial system. China is aware that one day it could be on the receiving end of the same sort of punitive financial sanctions that Washington has imposed on Russia in response to its invasion of Ukraine. A globally accepted yuan could also bolster its claim to represent a viable alternative order to the one led by the United States. China 'wants to be able to purchase what it needs from other countries using its own currency and its own payments systems. It wants to reduce its dependence on the dollar and achieve greater financial self-reliance' (Choyleva and McMahon, 2022: vii).

To make the yuan cheaper and more convenient to use, Beijing is improving the payments system used to transact in yuan. The launch of a digital currency – the e-CNY – and the development of CIPS (China's cross-border trade settlement and communications platform) are examples of what China is planning to do. Western financial sanctions against Russia will give the yuan a boost as Russian firms turn to CIPS as an alternative to SWIFT. Beijing formally launched its drive to make the yuan an international currency in 2009 and yet, despite China's status as the world's second-largest economy and the largest trading nation, its currency lags not just the dollar and the euro in terms of global usage, but the pound and the yen as well (Choyleva and McMahon, 2022).

The Russian invasion of Ukraine in 2022 and the resultant widespread sanctions on Russia by Western governments and corporations have brought the issue of de-dollarization to the fore. In June 2022, Putin said that the BRICS were working on developing a new reserve currency based on a basket of currencies for its member countries. BRICS has emerged as a 'rising power de-dollarization coalition,' bringing together the initiatives taken by members to reduce currency risk and bypass US sanctions. BRICS' 'coalitional de-dollarization initiatives' have established a critical infrastructure for a prospective alternative global financial system (Liu and Papa, 2022).

BRICS could develop something like the IMF's special drawing rights, a reserve currency based on a basket of largely Western currencies, around 40 per cent dollar, 30 per cent euro. BRICS certainly has the heft to do this: in the past two decades, the BRICS nations' share of global output at market prices has risen from 8.4 to 25.5 per cent, most of this due to the extraordinary growth of China. A BRICS currency challenging US hegemony in foreign exchange may further increase this dependence on Beijing. However, in such an alternative system the dollar's depreciation would also decrease the value of BRICS nations' large holdings of dollar-denominated assets, so it is unlikely that the US dollar will be replaced with another global hegemonic currency, despite the group's support for yuan internationalization. However, given BRICS' political and economic significance, its joint de-dollarization initiatives are likely to directly impact the US dollar's dominance and US leadership of the global financial system.

BRICS changing the geopolitics of the internet

A Russian study has noted that Asia will be the site of future developments in the technology of the internet, as 'massive data from China, India and other Asian countries will help pioneer many of the new technological developments' (Kulik and Korovkin, 2021: 81). In addition, the BRICS countries, especially Russia and China, have distinctive positions on how the internet should be governed, as cyberspace is becoming increasingly regionalized in terms of approaches to security (Thussu, 2021). Russia and India are seen as 'natural partners in the process of shaping the principles of the new digital world, and their efforts, if stepped up, would benefit the international community as a whole, not just the two countries' (Kulik and Korovkin, 2021: 91).

In the West, concerns of a security nature have arisen due to the potential for China's technical standards to fragment the internet. China's drive for technological dominance has resulted in the creation of native technologies which reflect local policies and politics, micromanagement of the internet from the top down and the use of international standards development organizations (SDOs), such as the ITU, to legitimize and protect these technologies in the global marketplace (Hoffmann et al., 2020). Alternative internet technologies based on a new 'decentralized internet infrastructure' are being developed in SDOs and marketed by Chinese companies. These alternative technologies and a suite of supporting standards could splinter the global internet's shared and ubiquitous architecture (ibid.).

This may also pave the way to a new form of internet governance, one that is multilateral instead of multistakeholder, according to Digital Policy and Cyber Security, Oxford Information Labs. China is promoting a 'decentralized internet infrastructure ... but the proposals would in fact lead to more centralised (i.e. government) control over networks and users' data', it says. Ultimately governments will be able to 'create an internet with more control over their citizens' (Hoffmann et al., 2020: 255). Similar apprehensions about the changing geopolitics of global technical standardization have also been voiced by French think tanks (see, e.g., Seaman, 2020).

Towards de-globalization?

The phase of US-led neo-liberal globalization, which lasted from the end of the Cold War to the 2008 economic crisis, has witnessed 'the rise of the rest', with China being the most important element in the new global geopolitical configuration. Kevin Rudd, a former Australian prime minister and China specialist, has advocated a 'managed strategic competition' between China and the United States to avoid war, as China represents 'the most politically and ideologically disciplined challenger it has ever faced during its century of geopolitical dominance' (Rudd, 2022). He cautions that US strategists should avoid 'mirror imaging' and 'should not assume that Beijing will act in ways that Washington would construe as rational or serving China's self-interests. The West won an ideological contest in the 20th century. But China is not the Soviet Union, not least because China now has the second-largest economy in the world' (Rudd, 2022).

Unlike the Soviet Union, the United States' ideological adversary during the Cold War, China is deeply integrated into the world economy and, despite very close economic ties with the West, it has retained its distinctive, state-led capitalist model (Weber, 2021). The leading Western governments and corporations based there have been complicit in supporting China's 'authoritarian' capitalism, contributing in a fundamental way to nourishing Beijing's hegemonic aspirations (Dirlik, 2017). China as a 'risen' country has been seen in the West as 'an externalised, separate, and self-contained 'Other', the premise serving to 'obscure rather than enlighten, and ultimately produces a distorted image of both China and the world' (Franceschini and Loubere, 2022: 5). Western strategists should focus, it has been argued, on the 'processes underpinning Chinese globalization – on the linkages and parallels, continuities and evolutions, as well as the ruptures, resulting from the intensification of Chinese entanglements in the global system' (ibid.: 58). An insider account attests to these, as observed by Cai Xia, a professor at the Central Party School of the Chinese Communist Party from 1998 to 2012. 'Xi has decided to directly challenge the United States and pursue a China-centric world order' (Xia, 2022: 98).

Sino-globalization via the Belt and Road Initiative

Sino-globalization is primarily visible in Asia, where it has been, traditionally, a civilizational power, along with India, which has shaped historical imagination, scientific discoveries and cultural exchanges. Many BRI projects are centred on Asia, the home of the Silk Route, and Afghanistan is the latest country to be integrated into this, given its rich mineral resources and geostrategic location at the crossroads of Central and South Asia, as well as China, Russia and Iran. As well as being its biggest trading partner, China is also the largest investor in mineral resources in Afghanistan, having acquired some of the largest mining contracts, including drilling rights in the Amu Darya Basin and exploration rights in the Aynak copper mine. Creation of transportation networks is crucial for the export of natural resources, and China is using its BRI infrastructure to develop these, especially extending the China-Pakistan Economic Corridor (CPEC) to Afghanistan (Johny and Krishnan, 2022).

In late 2022, China signed a $540 million deal with the Taliban regime to develop oil and gas fields – the first large investment in Afghanistan since the Taliban took power in August 2021. Such developments alarm India, which sees this as undermining India's traditional domination of the South Asian region (Pardesi, 2022). China is also investing in developing digital infrastructure including the PEACE (Pakistan and East Africa Connecting Europe) cable. As a flagship project of BRI, CPEC has been projected as a great success story, and China has, since 2015, organized a CPEC Media Forum with Pakistan, ensuring that Chinese projects receive good coverage in Pakistani media. In 2017 China launched a weekly newspaper *Huashang* (Pure Business) to communicate its achievements (Hassan, 2021). In Southeast Asia, where the Association of Southeast Asian Nations (ASEAN) is one of China's largest trading partners, Beijing has endeavoured to thwart the strategic autonomy of ASEAN, exploiting the differences among its members to limit criticisms of geopolitical issues such as Beijing's claims to the South China Sea (Emmerson, 2020).

The Middle East

The Gulf Cooperation Council (GCC) has close economic and security ties with China (Evron, 2019), which replaced the EU in 2020 as the GCC's largest trading partner, with bilateral trade valued at more than $161 billion. China's presence in major infrastructure projects, such as Qatar's Lusail Stadium and high-speed rail lines in Saudi Arabia, provides lucrative opportunities for Chinese companies (Ahmed, 2016). The UAE is China's largest export market and non-oil trading partner in the region, and the country has also been a hub for Chinese Covid-19 vaccine production (Zoubir and Tran, 2021). While China has been touted as a potential security partner, its primary interests in the region continue to be expanding its commercial reach and locking in energy supplies, while avoiding any security entanglements (Lons et al., 2019), though in recent years, China has sought to play a security role through the export of defence technology. A 2019 report about Saudi Arabia cooperating with China to develop missiles, for example, provoked considerable debate in the United States, even though Saudi Arabia sources only a tiny portion of its overall arms purchases from China (Freymann, 2021; Fulton, 2022).

Latin America

China's growing presence in Latin America and the Caribbean (LAC) has eroded traditional US dominance in the region: as many as 21 countries are participating in the BRI, with Argentina joining in 2022. Beijing's clout is also apparent in its ability to isolate Taiwan: Between 2017 and 2023, five countries in the region – Panama, the Dominican Republic, El Salvador, Nicaragua and Honduras – have severed their diplomatic relations with Taiwan, prompting Taipei to accuse Beijing of using 'coercion and intimidation' to lure away its few remaining allies.

A key explanation for this shift is economic: total China-LAC trade increased from almost $18 billion in 2002 to $318 billion in 2020. According to the China Global Investment Tracker database, maintained by the American Enterprise Institute, between 2005 and 2021, China's investments in the region amounted to $140 billion, with Brazil accounting for $64 billion, and energy projects accounting for 59 per cent of investments (American Enterprise Institute, 2022). Brazil also has the highest number of Confucius Institutes in the region, while Argentina is partnering with China for establishing an aerospace station in Patagonia. Creating telecommunication and information networks is a particularly crucial element for understanding the changes in China's messaging in the region, exemplified by *Program Hoy*, a TV show, a result of the partnership between CCTV Video News Agency (CCTV+) and Alianza Informativa Latinoamericana, the biggest non-profit television network alliance in the region. As many as 22 mainstream media outlets in 21 countries and regions have benefitted with deploying technology for 5G connectivity and satellite links via Huawei (Duarte et al., 2022).

The new 'scramble for Africa'

Perhaps the most important impact of Sino-globalization can be witnessed in Africa, where China is investing in infrastructure as part of the BRI. This includes such projects as a new railway linking Nairobi to the coastal port at Mombasa in Kenya, a new port in Alexandria in Egypt and copper mines and construction sites in Zambia, Africa's copper giant (Lee, 2017). China is also transforming the continent's information space by providing information and communication hardware to expand access to the internet and mobile phones; training African broadcasters via exchange programmes; and setting up an Africa-specific channel of CGTN, as well as Xinhua offering its content free of charge to some media organizations, to promote 'ideological biases' (Grassi, 2014; Umejei, 2020). One African scholar has discussed this in the context of dichotomies as 'upstairs' and 'downstairs' to indicate two different types of gatekeepers: those concerned with letting in issues that pertain to Chinese economic and political interests (Chinese gatekeepers or upstairs gatekeepers) versus African editors (downstairs), who are given the mandate to control information not pertaining to China, or not harmful to Chinese policies' (Umejei, 2020: 55).

Concern about Chinese aid to the continent is creating tensions with the West (Blair et al., 2022) but, unlike the West, China is not prone to delivering homilies to Africans on freedom, democracy and human rights, therefore making themselves less intrusive in governance, a situation favoured by African elites. China's media strategies for developing states, including those in Africa, may also entail policing the information space for geopolitics, security and citizenship (Zhang et al., 2016; Gagliardone, 2019).

Another sign of Chinese cultural presence is the expansion of Confucius Institutes, which, in some cases, such as that of Ethiopia, could be seen as 'pragmatic enticement' (Repnikova, 2022b). In 2022, a $40 million facility in Tanzania funded by the Chinese Communist Party was opened to train cadres from ruling parties: its 120 students from six countries, with all the political entities taking part, had ruled their countries without interruption since independence (Nyabiage, 2022).

Communicating Sino-globalization

In parallel with its economic and military prowess, under President Xi, China has heavily invested in promoting its soft power, to influence global public opinion, as well as to mitigate international criticism of the one-party state. This 'discourse power' is being deployed to legitimize a Chinese version of globalization, as well as to undermine the country's geopolitical adversaries. Building a global 'community with a shared future', as an alternative worldview to the dominant US-defined 'unilateral' approach, is a central theme in this discourse – which also emphasizes such principles as 'non-interference' in the internal affairs of other nations and protecting and preserving 'state sovereignty' (Thibaut, 2022).

Such efforts are part of the push to promote Chinese narratives and mitigate international criticism. Communication formed part of the concept of 'comprehensive national power' (*zonghe guoli*) under Deng Xiaoping but, in the past two decades, soft power has become a fashionable term in China. The expansion of Confucius Institutes formed part of the public diplomacy infrastructure envisaged as part of Sino-globalization (Hartig, 2015). As Chinese cultural presence is resented especially in the West, for example, in the case of Confucius Institutes (Sahlins, 2015), the communicating part has become more challenging as their coverage in the media has been generally negative (Brazys and Dukalskis, 2019).

In contrast with many other nations that are cutting costs on public diplomacy, China has 'devoted significant resources to communicating its values and culture amid the intensification of its global footprint' (Zhang and Schultz, 2022: 2), and

China's international media is contributing significantly to achieve this geopolitical goal (see Zhang et al., 2016). China has invested billions of dollars in the past two decades to communicate its version of geopolitics to a largely unresponsive, not to say apathetic, global audience (Fifield, 2020). To communicate BRI to such an audience, in 2017, the Chinese authorities created the Belt and Road News Network, comprising 208 media organizations from 98 countries and whose board is chaired by the *People's Daily*, to tell the stories about the BRI in a way that 'shapes healthy public opinion and helps the BRI yield more substantial results for people living in countries along the Belt and Road' (Belt and Road News Network, 2019; Fifield, 2020).

While this approach of legitimizing Sino-globalization has international ambitions, the focus seems to be on the global South, which is considered to be more amenable to Communist Party-approved narratives, given these countries' dependence on Chinese largesse. One strategy to achieve this is 'using international friends for international propaganda' relying on and co-opting the voices of influential foreigners to spread pro-China narratives. Chinese state media have regularly used foreign voices to speak out on China's interests, for example, Xinhua's 'Through Foreign Eyes' (Brown, 2020).

In a 2021 speech to the Central Committee, Xi stressed that China must 'expand [its] international communication through international friends', who will be the country's 'top soldiers of propaganda against the enemy' (Xinhua, 2021). This message was reiterated at the 20th National Congress of the party in October 2022 where the Chinese President instructed the party's Central Propaganda Department to 'accelerate the development of Chinese discourse and narrative systems, effectively communicate the voice of China, and portray a credible, lovable, and respectable image of China', a difficult task given the congress was taking place at a time of lockdowns precipitated by Covid-19.

The other strategy is what is referred to as 'borrowing a boat out to sea', using international platforms to spread propaganda, including expanding the media footprint, conducting propaganda campaigns and leveraging Beijing's influence to gain government support for its initiatives in multilateral settings like the UN, as well as Beijing-sponsored regional forums such as the Forum on China-Africa Cooperation (FOCAC), the Forum of China and the Community of Latin American and Caribbean States (China-CELAC Forum) and the China-Arab States Cooperation Forum (CASCF).

While the official Chinese media has been instrumental in propagating a Chinese version of globalization, there is also growing evidence of privately owned and professionally managed news media emanating from the one-party state, notably Caixin media group, providing authoritative financial and business news to a global audience. Caixin offers the English news via a 24/7 website and an English-language magazine *Caixin Weekly*, which started publication in 2010 and has a wide global readership (Meng and Zhang, 2022).

Mandarin TV, a bilingual Chinese and French TV channel, renamed *Europe TV* in 2021, broadcasts its programmes to 135 million homes across Europe. *Modern*

Silk Road (*Modernİpek Yolu*) was launched in 2017 in Türkiye, where leading newspapers such as *Hürriyet*, *Sabah*, and *Cumhuriyet* have published full-page advertorials about China. One outcome of such strategies is that Ankara has substantially toned down its criticisms of Chinese policy on Uyghur Muslims, which is appreciated by the Chinese side as a policy of 'strategic silence' (Üngör, 2022).

In 2018, Xinhua signed an agreement with Germany's national news agency *Deutsche Presse-Agentur* (DPA), to produce a newsletter called the Xinhua Silk Road Information Service, whose database continues to promote the BRI vision to the world (https://en.imsilkroad.com/). Media content that is controlled by the Chinese state has been published in outlets ranging from *Süddeutsche Zeitung* to *Handelsblatt*. The logic is that paid-for editorial content appearing in prestigious international publications gives it a credibility that would otherwise not be afforded if disseminated directly from Chinese media, raising concerns about growing Chinese influence in Europe (Ohlberg et al., 2018).

In addition to these legacy media, China has been actively using digital communication, including 'clickbaits' to compete for visibility in the global media sphere (Lu and Pan, 2021). An Australian think tank report claimed that 'foreign social media influencers are creating content about Xinjiang that's being used as part of a wider, global propaganda push by the Chinese state to counter critical reporting about human rights abuses in the region' (Ryan et al., 2021: 4). Between January 2020 and August 2021, 156 Chinese state-controlled accounts published at least 546 Facebook posts, Twitter posts and shared articles from CGTN, *Global Times*, Xinhua or *China Daily* websites that have amplified Xinjiang-related social media content from 13 influencer accounts. More than 50% of that activity occurred on Facebook (ibid.).

The government has used social media influencers to promote its agenda by generating lucrative traffic for the influencers by sharing videos with millions of followers on YouTube, Twitter and Facebook, platforms which the government blocks inside China to prevent the uncontrolled spread of information, 'as propaganda megaphones for the wider world' (Mozur et al., 2021). A 2020 report by Freedom House tellingly titled *Beijing's Global Megaphone* noted: 'Chinese officials are making a more explicit effort to present China as a model for other countries, and they are taking concrete steps to encourage emulation through trainings for foreign personnel and technology transfers to foreign state-owned media outlets' (Cook, 2020: 2).

Winning or fading influence?

Despite such multifaceted and multipronged attempts at legitimizing Chinese narratives on global affairs, China faces severe limitations. As one commentator has noted, 'So long as its political system denies, rather than enables, free human development, its propaganda efforts will face an uphill battle' (Shambaugh, 2015: 107) Lacking cultural and political appeal in many parts of the global South, suggests one US think tank report, China is promoting 'organized narratives around the "China story" in the form of disinformation and cyberwarfare' (Thibaut, 2022: 24).

'The major obstacle to China's rise on the international stage', writes another specialist, 'is not US hostility or internal foes. Rather, it is the authoritarian strand of CCP's core identity', adding that 'Chinese authoritarianism threatens to limit Beijing's ability to create a plausible new form of global order' (Mitter, 2021: 174). An Australian think tank report noted that the CCP influences WeChat. which 'has accelerated the growth of "CCP-aligned media" among Chinese in Australia' (Joske et al., 2020). Yet others accuse China of 'exporting digital systems that make authoritarianism more effective than ever' (Beckley, 2022).

The Chinese treatment of its Muslim minorities in Xinjiang has received much Western criticism, with reports of 're-education camps' where up to one million Muslims are forced to learn Mandarin and sing communist songs (Kuntz, 2018). Numerous such reports also regularly appear in the elite British and US media: in 2021 the BBC published at least 51 articles on the 'Uyghur Genocide'. One recent academic study also labelled it as 'cultural genocide' (Roberts, 2020).

In a think tank report about the Chinese media's criticism of the BBC's coverage of the Xinjiang issue, it was noted that the CCP instigated a campaign against the BBC using YouTube, Twitter and Facebook, claiming that it was biased against China and spread disinformation prompted by foreign actors and intelligence agencies. The report concluded that, for China, 'controlling global narratives around key public issues is fundamental to the pursuit of its foreign policy interests' (Zhang and Wallis, 2021).

Many of these narratives are drawn from material supplied by Western-based advocacy groups such as the Uyghur Human Rights Project, which 'promotes the rights of the Uyghur people through research-based advocacy, publishing reports and analysis in English and Chinese', and the Washington-based Oxus Society for Central Asian Affairs. For its part, China has viewed its Uyghur minority as potentially subversive elements, as separatists and even in league with transnational jihadist groups, influenced in no small measure by geopolitical considerations, including the fall of the Soviet Union and the rise of Islamic militancy in neighbouring Afghanistan (Kuo and Mylonas, 2022).

In 2021, CGTN published a 5,000-word rebuttal about Xinjiang, arguing that 'some anti-China forces in the West, including the United States, have 'concocted and disseminated plenty of false information' as Xinjiang-related issues were not about human rights, ethnicity or religion at all, but about combating violent terrorism and separatism. 'We have chosen some typical Xinjiang-related rumours and lies fabricated by anti-China forces, and debunked them with facts to set the record straight' (CGTN, 2021a).

In 2022, the UN human rights office, in a 48-page report, accused China of serious human rights violations that 'may constitute international crimes, in particular crimes against humanity', though it did not use the word 'genocide'. The report was described by a spokesman for China's foreign ministry as a 'farce orchestrated by the United States and a small number of Western powers'. China submitted a 131-page response that said the human rights office's 'so-called "assessment"' was 'based on disinformation and lies' and ignored China's success in stopping extremism in Xinjiang (Cumming-Bruce and Ramzy, 2022).

Another constraint is the Chinese media's inability to be more culturally sensitive. One striking example was the CCTV's annual Spring Festival Gala in 2021, watched by more than a billion people, which featured Chinese men and women smeared in dark makeup and dressed in mismatched costumes meant to evoke 'African tribal' attire (Hong, 2021). Chinese official media has not yet got over being steeped in stereotypes of a 'primitive' Africa, a stereotype historically associated with the imperial European gaze (Batchelor, 2022). One critic has suggested that the 2017 Chinese feature film *Wolf Warrior 2* infantilizes Africa and adopts the 'White Saviour Complex' transplanted to Chinese heroes (Galafa, 2019), reflecting a version of racism among the Chinese middle classes (Talmacs, 2020).

Media mishandling works against Chinese narratives: in 2018, a CGTN reporter was arrested on suspicion of assault on a human rights activist at the event hosted by Hong Kong Watch, a London-based human rights group, held on the sidelines of the Conservative Party of Britain's annual conference – a video of her being slapped went viral (Johnston, 2018). Australian journalist Cheng Lei, a former CGTN host, was detained in China in 2020, accused of divulging state secrets (Buckley, 2022). The 2021 episode when the Chinese tennis star Peng Shuai – a double champion at Wimbledon and French Open – disappeared for several days as a silenced #MeToo accuser, received extensive negative coverage in the Western media (Stevenson and Lee Myers, 2021).

Another example was when in an exclusive report Singapore's Channel News Asia captured rare footage leading up to the unexpected exit of former Chinese president Hu Jintao from the closing of the Communist Party Congress in October 2022; the footage went viral and was shown around the world to emphasize divisions in the highest echelons of the party (Siong, 2022). A survey of China-based international journalists, conducted by the Foreign Correspondents' Club of China (FCCC), a Beijing-based professional association comprising correspondents from over 25 countries, criticized the influence and pressure brought to bear on foreign journalists in China, which reflects how they ensure that their version of the 'China story' is circulated around the world. 'The continued decline in reporting conditions in China, year on year should be a concern for all media organizations and governments' (FCCC, 2020).

China is also increasingly talking back at the West, not least with its more assertive 'Wolf Worrier' diplomacy, which has received wide coverage in Western journalistic writing (Wong and Ng, 2020; Zheng, 2020), as well as academic interest (Dai and Luqiu, 2022; Chen, 2023). In 2021, CGTN published a detailed report issued by China's State Council Information Office, criticizing the West's 'hypocrisy and double standards on human rights'. The report said that Washington's pandemic policy led to tragic outcomes, as more than 500,000 Americans lost their lives. It also claimed that 'Money-tainted politics' had turned US elections into a 'one-man show' of the wealthy class, and people's confidence in the American democratic system had reached a 20-year low (CGTN, 2021b).

In 2023, CGTN published another scathing 11,000-word report on *Human Rights Violations in the United States*, suggesting that the United States, 'founded on colonialism, racist slavery and inequality in labor, possession and distribution, has further fallen into a quagmire of system failure, governance deficits, racial divide and social unrest' and that American politicians, 'serving the interests of oligarchs', 'wantonly use human rights as a weapon to attack other countries, creating confrontation, division and chaos in the international community, and have thus become a spoiler and obstructor of global human rights development' (CGTN, 2023).

As Western-style liberal democracy is seen as anathema in a one-party state, the Chinese propaganda machine robustly claims a different version. The State Council Information Office's special report *China: Democracy That Works* states unambiguously: 'China is a faithful and exemplary actor in pursuing, exploring and practicing democracy. It endeavors to increase democracy both within its own territory and between nations. . . . China proposes to build a global community of shared future and presses for a new model of international relations based on mutual respect, fairness and justice, and win-win cooperation' (State Council Information Office, 2021: 48).

It is instructive to note that while the rights of the Uyghur Muslims are robustly defended by the West, much of the Islamic world has kept a studied silence on the issue and the 2019 UN vote on this favoured China over the West (Yellinek and Chen, 2019), reflecting a geopolitical shift in influence. In addition, an EU-supported study reported that, while North America and South Asia hold a negative view of the BRI, 'most regions in the world hold a rather positive view' of it, and 'Central Asia and sub-Saharan Africa display [the] most positive' (García-Herrero and Schindowski, 2023: 16). Chinese foreign policy elites now frequently speak about the 'Belt and Road Cooperation' instead of 'Belt and Road Initiative,' which sounds less like a strategic push towards a nationalist goal. Besides, several new concepts have appeared that complement the BRI, notably the 'Global Development Initiative' and the 'Global Security Initiative' (ibid.: 17).

Changing geopolitics of 'digital for development'

From the modernization discourses of the Cold War to the digital empowerment narratives of recent decades, the issue of development is deeply ingrained with geopolitics. Although foreign aid was discussed in terms of modernization and development, it was in fact a key site of Cold War geopolitical competition and rivalry. Foreign aid enabled a variety of countries to create spheres of strategic influence and alliance during the Cold War, to project their economic, political and cultural power; to pursue their foreign policy objectives; to create particular kinds of states, and to sponsor (or counter) various kinds of revolution. USAID was involved in counter-insurgency practices not dissimilar from the ways in which the agency today seeks to advance neo-liberalization in recipient states.

Writing the foreword of the 2019 *Dictionary of Development*, Wolfgang Sachs (editor of its first edition, in 1992) notes how the geopolitics of development has 'imploded'. The changing geopolitics of aid, investment and South-South cooperation witnessed in the past two decades has demonstrated the limitations of the Western developmental model, according to which industrial nations would be the shining example for poorer countries: 'Globalization has almost dissolved the established North-South scheme' (Kothari el al., 2019: xiii and xiv). The emerging economies have also increasingly begun to develop an internationalist profile and to assert themselves globally as humanitarian, peacekeeping, peacebuilding and 'police-keeping' actors: their rise has also produced 'new or emancipatory modalities' of 'development', especially in the context of Africa (Power, 2019). In addition, given the existential challenges of climate change, which disproportionately impacts on the South, the question arises, 'What point is there in development, if there is no country that can be called "sustainably developed?"' (Sachs, 2020).

Such a shift has also been prompted by the recognition of the colonial roots of much development thinking, as Oxfam, one of the leading UK NGOs admitted in its 2023 Inclusive Language Guide, which was in English, the language of a colonizing nation: 'we recognize that the dominance of English is one of the key issues that must be addressed in order to decolonise our ways of working and shift power' (Oxfam, 2023: 7). As the global South gains salience in the geopolitical arena, the framing of developmental communication needs a reconfiguration and reassessment, especially with the success of non-Western, some hybrid models of development, using digital technology.

The Chinese model of development

The biggest challenge to Western hegemony in the developmental field has emerged from China's success in exporting its developmental model to other parts of the world and how this cooperation – though almost invariably covered in a sceptical if not hostile manner in mainstream Western media – is transforming a large section of the global South. Developmental geopolitics has emerged as an intellectual project in China, especially since the launch of the BRI (Cheng and Liu, 2021).

As the biggest aid provider, China has been instrumental in unleashing the structural transformation underway in many parts of the global South, partly because of growing South-South development aid and cooperation, part of the 'New Structural Economics' (Lin and Wang, 2017), though this is not without its drawbacks. A 2021 study of international development finance from China, which examined more than 13,000 projects worth $843 billion across 165 countries over an 18-year period, found that with annual international development finance commitments of $85 billion a year, China outspends the United States and other major powers on a 2-to-1 basis or more. It noted instances of debt trap and found that 35 per cent of the BRI infrastructure projects have encountered major implementation problems, though these are never highlighted in the Chinese narratives (Malik et al., 2021). Although China's public diplomacy is geared to presenting itself as 'a muscular and commercially savvy lender to the developing world', the terms and conditions of its lending remain obscure, notes a study, and the contracts contain confidentiality clauses that obscure borrowers from revealing the terms or, in some cases, even the existence of the debt (Gelpern et al., 2021).

In recent years, China has emerged as a major provider of 'emergency financing' – $240 billion – and much of this has been given to countries with geopolitical significance, for example, their strategic location or natural resources. In 2020, 15 of the 19 cobalt-producing mines in Congo were owned or financed by Chinese companies, of which the five biggest had been given $124 billion in credit lines by the Chinese government for their global operations (Searcey et al., 2021). In a three-part special series on 'Asia's age of hydro-politics', the Japanese newspaper *Asia Nikkei* called China the 'upstream superpower', highlighting the geopolitical dimensions of how control over water flow of the 'geopolitically critical' Brahmaputra can affect the ecological balance in south Asia: the mighty river which originates in Tibet provides about 30 per cent of India's freshwater resources, and 70 per cent for Bangladesh (Sharma et al., 2023).

Communication hardware and software are an integral part of Chinese aid packages, symbolizing the country's 'globalising internet' with a state-centric governance model with implications for debates around the internet governance (see essays in Hong and Harwit, 2022). Chinese internet connectivity could remove the existing digital divides in the global South: according to ITU, in 2022, some 2.7 billion people worldwide were still not online. In the world's poorest countries: for an average consumer the cheapest mobile broadband still costs over six times the global average. In Africa, on average only 40 per cent of the population were using the internet – among women the figure was 34 per cent, while only 23 per cent of people in rural areas had access (ITU, 2023). Such digital disconnect creates socio-digital inequalities conceptualized as 'systematic differences between individuals from different backgrounds in the opportunities and abilities to translate digital engagement into benefits and avoid the harm' (Helsper, 2021: 34).

Despite consistent criticism of China's developmental diplomacy in the Western media, the country has demonstrated that it has tackled one of the most pressing problems of development by raising over 850 million of its own people out of poverty over the past 40 years, according to the World Bank. In November 2020, China officially declared that it had eradicated extreme poverty. A 2021 White Paper of the Chinese government celebrated the ending of poverty thus: 'China is home to nearly one fifth of the world's population. Its complete eradication of extreme poverty – the first target of the UN 2030 Agenda for Sustainable Development – 10 years ahead of schedule is a milestone in the history of the Chinese nation and the history of humankind, making an important contribution to the cause of global poverty alleviation' (Government of China, 2021: 1–2).

In a three-part report, the CGTN published reflections from an Oxford graduate who has studied and lived in China, lauding the country's 'governing and philosophical system which acts as the macro foundation for China's success in alleviating extreme poverty' (Lamb, 2021a), noting that 'the Western methods of aid and intervention have proved ineffectual for eliminating extreme poverty in the global South' (Lamb, 2021b) and the raising of living conditions experienced by over a billion Chinese citizens 'deserves greater acknowledgment in the West' (Lamb, 2021c). Outside the Western orbit, Chinese achievements in this regard are routinely acknowledged, as is the case within multilateral organizations. However, this extraordinary success has not been without ecological and cultural costs: environmental degradation and its health consequences have taken a heavy toll on Chinese society (Huang, 2020).

With more than one trillion dollars of investment, the BRI is viewed as a 'global alternative infrastructure', forcing the United States and its allies to revise their approach to investing in the global South. The first reaction came from Japan, which launched in 2015 its Partnership for Quality Infrastructure: Investment for Asia's Future' (PQI), with an investment of $110 billion (Ministry of Foreign Affairs of Japan, 2015). The West reacted later: in 2019, the Trump administration announced the creation of a new agency, the US international Development Finance Corporation (DFC), with access to $60 billion in financial capital to help US businesses invest in emerging markets, with lending intended for private investors, not governments. The Overseas Private Investment Corporation, which became part of the DFC, launched its 'Connect Africa' initiative, which will invest more than $1 billion in projects in Africa that support transportation, communications and 'value chains'.

In 2021, the United States launched the 'Build Back Better' project, aimed to reduce the $40 trillion infrastructure gap in low- and middle-income countries (White House, 2021). Britain then announced its Clean Green Initiative – $3.4 billion over five years (2021–2026) (UK Government, 2021), while in December of the same year the EU set out a $298 billion Global Gateway strategy to support infrastructure projects across the world with a view to enhance connectivity (European Commission, 2021). In 2022, the G7's new Global Investment and Infrastructure Partnership Plan aimed to raise $600 billion from private and public funds by 2027, with $200 billion coming from the United States (White House, 2022). These Western initiatives appear to be influenced by geopolitical considerations rather than having clear developmental goals but claim to be qualitatively superior to the BRI, as the projects promote democratic values, operate high standards and conform to the principles of good governance and transparency.

An Indian model in the making

While China's impressive developmental success has been acknowledged – grudgingly in some cases by the custodians of development – the achievement of India in using digital technology for development over the past decade has received scant attention. Since 2015, when it launched a 'Digital India' programme, supported by $75 billion from public and private investment in a phased manner, the country has witnessed a transformation that is now being exported to other parts of the global South. In stark contrast to its large eastern neighbour, with its party-state monopoly on power and discourse, that a multi-party, multi-lingual, and multi-cultural democracy could achieve this is a testimony of the remarkable resilience of its polity.

India's digital infrastructure is designed around *Aadhaar* (Sanskrit for foundation), the unique identity number which, since its launch in 2010, has been provided to over 1.3 billion Indians – the world's largest identity project (Sharma, 2020). The IDs are the foundation of the instant payment system, known as the Unified Payments Interface (UPI), an initiative of India's central bank, the Reserve Bank of India (RBI), but run by a non-profit organization, offering services from banks and mobile payment apps, with no transaction fees. According to India's Ministry of Finance, UPI transactions are running at $1.7 trillion per annum.

Combining this with the rapid expansion of mobile technology has transformed the digital space. The JAM trinity (short for Jan Dhan-Aadhar-Mobile, a system designed to eliminate intermediaries and leakages in the transfer of government subsidies to intended beneficiaries) has made a substantial difference to millions of Indians living on the bottom of the socio-economic pyramid. Average data traffic per smartphone in India is the highest globally, and 76 per cent of total mobile subscriptions were using a mostly Chinese-made smartphones in 2022. Such traffic is expected to grow exponentially following the launch of 5G services in October 2022, as India witnesses an 'aggressive 5G network deployments by service providers', with 5G subscriptions expected to reach, according to industry estimates, 700 million, accounting for 57 per cent of subscriptions by 2028 (Ericsson, 2023: 20).

This transformation of the digital space has been done with the guiding principle of viewing payments- and settlements-related services as a public good that ought to be provided publicly. This 'digital public infrastructure', has extended the reach of government programmes and tax collection. From just 17 per cent of Indians having a bank account in 2008, the proportion is now over 80 per cent. India's indigenous instant payment system has remade commerce and pulled millions into the formal economy (Acharya, 2023; Nageswaran and Kaur, 2023). The system has grown rapidly and is used by 300 million individuals and 50 million merchants (Mashal and Kumar, 2023).

The value of instant digital transactions in India in 2022 was far more than in the United States, Britain, Germany and France: 'Combine the four and multiply by four – it is more than that', an Indian cabinet minister told the World Economic Forum (cited in Mashal and Kumar, 2023). Information has fundamentally reshaped development discourse and practice, with political implications of information for poverty alleviation, if not eradication (Srinivasan, 2022). This public-private model is one India wants to export to other countries in the global South that are dealing with the same challenge of a digital divide that India was facing a decade ago. India's public-utility approach has differed from the mostly private but concentrated model of digitization in China and the private but heavily fragmented model of digitization in the United States. During India's presidency of the G2O in 2023, the country pushed for a Global Initiative on Digital Health to focus on building an institutional framework for an inter-linked health ecosystem for the world.

India has been trying to promote the use of Indian rupee for settlement in trade with other countries after sanctions were imposed on Russia by the United States and the EU following its invasion of Ukraine. In 2023, eight countries had opened a Special Rupee vostro Account (SRVA) to facilitate trade in rupee: Russia, Sri Lanka, Mauritius, Malaysia, Singapore, Myanmar, Israel and Germany. The RBI has issued guidelines on cross-border trade transactions in the rupee and announced a new trade mechanism to settle international trade in Indian currency (Sharma, 2023). India is increasingly shifting towards a regulatory model primarily focused on maximizing the economic and social benefits of data and data-driven sectors for its citizens and the domestic economy and minimizing revenue flows to foreign corporations.

In addition, India has also strengthened its space communication capabilities. The strategy and resource ambitions of China and India in the space sector challenges Western predominance in this area (Goswami and Garretson, 2020). In April 2023, the Indian Space Research Organization (ISRO) – since 1969, the only agency for India's space-related outreaches – released its space policy, with a clear encouragement of private participation across 'the entire chain of the space economy'. Its vision includes 'to augment space capabilities; enable, encourage and develop a flourishing commercial presence in space; use space as a driver of technology development and derived benefits in allied areas' (ISRO, 2023: 5).

The presence of private capital in the space industry preceded the announcement: in November 2022, Skyroot Aerospace launched the Vikram-S rocket, becoming the first Indian private company to reach outer space. In August 2023, ISRO gained international attention when its *Chandrayaan-3* ('moon craft' in Sanskrit) landed on the lunar surface, making India the fourth country after the United States, Russia and China to have managed the feat. With a small annual budget of about $1.5 billion – as against the $25 billion allocated to NASA and the $12 billion budgeted for the Chinese space agency – the Indian space companies can offer relatively cheap services, especially attractive to resource-poor global South. The global space economy is currently valued at about $360 billion, of which India accounts for barely two per cent yet it is working towards higher ambitions and has a good record of expertise in this field (ISRO, 2023). ISRO launched 36 Low Earth Orbit satellites simultaneously for OneWeb, the Bharti Airtel-led consortium, prompting calls for closer Europe-India space cooperation (Aliberti, 2018).

Sustainable digitization and development

A superior attitude towards their own values and products is not atypical of major Western governments and corporations, who have deployed media and communication channels to promote their developmental agendas and mitigate any criticism. A striking example is the attitude towards global warming: in 2020, the attorney general of Minnesota in the United States sued ExxonMobil, among others, for launching a 'campaign of deception' which deliberately tried to undermine the science supporting global warming (Keane, 2020). Climate lobbying and propaganda by fossil fuel interests has been described as a 'vast blind spot' of major climate assessments – ignored in all but the most recent Intergovernmental Panel on Climate Change (IPCC) assessment report.

Studies have shown that although the ExxonMobil scientists during the 1970s and 1980s accurately modelled global warming and predicted when it would be detected, they denied this information to the public (Supran et al., 2023). Others have argued that the anti-environmental movement was formulated by 'a small network of doubt-mongers' financed by conservative think-tanks (Oreskes and Conway, 2010: 213). A joint report by Rainforest Action Network noted that 'fossil fuel financing from the world's 60 largest banks has reached $4.6 trillion in the six years since the adoption of the Paris Agreement' and that overall fossil fuel financing remains dominated by four US banks – JPMorgan Chase, Citi, Wells Fargo and Bank of America – who together account for one quarter of all fossil fuel financing identified over the past six years (Rainforest Action Network et al., 2023).

It is not surprising then that, even after three decades of campaigns (starting in Rio de Janeiro in 1992), an effective treaty to reduce global greenhouse gas emissions remains elusive. Geopolitics and geo-economics of the leading powers and polluters are among the biggest hurdles. The United States rejected the 1997 Kyoto Protocol, arguing that it ignored non-Western polluters, including China and India. Although the 2015 Paris agreement included developing countries in the discussion, there was no mechanism for enforcement and, since the United States withdrew in 2017, the process was doomed. The United States is now suggesting a Western 'carbon customs alliance', which would have a 'harmonized carbon price among its members, paired with a common trade policy applied to countries outside the alliance. The alliance would shape the rules of trade governing carbon intensive goods and also partly determine which economies will dominate the energy industries of the future' (Baker et al., 2020: 37). The 2022 UN Environment Programme report shows that updated national pledges since COP26 – held in 2021 in Glasgow – make a negligible difference to predicted 2030 emissions and that the world is very far from the Paris Agreement goal of limiting global warming to well below 2°C (UNEP, 2022). While Russia's invasion of Ukraine sparked 'a global energy crisis', it created a $2 trillion windfall for fossil fuel producers above their 2021 net income (World Energy Outlook, 2022).

In the crucial global food sector, too, the US imprint is very visible, with such digital powerhouses as Microsoft and Amazon connecting with the companies that supply products to farmers (pesticides, tractors, drones, etc.) and with those that control the flow of data and have access to food consumers. According to the Barcelona-based group GRAIN, agribusiness is getting farmers to use their mobile phone apps to supply them with data, on the basis that the experts can give 'advice' to the farmers, while the big e-platforms are taking control of food distribution. Microsoft is building up a digital farming platform called Azure FarmBeats that operates through the company's global cloud technology Azure, while Amazon Web Services, the world's largest cloud service platform, is developing its own digital agriculture platform.

As with the 1960s Green Revolution, this modernization of the food sector, critics suggest, favours the use of chemical inputs and costly machinery, as well as the production of commodities for corporate buyers not local markets (see www.grain.org), with negative impacts on local producers. In January 2022, the US Department of Agriculture ordered new labelling for genetically modified foods: 'genetically engineered' (GE) ingredients or 'genetically modified organisms' (GMOs) will now be labelled as 'bioengineered' (Reiley, 2022). Such changes are likely to have an impact on the campaigns for organic farming. Electronic waste is another major issue of concern: not just in relation to e-waste being exported to the global South but the more harmful 'externalities' arising from the mining for, and the manufacture of, electronics in terms of their 'tonnage, toxicity, and harms' (Lepawsky, 2018).

Despite the assault on sustainable ecology there are also signs of optimism, for instance, in the impressive use of alternative source of energy, as a report noted: 'A blend of policy subsidies, market incentives, and expanded productive capacity helped drop the price of photovoltaic solar energy by roughly 90 per cent between 2010 and 2020'. Solar power now offers the world's lowest levelled cost of energy (Kharas et al., 2022: 8). India has been aiming to meet its domestic renewable capacity target of 500 gigawatts in 2030, and renewables meet nearly two-thirds of the country's rapidly rising demand for electricity, says the *World Energy Outlook*. It may be achievable with the discovery in 2023 of 5.9 million tonnes of inferred lithium ore, which can be used in the production of batteries for electronic vehicles, solar panels and electronic devices (Mishra, 2023).

Digital for development relies on more equal access to the resources of the internet. The Broadband Commission for Sustainable Development, devised by ITU and UNESCO, counsels for a liberal global regulatory environment for broadband services to attract more investment (Broadband Commission for Sustainable Development, 2023). However, the digital empires continue to tighten their grip on humanity (Suleyman, 2023) and the call to 'deprivatize the internet . . . where people, and not profit, rule,' an increasingly improbable dream (Tarnoff, 2022).

Decolonizing the study of geopolitics and global communication

As noted consistently in the preceding chapters, the running thread through this book is the idea of empire: from the territorial imperialism of the 19th century to the communication and digital imperialism of the 21st century and its various competing and converging manifestations. This imperial imprint can also be found on the research and scholarship in the field of global communication.

As with the other fields of social sciences, the study of communication is also deeply influenced and shaped by a Eurocentric approach that privileges a Western understanding of geopolitics. If anything, given the relatively recent origins of this field, it is more susceptible to these intellectual constraints and yet, as argued below, the subject also opens up huge possibilities to decolonize the discourse and address the imperial legacy, as well as to confront the new and emerging issues for a 'post-Western', multi-polar world.

The absence of non-Western international theory has been explained by two leading scholars in the field on the grounds of 'ideational and perceptual forces, which fuel, in varying mixtures, both Gramscian hegemonies, and ethnocentrism and the politics of exclusion. Some of these explanations are located within the West, some within the non-West and some in the interaction between the two' (Acharya and Buzan, 2010: 2). In their 2019 book, marked to celebrate a century of the establishment of international relations as an academic field, they note that IR has remained 'too parochially Eurocentric for too long and needs to show greater inclusiveness' (Acharya and Buzan, 2019: 1).

One way of doing this would be to reconsider the hegemonic nature of various historiographies and how they have historicized the world outside the West. Some scholars have even challenged the well-established notion that the modern international system began in 1648 with the Peace of Westphalia, taking it back more than four centuries to 1206, when Genghis Khan ruled a large part of the Eurasian region and created the 'Chinggisid order,' whose legacies survived in Ming, Mughal, Safavid and Timurid empires, respectively, in present-day China, India, Iran and Uzbekistan (Zarakol, 2022). This has also been noted in the context of how Western scholars interpret Indian traditions, viewed primarily through an implicitly Judeo-Christian lens (Fárek, 2022). Similar observations have been made in relations to Islam (Said, 1978; Al-Azmeh, 1993) and Africa (Elkins, 2022).

In the case of British colonialism, the 'imperial ethos' took the form of a 'civilizing mission': given their belief in their 'superior race, Christian values and economic knowhow', the British felt they had 'a moral obligation to redeem the backward heathens of the world' (Elkins, 2005: 5). In the realm of international law, too, imperialism often meant 'transplanting' an entire legal system onto its colonies, based on mostly European principles (Watson, 1993) which is also in evidence today, for example, in the field of intellectual property law (Birnhack,

2021). Understanding the historical context, therefore, is essential to comprehend contemporary geopolitics.

While in the new geopolitics of the 21st century, Africa is sometimes projected as a 'rising' market, the historical context of how the continent is represented in the media should not be overlooked (Bunce et al., 2017). The representation of its history remains deeply problematic, being racist and colonial in its approach and ideology (Green, 2020; French, 2022). The atrocities in the continent have been well documented: most prominently, the violence and excesses of French colonialism (Smith, 2023); the German killing of Herero and Nama people in Namibia – then known as German Southwest Africa – considered as the first genocide of the 20th century (Erichsen and Olusoga, 2010); or the horrendous Belgian atrocities in Congo (Hochschild, 1999).

Like their other colonial cousins, the British aimed to 'bring light' to the 'Dark Continent', by transforming the so-called natives into progressive citizens, a process which included the 'murderous campaign to eliminate' tens of thousands of Kikuya people in Kenya (Elkins, 2005: xvi). Though projecting itself as a liberal empire, Britain's use of systematic violence in its colonies was widespread, but, given its domination of communication, it was better at hiding the atrocities (Elkins, 2022). Calls have been made to challenge the 'white' media philosophy and develop a 'Black media philosophy' which 'requires recognition of the racial politics of the Western episteme and a complex understanding of the projects that challenge such an episteme' (Towns, 2022: 9).

While much of decolonial discourse is centred on Western European powers, Russia as a vast imperial enterprise needs more attention and critical scrutiny. Although Russia projects itself as an anti-colonial power, its imperial imprint is visible across large swathes of the Eurasian region. In parts of central and eastern Asia, not unlike its European counterparts, Moscow, too, conformed to the 'white man's burden' in pursuing the mission to 'civilize the natives'.

However, it was the natives who articulated an intellectual response to such a mission. The decolonization debate emerged from within the colonized countries. The 1947 Asian Relations Conference in Delhi set the foundations for an anti-imperialist discourse – 'the opening act of decolonial solidarity' (Thakur, 2019) – though in a Eurocentric reading, of this 'Third World' event it was invariably placed within the context of Cold War geopolitics and thus depriving it of any understanding of its historical relevance. This seminal conference was followed by the better known 'Bandung Conference', the first major Asian-African conference with decolonization as the main agenda item (Chakrabarty, 2010). This decolonization discourse, in its regional and local variations, was crucial in the anti-colonial movements across Asia, Africa and the Middle East and also informed the 1970s discussions of the New World Information and Communication Order (see Chapter 1).

Reclaiming the language of geopolitics

In Eurocentric historiography, it has been argued, a hierarchy exists 'not only between philosophy and history but also between history and history – between a history that claims to be philosophically and normatively salient, and other histories, such as histories from the global South, that cannot make such a claim' (Banerjee, 2020: 5–6). Connell summarized the 'Northernness' of general theory thus: 'The consequences of metropolitan geopolitical location can be seen . . . in four characteristic textual moves: the claim of universality; reading from the centre; gestures of exclusion; and grand erasure' (Connell, 2007: 44).

Al-Azmeh has criticized the use of formulations such as 'Islamic economies', 'Islamic polities' and 'Islamic history' as concepts which are 'disassociated from their historical, social, cultural and other contexts, and reduced to this substantive Islamism of European imagination' (Al-Azmeh, 1993: 139). Others have argued for including an 'Islamic worldview' and thus contributing to 'de-Westernising' the study of journalism (Basyouni, 2022). In the realm of 'security studies', too, Eurocentrism is evident in using 'Europe to explain Asia', for example, in relation to China, with such archaic references as the 'Thucydides Trap' (Allison, 2017) as if they were relevant to contemporary geopolitics. As once commentator has observed: 'Eurocentrism, hybridity, and mimicry have served to obscure fundamental differences in how security is understood and how it operates in different places. Accounting for history, culture, and ideology reveals the limits of universal theorizing' (Nyman, 2023: 692).

Recent calls in the West to decolonize the curriculum have gained ground 'to situate the histories and knowledges that do not originate from the West in the context of imperialism, colonialism and power and to consider why these have been marginalised and decentred' (Schucan and Pitman, 2020). Others speak of 'the subaltern geopolitics of development', which would look beyond the Area Studies lens – a colonial project – and resist the traditional mapping of regions of the world as 'The Tropics' or the 'Third World', particularly in the context of theorizing Africa (Power, 2019). This would require a radical rethinking of how geopolitics is taught at universities worldwide. Decolonization is much needed, for example, in apartheid-shaped higher education in South Africa, even after three decades of the formal ending of an institutionally racist governance structure (Chasi and Rodny-Gumede, 2019).

Scholars have questioned the 'power matrices that are embedded within, and its over-reliance on Western epistemes, that dis-members its citizenry; de-contextualises; and de-positions; by privileging "numbers"/quantification; objectivity and politics as a "science"' (Karam and Mutsvairo, 2022: 7). Moyo has argued that Africa should produce its own theories and resist being used as a platform to test Eurocentric ideas (Moyo, 2020), a perspective which has been given impetus by the arguments for creating an 'Afrokology' (Milton and Mano, 2021), while some have argued for 'a decolonial approach that privileges qualitative methods in ways that position African digital experiences as 'epistemic sites' of knowledge production in their own right (Schoon et al., 2020).

More radical readings have argued for 'decolonizing' political-economy paradigms as well as world-system analysis, and to propose 'an alternative decolonial conceptualization of the world-system' (Grosfoguel, 2007: 212). To deal with what Dipesh Chakraborty accurately labelled as 'asymmetric ignorance' (2000: 28), there is a pressing need to address the structural inequality in 'the geopolitics of knowledge production and how we can intervene in that to reorient the unequal directions of knowledge flows and re-engage or rediscover histories of media that were never allowed to be histories' (Shome, 2017: 68).

Western philosophy privileges the 'ego politics of knowledge' over the 'geopolitics of knowledge' and the 'body-politics of knowledge', which has allowed, historically, the 'Western man' to represent his knowledge as the only one capable of achieving a universal consciousness, and to dismiss non-Western knowledge as particularistic and, thus, unable to achieve universality' (ibid.: 214). Traces of such colonial frameworks have been noted in the study of French sociology, where leading figures, notably Raymond Aron, Jacques Berque, Georges Balandier and Pierre Bourdieu, closely worked with colonial governments to theorize such 'social problems' as detribalization, urbanization, poverty and migration (Steinmetz, 2023). Bringing these marginalized perspectives to the fore would contribute also to the notion of 'global history' (Conrad, 2016).

Others speak of the need to articulate a 'collective voice in the fight against marginalization, injustice and epistemicide' (Medrado and Rega, 2023), while ending the dependency on the 'new developmentalism' has been called for in South America (de Oliveira, 2022), and in India arguments have been advanced for de-centring histories of 'global order-making' and to negotiate 'alternative visions of the international in an increasingly multipolar world order' (Raghavan et al., 2022).

The crisis in communication studies

As a relatively modern field of academic inquiry, communication studies has always had a profound Western or more specifically US cultural and intellectual imprint, led by the globalization of the American model of 'mass communication studies', with its intercultural, developmental, health, interpersonal and organizational variants. As noted in Chapter 1, the Cold War matrix ensured that the US model of communication studies became the dominant one, particularly in what was then called the Third World, largely because of a dependency syndrome in the field of research and the primacy of English-language scholarship, evident in the content of courses and syllabi, the import of textbooks, journals, citations and employment of experts, as well as the funding of research projects (Thussu, 2019).

In exporting theory from the Western academy, colonialism brought with it the assumption that 'theory is the product of Western tradition and that the aim of academies outside the West is to apply it' (Mamdani, 2018). Attempts to challenge this 'epistemological essentialism', rooted within a Euro-Atlantic intellectual and cultural tradition, were thwarted (Thussu, 2009). Even today most books and journals in the field emanate from the United States, closely followed by Britain. With the end of the Cold War there was talk of 'de-Westernizing' media studies, part of 'a growing reaction against the self-absorption and parochialism of much Western media theory' (Curran and Park, 2000: 3). Yet endeavours to provide comparative models of media systems have ignored work beyond the Euro-American arena, despite the extraordinary expansion of the media, especially in Asia (Hallin and Mancini, 2004). Hallin and Mancini's 2012 widely cited edited collection *Comparing Media Systems Beyond the Western World* does not include any discussion of India, one of the largest and most complex media systems 'beyond the Western world'.

To further 'internationalize' communication research (Lee, 2015), a re-evaluation of pedagogic parameters, as well as research agendas and methods, is warranted. One area that needs particular attention is to explore in more detail the dynamics between religion and communication – a largely ignored area of research, especially among critical scholars. Some scholars speak of 'transnational interdisciplinarity' which encourages researchers to 'engage in, and try to connect to, knowledge formations and vocabularies that reside in other modernities and other temporalities that are either refused recognition, or are not adequately translated, in machines of knowledge production' (Shom, 2006: 3).

Proponents of the democratizing potential of digital technologies have argued that 'knowledge-building communities' on such platforms as Wikipedia can act as creating a kind of 'distributed cognition', beneficial to knowledge dissemination and consumption. (Bruckman, 2022). Such search engines as Google Scholar have emerged in the past decade as an extensive source for academic material, providing access to knowledge to millions of researchers across the world. An international survey conducted by Renew Consultants, examining the trends from 2005–2020, reported that Google Scholar, was the most important 'discovery resource' for Humanities and Social Sciences (Gardner and Inger, 2021). Many leading Western university presses now provide open-access books, and there are some open-access publishers: notably Intech Open with over 5,000 titles.

Such developments are particularly important to strengthen academic research and scholarship in the global South where resource constraints limit intellectual production. These are positive steps towards knowledge becoming a 'global public good' (Baldwin, 2023: 14). The downside of this democratization of knowledge is the fact that digital search systems privilege work which is easily measurable and creates a digital hierarchy in which the academic careers are 'heavily determined by the ability to get published and quoted by others' (Morozov, 2013: 249). Scholarship from the global South faces severe limitations since what Lamdan has called 'the academic information industry' is entirely monetized and dominated by a few oligopolies such as RELX's Elsevier, which has launched academic metrics products like Scopus and Clarivate to create databases for indexing journal articles and evaluating their impact (Lamdan, 2022). In such a political economy of academic life, predatory publishers, too, have emerged: OMICS Publishing Group, one of the largest in the world, and the World Academy of Science, Engineering and Technology are two leading examples of how fake conferences and journals can create a multimillion-dollar organization (Oberhaus, 2018).

In order to build a more inclusive understanding of the rapidly changing geopolitics of global communication, internationalization is a prerequisite. At a time when in the United States, and more broadly in the West, 'woke capitalism' has become intellectually fashionable (Ramaswamy, 2021), the global South is waking up to reasserting its place in the international order. The digital transformation, especially in the very large countries with long histories and rising economic and cultural power – notably China and India, the two ancient civilizations with huge potential to influence the emerging global order – is likely to affect the way global geopolitics is conducted and communicated (Hobson, 2004, 2020). Indeed, scholars speak of possibilities of a 'post-Western', 'sustainable modernity', based on Asian histories and cultures (Duara, 2014). A decolonized geopolitics, for example, would acknowledge that science is not, and has never been, a uniquely European endeavour (Poskett, 2022); that the world's oldest surviving university is in Morocco, not in Europe, and that Admiral Zheng He from China traversed the oceans nearly a century before Christopher Columbus.

As noted in Chapter 1, British imperialism had a profound impact on global communication hardware and software. Its cultural and political successor, the United States, took the baton from it and imperialism in its various avatars – liberal, neo-liberal and digital – continues to shape global geopolitics and how it is communicated as outlined in this book. These continuities persist alongside the significant changes in geopolitics and communication that are reconfiguring and transforming the global order.

BIBLIOGRAPHY

Abdullah, Rasha (2011) The revolution will be Tweeted. *The Cairo Review of Global Affairs*. 3: 41–49. https://www.thecairoreview.com/essays/the-revolution-will-be-tweeted/

Abdullah, Rasha (2014) *Egypt's Media in the Midst of Revolution*. Washington: Carnegie Endowment for International Peace.

Abdul-Nabi, Zainab (2022) *Al-Jazeera's 'Double Standards' in the Arab Spring: A Peace Journalism Analysis (2011–2021)*. London: Palgrave-Macmillan.

Abrahamian, Ervand (2013) *The Coup: 1953, the CIA, and the Roots of Modern US-Iran Relations*. New York: New Press.

Abramowitz, Michael (2011) Libya intervention shows shift in thinking about mass atrocities. *Washington Post*, 1 April.

Abu-Nasr, Donna and Pendleton, Devon (2016) Syria's super-rich are waiting for war to end to return and rebuild their homeland. *Bloomberg*, 14 June.

Acharya, Amitav and Buzan, Barry (2010) Why is there no Non-Western international relations theory? An introduction. In Acharya, Amitav and Buzan, Barry (eds.) *Non-Western International Relations Theory: Perspectives on and beyond Asia*, pp. 1–25. London: Routledge.

Acharya, Amitav and Buzan, Barry (2019) *The Making of Global International Relations*. Cambridge: Cambridge University Press.

Acharya, Viral (2023) *India at 75: Replete with Contradictions, Brimming with Opportunities, Saddled with Challenges* (Brookings Papers on Economic Activity). Washington: Brookings Institute.

Acker, Amelia and Chaiet, Mitch (2020) The weaponization of web archives: Data craft and COVID-19 publics. *The Harvard Kennedy School (HKS) Misinformation Review*, 1(3). https://doi.org/10.37016/mr-2020-54

Aday, Sean, Cluverius, John and Livingston, Steven (2005) As goes the statue, so goes the war: The emergence of the victory frame in television coverage of the Iraq War. *Journal of Broadcasting & Electronic Media*, 49(3): 314–331.

African Union (2020) *The Digital Transformation Strategy for Africa 2020–2030*. Addis Ababa: African Union. https://au.int/en/documents/20200518/digital-transformation-strategyafrica-2020-2030.

Aggarwal, Neil Krishan (2016) *The Taliban's Virtual Emirate: The Culture and Psychology of an Online Militant Community*. New York: Columbia University Press.

Agnew, John (2003) *Geopolitics: Re-visioning World Politics*, 2nd ed. London: Routledge.
Agrawal, Ravi (2018) *India Connected: How the Smartphone is Transforming the World's Largest Democracy*. New York: Oxford University Press.
Ahen, Frederick (2021) International mega-corruption Inc.: The structural violence against sustainable development. *Critical Perspectives on International Business*, 18(2): 178–200.
Ahmed, Faisal and Lambert, Alexandre (2022) *The Belt and Road Initiative: Geopolitical and Geoeconomic Aspects*. London: Routledge.
Ahmed, Gafar (2016) In search of a strategic partnership: China-Qatar energy cooperation, from 1988 to 2015. In Tim, Niblock, Degang, Sun and Alejandra, Galindo (eds.) *The Arab States of the Gulf and BRICS: New Strategic Partnerships in Politics and Economics*. Berlin: Gerlach Press.
AIDP (2017) *Artificial Intelligence Development Plan*. Beijing: State Council (English Translation). www.newamerica.org/cybersecurity-initiative/digichina/blog/full-translation-chinas-newgeneration-artificial-intelligence-development-plan-2017
Akhavan, Niki (2013) *Electronic Iran: The Cultural Politics of an Online Evolution*. New Brunswick, NJ: Rutgers University Press.
Al-Abed, Bana (2017) *Dear World: A Syrian Girl's Story of War and Plea for Peace*. New York: Simon & Schuster.
Al-Azmeh, Aziz (1993) *Islams and Modernities*. London: Verso.
Aldrich, Richard (2002) *The Hidden Hand: Britain, America and Cold War Secret Intelligence*. London: John Murray.
Al-Hlou, Yousur, Froliak, Masha and Hill, Evan (2023) 'Putin is a fool': Intercepted calls reveal Russian army in disarray. *New York Times*, 28 September.
Aliberti, Marco (2018) *India in Space: Between Utility and Geopolitics*. New York: Springer.
Allison, Graham (2017) *Destined for War: Can America and China Escape Thucydides's Trap?* Boston, MA: Houghton Mifflin Harcourt.
Allison, Graham, Kevin, Klyman, Karina, Barbesino and Hugo, Yen (2021) *The Great Tech Rivalry: China vs the U.S.* Boston: Belfer Center for Science and International Affairs, Harvard Kennedy School.
Almén, Oscar and Weidacher Hsiung, Christopher (2022) *China's Economic Influence in the Arctic Region: The Nordic and Russian Cases*. Stockholm: Swedish Defence Research Agency.
Alperovitch, Dmitri (2022) The dangers of Putin's Paranoia. Why isolation encourages escalation. *Foreign Affairs*, 18 March.
Al-Rodhan, Nayef (2009) *Neo-statecraft and Meta-geopolitics: Reconciliation of Power, Interests and Justice in the 21st Century*. Reihe: Geneva Centre for Security Policy.
Aly, Anne, Macdonald, Stuart, Jarvis, Lee and Chen, Thomas (eds.) (2016) *Violent Extremism Online: New Perspectives on Terrorism and the Internet*. London: Routledge.
American Enterprise Institute (2022) *China Global Investment Tracker Database*. Washington: American Enterprise Institute. www.aei.org/china-global-investment-tracker/
Ameyaw-Brobbey, Thomas (2021) A critical juncture? COVID-19 and the fate of the US-China struggle for supremacy. *World Affairs*, 184(3): 260–293.
Amin, Samir (1989) *Eurocentrism*. London: Monthly Review Press.
Amnesty International (2021) *China: 'Like We Were Enemies in a War': China's Mass Internment, Torture, and Persecution of Muslims in Xinjiang*, June. https://www.amnesty.org/en/documents/asa17/4137/2021/en/
Anderson, Jack and Van Atta, Dale (1990) Saddam Hussein's house of horrors. *Washington Post*, 13 August.
Andrew, Christopher and Mitrokhin, Vasili (2005) *The World Was Going Our Way: The KGB and the Battle for the Third World*. New York: Basic Books.
Anduaga, Aitor (2009) *Wireless and Empire: Geopolitics, Radio Industry, and Ionosphere in the British Empire, 1918–1939*. New York: Oxford University Press.

Anonymous (2021) To counter China's rise, the U.S. should focus on Xi: A proposal for a full reboot of American strategy toward China. *Politico*, 28 January. https://www.politico.com/news/magazine/2021/01/28/china-foreign-policy-long-telegram-anonymous-463120

Aouragh, Miriyam and Chakravartty, Paula (2016) Infrastructures of empire: Towards a critical geopolitics of media and information studies. *Media, Culture & Society*, 38(4): 559–575.

AP (2023) *The Cyber Gulag: How Russia Tracks, Censors and Controls Its Citizens*. Associated Press, May 23.

Aral, Sinan (2020) *The Hype Machine: How Social Media Disrupts Our Elections, Our Economy and Our Health*. New York: Currency.

Archetti, Cristina (2013) *Understanding Terrorism in the Age of Global Media: A Communication Approach*. London: Palgrave Macmillan.

Arnove, Robert (ed.) (1982) *Philanthropy and Cultural Imperialism: The Foundations at Home and Abroad*. Bloomington: Indiana University Press.

Arora, Payal (2019) *The Next Billion Users: Digital Life Beyond the West*. Cambridge, MA: Harvard University Press.

Arquilla, John (2021) *Bitskrieg: The New Challenge of Cyberwarfare*. Cambridge: Polity.

Arslanalp, Serkan, Eichengreen, Barry and Simpson-Bell, Chima (2022) *The Stealth Erosion of Dollar Dominance: Active Diversifiers and the Rise of Non-traditional Reserve Currencies*. Washington: International Monetary Fund Working Paper WP/22/58.

Article 19 (2020) *Iran: Tightening the Net 2020 after Blood and Shutdowns*. London: Article 19.

Article 19 (2022) *The Global Expression Report 2022: The Intensifying Battle for Narrative Control*. London: Article 19.

Arutunyan, Anna (2022) *Hybrid Warriors: Proxies, Freelancers and Moscow's Struggle for Ukraine*. London: Hurst.

Asada, Kenji, Munakata, Aiko, Zhou, Marrian, Zhou, Cissy and Li, Grace (2022) China's online nationalist army-How social media users weaponized patriotism. *Nikkei*, 27 November.

Ashford, Emma and Cooper, Evan (2023) *Assumption Testing: Multipolarity is More Dangerous Than Bipolarity for the United States*. Washington: Stimson Center, October. https://www.stimson.org/2023/assumption-testing-multipolarity-is-more-dangerous-than-bipolarity-for-the-united-states/

Assange, Julian (2014) *When Google Met WikiLeaks*. New York: O/R Books.

Asthana, Sanjay (2019) *India's State-Run Media: Broadcasting, Power, and Narrative*. Cambridge: Cambridge University Press.

Atlantic Council (2018) *Disinfo Portal*. https://disinfoportal.org/

Atlantic Council (2021a) *The China Plan: A Transatlantic Blueprint for Strategic Competition*. Washington: The Scowcroft Center for Strategy and Security.

Atlantic Council (2021b) *The Longer Telegram: Toward A New American China Strategy*. Washington: The Scowcroft Center for Strategy and Security, March.

Atton, Chris (2004) *An alternative Internet: Radical Media, Politics and Creativity*. Edinburgh: Edinburgh University Press.

Avaaz (2019) Yellow Vests flooded by fake news over 100m views of disinformation on Facebook. *Avaaz*, 15 March.

Ayres, Alyssa (2018) *Our Time has Come: How India is Making its Place in the World*. New York: Oxford University Press.

Badrinathan, Sumitra, Kapur, Devesh, Kay, Jonathan and Vaishnav, Milan (2021) *Social Realities of Indian Americans: Results From the 2020 Indian American Attitudes Survey*. Washington: Carnegie Endowment for International Peace.

Baik, Jiwoon (2019) 'One Belt One Road' and the geopolitics of empire. *Inter-Asia Cultural Studies*, 20(3): 358–376.

Bajpai, Kanti (2021) *India Versus China: Why They Are Not Friends*. New Delhi: Juggernaut Books.
Bajpai, Kanti, Ho, Salina and Miller Chatterjee, Manjari (eds.) (2020) *Routledge Handbook of China-India Relations*. London: Routledge.
Baker, James, Shultz, George and Halstead, Ted (2020) The strategic case for U.S. Climate leadership: How Americans can win with a pro-market solution. *Foreign Affairs*, 99(3): 28–38.
Baker, Simon (2023) China overtakes United States on contribution to research in nature index. *Nature*, 19 May. www.nature.com/articles/d41586-023-01705-7
Bakker, Gerben (2008) *Entertainment Industrialized: The Emergence of the International Film Industry, 1890–1940*. Cambridge: Cambridge University Press.
Baldwin, Peter (2023) *Athena Unbound: Why and How Scholarly Knowledge Should Be Free for All*. Cambridge: MIT Press.
Bandurski, David (2022) *China and Russia are Joining Forces to Spread Disinformation*. Brookings: TechStream.
Banerjee, Prathama (2020) *Elementary Aspects of the Political: Histories from the Global South*. Durham: Duke University Press.
Barder, Alexander (2021) *Global Race War: International Politics and Racial Hierarchy*. Oxford: Oxford University Press.
Barnes, Julian and Wong, Edward (2022) U.S. and Ukrainian Groups Pierce Putin's Propaganda Bubble. *New York Times*, 13 April.
Barnes, Julian, Cooper, Helene, Gibbons-Neff, Thomas, Schwirtz, Michael and Schmitt, Eric (2023) Leaked documents reveal depth of U.S. Spy efforts and Russia's military struggles. *New York Times*, 8 April.
Barnhisel, Greg (2015) *Cold War Modernists: Art, Literature and American Cultural Diplomacy*. New York: Columbia University Press.
Barrinha, André and Christou, George (2022) Speaking sovereignty: The EU in the cyber domain. *European Security*, 31(3): 356–376.
Barrinha, André and Renard, Thomas (2018) Cyber-diplomacy: The making of an international society in the digital age. *Global Affairs*, 3 (4–5): 353–364.
Barry, Ellen (2022) 'In the end, you're treated like a spy,' says M.I.T. Scientist. *The New York Times*, 24 January.
Basrur, Rajesh (2019) India and China: A managed nuclear rivalry. *The Washington Quarterly*. 42(3): 151–170.
Bass, Gary (2013) *The Blood Telegram: Nixon, Kissinger, and a Forgotten Genocide*. New York: Alfred Knopf.
Basyouni, Ibrahim Hamada (2022) Islamic worldview as a model for de-westernising journalism studies and profession. *Javnost – The Public*, 29(4): 354–370.
Batchelor, Kathryn (2022) Images of 'Africa' in China-Africa cooperation. *China Information* 36(2): 221–240.
Baudrillard, Jean (1994) *The Illusion of the End*. Translated by C. Turner. Cambridge: Polity. First published in 1992 as *L'illusion de la fin*. Paris: Editions Galilee.
Baughan, Emily (2021) *Saving the Children-Humanitarianism, Internationalism, and Empire*. Los Angeles: University of California Press.
Baumgartner, Maik et al. (2022a) Hackers, Spies and contract killers-how Putin's agents are infiltrating Germany. *Der Spiegel*, 1 September.
Baumgartner, Maik et al. (2022b) Sabotage in the Baltic Attacks Expose Vulnerability of European Infrastructure. *Der Spiegel*, 30 September.
Bayly, Christopher (1996) *Empire and Information: Intelligence Gathering and Social Communication in India, 1780–1870*. Cambridge: Cambridge University Press.
Bayly, Christopher (2004) *The Birth of the Modern World, 1780–1914: Global Connections and Comparisons*. Malden, MA: Blackwell.

BBC (2020a) Li Wenliang: Coronavirus kills Chinese whistleblower doctor. *BBC News*, 7 February. www.bbc.com/news/world-asia-china-51403795.
BBC (2020b) *Enabling Media Markets to Work for Democracy: An International Fund for Public Interest Media Feasibility Study*. London: BBC.
BBC (2022a) How Ukraine is winning the social media war. *BBC*, 16 October.
BBC (2022b) *Russia 1985–1999: TraumaZone. A seven-part series by Adam Curtis*. London: BBC.
BBC (2022c) Africa is a hostage of Russia's war on Ukraine, Zelensky says. *BBC*. https://www.bbc.com/news/world-europe-61864049
Becker, Jeffrey (2020) *China Maritime Report No. 11: Securing China's Lifelines across the Indian Ocean*. Newport, RI: China Maritime Studies Institute, U.S. Naval War College.
Beckley, Michael (2022) Enemies of my enemy: How fear of China is forging a new world order. *Foreign Affairs*, March/April.
Beijing: The State Council Information Office of the People's Republic of China, March.
Belt and Road News Network (2019) A brief introduction to the belt and road news network. *BRNN*, 11 April, http://en.brnn.com/n3/2019/0411/c414872-9565686.html.
Belton, Catherine (2020) *Putin's People: How the KGB Took Back Russia and Then Took on the West*. London: HarperCollins.
Belton, Catherine (2023) Khodorkovsky warns West of war with China if Russia wins in Ukraine. *Washington Post*, 15 February.
Belton, Catherine, Mekhennet, Souad and Harris, Shane (2023) WP Exclusive-Kremlin tries to build antiwar coalition in Germany. *Washington Post*, 21 April.
Benkler, Yochai (2006) *The Wealth of Networks: How Social Production Transforms Markets and Freedom*. New Haven: Yale University Press.
Benkler, Yochai, Faris, Robert and Roberts, Hal (2018) *Network Propaganda: Manipulation, Disinformation and Radicalization in American Politics*. New York: Oxford University Press.
Bennett, Lance and Livingston, Steven (2018) The disinformation order: Disruptive communication and the decline of democratic institutions. *European Journal of Communication*, 33(2): 122–139.
Bennett, Lance and Segerberg, Alexandra (2013) *The Logic of Connective Action: Digital Media and the Personalization of Contentious Politics*. Cambridge: Cambridge University Press.
Benton, Lauren and Ford, Lisa (2016) *Rage for Order: The British Empire and the Origins of International Law, 1800–1850*. Cambridge, MA: Harvard University Press.
Bergen, Peter, Salyk-Virk, Melissa and Sterman, David (2020) *Introduction: How We Became a World of Drones*. New America, 30 July.
Bergengruen, Vera (2023) Despite Rift with Putin, the Wagner Group's global reach is growing. *Time*, 2 August.
Bergman, Ronan (2018) *Rise and Kill First: The Secret History of Israel's Targeted Assassinations*. New York: Random House (The secret history of Israel's targeted assassinations).
Bergman, Ronan and Fassihi, Farnaz (2021) The scientist and the A.I.-Assisted, remote-control killing machine. *New York Times*, 18 September.
Bergman, Ronen and Mazzetti, Mark (2022) The battle for the world's most powerful cyberweapon. *New York Times Magazine*, 28 January.
Bergsten, Fred (2022) *The United States vs. China: The Quest for Global Economic Leadership*. London: Polity.
Berkhoff, Karel (2012) *Motherland in Danger: Soviet Propaganda during World War II*. Cambridge, MA: Harvard University Press.
Berman, Edward (1983) *The Influence of the Carnegie, Ford, and Rockefeller Foundations on American Foreign Policy: The Ideology of Philanthropy*. New York: State University of New York Press.
Bernstein, Carl (1977) The CIA and the media: How Americas most powerful news media worked hand in glove with the central intelligence Agency and why the church

committee covered it up. *Rolling Stone*, Rolling-stone-10-20-1977?rq=the%20cia%20 and%20the%20media

Berth, Christiane (2020) ITU, the development debate, and technical cooperation in the global South, 1950–1992. In Balbi, Gabriele and Fickers, Andreas (eds.) *History of the International Telecommunication Union (ITU): Transnational Techno-diplomacy from the Telegraph to the Internet*, pp. 77–106. Berlin: De Gruyter.

Bhattacharjee, Yudhijit (2023) The daring ruse that exposed China's Campaign to steal American secrets. *New York Times Sunday Magazine*, 12 March.

Bichler, Shimshon and Nitzan, Jonathan (1996) Putting the state in its place: US foreign policy and differential capital accumulation in Middle East 'energy conflicts'. *Review of International Political Economy*, 3(4): 608–662.

Biddle, Sam (2023) U.S. Special forces want to use deepfakes for Psy-Ops. *The Intercept*, 7 March.

Biden, Joseph (2020) Why America must lead again: Rescuing U.S. Foreign policy after Trump. *Foreign Affairs*, March/April.

Bigo, Didier, Isin, Engin and Ruppert, Evelyn (eds.) (2019) *Data Politics-Worlds, Subjects, Rights*. London: Routledge.

Birnhack, Michael (2021) A post-colonial framework for researching intellectual property history. In Irene, Calboli and Maria Lillà, Montagnani (eds.) *Handbook on Intellectual Property Law Research: Lenses, Methods, and Approaches*. Oxford: Oxford University Press.

Bjola, Corneliu and Pamment, James (eds.) (2019) *Countering Online Propaganda and Extremism: The Dark Side of Digital Diplomacy*. London: Routledge.

Blair, Ann, Duguid, Paul, Goeing, Anja-Silvia and Grafton, Anthony (eds.) (2021) *Information-A Historical Companion*. Princeton: Princeton University Press.

Blair, Robert, Marty, Robert and Roessler, Philip (2022) Foreign aid and soft power: Great power competition in Africa in the early twenty-first century. *British Journal of Political Science*, 52(3): 1355–1376.

Blanchfield, Mike and Hampson, Osler Fen (2021) *The Two Michaels: Innocent Canadian Captives and High Stakes Espionage in the US-China Cyber War*. Toronto: Sutherland House.

Bleiker, Roland (ed.) (2018) *Visual Global Politics*. London: Routledge.

Blondheim, Menahem (1994) *News Over the Wires: The Telegraph and the Flow of Public Information in America, 1844–1897*. Cambridge, MA: Harvard University Press.

Boao Forum for Asia (2020) *Asia Poverty Reduction Report 2020: Asia Poverty under Globalization Changes and Public Crises*. Beijing: Boao Forum for Asia.

Boburg, Shawn (2013) Leaked files reveal reputation-management firm's deceptive tactics. *Washington Post*, 17 February.

Bodner, John, Welch, Wendy and Brodie, Ian (2020) *COVID-19 Conspiracy Theories: Qanon, 5G, the New World Order and Other Viral Ideas*. Jefferson, NC: McFarland.

Bonea, Amelia (2016) *The News of Empire: Telegraphy, Journalism and the Politics of Reporting in Colonial India*. New Delhi: Oxford University Press.

Boot, Max (2023) How a tech executive uses the 'Silicon Valley playbook' to equip Ukraine. *Washington Post*, 1 May.

Bordoff, Jason and O'Sullivan, Meghan (2022) Green Upheaval: The new geopolitics of energy. *Foreign Affairs*, January/February.

Bowen, Bleddyn (2020) *War in Space: Strategy, Spacepower, Geopolitics*. Edinburgh: Edinburgh University Press.

Bowley, Graham (2013) An Afghan Media Mogul, pushing boundaries. *New York Times*, 27 July.

Boyd-Barrett, Oliver (1980) *The International News Agencies*. London: Constable.

Boyd-Barrett, Oliver (2014) *Media Imperialism*. London: Sage.

Boyd-Barrett, Oliver (2022) *Conflict Propaganda in Syria Narrative Battles*. London: Routledge.

Boyd-Barrett, Oliver and Mirrlees, Tanner (eds.) (2019) *Media Imperialism: Continuity and Change*. Cambridge: Polity.
Brandimarte, Italo (2023) Breathless war: Martial bodies, aerial experiences and the atmospheres of empire. *European Journal of International Relations*, 1–28. https://doi.org/10.1177/13540661231153259
Brands, Hal and Gaddis, John Lewis (2021) The new cold war: America, China, and the Echoes of history. *Foreign Affairs*, 100(6): 10–20.
Braw, Elisabeth (2022) *The Defender's Dilemma: Identifying and Deterring Gray-Zone Aggression*. Washington: American Enterprise Institute Press
Brayton, Steven (2002) Outsourcing war: Mercenaries and the privatization of peacekeeping. *Journal of International Affairs*, 55(2): 303–329.
Brazys, Samuel and Alexander Dukalskis (2019) Rising powers and grassroots image management: Confucius institutes and China in the media. *The Chinese Journal of International Politics*, 12(4): 557–584.
Bremmer, Ian (2021) The technopolar moment: How digital powers will reshape the global order. *Foreign Affairs*, 100(6): 112–128.
Brennan, James (2015) International news in the age of empire. In John, Richard R. and Jonathan, Silberstein-Loeb (eds.) *Making News: The Political Economy of Journalism from the Glorious Revolution to the Internet*, pp. 107–132. Oxford: Oxford University Press.
Briant, Emma Louise (2015) *Propaganda and Counter-Terrorism: Strategies for Global Change*. Manchester: Manchester University Press.
Briggs, Asa (1970) *A History of Broadcasting in the United Kingdom, Vol. III: The War of Words*. Oxford: Oxford University Press.
Brinkerhoff, Jennifer (2009) *Digital Diasporas*. Cambridge: Cambridge University Press.
Britton, John (2013) *Cables, Crises, and the Press: The Geopolitics of the New International Information System in the Americas, 1866–1903*. Albuquerque: University of New Mexico Press.
Broadband Commission for Sustainable Development (2022) *The State of Broadband: Accelerating Broadband for New Realities*. New York: ITU/UNESCO Broadband Commission for Sustainable Development.
Broadband Commission for Sustainable Development (2023) *The State of Broadband: Digital connectivity a transformative opportunity*. New York: ITU/UNESCO Broadband Commission for Sustainable Development, September.
Broge, Tasneem and Marsh, Alastair (2021) Goldman Sachs, Harvard team up with Al Gore's investment firm. *Bloomberg*, 27 October.
Brousseau, Eric, Marzouki, Meryem and Méadel, Cécile (eds.) (2012) *Governance, Regulation, and Powers on the Internet*. Cambridge: Cambridge University Press.
Brown, Katherine (2019) *Your Country, Our War-The Press and Diplomacy in Afghanistan*. New York: Oxford University Press.
Brown, Kerry (2018) *China's Dreams: The Culture of the Chinese Communism and the Secret Source of its Power*. London: Polity.
Brown, Kerry (2020) Chinese Storytelling in the Xi Jinping Era. *The Hague Journal of Diplomacy*, 16(2–3): 323–333.
Browne, Malachy, Koettl, Christoph, Singhvi, Anjali, Reneau, Natalie, Marcolini, Barbara, al Hlou, Yousur and Jordan, Drew (2018) Douma chemical attack: One building, one bomb: How Assad gassed his own people. *The New York Times*, 25 June.
Brubaker, Rogers (2023) *Hyperconnectivity and its Discontents*. Cambridge: Polity.
Bruckman, Amy (2022) *Should You Believe Wikipedia? Online Communities and the Construction of Knowledge*. Cambridge: Cambridge University Press.
Bruns, Axel, Harrington, Stephen and Hurcombe, Edward (2020) 'Corona? 5G? Or both?': The dynamics of COVID-19/5G conspiracy theories on Facebook. *Media International Australia*, 177(1): 12–29.
Buckley, Chris (2022) Australian journalist who worked for Chinese media stands trial in Beijing. *New York Times*, 31 March.

Bunce, Mel, Franks, Suzanne and Paterson, Chris (eds.) (2017) *Africa's Media Image in the 21st Century: From the 'Heart of Darkness' to 'Africa Rising'*. London: Routledge.
Burke, Jason and Akinwotu, Emmanuel (2022) Russian mercenaries linked to civilian massacres in Mali exclusive: Internal Malian army documents show Wagner operatives took part in 'mixed missions'. *The Guardian*, 4 May.
Burns, John (2003) The world; How many people has Hussein killed? *The New York Times*, 26 January.
Burri, Mira (2017) The regulation of data flows through trade agreements. *Georgetown Journal of International Law*, 48(1): 408–448.
Bush, Sarah Sunn and Lauren Prather (2022) *From Monitors to Meddlers: How Foreign Actors Influence Local Trust in Elections*. Cambridge: Cambridge University Press.
Büthe, Tim and Mattli, Walter (2011) *The New Global Rulers: The Privatization of Regulation in the World Economy*. Princeton: Princeton University Press.
Butter, Michael and Knight, Peter (eds.) (2020) *Routledge Handbook of Conspiracy Theories*. New York: Routledge.
Byler, Darren, Franceschini, Ivan and Loubere, Nicholas (eds.) (2021) *Xinjiang Year Zero*. Canberra: Australian National University Press.
Byman, Daniel (2019) *Road Warriors: Foreign Fighters in the Armies of Jihad*. New York: Oxford University Press.
Byman, Daniel (2021) The good enough doctrine: Learning to live with terrorism. *Foreign Affairs*, 100(5): 32–43.
Byrd, William and Noorani, Javed (2017) *Industrial-Scale Looting of Afghanistan's Mineral Resources*. Washington: United States Institute of Peace, Special Report 404.
Cadwalladr, Carole and Graham-Harrison, Emma (2018) Revealed: 50 million Facebook profiles harvested for Cambridge Analytica in major data breach. *The Guardian*, 17 March.
Caesar, Ed (2021) The incredible rise of North Korea's Hacking Army. *New Yorker*, 9 April.
Cairncross, Frances (1997) *The Death of Distance: How the Communications Revolution will Change Our Lives*. London: Orion Business Books.
Cairo, Heriberto (2006) 'Portugal is not a small country': Maps and propaganda in the Salazar Regime. *Geopolitics*, 11(3): 367–395.
Calhoun, Craig, Gaonkar, Dilip and Taylor, Charles (2022) *Degenerations of Democracy*. Cambridge, MA: Harvard University Press.
Carlson, Matt, Robinson, Sue and Lewis, Seth (2021) *News After Trump: Journalism's Crisis of Relevance in a Changed Media Culture*. New York: Oxford University Press.
Casey, Steven (2008) *Selling the Korean War: Propaganda, Politics, and Public Opinion 1950–1953*. New York: Oxford University Press.
Castells, Manuel (2000) *The Information Age: Economy, Society and Culture, Vol. 3: End of Millennium*, 2nd ed. Oxford: Blackwell.
Castells, Manuel (2009) *Communication Power*. Oxford: Oxford University Press.
Cave, Damien (2023) How 'decoupling' from Chine became 'de-risking'. *New York Times,* 22 May.
Cave, Damien and Chien, Amy Chang (2022) How Taiwan's 'adorable' and ambitious diplomacy aims to keep the Island safe. *New York Times*, 2 October.
Cave, Danielle, Samantha Hoffman, Alex Joske, Fergus Ryan, and Elise (2019) *Mapping China's technology giants*. International Cyber Policy Centre, Australian strategic Policy Institute, Issue paper report no. 15, 18 April.
CCDH (2021) The disinformation dozen: Why platforms must act on twelve leading online anti-vaxxers. *Center for Countering Digital Hate*, 24 March.
Center for New American Security (2020) *Dangerous Synergies: Countering Chinese and Russian Digital Influence Operations*. Washington: Centre for New American Security.
Center for Responsive Politics (2021a) *Capitalizing on Conflict: How Defense Contractors and Foreign Nations Lobby for Arms Sales*. Washington: Center for Responsive Politics.
Centre for Responsive Politics (2021b) *Lobbying Spending Nears Record High in 2020 Amid Pandemic*. Washington: Centre for Responsive Politics.

Ceruzzi, Pauk (2021) Satellite navigation and the military-civilian dilemma: The geopolitics of GPS and its rivals. In Alexander C. T. Geppert, Brandau, Daniel and Siebeneichner, Tilmann (eds.) *Militarizing Outer Space*. London: Palgrave Macmillan.
CGTN (2021) *Is Virus Tracing for COVID-19 Politicized?* Beijing: CGTN Think Tank Online Survey.
CGTN (2021a) *Fact Check: Lies on Xinjiang-related Issues vs. the Truth*. Beijing: CGTN, 6 February.
CGTN (2021b) *China Issues Report Urging U.S. to Drop Double Standard on Human Rights*. Beijing: China Central Television Network 24 March.
CGTN (2023) *The Report on Human Rights Violations in the United States in 2022*. Chakrabarty, Dipesh (2000) *Provincializing Europe: Postcolonial Thought and Historical Difference*. Princeton,(NJ): Princeton University Press.
Chakrabarty, Dipesh (2010) The legacies of Bandung: Decolonization and the politics of culture. In Christopher, Lee (ed.) *Making a World After Empire: The Bandung Moment and its Political Afterlives*, pp. 45–68. Athens, OH: Ohio University Press.
Chakravorty, Sanjoy; Kapur, Devesh, and Singh, Nirvikar (2017) *The Other One Percent: Indians in America*. New York: Oxford University Press.
Chambers, John (2012) The internet of everything: Let's get this right. *Wired*, 14 December.
Chan, Anita Say (2014) *Networking Peripheries: Technological Futures and the Myth of Digital Universalism*. Cambridge: MIT Press.
Chandler, Robert W. (1981) *War of Ideas: The US Propaganda Campaign in Vietnam*. Boulder, CO: Westview Press.
Chang, Gordon G. (2020) *The Great U.S.-China Tech War*. New York: Encounter Books.
Chari, Raj, Hogan, John, Murphy, Gary and Crepaz, Michele (2019) *Regulating Lobbying: A Global Comparison*, 2nd ed. Manchester: Manchester University Press.
Chasi, Colin and Rodny-Gumede, Ylva (2019) No pain no gain? Reflections on decolonization and higher education in South Africa. *Africa Education Review*, 16(5): 120–133.
Chaturvedi, Sachin and Saha, Sabyasachi (2021) The BRICS way to multilateralism amid crisis. In *The Future of BRICS*, pp. 6–13. New Delhi: Observer Research Foundation, and Research and Information System for Developing Countries. https://www.orfonline.org/wpcontent/uploads/2021/08/Future_of_BRICS.pdf
Chayes, Sarah (2015) *Thieves of State: Why Corruption Threatens Global Security*. New York: W. W. Norton.
Chen, Lulu Yilun (2023) *Influence Empire: Inside the Story of Tencent and China's Tech Ambition*. New York: Hodder.
Cheng, Dean (2016) *Cyber Dragon: Inside China's Information Warfare and Cyber Operations*. Santa Barbara, CA: Praeger.
Cheng, Han and Liu, Weidong (2021) Disciplinary geopolitics and the rise of international development studies in China. *Political Geography*, 89: 1–11.
Chernobrov, Dmitry (2022) Diasporas as cyberwarriors: Infopolitics, participatory warfare and the 2020 Karabakh war. *International Affairs*, 98(2): 631–651.
Cheshkin, Ammon and Kachuyevski, Angela (2018) The Russian-speaking populations in the post-Soviet space: Language, politics and identity. *Europe-Asia Studies*, 71(1): 1–23.
Cheung, Tai Ming (2018) The rise of China as a cybersecurity industrial power: Balancing national security, geopolitical, and development priorities. *Journal of Cyber Policy*, 3(3): 306–326.
Chifu, Iulian and Simons, Greg (2023) *Rethinking Warfare in the 21st Century: The Influence and Effects of the Politics, Information and Communication Mix*. Cambridge: Cambridge University Press.
Chin, Josh and Lin, Liza (2022) *Surveillance State: Inside China's Quest to Launch a New Era of Social Control*. New York: St. Martin's Press.
China Daily (2021) Things to know about all the lies on Xinjiang: How have they come about? *China Daily*, 30 April, pp. 9–11.
China Daily (2023a) Report reveals US' pique at Hong Kong's progress in disempowering its proxies. *China Daily* (editorial), 2 April.

China Daily (2023b) China's law-based cyberspace governance in the New Era. *China Daily*, 17 March.
China Daily (2023c) USA is universal spying agency (editorial). *China Daily* (Hong Kong edition), 20 April.
China Task Force Report (2020) *U.S. House of Representatives China Task Force*, 30 September, 116th Congress, Washington.
Chkhaidze, Nicholas, Yurov, Ivan and Kuzio, Taras (2022) *Opposition in Russia to the Invasion of Ukraine: How Much of a Threat Is It to Putin's Regime?* London: The Henry Jackson Society.
Cho, Joshua (2021) Corporate media oppose Afghan control of Afghanistan. Fairness and Accuracy in Reporting. *FAIR*, 11 May.
Chomsky, Noam, Roberts, Ian and Watumull, Jeffrey (2023) The false promise of ChatGPT. *New York Times*, 8 March.
Choudhury-Lahiri, Deep (2010) *Telegraphic Imperialism: Crisis and Panic in the Indian Empire, c.1830–1920*. London: Palgrave/Macmillan.
Choudry, Aziz and Kapoor, Dip (eds.) (2013) *NGOization: Complicity, Contradictions and Prospects*. London: Zed books.
Choyleva, Diana and McMahon, Dinny (2022) China's quest for financial self-reliance: How Beijing plans to decouple from the dollar-based global trading and financial system. *Enodo Economics and Wilson Center*, August. endoeconomics.com
Chwieroth, Jeffrey (2010) *Capital Ideas: The IMF and the Rise of Financial Liberalization*. Princeton: Princeton University Press.
CISA (2023) *China Cyber Threat Overview and Advisories, Cybersecurity & Infrastructure Security Agency*. Washington: U.S. Department of Homeland Security.
Clarke, Roger (2019) Risks inherent in the digital surveillance economy: A research agenda. *Journal of Information Technology*, 34(1): 59–80.
Clifford, Mark (2022) *Today Hong Kong, Tomorrow the World: What China's Crackdown Reveals about Its Plans to End Freedom Everywhere*. New York: St. Martin's.
Clifton, Eli (2021) Top defense firms spent $1B on Lobbying during Afghan War, saw $2T return. *Responsible Statecraft*, 2 September.
CNBC (2013) Bill Clinton: we could have saved 300,000 lives in Rwanda. *CNBC*, 13 March.
CNN (2002) Rice: Iraq trained al Qaeda in chemical weapons. *CNN*, 26 September. https://edition.cnn.com/2002/US/09/25/us.iraq.alqaeda/
Coll, Steve and Entous, Adams (2021) The secret history of the U.S. Diplomatic failure in Afghanistan. *New Yorker*, 20 December.
Colley, Thomas, Moore, Martin (2022) News as geopolitics: China, CGTN and the 2020 US presidential election. *The Journal of International Communication*, 16(3): 1–22.
Collini, Francesco et al. (2022) Beijing's Long Arm-China's Secret Police Stations in Europe. *Der Spiegel*, 4.11 or 11.4 (check)
Conflict Armament Research (2017) *Weapons of the Islamic State*. London: Conflict Armament Research. www.conflictarm.com/reports/weapons-of-the-islamic-state/
Congressional Research Service (2022a) *Defense Primer: Electronic Warfare*. Washington: Congressional Research Service. https://crsreports.congress.gov/product/pdf/IF/IF11118
Congressional Research Service (2022b) *Restrictions on Huawei Technologies: National Security, Foreign Policy, and Economic Interests*, 5 January. R47012U.S. www.everycrsreport.com/files/2022-01
Connell, Raewyn (2007) *Southern Theory: Social Science and the Global Dynamics of Knowledge*. Cambridge: Polity.
Connelly, Matthew (2023) *The Declassification Engine: What History Reveals About America's Top Secrets*. New York: Pantheon.
Conrad, Sebastian (2016) *What Is Global History?* Princeton: Princeton University Press.
Convergence (2022) Conspiracy Theories in Digital Environments, special issue. *Convergence*, 28: 4.

Cook, Chris, Staton, Bethan, Harlow, Max and Schipani, Andres (2021) The essay mills undermining academic standards around the world. *The Financial Times*, 6 November.

Cook, Sarah (2020) *Beijing's Global Megaphone: The Expansion of Chinese Communist Party Media Influence since 2017*. Washington: Freedom House.

Cooper, Helene and Mashal, Mujib (2017) U.S. Drops 'mother of all bombs' on ISIS caves in Afghanistan. *New York Times*, 13 April.

Cooper, Helene and Schmitt, Eric (2023) Ukraine War Plans Leak Prompts Pentagon Investigation classified documents detailing secret American and NATO plans have appeared on Twitter and Telegram. *New York Times*, 6 April.

Cooper, Richard and Kohler, Juliette Voïnov (eds.) (2009) *Responsibility to Protect: The Global Moral Compact for the 21st Century*, London: Palgrave Macmillan.

Copeland, Dale (2022) When trade leads to war-China, Russia, and the limits of interdependence. *Foreign Affairs*, 23 August.

Copp, Tara (2018) Here's the blueprint for Erik Prince's $5 billion plan to privatize the Afghanistan War. *Military Times*. www.militarytimes.com/news/your-military/2018/09/05/heres-the-blueprint-forerik-princes-5-billion-plan-to-privatize-the-afghanistan-war/

Cornish, Chloe and Parkin, Benjamin (2022) Asia's richest man Gautam Adani reveals global media ambitions. *Financial Times*, 25 November. www.ft.com/content/d6c5ffa0-0b9b-436f-8c8b-ef4170bedfe3

Corporate Europe Observatory (2020) *Big Tech Lobbying: Google, Amazon & Friends and their Hidden Influence*. Brussels: Corporate Europe Observatory. https://corporateeurope.org/en/2020/09/big-tech-lobbying

Cosentino, Gabriele (2023) *The Infodemic: Disinformation, Geopolitics and the COVID-19 Pandemic*. London: Bloomsbury Academic.

Costs of War Project (2022) *Watson Institute of International & Public Affairs*. Brown University. https://watson.brown.edu/costsofwar.

Cottle, Simon and Cooper, Glenda (eds.) (2015) *Humanitarianism, Communications and Change*. New York: Peter Lang.

Couldry, Nick and Mejías, Ulises (2019) *The Costs of Connection: How Data is Colonizing Human Life and Appropriating it for Capitalism*. Los Angeles: Stanford University Press.

Couture, Stephane and Toupin, Sophie (2019) What does the notion of 'sovereignty' mean when referring to the digital? *New Media & Society*, 21(2): 2305–2322. https://doi.org/10.1177/1461444819865984

Coy, Peter (2023) To see one of A.I.'s Greatest dangers, look to the military. *New York Times*, 19 May.

Creemers, Rogier (2020) China's conception of cyber sovereignty. In Broeders, Dennis and Bibi Berg (eds.) *Governing Cyberspace: Behavior, Power and Diplomacy*, pp. 107–145. Lanham: Rowman & Littlefield.

Creemers, Rogier, Triolo, Paul and Webster, Graham (2018) China's new top Internet official lays out agenda for Party control online. *DigiChina*, 24 September. www.newamerica.org/cybersecurity-initiative/digichina/blog/translation-chinas-new-top-Internetofficial lays-out-agenda-for-party-control-online/.

Crilley, Rhys and Chatterje-Doody, Precious (2022) Emotions and war on YouTube: Affective investment in RT's visual narratives of the conflict in Syria. *Cambridge Review of International Affairs*, 33(5): 713–733.

Crilley, Rhys, Gillespie, Marie, Vidgen, Bertie and Wills, Alistair (2022) Understanding RT's audiences: Exposure not endorsement for twitter followers of Russian state-sponsored media. *The International Journal of Press/Politics*, 27(1): 220–242.

Crisp, James (2022) Why Putin would want to blow up Nord Stream 2, and the advantages it gives him. *The Telegraph*, 28 September.

Critchlow, James (1995) *Radio Hole-in-the-Head: Radio Liberty: An Insider's Story of Cold War Broadcasting*. Washington: American University Press.

Cronau, Peter (2022) *Massive Anti-Russian 'Bot Army' Exposed by Australian Researchers*, 3 November. https://declassifiedaus.org/2022/11/03/strongmassive-anti-russian-bot-army-exposed-by-australian-researchers-strong/

Crowley, Michael and Wong, Edward (2023) U.S. Officials overseeing Aid say Ukrainian leaders are tackling corruption. *New York Times*, 27 January.

CRS (2020a) *Intellectual Property Rights and International Trade*. Washington: Congressional Research Service.

CRS (2020b) *US EU Data Protection Rules and U.S. Implications*. Washington: Congressional Research Service.

Crystal, David (2003) *English as a Global Language*, 2nd ed. Cambridge: Cambridge University Press.

CSIS (2020) Criteria for security and trust in telecommunications networks and services. *CSIS Working Group on Trust and Security in 5G Networks, Center for Strategic and International Studies*, 13 May.

Cull, Nicholas (2009) *The Cold War and the United States Information Agency: American Propaganda and Public Diplomacy 1945–1989*. Cambridge: Cambridge University Press.

Culpepper, Pepper D. and Thelen, Kathleen (2020). Are we all Amazon primed? Consumers and the politics of platform power. *Comparative Political Studies*, 53(2): 288–318.

Cumming-Bruce, Nick and Ramzy, Austin (2022) U.N. Says China may have committed 'crimes against humanity' in Xinjiang. *New York Times*, 31 August.

Cummings, Richard (2010) *Radio Free Europe's 'Crusade for Freedom': Rallying Americans behind Cold War Broadcasting, 1950–1960*. Jefferson, NC: McFarland & Co.

Curran, James and Park, Myung-Jin (eds.) (2000) *De-Westernizing Media Studies*. London: Routledge.

Dagres, Holly (2022) *Iranians on #SocialMedia*. Washington: Atlantic Council.

Dahm, Michael (2020) *Chinese Debates on the Military Utility of Artificial Intelligence.*, Washington: War on the Rocks.

Dai, Yaoyao and Luqiu, Luwei Rose (2022) Wolf warriors and diplomacy in the New Era: An empirical analysis of China's diplomatic language. *China Review*, 22(2): 253–283.

Daoud, Ziad and Johnson, Scott (2023) A World Made of BRICS. *Bloomberg*, 8 November. https://www.bloomberg.com/news/articles/2023-11-07/a-world-made-of-brics#xj4y7vzkg

Dapiran, Antony (2020) *City on Fire: The Fight for Hong Kong*. London: Scribe.

Daudin, Guillaume, Morys, Matthias and O'Rourke, Kevin H. (2010) Globalization, 1870–1914. In Stephen Broadberry and Kevin O'Rourke (eds.) *The Cambridge Economic History of Modern Europe*, pp. 5–29. Cambridge: Cambridge University Press.

Davenport, Christian (2018) *The Space Barons: Elon Musk, Jeff Bezos, and the Quest to Colonize the Cosmos*. New York: PublicAffairs.

David, Alexander, Thakur, Vineet and Vale, Peter (2020) *The Imperial Discipline: Race and the Founding of International Relations*. London: Pluto Press.

Davis, Aeron (2002) *Public Relations Democracy: Politics, Public Relations and the Mass Media in Britain*. Manchester: Manchester University Press.

Davis, Aeron (2011) Mediation, financialization, and the global financial crisis: An inverted political economy perspective. In Winseck, D. and Jin, D. Y. (eds.) *The Political Economies of Media: The Transformation of the Global Media Industries*, pp. 241–254. London: Bloomsbury Academic.

Davis, Stuart H. and Ness, Immanuel (eds.) (2021) *Sanctions as War: Anti-imperialist Perspectives on American Geo-economic Strategy*. Boston, MA: Brill.

Davydov, Sergey (ed.) (2020) *Internet in Russia: A Study of the Runet and its Impact on Social Life*. Berlin: Springer.

De Groot, Tom and Regilme, Salvador (2022) Private military and security companies and the militarization of humanitarianism. *Journal of Developing Societies*, 38(1): 50–80.

De La Chapelle, Bertrand and Porciuncula, Lorrayne (2021) *We Need to Talk about Data: Framing the Debate Around the Free Flow of Data and Data-Sovereignty*. www.internetjurisdiction.net

de Oliveira, Felipe Antunes (2022) Lost and found: Bourgeois dependency theory and the forgotten roots of neo-developmentalism. *Latin American Perspectives*, 49(1): 36–56.

De Witte, Ludo (2003) *The Assassination of Lumumba*, 2nd ed. London: Verso (translated from the original Dutch by Renee Fenby and Ann Wright).

Defense Intelligence Agency (2022) *2022 Challenges to Security in Space: Space Reliance in an Era of Competition and Expansion*. Washington: Defense Intelligence Agency. www.dia.mil/Military-Power-Publications.

Deibert, Ron (2015) The geopolitics of cyberspace after Snowden. *Current History*. www.currenthistory.com/Deibert_CurrentHistory.pdf.

Dely, Angela (2019) Algorithmic oppression with Chinese characteristics: AI against Xinjiang's Uyghurs. *Global Information Society Watch*. www.giswatch.org/node/6165#_ftn33

DeNardis, Laura (2014) *The Global War for Internet Governance*. New Haven: Yale University Press.

DeNardis, Laura (2020) *The Internet in Everything: Freedom and Security in a World with No Off Switch*. New Haven: Yale University Press.

DeNardis, Laura (ed.) (2011) *Opening Standards: The Global Politics of Interoperability*. New Haven: Yale University Press.

Denyer, Simon (2016) China's Scary Lesson to the World: Censoring the Internet Works. *Washington Post*, 23 May.

Department of Defense (2009) *Dictionary of Military and Associated Terms*. Washington: Department of Defense. www.dtic.mil/doctrine/jel/new_pubs/jp1_02.pdf

Department of Defense (2022) *Military and Security Developments Involving the People's Republic of China 2022*. Washington: Department of Defense.

Department of Justice (2019) *U.S. and UK Sign Landmark Cross-Border Data access Agreement to Combat Criminals and Terrorists Online, 3 October*. Washington: Department of Justice.

Department of State (2023) *Hong Kong Policy Act Report, 32*. Washington: U.S. Department of State, Bureau of East Asian and Pacific Affairs.

Der Derian, James (2009) *Virtuous War: Mapping the Military Industrial-Media-Entertainment Network*, 2nd ed. London: Routledge.

Der Derian, James and Wendt, Alexander (2020) 'Quantizing international relations': The case for quantum approaches to international theory and security practice. *Security Dialogue*, 51(5): 399–413.

Der Derian, James and Wendt, Alexander (2022) Quantum international relations: The case for new human science for world politics. In Der Derian, James and Wendt, Alexander (eds.) *Quantum International Relations: A Human Science for World Politics*, pp. 3–26. New York: Oxford University Press.

Desai, Radhika (2023) *Capitalism, Coronavirus and War: A Geopolitical Economy*. London: Routledge.

Desmond, Robert (1978) *The Information Process: World News Reporting to the Twentieth Century*. Iowa City: University of Iowa Press.

Deudney, Daniel (2021) *Dark Skies: Space Expansionism, Planetary Geopolitics, and the Ends of Humanity*. Oxford: Oxford University Press.

Devaux, Axelle, Grand-Clément, Sarah and Hoorens, Stijn (2022) *Truth Decay in Europe: Exploring the Role of Facts and Analysis in European Public Life*. Brussels: RAND Europe.

Diamond, Larry (2010) Liberation technology. *Journal of Democracy*, 21(3): 69–83.

Diamond, Larry (2019) *Ill Winds: Saving Democracy from Russian Rage, Chinese Ambition, and American Complacency*. New York: Penguin.

Diesen, Glenn (2022) *Russophobia-Propaganda in International Politics*. London: Palgrave/Macmillan.
Dijck, José van, Poell, Thomas and de Waal, Martijn (2018) *The Platform Society: Public Values in a Connected World*. Oxford: Oxford University Press.
Dikötter, Frank (2022) *China After Mao: The Rise of a Superpower*. London: Bloomsbury.
DiMaggio, Anthony R. (2022) Conspiracy theories and the manufacture of dissent: QAnon, the "Big Lie," COVID-19, and the rise of rightwing propaganda. *Critical Sociology*, 48: 1025–1048.
Dirlik, Arif (2017) *Complicities: The People's Republic of China in Global Capitalism*. Chicago, IL: Prickly Paradigm Press.
Dittmer, Jason (2007) The Tyranny of the serial: Popular geopolitics, the nation, and comic book discourse. *Antipode*, 39(2): 247–268.
Dixon, Deborah (2015) *Feminist Geopolitics: Material States*. London: Routledge.
Dixon, Paul (2009) 'Hearts and minds'? British counter-insurgency from Malaya to Iraq. *Journal of Strategic Studies*, 32(3): 353–381.
Doboš, Bohumil (2019) *Geopolitics of the Outer Space: A European Perspective*. Cham: Springer.
Dodds, Klaus (2003) Licensed to stereotype: Popular geopolitics, James Bond and the spectre of Balkanism. *Geopolitics*, 8(2): 125–156.
Dodds, Klaus and Ingram, Alan (eds.) (2009) *Spaces of Security and Insecurity: Geographies of the War on Terror*. London: Routledge.
Dogan, Taner (2021) *Communication Strategies in Turkey: Erdoğan, the AKP and Political Messaging*. London: I.B. Tauris.
Dogra, Nandita (2012) *Representations of Global Poverty: Aid, Development and International NGOs*. London: I. B. Tauris.
Dollar, David and Huang, Yiping (2022) *The Digital Financial Revolution in China*. Washington: Brookings Institution Press.
Donaldson, Dave and Storeygard, Adam (2016). The view from above: Applications of satellite data in economics. *Journal of Economic Perspectives*, 30(4): 171–198.
Donati, Jessica (2021) *Eagle Down-The Last Special Forces Fighting the Forever War*. New York: PublicAffairs.
Donnan, Shawn (2011) Think again. *Financial Times Magazine*, 8 July.
Dorfman, Zach (2020a) China used stolen data to expose CIA operatives in Africa and Europe. The discovery of U.S. Spy networks in China fueled a decade long global war over data between Beijing and Washington. *Foreign Policy*, 21 December.
Dorfman, Zach (2020b) Beijing ransacked data as U.S. Sources went dark in China as Xi consolidated power, U.S. officials struggled to read China's new ruler. *Foreign Policy*, 22 December.
Dorfman, Zach (2020c) Tech giants are giving China a vital edge in Espionage U.S. Officials say private Chinese firms have been enlisted to process stolen data for their country's spy agencies. *Foreign Policy*, 23 December.
Dorfman, Zach (2022) Exclusive: Secret CIA training program in Ukraine helped Kyiv prepare for Russian invasion. *Yahoo News*, 16 March.
Doshi, Rush (2021) *The Long Game: China's Grand Strategy to Displace American Order*. Oxford: Oxford University Press.
Doshi, Rush, Dale-Huang, Alexis and Zhang, Gaoqi (2021) *Northern Expedition: China's Arctic Activities and Ambitions*. Washington: Brookings Institution.
Doshi, Rush, De La Bruyère, Emily, Picarsic, Nathan and Ferguson, John (2021) *China as a 'Cyber Great Power': Beijing's Two Voices in Telecommunications*. Washington: Brookings.
Dourish, Paul (2015) Protocols, packets, and proximity: The materiality of internet routing. In Parks, Lisa and Starosielski, Nicole (eds.) *Signal Traffic: Critical Studies of Media Infrastructures*, pp. 183–204. Chicago: University of Illinois Press.
Douthat, Ross (2011) A very liberal intervention. *New York Times*, 20 March.

Dreher, Axel, Fuchs, Andreas, Parks, Bradley, Strange, Austin and Tierney, Michael (2022) *Banking on Beijing: The Aims and Impacts of China's Overseas Development Program*. Cambridge: Cambridge University Press.

Drezner, Daniel, Farrell, Henry and Newman, Abraham (eds.) (2021) *The Uses and Abuses of Weaponized Interdependence*. Washington: Brookings Institution Press.

Duara, Prasenjit (2014) *The Crisis of Global Modernity: Asian Traditions and a Sustainable Future*. Cambridge: Cambridge University Press.

Duarte, Luiza, Albro, Robert and Hershberg, Eric (2022) *Communicating Influence: China's Messaging in Latin America and the Caribbean*. American University's Center for Latin American and Latino Studies (CLALS), CLALS Working Paper Series No. 35, February.

Dubrofsky, Rachel and Magnet, Shoshana (eds.) (2015) *Feminist Surveillance Studies*. Durham, NC: Duke University Press.

Dugast, J., and Foucault, T. (2018). Data abundance and asset price informativeness. *Journal of Financial Economics*, 130(2): 367–391.

Dutta, Soumitra and Lanvin, Bruno (eds.) (2021) *The Network Readiness Index 2021* Washington: Portulans Institute.

Dyer-Witheford, Nick and De Peuter, Greig (2009) *Games of Empire: Global Capitalism and Video Games*. Minneapolis: University of Minnesota Press.

Eady, Gregory, Paskhalis, Tom, Zilinsky, Jan et al. (2023) Exposure to the Russian Internet Research Agency foreign influence campaign on Twitter in the 2016 US election and its relationship to attitudes and voting behavior. *Nature Communication*, 14(62): 1–11.

Eaton, Charlie (2021) *Bankers in the Ivory Tower-The Troubling Rise of Financiers in US Higher Education*. Chicago: Chicago University Press.

Ebel, Francesca (2023) The rise and violent demise of pro-Russian war blogger. *Washington Post*, 30 April.

Eberstadt, Nicholas (2019) With great demographics comes great power: Why population will drive geopolitics. *Foreign Affairs*, 98(4): 146–157.

Ebert, Hannes and Maurer, Tim (2013) Contested cyberspace and rising powers. *Third World Quarterly*, 34(6): 1054–1074.

ECFR (2021) *Network Effects: Europe's Digital Sovereignty in the Mediterranean. ECFR/393*, May. London: The European Council on Foreign Relations.

Economist (2019) The Redmond doctrine: Lessons from Microsoft's corporate foreign policy. *The Economist*, September 12.

Economy, Elizabeth (2022) *The World According to China*. Cambridge: Polity.

EEAS (2022) *Strategic Communications, Task Forces and Information Analysis (STRAT. 2)* 2022 Report on EEAS Activities to Counter FIMI. Brussels: European External Action Service.

Electronic Frontier Foundation (2018) *The Malicious Use of Artificial Intelligence: Forecasting, Prevention, and Mitigation*. San Francisco, CA: Electronic Frontier Foundation. https://www.eff.org/files/2018/02/20/malicious_ai_report_final.pdf

Elkins, Caroline (2005) *Imperial Reckoning: The Untold Story of Britain's Gulag in Kenya*. New York: Henry Holt.

Elkins, Caroline (2022) *Legacy of Violence: A History of the British Empire*. New York: Knopf.

Ellul, Jacques (1965) *Propaganda: The Formation of Men's Attitudes*. New York: Alfred Knopf.

Elmi, Nima (2020) Is big tech setting Africa back? *Foreign Policy*, 11 November.

Elswah, Mona and Howard, Philip (2020) 'Anything that Causes Chaos': The Organizational Behaviour of Russia Today (RT). *Journal of Communication*, 70(5): 623–645.

Elswah, Mona and Howard, Philip (2022) Where news could not inspire change: TRT World as a party broadcaster. *Journalism*, 23(10): 2079–2095.

Emmerson, Donald (ed.) (2020) *The Deer and the Dragon: Southeast Asia and China in the 21st Century*. Stanford: Walter H. Shorenstein Asia-Pacific Research Center, Stanford University, Brookings Institution Press.

Engstrom, Jeffrey (2018) *System Confrontation and System Destruction Warfare: How the Chinese People's Liberation Army Seeks to Wage Modern Warfare*. Santa Monica: RAND Corporation.

Epifanova, Alena (2020) *Deciphering Russia's 'Sovereign Internet Law': Tightening Control and Accelerating the Splinternet*. Berlin: The German Council on Foreign Relations, Analysis.

Epstein, Helen (2017) *Another Fine Mess: How America Looked on as Uganda Kindled the Rwanda Genocide*. New York: Columbia Global Reports.

Erichsen, Casper and Olusoga, David (2010) *The Kaiser's Holocaust: Germany's Forgotten Genocide and the Colonial Roots of Nazism*. London: Faber.

Ericsson (2023) *Ericsson Mobility Report*, June. ericsson.com/mobility-report

Erisman, Porter (2015) *Alibaba's World: How a Remarkable Chinese Company Is Changing the Face of Global Business*. New York: Palgrave Macmillan.

Erwin, Sandra (2022) As Russia prepared to invade, U.S. opened commercial imagery pipeline to Ukraine. *Space News*, 6 April.

European Commission (2021a) *2030 Digital Compass: The European Way for the Digital Decade*. Communication from the Commission to the European Parliament, the Council, the European economic and social committee and the committee of the regions, COM (p. 118). https://ec.europa.eu/info/sites/default/files/communication-digital-compass-2030_en.pdf

European Commission (2021b) *Global Gateway*. https://ec.europa.eu/info/strategy/priorities-2019–2024/stronger-europe-world/global-gateway_en

European Commission (2022) *Statement by President von der Leyen on Further Measures to Respond to the Russian Invasion of Ukraine*. Brussels: European Commission. https://ec.europa.eu/commission/presscorner/detail/en/statement_22_1441.

European Parliament (2022) European Parliament resolution of 9 March 2022 on foreign interference in all democratic processes in the European Union, including disinformation (2020/2268(INI)). https://www.europarl.europa.eu/doceo/document/TA-9-2022-0064_EN.html

European Union (2022) *A Strategic Compass: For Security and Defence*. Brussels: European Union.

European Values Centre (2018) 2018 Ranking of countermeasures by the EU28 to the Kremlin's subversion operations. *Kremlin Watch Report*. www.kremlinwatch.eu/userfiles/2018-ranking-of-countermeasures-by-the-eu28-to-the-kremlin-s-subversion-operations.pdf

Evans, Heidi (2010) 'The path to freedom'? Transocean and German wireless telegraphy, 1914–1922. *Historical Social Research*, 35(1): 209–233.

Evron, Yoram (2019) The challenge of implementing the belt and road initiative in the Middle East: Connectivity projects under conditions of limited political engagement. *China Quarterly* 237: 196–216.

Fang, Kecheng (2022) 'Rumor-Debunking' as a propaganda and censorship strategy in China: The case of the COVID-19 outbreak. In Wasserman, Herman and Madrid-Morales, Dani (eds.) *Disinformation in the Global South*, pp. 108–122. Hoboken: Wiley.

Fang, Lee (2022) Former NSA chief signed deal to train Saudi hackers months before Jamal Khashoggi's murder. *Intercept*, 27 September.

Fang, Lee, Klippenstein, Ken and Boguslaw, Daniel (2023) New FTX filing pulls back the curtain on Sam Bankman-Fried's massive influence-peddling operation. *The Intercept*, 31 January.

Farahany, Nita (2023) *The Battle for Your Brain: Defending Your Right to Think Freely in the Age of Neurotechnology*. New York: St Martin's Press.

Fárek, Martin (2022) *India in the Eyes of Europeans: Conceptualization of Religion in Theology and Oriental Studies*. Chicago: University of Chicago Press.

Farrell, Henry and Newman, Abraham (2019) Weaponized interdependence: How global economic networks shape state coercion. *International Security*, 44: 42–79.

Farrell, Henry, Newman, Abraham and Wallace, Jeremy (2022) Spirals of delusion: How AI distorts decision-making and makes dictators more dangerous. *Foreign Affairs*, September/October.

Faulconbridge, Guy (2022) *Britain Secretly Funded Reuters in 1960s and 1970s – Documents*. London: Reuters.

FCCC (2020) *Control, Halt, Delete: Reporting in China under Threat of Expulsion*. Beijing: Foreign Correspondents' Club of China.

Feldman, Bob (2007) Report from the field: Left media and left think tanks–foundation-managed protest? *Critical Sociology*, 33: 427–446.

Felman, Josh and Subramanian, Arvind (2022) Why India can't replace China. *Foreign Affairs*, December.

Ferracane, Martina, Lee-Makiyama, Hosuk and van der Marel, Erik (2018) *Digital Trade Restrictiveness Index*. Brussels: European Center for International Political Economy.

Ferretti, Federico (2021) Geopolitics of decolonization: The subaltern diplomacies of Lusophone Africa (1961–1974). *Political Geography*, 85: 1–11.

FICCI/EY (2023) *Windows of Opportunity April 2023 India's Media & Entertainment Sector – Maximizing across Segments*. Mumbai: Federation of Indian Chambers of Commerce and Industry in collaboration with Ernst & Young.

Fifield, Anna (2020) China is waging a global propaganda war to silence critics Abroad, report warns. *Washington Post*, 15 January.

Fisher, Aleksandr (2020) Demonizing the Enemy: The Influence of Russian State-Sponsored Media on American Audiences. *Post-Soviet Affairs*, 36(4): 281–296.

Fivenson, Adam, Petrenko, Galyna, Víchová, Veronika and Poleščuk, Andrej (2023) *Shielding Democracy: Civil Society Adaptations to Kremlin Disinformation about Ukraine*. Washington: National Endowment for Democracy.

Flew, Terry (2021) *Regulating Platforms*. Cambridge: Polity.

Flint, Colin (2022) *Introduction to Geopolitics*, 4th ed. London: Routledge.

Fly, J., Rosenberger, L., and Salvo, D. (2018) *Policy Blueprint for Countering Authoritarian Interference in Democracies, no. 27*. Berlin: The German Marshall Fund of the United States

Fok, James (2021) *Financial Cold War: A View of Sino-US Relations from the Financial Markets*. Cambridge: Wiley.

Foroudi, Layli and Rose Michael (2023) Macron criticised for saying Europe should take independent stance on Taiwan. *Reuters*, 10 April.

Fortune (2024) Fortune global 500. *Fortune*, August. https://fortune.com/ranking/global500/

Fox, Christine and Probasco, Emelia (2022) Big tech goes to war: To help Ukraine, Washington and Silicon Valley must work together. *Foreign Affairs*, 19 October.

Franceschini, Ivan and Loubere, Nicholas (2022) *Global China as Method*. Cambridge: Cambridge University Press.

Frankopan, Peter (2018) *The New Silk Roads: The Present and Future of the World*. London: Bloomsbury.

Franks, Suzanne (2013) *Reporting Disasters: Famine, Aid, Politics and the Media*. London: Hurst.

Frau-Meigs, Divina, Nicey, Jérémie, Palmer, Michael, Pohle, Julia and Tupper, Patricio (eds.) (2012) *From NWICO to WSIS: 30 Years of Communication Geopolitics Actors and Flows, Structures and Divides*. Bristol: Intellect.

Freedman, Des (2008) *The Politics of Media Policy*. Cambridge: Polity.

Freeman, Ben (2012) *The Foreign Policy Auction-Foreign Lobbying in America*. Scotts Valley: CreateSpace Independent Publishing Platform.

Freeman, Ben (2020) *U.S. Government and contractor funding of America's Top 50 think tanks*. Washington: Foreign Influence Transparency Initiative (FITI); Center for International Policy.

French, Howard (2022) *Born in Blackness: Africa and the Making of the Modern World: Africa, Africans, and the Making of the Modern World, 1471 to the Second World War*. New York: WW Norton.

Freymann, Eyck (2020) *One Belt One Road: Chinese Power Meets the World*. Cambridge, MA: Harvard University Press.

Freymann, Eyck (2021) Influence without entanglement in the Middle East. *Foreign Policy*, 25 February.

Fried, Daniel and Polyakova, Alina (2018) *Democratic Defense Against Disinformation*. Washington: Atlantic Council.

Friedman, Tom (2020) A geopolitical Earthquake just hit the Mideast. *The New York Times*, 13 August.

Friel, Howard and Falk, Richard (2004) *The Record of the Paper: How the New York Times Misreports US Foreign Policy*. London: Verso.

Frisch, Nicholas, Belair-Gagnon, Valerie and Agur, Colin (2018) Media capture with Chinese characteristics: Changing patterns in Hong Kong's news media system. *Journalism*, 19(8): 1165–1181.

Fuchs, Christian (2016) Baidu, Weibo and Renren: The global political economy of social media in China. *Asian Journal of Communication*, 26(1): 14–41.

Fuchs, Christian (2018) *Digital Demagogue: Authoritarian Capitalism in the Age of Trump and Twitter*. London: Pluto.

Fukuyama, Francis (2020) 30 years of world politics-what has changed? *Journal of Democracy*, 31(1): 11–21.

Fukuyama, Francis, Richman, Barak, and Goel, Ashish (2021) How to save democracy from technology: Ending big tech's information monopoly. *Foreign Affairs*, 100(1): 98–110.

Fulton, Jonathan (2022) *China is Trying to Create a Wedge between the US and Gulf Allies. Washington Should Take Note*. Washington: Atlantic Council.

Gagliardone, Iginio (2019) *China, Africa, and the Future of the Internet: New Media, New Politics*. London: Zed Books.

GAIA-X (2022) *Gaia-x – Architecture Document*. Brussels, April. https://gaia-x.eu/wp-content/uploads/2022/06/Gaia-x-Architecture-Document-22.04-Release.pdf

Gaida, Jamie, Wong-Leung, Jennifer, Robin, Stephan and Cave, Danielle (2023) *Critical Technology Tracker: The global race for future power*. Canberra: Australian Strategic Policy Institute, International Cyber Policy Centre (Policy Brief, Report No. 69/2023).

Galafa, Beaton (2019) The new 'heart of darkness': Exploring images of Africa in Wolf Warrior 2. *Asia-Pacific Journal: Japan Focus*, 17(4).

Gall, Carlotta (2023) Now fighting for Ukraine: Volunteers seeking revenge against Russia. *New York Times*, 8 January.

Gallagher, Kevin and Kozul-Wright, Richard (2021) *The Case for a New Bretton Woods*. Cambridge: Polity.

Galloni, Alessandra (2022) *Tanks, TikTok and Trust: Journalism in a Time of Turmoil*. Oxford: Reuters Memorial Lecture, Reuters Institute.

Gambhir, Harleen (2016) *The Virtual Caliphate: ISIS's Information Warfare*. Washington: Institute for the Study of War.

Gamlen, Alan (2019) *Human Geopolitics: States, Emigrants, and the Rise of the Diaspora Institutions*. Oxford: Oxford University Press.

Gao, Henry (2012) The shifting stars: The rise of China, emerging economies and the future of world trade governance. In Bellmann, Meléndez-Ortiz Christophe and Mendoza, Miguel Rodriguez (eds.) *The Future and the WTO: Confronting the Challenges*, pp. 74–79. Geneva: International Centre for Trade and Sustainable Development.

García-Herrero, Alicia and Schindowski, Robin (2023) *Global trends in countries' perceptions of the Belt and Road Initiative*. Working Paper 04, April, Brussels: Bruegel.

Gardner, Kyle (2021) *The Frontier Complex: Geopolitics and the Making of the Indo-China Border, 1846–1962*. Cambridge: Cambridge University Press.

Gardner, Tracy and Inger, Simon (2021) How readers discover content in scholarly publications. *Renew Consultants*, July. renew.pub/discovery2021

Garlick, Jeremy (2019) *The Impact of China's Belt and Road Initiative: From Asia to Europe*. London: Routledge.

Garner, Ian (2023) *Z Generation: Into the Heart of Russia's Fascist Youth*. London: Hurst.

Garsten, Christina and Sorbom, Adrienne (2018) *Discreet Power: How the World Economic Forum Shapes Market Agendas*. Los Angeles: Stanford University Press.

Gaub, Florence (2016) An unhappy marriage: Civil-military relations in Post-Saddam Iraq. *Carnegie Middle East Center*, January.

Gavra, Dmitry and Bykova, Elena (2021) Russian soft power from USSR to Putin's Russia. In Thussu, Daya Kishan and Nordenstreng, Kaarle (eds.) *BRICS Media: Reshaping the Global Communication Order?*, pp. 177–192. London: Routledge.

GCS (2019) *RESIST Disinformation: A Toolkit*. London: Government Communication Service.

Gelpern, Anna, Horn Sebastian, Morris, Scott, Parks, Brad and Trebesch, Christoph (2021) *How China Lends: A Rare Look into 100 Debt Contracts with Foreign Governments*. Copblished by AidData at William and Mary; The Kiel Institute for the World Economy and the Peterson Institute for International Economics, March. www.cgdev.org/publication/how-china-lends-rare-look-into-100-debt-contracts-foreign-governments

Gerard, Emmanuel and Kuklick, Bruce (2015) *Death in the Congo: Murdering Patrice Lumumba*. Harvard: Harvard University Press.

Gerges, Fawaz (2017) *ISIS: A History*. Princeton: Princeton University Press.

Gerlitz, Carolin and Helmond, Anne (2013) The like economy: Social buttons and the data-intensive web. *New Media & Society*, 15(8): 1348–1365.

German Presidency of the EU Council (2020) *Together for Europe's Recovery: Programme for Germany's Presidency of the Council of the European Union (1 July to 31 December 2020)*. Berlin: Council of the European Union.

German Presidency of the European Council (2020) *Together for Europe's Recovery: Programme for Germany's Presidency of the Council of the European Union*. 1 July to 31 December 2020. Berlin. www.auswaertiges-amt.de

Gerstle, Gary (2022) *The Rise and Fall of the Neoliberal Order: America and the World in the Free Market Era*. Oxford: Oxford University Press.

Gessen, Masha (2022) Inside Putin's propaganda machine. *New Yorker*, 18 May.

Gessen, Masha (2023) How Russian journalists in exile are covering the war in Ukraine. *New Yorker*, 13 March.

Gettleman, Jeffrey (2022) An American in Ukraine finds the war he's been searching for. *New York Times*, 9 October.

Ghiasy, Richard and Zhou, Jiayi (2017) *The Silk Road Economic Belt: Considering Security Implications and EU-China Cooperation Prospects*. Stockholm: SIPRI.

Ghiasy, Richard, Su, Fei and Saalman, Lora (2018) *The 21st Century Maritime Silk Road: Security Implications and Ways Forward for the European Union*. Stockholm: Stockholm International Peace Research Institute, in collaboration with Friedrich Ebert Stiftung.

Gibson, Liam (2022) Suspected Chinese hackers spied on gov'ts, NGOs, media: Report. *Al Jazeera*, 18 August.

Giles, Keir (2016) *Russia's 'New' Tools for Confronting the West – Continuity and Innovation in Moscow's Exercise of Power*. London: Chatham House Research Paper

Giustozzi, Antonio (2019) *The Taliban at War, 2001–2018*. London: Hurst.

Gleeson, John (1950) *The Genesis of Russophobia in Great Britain*. Cambridge: Harvard University Press.

Global Engagement Centre (2023a) *Disinformation Roulette: The Kremlin's Year of Lies to Justify an Unjustifiable War*, 23 February. Washington: Global Engagement Centre.

Global Engagement Center (2023b) *The Kremlin's Never-Ending Attempt to Spread Disinformation about Biological Weapons*. Washington: Global Engagement Center.

GLOBSEC-NED (2022) *Ukrainian Economy at War: State of Play and Pathways Towards Recovery*. Bratislava: GLOBSEC and National Endowment for Democracy.

Golden, Tim (1994) The voice of the Rebels has Mexicans in his spell. *New York Times*, 8 February.

Goldsmith, Jack (2018) *The Failure of Internet Freedom: Probing the Demise of a Non-Regulation, Anti-Censorship, Global Internet Agenda*. 13 June, Knight First Amendment Institute, Columbia University. https://knightcolumbia.org/content/failure-Internet-freedom

Goldsmith, Jack and Wu, Tim (2006) *Who Controls the Internet?* New York: Oxford University Press.

González, Roberto and Gusterson, Hugh (2019) Introduction. In González, Roberto, Gusterson, Hugh and Houtman, Gustaff (eds.) *Militarization: A Reader*, pp. 1–26. Durham: Duke University Press.

Goodfriend, Sophia (2022) How the occupation Fuels Tel Aviv's booming AI sector. *Foreign Policy*, 21 February.

Gordon, David, Tong, Haoyu and Anderson, Tabatha (2020) *Beyond the Myths – Towards a Realistic Assessment of China's Belt and Road Initiative: The Security Dimension*. London: The International Institute for Strategic Studies. September, especially Chapter 4. The BRI's Cyber Dimension – The Digital Silk Road

Gorwa, Robert (2019) What is platform governance? *Information, Communication & Society*, 22(6): 854–871.

Goswami, Namrata and Garretson, Peter (2020) *Scramble for the Skies-The Great Power Competition to Control the Resources of Outer Space*. London: Lexington Books.

Government of China (2010) *Chapter 6: The Internet in China*. Beijing: Information Office of the State Council of the People's Republic of China.

Government of China (2021) *Poverty Alleviation: China's Experience and Contribution* (The State Council Information Office of the People's Republic of China). Beijing: Foreign Languages Press.

Government of China (2023) *The Belt and Road Initiative: A Key Pillar of the Global Community of Shared Future*. Beijing: State Council Information Office. http://www.scio.gov.cn/zfbps/zfbps_2279/202310/t20231010_773734.html

Graddol, David (2006) *English Next: Why Global English May Mean the End of 'English as a Foreign Language'*. London: British Council.

Graff, Garret (2023) Orders of disorder: Who disbanded Iraq's Army and De-Baathified its Bureaucracy? *Foreign Affairs*, May.

GRAIN (2021) *Digital Control: How Big Tech Moves Into Food and Farming (and What It Means)*. Barcelona: GRAIN. www.grain.org

Graphika (2021) *Ants in a Web Deconstructing Guo Wengui's Online 'Whistleblower Movement*. Graphika. https://public-assets.graphika.com/reports/graphika_report_ants_in_a_web.pdf

Graphika and Stanford Internet Observatory (2022) *Unheard Voice: Evaluating Five Years of Pro-Western Covert Influence Operations*. Los Angles: Graphika and Standard Internet Observatory. https://stacks.stanford.edu/file/druid:nj914nx9540/unheard-voice-tt.pdf

Grassi, Sergio (2014) *Changing the Narrative: China's Media Offensive in Africa*. Berlin: Friedrich-Ebert-Stiftung.

Green, Toby (2020) *A Fistful of Shells: West Africa from the Rise of the Slave Trade to the Age of Revolution*. London: Penguin.

Green, Yasmin, Gully, Andrew, Roy, Abhishek, Roth, Yoel, Tucker, Joshua and Wanless, Alicia (2022) *Evidence-Based Misinformation Interventions: Challenges and Opportunities for Measurement and Collaboration*. Washington: Carnegie Endowment for International Peace.

Greenwald, Glenn (2014) *No Place to Hide: Edward Snowden, the NSA, and the US Surveillance State*. New York: Metropolitan.

Griffin, Michael (2010) Media images of war. *Media, War & Conflict*, 3(1): 7–41.
Griffiths, James (2019) *The Great Firewall of China: How to Build and Control an Alternative Version of the Internet*. London: Zed.
Grimm, D. (2015) *Sovereignty: The Origin and Future of a Political and Legal Concept*. Columbia: Columbia University Press.
Grincheva, Natalia (2022) Beyond the scorecard diplomacy: From soft power rankings to critical inductive geography. *Convergence: The International Journal of Research into New Media Technologies*, 28(1): 70–91.
Grosfoguel, Ramón (2007) The epistemic decolonial turn: Beyond political-economy paradigms. *Cultural Studies*, 21(2–3): 211–223. https://doi.org/10.1080/09502380601162514
GSMA (2022) *The Mobile Economy 2022*. London: Global System for Mobile Communications.
Gunn, Geoffrey (2022) *Imagined Geographies-The Maritime Silk Roads in World History, 100–1800*. Hong Kong: Hong Kong University Press.
Gupta, A. (2021) The middle power dilemma: India's hegemony over global cricket. *The Round Table*, 110(6): 709–719.
Guriev, Sergie and Treisman, Daniel (2022) *Spin Dictators: The Changing Face of Tyranny in the 21st Century*. Princeton: Princeton University Press.
Ha, Louisa and Willnat, Lars (eds.) (2022) *The U.S.–China Trade War-Global News Framing and Public Opinion in the Digital Age*. East Lansing, MI: Michigan State University Press.
Ha, Mathew and Maxwell, David (2018) *Kim Jong Un's 'All-Purpose Sword': North Korean Cyber-Enabled Economic Warfare*. Washington: Foundation for Defense of Democracies, October.
Haas, Peter (2016) *Epistemic Communities, Constructivism, and International Environmental Politics*. London: Routledge.
Haas, Peter M. (1992) Introduction: Epistemic communities and international policy coordination. *International Organization*, 46: 1–32.
Haass, Richard and Kupchan, Charles (2021) The new concert of powers how to prevent catastrophe and promote stability in a multipolar world. *Foreign Affairs*, March.
Hafez, Kai and Grüne, Anne (2022) *Foundations of Global Communication: A Conceptual Handbook*. London: Routledge.
HAI (2023) *Artificial Intelligence Index Report 2023 (Stanford Institute for Human-Centered Artificial Intelligence)*. Stanford: Stanford University.
Hakelberg, Lukas (2020) *The Hypocritical Hegemon: How the United States Shapes Global Rules against Tax Evasion and Avoidance*. Ithaca: Cornell University Press.
Hale, Julian (1975) *Radio Power: Propaganda and International Broadcasting*. London: Paul Elek.
Hallin, Daniel (1986) *The Uncensored War: The Media and Vietnam*. Oxford: Oxford University Press.
Hallin, Daniel and Mancini, Poulo (2004) *Comparing Media Systems: Three Models of Media and Politics*. Cambridge: Cambridge University Press.
Hallin, Daniel and Mancini, Paolo (eds.) (2012) *Comparing Media Systems beyond the Western World*. Cambridge: Cambridge University Press.
Hamid, Shadi (2017) *Islamic Exceptionalism: How the Struggle Over Islam is Reshaping the World*. New York: St. Martin's Press.
Hamilton, Daniel and Quinlan, Joseph (2022) *The Transatlantic Economy 2022: Annual Survey of Jobs, Trade and Investment between the United States and Europe*. Washington: Foreign Policy Institute, Johns Hopkins University SAIS/Transatlantic Leadership Network.
Hamilton, Peter (2021) *Made in Hong Kong: Transpacific Networks and a New History of Globalization*. New York: Columbia University Press.
Hanania, Richard (2020) Worse than nothing: Why US intervention made government atrocities more likely in Syria. *Survival*, 62(5): 173–192.

Hannah, Mark and Gray, Caroline (2021) *Democracy in Disarray: How the World Sees the U.S. and Its Example*. New York: Eurasia Group Foundation.
Hannas, William and Tatlow, Didi Kirsten (eds.) (2020) *China's Quest for Foreign Technology: Beyond Espionage*. London: Routledge.
Haqqani, Husain (2013) *Magnificent Delusions: Pakistan, the United States, and an Epic History of Misunderstanding*. New York: PublicAffairs.
Harding, Luke (2022) *Invasion: Russia's Bloody War and Ukraine's Fight for Survival*. London: Faber.
Harding, Luke, Simeonova, Stiliyana, Ganguly, Manish and Sabbagh, Dan (2023) 'Vulkan files' leak reveals Putin's global and domestic cyberwarfare tactics. *Guardian*, 30 March.
Harkov, Lahav (2022) Russia-Ukraine War made President Volodymyr Zelensky a global icon No. 1. *Jerusalem Post*, 25 September.
Harper, Tim (2020) *Underground Asia-Global Revolutionaries and the Assault on Empire*. London: Allen Lane.
Harris, Bryan and Leahy, Joe (2023) Lula Vows partnership with China to 'balance world geopolitics. *Financial Times*, 15 April.
Harris, Shane (2021) CIA creates new mission center to counter China. *Washington Post*, 7 October.
Hartig, Falk (2015) *Chinese Public Diplomacy: The Rise of the Confucius Institute*. London: Routledge.
Hartung, William (2021) *Profits of War: Corporate Beneficiaries of the Post-9/11 Pentagon Spending Surge*. Washington: Center for International Policy, Watson Institute International and Public Affairs, Brown University.
Harwit, Eric (2008) *China's Telecommunications Revolution*. New York: Oxford University Press.
Harwit, Eric (2016) WeChat: Social and political development of China's dominant messaging app. *Chinese Journal of Communication*, 10(3): 312–327.
Haslam, Jonathan (2005) *The Nixon Administration and the Death of Allende's Chile: A Case of Assisted Suicide*. London: Verso.
Hassan, Kiran (2021) *How is China-Pakistan Media Collaboration booming under CPEC*. Lahore: Centre for Public Policy and Governance (Discussion Paper, 2, August).
Hawkins, Amy (2023a) Xi Jinping's wants a 'multipolar world', as China accelerates its shift away from the West. *The Guardian*, 9 October.
Hawkins, Amy (2023b) China spent $240bn on belt and road bailouts from 2008 to 2021, study finds. *The Guardian*, 28 March.
Headrick, Daniel (1981) *The Tools of Empire: Technology and European Imperialism in the Nineteenth Century*. New York: Oxford University Press.
Headrick, Daniel (1991) *The Invisible Weapon: Telecommunications and International Politics, 1851–1945*. New York: Oxford University Press.
Headrick, Daniel and Griset, Pascal (2001) Submarine telegraph cables: Business and politics, 1838–1939. *Business History Review*, 75(3): 543–578.
Hearns-Branaman, Jesse Owen and Bergman, Tabe (2023) (eds.) *Journalism and Foreign Policy: How the US and UK Media Cover Official Enemies*. London: Routledge.
Helbing, Dirk et al. (2017) Will democracy survive big data and artificial intelligence? *Scientific American*, 25 February. https://www.scientificamerican.com/article/will-democracy-survive-big-data-and-artificial-intelligence/
Helsper, Ellen (2021) *The Digital Disconnect: The Social Causes and Consequences of Digital Inequalities*. London: Sage.
Hersh, Seymour (2023) *How America Took Out the Nord Stream Pipeline*, 8 February. https://seymourhersh.substack.com/p/how-america-took-out-the-nord-stream
Herwig, Holger (2016) *The Demon of Geopolitics: How Karl Haushofer 'Educated' Hitler and Hess*. Lanham: Rowman & Littlefield.
Hewson, Jack (2023) A private company is using social media to track down Russian soldiers. *Foreign Policy*, 2 March.

Higgins, Eliot (2021) *We Are Bellingcat: Global Crime, Online Sleuths, and the Bold Future of News*. New York: Bloomsbury.
Hill, Richard (2014) *The New International Telecommunication Regulations and the Internet: A Commentary and Legislative History*. Berlin: Springer.
Hille, Kathrin, Olcott, Eleanor and Kynge, James (2021) US-China business: The necessary reinvention of Huawei. *Financial Times*, 29 September, p. 5.
Hillman, Jonathan (2019) *Influence and Infrastructure: The Strategic Stakes of Foreign Projects*. Washington: CSIS.
Hills, Jill (2007) *Telecommunications and Empire: Power Relations within the Global Telecommunications Empire*. Chicago: University of Illinois Press.
Himelboim, Itai et al. (2023) What do 5G networks, Bill Gates, Agenda 21, and QAnon have in common? Sources, distribution, and characteristics. *New Media & Society*. https://doi.org/10.1177/14614448221142800
Hindman, Matthew and Barash, Vladimir (2018) *Disinformation, 'Fake News' and Influence Campaigns on Twitter*. Miami, FL: Knight Foundation.
Hobson, John (2004) *The Eastern Origins of Western Civilization*. Cambridge: Cambridge University Press.
Hobson, John (2020) *Multicultural Origins of the Global Economy: Beyond the Western-Centric Frontier*. Cambridge: Cambridge University Press.
Hobson, John (2020) *Multicultural Origins of the Global Economy: Beyond the Western-Centric Frontier*. Cambridge: Cambridge University Press.
Hochfelder, David (2012) *The Telegraph in America, 1832–1920*. Baltimore: Johns Hopkins University Press.
Hochschild, Adam (1999) *King Leopold's Ghost: A Story of Greed, Terror, and Heroism in Colonial Africa*. Boston: Houghton Mifflin.
Hoffman, Andrew (2021) *The Engaged Scholar-Expanding the Impact of Academic Research in Today's World*. Stanford: Stanford University Press.
Hoffman, Samantha and Attrill, Nathan (2021) *Mapping China's Technology Giants: Supply Chains and the Global Data Collection Ecosystem*. London: International Cyber Policy Centre, Australian Strategic Policy Institute, Policy Brief, Report no. 45.
Hoffmann, Stacie, Bradshaw, Samantha and Taylor, Emily (2019) *Networks and Geopolitics: How Great Power Rivalries Infected 5G*. Oxford: Oxford Information Labs.
Hoffmann, Stacie, Lazanski, Dominique and Taylor, Emily (2020) Standardising the splinternet: how China's technical standards could fragment the internet. *Journal of Cyber Policy*, 5(2): 239–264.
Holt, Jennifer and Vonderau, Patrick (2015) 'Where the internet lives': Data centers as cloud infrastructure. In Parks, Lisa and Starosielski, Nicole (eds.) *Signal Traffic: Critical Studies of Media Infrastructures*, pp. 71–93. Chicago: University of Illinois Press.
Hong, Brendon (2021) One of the world's most watched TV shows keeps using blackface. *Daily Beast*, 12 February.
Hong, Nong (2020) *China's Role in the Arctic. Observing and Being Observed*. London: Routledge.
Hong, Yanyan (2021) The power of Bollywood: A study on opportunities, challenges, and audiences' perceptions of Indian cinema in China. *Global Media and China*, 6(3): 345–363.
Hong, Yu (2017) *Networking China: The Digital Transformation of the Chinese Economy*. Urbana: University of Illinois Press.
Hong, Yu and Goodnight, Thomas (2020) How to think about cyber sovereignty: The case of China. *Chinese Journal of Communication*, 13(1): 8–26.
Hong, Yu and Harwit, Eric (eds.) (2022) *China's Globalizing Internet: History, Power, and Governance*. London: Routledge.
Hoover Institution (2018) *Chinese Influence & American Interests: Promoting Constructive Vigilance*. Los Angles: Hoover Institution Press.

Horten, Gerd (2002) *Radio Goes to War: The Cultural Politics of Propaganda during World War II*. Berkeley: Stanford University Press.
Horwitz, Jeff (2021) Facebook says its rules apply to all. Company. Documents reveal a secret Elite that's exempt. *The Wall Street Journal*, 13 September.
Howard, Philip (2015) *Pax Technica: How the Internet of Things May Set us Free or Lock us up*. London: Yale University Press.
Howard, Philip and Hussain, Muzammil (2013) *Democracy's Fourth Wave? Digital Media and the Arab Spring*. Oxford: Oxford University Press.
Huang, Yanzhong (2020) *Toxic Politics: China's Environmental Health Crisis and Its Challenge to the Chinese State*. New York: Cambridge University Press
Huang, Yanzhong (2022) *The COVID-19 Pandemic and China's Global Health Leadership*. Washington: Council on Foreign Relations. Council Special Report No. 92 January.
Hudson, John and Khurshudyan, Isabelle (2023) Ukraine begins firing U.S.-provided cluster munitions at Russian forces. *Washington Post*, 20 July.
Hugill, Peter (1999) *Global Communications since 1844: Geopolitics & Technology*. Baltimore: Johns Hopkins University Press.
Hui, Mary (2019) The Hong Kong protests are the most live-streamed protests ever. *Quartz*, 11 November.
Human Rights Watch (2014) *With Liberty to Monitor All: How Large-Scale US Surveillance is Harming Journalism, Law, and American Democracy*. Washington: Human Rights Watch.
Human Rights Watch (2019) *China's Algorithms of Repression: Reverse Engineering a Xinjiang Police Mass Surveillance App*. New York: Human Rights Watch.
Human Rights Watch (2023) *Ukraine: Banned Landmines Harm Civilians* Hung, Ho-fung (2022) *City on the Edge: Hong Kong under Chinese Rule*. New York: Cambridge University Press.
Huntington, Samuel (1996) *The Clash of Civilizations and Remaking of the World Order*. New York: Simon & Schuster.
Hurel, Louise and Lobato, Luisa (2018) Unpacking cyber norms: Private companies as norms entrepreneurs. *Journal of Cyber Policy*, 3(1): 61–76.
Hurel, Louise Marie and Lobato, Luisa Cruz (2020) Cyber-norms entrepreneurship? Understanding Microsoft's advocacy on cybersecurity. In Dennis, Broeders and Bibi, van den Berg (eds.) *Governing Cyberspace: Behavior, Power, and Diplomacy*, pp. 285–313. London: Rowman & Littlefield.
Hvistendahl, Mara, Fahrenthold, David, Chutel, Lynsey and Jhaveri, Ishaan (2023) A global web of Chinese propaganda leads to a U.S. Tech Mogul. *New York Times*, 5 August.
IEA (2022) *World Energy Outlook 2022*. Paris: International Energy Agency.
IIPA (2022) *Copyright Industries in the U.S. Economy: The 2022 Report*. Washington: International Intellectual Property Alliance. www.iipa.com
IISS (2018) *Russian Incentives for Nuclear Hopefuls in Africa*. London: International Institute for Strategic Studies.
IISS (2021) *Cyber Capabilities and National Power: A Net Assessment*. London: International Institute for Strategic Studies.
IMF (2013) *Navigating Global Divergences: World Economic Outlook*. Washington: International Monetary Fund.
IMF (2023) *World Economic Outlook: Navigating Global Divergences*. Washington: International Monetary Fund.
Inkster, Nigel (2022) China is running covert operations that could seriously overwhelm us. *New York Times*, 14 September.
Innis, Harold (1972) *Empire and Communications*, revised ed. Toronto: University of Toronto Press (Originally published in 1950 by Oxford University Press).
Internet Association (2023) *Digital Trade. Internet Association*. https://internetassociation.org/positions/trade/

Internet Society (2017) *2017 Internet Society Global Internet Report: Paths to Our Digital Future*. Geneva: Internet Society.
Internet Society (2022) *Navigating Digital Sovereignty and its Impact on the Internet*, December. www.internetsociety.org/wp-content/uploads/2022/11/Digital-Sovereignty.pdf
Internet Society (n.d.) *Internet Way of Networking*. www.internetsociety.org/issues/internet-way-of-networking/
Iosifidis, Petros (2011) *Global Media and Communication Policy*. London: Palgrave/Macmillan.
Isin, Engin and Ruppert, Evelyn (2019) Data's empire: Postcolonial data politics. In Bigo, Didier, Isin, Engin and Ruppert, Evelyn (eds.) *Data Politics: Worlds, Subjects, Rights*, pp. 207–228. London: Routledge.
ISRO (2023) *Enhancing the Private Participation in Space Activities: India on a Track to Serve Global Needs*. Bengaluru: Indian Space Research Organization.
ITU (1999) *Trends in Telecommunication Reform*. Geneva: International Telecommunication Union.
ITU (2023) *Measuring Digital Development: Facts and Figures 2023*. Geneva: International Telecommunication Union.
Jackson, Sarah, Bailey, Moya and Foucault Welles, Brooke (2020) *#HashtagActivism: Networks of Race and Gender Justice*. Cambridge, MA: MIT Press.
Jacobsen, Katherine (2016) How a fictional president is helping Ukrainians rethink their absurd politics. *Foreign Policy*, December.
Jaramillo, Deborah (2009) *Ugly War, Pretty Package: How CNN and Fox News Made the Invasion of Iraq High Concept*. Bloomington: Indiana University Press.
Jervis, Robert (2017) *Perception and Misperception in International Politics*, New ed. Princeton: Princeton University Press.
Jia, Lianrui and Winseck, Dwayne (2018) The political economy of Chinese internet companies: Financialization, concentration and capitalization. *International Communication Gazette*, 80(1): 30–59.
Jili, Bulelani (2022) *China's Surveillance Ecosystem and the Global Spread of Its Tools*. Washington: Atlantic Council.
Jin, Dal Yong (2015) *Digital Platforms, Imperialism and Political Culture*. New York: Routledge.
Jinghua, L. (2020) The race of Chinese companies in the 5G competition. In Samuele, Dominioni and Fabio, Rugge (eds.) *The Geopolitics of 5G*. www.ispionline.it/sites/default/files/pubblicazioni/dossier_cyber_5g_september_2020.pdf
Johnson, Ross (2010) *Radio Free Europe and Radio Liberty: The CIA Years and beyond*. Berkeley: Stanford University Press.
Johnson, Ross and Parta, Eugene (eds.) (2010) *Cold War Broadcasting – Impact on the Soviet Union and Eastern Europe: A Collection of Studies and Documents*. Budapest: Central European University Press.
Johnston, Neil (2018) Kong Linlin: Reporter for Chinese state TV charged with slapping Tory delegate. *The Times*, 26 October.
Johny, Stanly and Krishnan, Ananth (2022) *Comrades and the Mullahs: China, Afghanistan and the New Asian Geopolitics*. New Delhi: HarperCollins.
Jones, Andrew (2021) China, Russia reveal roadmap for international moon base. *SpaceNews*, 16 June. https://spacenews.com/china-russia-reveal-roadmap-for-international-moon-base/
Joske, Alex, Li, Lin, Pascoe, Alexandra and Attrill, Nathan (2020) *The Influence Environment: A Survey of Chinese-language Media in Australia*. Canberra: International Cyber Policy Centre, Australian Strategic Policy Institute. Policy Brief, Report No. 42.
Kagan, Robert (2023) *The Ghost at the Feast: America and the Collapse of World Order, 1900–1941*. New York: Alfred Knopf.

Kagubare, Ines (2022a) Cyber Command chief confirms US took part in offensive cyber operations. *The Hill*, 1 June. https://thehill.com/policy/cybersecurity/3508639-cyber-command-chief-confirms-us-took-part-in-offensive-cyber-operations/
Kagubare, Ines (2022b) US, EU cyber investments in Ukraine pay off amid war. *The Hill*, 13 March. https://thehill.com/policy/technology/597921-us-eu-cyber-investments-in-ukraine-pay-off-amid-war/
Kahl, Colin and Wright, Thomas (2021) *Aftershocks: Pandemic Politics and the End of the Old International Order*. New York: St. Martin's Press.
Kalliney, Peter (2022) *The Aesthetic Cold War: Decolonization and Global Literature*. Princeton: Princeton University Press.
Kanozia, Rubal and Arya, Ritu (2021) 'Fake news', religion, and COVID-19 vaccine hesitancy in India, Pakistan, and Bangladesh. *Media Asia*, 48(4): 313–321. https://doi.org/10.1080/01296612.2021.1921963
Kaplan, Robert (2003) Supremacy by stealth. *Atlantic Monthly*, July–August. www.theatlantic.com/magazine/archive/2003/07/supremacy-by-stealth/302760
Kapoor, Ilan (2013) *Celebrity Humanitarianism: The Ideology of Global Charity*. London: Routledge.
Karam, Beschara and Mutsvairo, Bruce (2022) Reframing African ontologies in the era of decolonisation. In Karam, Beschara and Mutsvairo, Bruce (eds.) *Decolonising Political Communication in Africa: Reframing Ontologies*, pp. 1–8. London: Routledge.
Karatnycky, Adrian (2019) The world just witnessed the first entirely virtual presidential campaign. *Politico*. www.politico.com/magazine/story/2019/04/24/ukraine-president-virtual-campaign-226711
Kardon, Isaac (2023) *China's Law of the Sea: The New Rules of Maritime Order*. New Haven: Yale University Press.
Karnad, Bharat (2018) *Staggering Forward: Narendra Modi and India's Global Ambition*. New Delhi: Penguin.
Kashlev, Yuri (1984) *Information Imperialism*. Moscow: Novosti Press.
Kasturi, Charu (2022) Is the INSTC Russia's new economic escape route? *Al Jazeera*, 27 July.
Katz, Brian et al. (2021) *Maintaining the Intelligence Edge: Reimagining and Reinventing Intelligence through Innovation*. Washington: Center for Strategic and International Studies.
Katzman, Kenneth (2021) Iran sanctions. *Congressional Research Service*, 6 April. https://fas.org/sgp/crs/mideast/RS20871.pdf
Kaufman, Michael (2002) *Soros: The Life and Times of a Messianic Billionaire*. New York: Alfred Knopf.
Kavanagh, Jennifer and Rich, Michael (2018) *Truth Decay – An Initial Exploration of the Diminishing Role of Facts and Analysis in American Public Life*. Santa Monica, CA: RAND Corporation (RR-2314-RC).
Keane, Michael, Haiqing, Yu, Elaine, Jing Zhao and Susan, Leong (2021) *China's Digital Presence in the Asia-Pacific: Culture, Technology and Platforms*. London: Anthem Press.
Keane, Michael, Yecies, Brian and Flew, Terry (2018) *Willing Collaborators: Foreign Partners in Chinese Media*. London: Rowman & Littlefield.
Keane, Phoebe (2020) How the oil industry made us doubt climate change. *BBC News*, 20 September.
Kearns, Gerry (2009) *Geopolitics and Empire: The Legacy of Halford Mackinder*. Oxford: Oxford University Press.
Kennedy, Paul (1988) *The Rise and Fall of the Great Powers: Economic Change and Military Conflict from 1500 to 2000*. London: Unwin.
Kennedy, Paul (1971) Imperial cable communications and strategy, 1879–1914. *English Historical Review*, 86: 728–752.
Kerbaj, Richard (2022) *The Secret History of The Five Eyes: The Untold Story of the International Spy Network*. London: John Blake.

Kharas, Homi, McArthur, John and Ohno, Izumi (eds.) (2022) Breakthroughs: Why we need them for sustainable development. In Kharas, Homi, McArthur, John and Ohno, Izumi (eds.) *Breakthrough: The Promise of Frontier Technologies for Sustainable Development*, pp. 1–21. Washington: Brookings Institution Press.

Khurshudyan, Isabelle, Sonne, Paul, Morgunov, Serhiy and Hrabchuk, Kamila (2022) Inside the Ukrainian counteroffensive that shocked Putin and reshaped the war. *Washington Post*, 29 December.

Kim, Young-Chan (ed.) (2020) *China-India Relations: Geo-political Competition, Economic Cooperation, Cultural Exchange and Business Ties*. Cham: Springer.

Kirchgaessner, Stephanie, Ganguly, Manisha, Pegg, David, Cadwalladr, Carole and Burke, Jason (2023) Revealed: The hacking and disinformation team meddling in elections. *The Guardian*, 15 February.

Kissinger, Henry (2020) The Coronavirus pandemic will forever alter the world order. *Wall Street Journal*, 3 April. www.wsj.com/articles/the-coronavirus-pandemic-will-forever-alter-the-world-order-11585953005

Kissinger, Henry, Schmidt, Eric and Huttenlocher, Daniel (2021) *The Age of AI: And Our Human Future*. New York: Little, Brown and Company.

Klauser, Francisco (2022) Policing with the drone: Towards an aerial geopolitics of security. *Security Dialogue*, 53(2): 148–163.

Kliman, Daniel, Kendall-Taylor, Andrea, Lee, Kristine, Fitt, Joshua and Nietsche, Carisa (2020) *Dangerous Synergies: Countering Chinese and Russian Digital Influence Operations*. Washington: Center For a New American Security.

Klyukanov, Igor (2022) *Communication: A House Seen from Everywhere*. New York: Berghahn.

Knake, Robert (2020) *Weaponizing Digital Trade: Creating a Digital Trade Zone to Promote Online Freedom and Cybersecurity*. Council Special Report No. 88, September Washington: Council on Foreign Relations.

Knight, Jane (2022) *Knowledge Diplomacy in International Relations and Higher Education*. Cham: Springer.

Kohli, Atul (2020) *Imperialism and the Developing World: How Britain and the United States Shaped the Global Periphery*. New York: Oxford University Press.

Koivurova, Timo and Kopra, Sanna (eds.) (2020) *Chinese Policy and Presence in the Arctic*. Leiden: Brill.

Kokas, Aynne (2022) *Trafficking Data: How China is Winning the Battle for Digital Sovereignty*. New York: Oxford University Press.

Konda, Thomas Milan (2019) *Conspiracies of Conspiracies: How Delusions Have Overrun America*. Chicago: Chicago University Press.

Koo, Se-Woong (2020) Why the Western media keeps getting North Korea wrong. *Al Jazeera*, 6 May.

Koshiw, Isobel (2023) Anti-Putin militias mount cross-border incursion in western Russia. *Washington Post*, 23 May.

Kotasthane, Pranay and Manchi, Abhiram (2023) *When the Chips Are Down: A Deep Dive into a Global Crisis*. New Delhi: Bloomsbury.

Kothari, Ashish, Salleh, Ariel, Escobar, Arturo, Demaria, Federico and Acosta, Alberto (eds.) (2019) *Pluriverse: A Post-Development Dictionary*. New Delhi: Tulika Books.

Kraidy, Marwan (2016) *The Naked Blogger of Cairo: Creative Insurgency in the Arab World*. Cambridge, MA: Harvard University Press.

Kraidy, Marwan (2017) The projectilic image: Islamic State's digital visual warfare and global networked affect. *Media, Culture & Society*, 39(8): 1194–1209. https://doi.org/10.1177/0163443717725575

Krauthammer, Charles (1990) The unipolar moment: The America and the world 1990. *Foreign Affairs*. www.foreignaffairs.com/articles/1990-01-01/unipolar-moment

Krebs, Ronald (2015) *Narrative and the Making of US National Security*. Cambridge: Cambridge University Press.

Krishnan, Ananth and Johnny, Stanly (2022) *The Comrades and The Mullahs: China, Afghanistan, and the New Asian Geopolitics*. New Delhi: Harper-Collins.

Kroenig, Matthew (2020) *The Return of Great Power Rivalry: Democracy Versus Autocracy from the Ancient World to the U.S. and China*. New York: Oxford University Press.

Krugman, Paul (2003) Man on horseback. *The New York Times*, 6 May.

Kugelman, Michael (2017) Why Pakistan hates Malala. *Foreign Policy*, 15 August.

Kulik, Lydia and Korovkin, Vladimir (2021) *India Goes Digital: From Local Phenomenon to Global Influencer*. Moscow: SKOLKOVO Institute for Emerging Market Studies (IEMS).

Kumar, Anilesh (2023) 'Virus Jihad': The (mis)representation of Muslims during COVID 19 outbreak in Indian media. *Howard Journal of Communication*. https://doi.org/10.1080/10646175.2023.2213181

Kumar, Deepa (2021) *Islamophobia and the Politics of Empire: Twenty Years after 9/11*, 2nd revised ed. London: Verso.

Kuntz, Katrin (2018) The disappeared: An inside look at China's reeducation camps. *Der Spiegel*, 13 November.

Kuo, Kendrick and Mylonas, Harris (2022) *The Geopolitics of 'Fifth-Column' Framing in Xinjiang*. In Harris, Mylonas and Scott, Radnitz (eds.) *Enemies Within*, pp. 101–126. Oxford: Oxford University Press.

Kupfer, Matthew and Query, Alexander (2020) Shadowy organization adds former Western top officials to 'enemies of Ukraine' list. *Kyiv Post*, 17 February. https://archive.kyivpost.com/ukraine-politics/shadowy-organization-adds-former-western-top-officials-to-enemies-of-ukraine-list.html

Kurbjuweit, Dirk and Neukirch, Ralf (2022) Kremlin Threats: Europe has to learn to defend itself, but how? *Der Spiegel*, 9 June.

Kurlantzick, Joshua (2017) *A Great Place to Have a War: America in Laos and the Birth of a Military CIA*. New York: Simon & Schuster.

Kurlantzick, Joshua (2023) *Beijing's Global Media Offensive: China's Uneven Campaign to Influence Asia and the World*. New York: Oxford University Press.

Kushner, Barak (2007) *The Thought War: Japanese Imperial Propaganda*. Honolulu: University of Hawaii Press.

Kuzio, Taras (2022) *Russian Nationalism and the Russian-Ukrainian War*. London: Routledge.

Kwet, Michael (2019) Digital colonialism: US empire and the new imperialism in the Global South. *Race & Class*, 60(4): 3–26.

LaFeber, Walter (2000) Technology and U.S. Foreign relations. *Diplomatic History*, 24(1): 1–19.

Lake, David (2009) *Hierarchy in International Relations*. Ithaca, NY: Cornell University Press.

Lamarre, Eric, Smaje, Kate and Zemmel, Rodney (2023) *Rewired: The McKinsey Guide to Outcompeting in the Age of Digital and AI*. Hoboken: Wiley.

Lamb, Christina (2021) Chronicle of a defeat foretold: Why America failed in Afghanistan. *Foreign Affairs*, 100(4): 174–179.

Lamb, Keith (2021a) How to eradicate extreme poverty: Part 1 – China's governing system. CGTN, 22 February.

Lamb, Keith (2021b) How to eradicate extreme poverty: Part 2 – What did China do? CGTN, 24 February.

Lamb, Keith (2021c) How to eradicate extreme poverty: Part 3 – A lived experience. CGTN, 26 February.

Lamdan, Sarah (2022) *Data Cartels: The Companies That Control and Monopolize Our Information*. Los Angles: Stanford University Press.

Lander, Mark and Risen, James (2017) Trump finds reason for the U.S. to remain in Afghanistan: Minerals. *New York Times*, 26 July, p. A1.

Langa, Mahesh (2019) Mukesh Ambani urges Modi to take steps against data colonization by global corporations. *The Hindu*, 18 January. www.thehindu.com/news/national/mukesh-ambani-urges-modi-to-take-steps-against-data-colonisation/article26025076.ece

Lashinsky, Adam (2017) How Alibaba's Jack Ma is building a truly global retail empire. *Fortune*, 24 March.

Lashmar, Paul, Gilby Nicholas and Oliver, James (2021) Revealed: how UK spies incited mass murder of Indonesia's communists. *Observer*, 17 October.

Lasswell, Harold (1927) *Propaganda Techniques in the World War*. New York: Alfred Knopf.

Laville, Helen (2002) *Cold War Women: The International Activities of American Women's Organisations*. Manchester: Manchester University Press.

Laville, Helen and Wilford, Hugh (eds.) (2006) *The US Government, Citizen Groups and the Cold War: The State-Private Network*. London: Routledge.

Law, Nathan (with Evan Fowler) (2021) *FREEDOM: How We Lose It and How We Fight Back*. London: Bantam Press.

Lawrence, Felicity, Evans, Rob, Pegg, David, Barr, Caelainn and Duncan, Pamela (2019) How the right's radical thinktanks reshaped the Conservative party. *The Guardian*, 29 November.

Lawson, Brendan T. (2021) Hiding behind databases, institutions and actors: How journalists use statistics in reporting humanitarian crises. *Journalism Practice*, 17(4): 664–682.

Lazer, D., Baum, M., Grinberg, N., Friedland, L., Joseph, K., Hobbs, W. and Mattsson, C. (2017) *Combating Fake News: An Agenda for Research and Action*. Shorenstein Center. https://shorensteincenter.org/wp-content/uploads/2017/05/Combating-Fake-News-Agenda-for-Research-1.pdf

Leali, Georgio (2022) France not opposed in principle to cutting Russia from SWIFT: Bruno Le Maire. *Politico*, 25 February. https://www.politico.eu/article/frances-le-maire-not-against-cutting-russia-out-of-swift/

Ledwidge, Frank (2023) The Pentagon leaks reveal the rot at the heart of US intelligence – But they haven't hurt Ukraine. *The Guardian*, 17 April. www.theguardian.com/commentisfree/2023/apr/17/pentagon-leaks-reveal-rot-us-intelligence-ukraine

Lee Myers, Steven and Shanker, Thom (2012) State department and Pentagon plan for Post-Assad Syria. *New York Times*, 4 August. https://www.nytimes.com/2012/08/05/world/middleeast/state-dept-and-pentagonplanning-for-post-assad-syria.html.

Lee, Chin-Chuan (ed.) (2015) *Internationalizing International Communications: A Critical Intervention*. Ann Arbor: University of Michigan Press.

Lee, Ching Kwan (2017) *The Specter of Global China: Politics, Labor, and Foreign Investment in Africa*. Chicago, IL: The University of Chicago Press.

Lee, Francis and Chan, Joseph (2018) *Media and Protest Logics in the Digital Era: The Umbrella Movement in Hong Kong*. New York: Oxford University Press.

Lee, Kai-fu (2018) *AI Superpowers: China, Silicon Valley and the New World Order*. Boston: Houghton Mifflin Harcourt.

Lee, Micky and Jin, Dal Yong (2018) *Understanding the Business of Global Media in the Digital Age*. London: Routledge.

Lehdonvirta, Vili (2022) *Cloud Empires: How Digital Platforms Are Overtaking the State and How We Can Regain Control*. Cambridge, MA: MIT Press.

Lele, Ajey and Roy, Kritika (2019) *Analysing China's Digital and Space Belt and Road Initiative* (IDSA Occasional Paper No. 55). New Delhi: Institute for Defence Studies and Analyses.

Lennon, Alexander (ed.) (2003) *The Battle for Hearts and Minds: Using Soft Power to Undermine Terrorist Networks*. New Haven: MIT Press.

Lenoir, Tim and Caldwell, Luke (2018) *The Military-Entertainment Complex*. Cambridge, MA: Harvard University Press.

Lepawsky, Josh (2018) *Reassembling Rubbish-Worlding Electronic Waste*. Cambridge: MIT Press.

Levin, Dov (2020) *Meddling in the Ballot Box: The Causes and Effects of Partisan Electoral Interventions*. Oxford: Oxford University Press.

Levine, Alexandra (2023) The words TikTok parent ByteDance may be watching you say. *Forbes*, 5 May. www.forbes.com/sites/alexandralevine/2023/05/05/tiktok-bytedance-sensitive-words-suppression-china/?sh=1884c78b69c9

Levitsky, Steven and Way, Lucan (2022) *Revolution and Dictatorship-The Violent Origins of Durable Authoritarianism*. Princeton: Princeton University Press.

Lewis, Angela (2024) *Chinese Television and Soft Power in Africa*. London: Routledge.

Lewis, Justin and Brookes, Rod (2004) How British television news represented the case for war. In Allan, Stuart and Zelizer, Barbie (eds.) *Reporting War*. London: Routledge.

Lewis, Rebecca (2018) Alternative influence: Broadcasting the reactionary right on YouTube. *Data & Society Research Institute*. https://datasociety.net/wp-content/uploads/2018/09/DS_Alternative_Influence.pdf

Li, Congjun (2011) Toward a new world media order. *Wall Street Journal*, 1 June. www.wsj.com/articles/SB10001424052748704816604576335563624853594

Li, Siyuan (2022) A Foucauldian power analysis of China's Confucius institute in Africa: Power, knowledge and the institutionalisation of China's Foreign policy. *Journal of Asian and African Studies*, 58(8): 1–17.

Li, Xiaobing and Fang, Qiang (2022) *Sino-American Relations: A New Cold War*. Amsterdam: Amsterdam University Press.

Lieberman, Evan (2022) *Until We Have Won Our Liberty: South Africa After Apartheid*. Princeton: Princeton University Press.

Liebermann, Oren (2022) How Ukraine is using resistance warfare developed by the US to fight back against Russia. *CNN*, 27 August. https://edition.cnn.com/2022/08/27/politics/russia-ukraine-resistance-warfare/index.html

Lima, Cirstiano (2021) A whistleblower's power: Key takeaways from the Facebook Papers. *The Washington Post*, 26 October. www.washingtonpost.com/technology/2021/10/25/what-are-the-facebook-papers/

Lin, Justin Yifu and Wang, Yan (2017) *Going Beyond Aid: Development Cooperation for Structural Transformation*. Cambridge: Cambridge University Press.

Ling, Justin (2023) Russian mercenaries are pushing France out of central Africa. *Foreign Policy*, 18 March. https://foreignpolicy.com/2023/03/18/russian-mercenaries-are-pushing-france-out-of-central-africa/

Lipton, Eric (2023) Start-ups bring silicon valley ethos to a lumbering military-industrial complex. *New York Times*, 21 May. www.nytimes.com/2023/05/21/us/politics/start-ups-weapons-pentagon-procurement.html?alg

Lipton, Eric and Williams, Brooke (2016) How think tanks amplify corporate America's influence. *New York Times*, 7 August. www.nytimes.com/2016/08/08/us/politics/think-tanks-research-and-corporate-lobbying.html

Lister, Tim, Shukla, Sebastian and Ward, Clarissa (2021) It was our children they killed. *CNN*, 15 June. https://edition.cnn.com/2021/06/15/africa/central-african-republic-russian-mercenaries-cmd-intl/index.html

Liu, Jiaqi (2022) When diaspora politics meet global ambitions: Diaspora institutions amid China's geopolitical transformations. *International Migration Review*, 56(4): 1255–1279.

Liu, Zongyuan Zoe and Papa, Mihaela (2022) *Can BRICS De-Dollarize the Global Financial System?* New York: Cambridge University Press.

Loewenstein, Antony (2023) *The Palestine Laboratory: How Israel Exports the Technology of Occupation Around the World*. London: Verso.

Lons, Camille et al. (2019) *China's Great Game in the Middle East, Policy Brief.* London: European Council on Foreign Relations. www.ecfr.eu/publications/summary/china_great_game_middle_east.

Loory, Stuart (1974) The CIA's use of the press: A mighty Wurlitzer. *Columbia Journalism Review*, xiii(3): 9–18.

Lord, Carnes (1998) The past and future of public diplomacy. *Orbis*, Winter: 49–72.

Lord, Strang (1963) *The Unavowable Information Services of Her Majesty's Government Overseas, Report on the Foreign Office Information Research Department, CAB 301/399.* http://discovery.nationalarchives.gov.uk/details/r/C16747784?fbclid=IwAR2ZWFE2xPU8_bj3t_P6su89bRnYFWxZbZcJkWo96i9mKgmtYZrlgd8o644

Louro, Michele, Stolte, Carolien, Streets-Salter, Heather and Tannoury-Karam, Sana (eds.) (2020) *The League against Imperialism: Lives and Afterlives.* Chicago: University of Chicago Press.

Lovell, Stephen (2015) *Russia in the Microphone Age: A History of Soviet Radio, 1919–1970.* Oxford: Oxford University Press.

Lowenthal, Mark (2005) Open source intelligence: new myths, new realities, in George, Roger and Kline, Robert (eds.) *Intelligence and the National Security Strategist: Enduring Issues and Challenges.* Lanham: Rowman and Littlefield.

Lu, Yingdan and Pan, Jennifer (2021) Capturing clicks: How the Chinese government uses clickbait to compete for visibility. *Political Communication*, 38(1–2): 23–54.

Lugo-Ocando, Jairo (2014) *Blaming the Victim: How Global Journalism Fails Those in Poverty.* London: Pluto Press.

Lugo-Ocando, Jairo (2020) *Foreign Aid and Journalism in the Global South: A Mouthpiece for Truth.* London: Lexington Books.

Lugo-Ocando, Jairo and Nguyen, An (2017) *Developing News: Global Journalism and the Coverage of 'Third World' Development.* London: Routledge.

Luqiu, Rose Luwei (2021) *Covering the 2019 Hong Kong Protests.* London: Palgrave/Macmillan.

Luther, Sarah (1988) *The United States and the Direct Broadcast Satellite: The Politics of International Broadcasting in Space.* New York: Oxford University Press.

Lüthi, Lorenz (2016) The non-aligned movement and the Cold War, 1961–1973. *Journal of Cold War Studies*, 18(4): 98–147. https://doi.org/10.1162/JCWS_a_00682.

Lutsevych, Orysia (2023) Ukraine is locked in a war with corruption as well as Putin – it can't afford to lose either. *The Guardian*, 30 January.

Lyon, David (2015) *Surveillance After Snowden.* Cambridge: Polity.

Ma, Winston (2021) *The Digital War: How China's Tech Power Shapes the Future of AI, Blockchain, and Cyberspace.* Cambridge: Wiley.

Maass, Peter (2011) The Toppling: How the media inflated a minor moment in a long war. *The New Yorker*, 2 January. www.newyorker.com/magazine/2011/01/10/the-toppling

Maçães, Bruno (2018) *Belt and Road: A Chinese World Order.* London: Hurst & Co.

MacBride Report (1980) *Many Voices, One World: Communication and Society Today and Tomorrow. International Commission for the Study of Communication Problems.* Paris: UNESCO.

MacLean, Donald (1999) Open doors and open questions: Interpreting the results of the 1998 ITU Minneapolis plenipotentiary conference. *Telecommunications Policy*, 23: 147–58.

Macleod, Alan (2021) Geopolitics, profit, and poppies: How the CIA turned Afghanistan into a failed narco-state. *Monthly Review*, 25 June.

Macleod, Alan (2021) *Support the Tropes: How Media Language Encourages the Left to Support Wars, Coups and Intervention.* Washington: FAIR (Fairness and Accuracy in Reporting).

Mahbubani, Kishore (2022) *The Asian 21st Century.* Singapore: Springer.

Mahl, Daniela, Schäfer, Mike and Zeng, Jing (2023) Conspiracy theories in online environments: An interdisciplinary literature review and agenda for future research. *New Media and Society*, 25(7): 1781–1801. https://doi.org/10.1177/14614448221075759.

Mahler, Jonathan (2018) How one conservative think tank is stocking Trump's government. *New York Times Magazine*, 20 June.

Mahtani, Shibani and McLaughlin, Timothy (2023) *Among the Braves: Hope, Struggle, and Exile in Battle for Hong Kong and the Future of Global Democracy*. Paris: Hachette.

Malik, Ammar A. (2019) India, China, and the BRI. In Harsh, Pant (ed.) *China Ascendant: Its Rise and Implications*, pp. 86–96. New Delhi: HarperCollins.

Malik, Ammar A., Parks, Bradley, Russell, Brooke, Lin, Joyce Jiahui, Walsh, Katherine, Solomon, Kyra, Zhang, Sheng, Elston, Thai-Binh and Goodman, Seth (2021) *Banking on the Belt and Road: Insights from a New Global Dataset of 13,427 Chinese Development Projects*. Williamsburg, VA: AidData at William & Mary.

Malkasian, Carter (2021) *The American War in Afghanistan-A History*. Oxford: Oxford University Press.

Mallorquin, Carlos (2021) *A Southern Perspective on Development Studies*. Santiago: Ariadna Ediciones.

Malmvig, Helle (2020) Soundscapes of war: The audio-visual performance of war by Shi'a militias in Iraq and Syria, *International Affairs*, 96(3): 649–666.

Mamdani, Mahmood (2010) *Saviors and Survivors: Darfur, Politics, and the War on Terror*. New York: Doubleday.

Mamdani, Mahmood (2018) The African University. *London Review of Books*, 40(14).

Mandaville, Peter (2020) *Islam and Politics*, 3rd ed. London: Routledge.

Mankoff, Jeffrey (2022) *Empires of Eurasia: How Imperial Legacies Shape International Security*. New Haven: Yale University Press.

Manuel, Anja (2016) *This Brave New World: India, China and the United States*. New York: Simon & Schuster.

Marashi, Ibrahim (2023) My plagiarised work was used to justify the war on Iraq. *Al-Jazeera*, 21 March.

Markey, Daniel (2020) *China's Western Horizon: Beijing and the New Geopolitics of Eurasia*. New York: Oxford University Press.

Marquardt, Alex (2022) Exclusive: Musk's SpaceX says it can no longer pay for critical satellite services in Ukraine, asks Pentagon to pick up the tab. *CNN*, 14 October.

Marquardt, Alex (2023) CIA launches video to recruit Russian spies. *CNN*, 16 May. https://edition.cnn.com/2023/05/15/politics/cia-russia-spy-recruitment-video/index.html

Marsh, Vivien (2023) *Seeking Truth in International TV News: China, CGTN and the BBC*. London: Routledge.

Marsh, Vivien, MaDrid-Morales, Dani and Paterson, Chris (2023) Global Chinese media and a decade of change. *International Communication Gazette*, 85(1): 3–14.

Martin, Jamie (2022) *The Meddlers: Sovereignty, Empire, and the Birth of Global Economic Governance*. Cambridge, MA: Harvard University Press.

Martin, Peter (2021) *China's Civilian Army: The Making of Wolf Warrior Diplomacy*. Oxford: Oxford University Press.

Martinez Machain, Carla (2021) Exporting influence: US military training as soft power. *Journal of Conflict Resolution*, 65(3): 313–341.

Mashal, Mujib and Kumar, Hari (2023) Where digital payments, even for a 10-cent chai, are colossal in scale. *New York Times*, 1 March.

Masmoudi, Mustafa (1979) The new world information order. *Journal of Communication*, 29(2): 172–185.

Massing, Michael (2021) The story the media missed in Afghanistan. *The New York Review of Books*, 20 October.

Matlock, Jack (2011) *Superpower Illusions: How Myths and False Ideologies Led America Astray-and How to Return to Reality*. New Haven: Yale University Press.

Matloff, Judith (2022) Ukraine's latest weapon in the War-Jokes. *Al Jazeera*, 6 September. www.aljazeera.com/features/2022/9/6/ukraine-latest-weapon-in-the-war-jokes

Mattelart, Armand (1994) *Mapping World Communication: War, Progress, Culture*, Emanuel, S. and Cohen, J. (trans.). Minneapolis: University of Minnesota Press (Originally published in 1991 as *La Communication-monde, Histoire des idées et des stratégies*, Paris: Editions La Découverte).

Mattelart, Armand (2000) *Networking the World, 1794–2000*. Minneapolis, MN: University of Minnesota Press.

Mattingly, Daniel and Yao, Elaine (2022) How soft propaganda persuades. *Comparative Political Studies*, 55(9): 1569–1594.

Mattis, Peter (2023) How to spy on China: Beijing is a hard target – but better tech could make it Easier. *Foreign Affairs*, 28 April.

Mattli, Walter (2019) *Darkness by Design-The Hidden Power in Global Capital Markets*. Princeton: Princeton University Press.

Mavroidis, Petros and Sapir, Andre (2021) *China and the WTO: Why Multilateralism Still Matters*. Princeton: Princeton University Press.

Mayer-Schoenberger, Viktor and Cukier, Kenneth (2013) *Big Data: A Revolution That Will Transform How We Live, Work and Think*. New York: Houghton Mifflin Harcourt.

Mayer-Schöenberger, Viktor and Ramge, Thomas (2018) *Reinventing Capitalism in the Age of Big Data*. London: John Murray.

Mazzetti, Mark and Younes, Ali (2016) C.I.A. Arms for Syrian Rebels supplied black market, officials say. *New York Times*, 26 June. www.nytimes. com/2016/06/27/world/middleeast/cia-arms-for-syrian-rebels-suppliedblack-market-officials-say.html.

McChesney, Robert (2013) *Digital Disconnect: How Capitalism is Turning the Internet against Democracy*. New York: The New Press.

McCoy, Alfred (2003) *The Politics of Heroin: CIA Complicity in the Global Drug Trade*, 2nd revised ed. Chicago: Lawrence Hill.

McDonald, Oonagh (2015) *Lehman Brothers: A Crisis of Value*. Manchester: Manchester University Press.

McFadden, Mark, Jones, Kate, Taylor, Emily and Osborn, Georgia (2021) *Harmonising Artificial Intelligence: The Role of Standards in the EU AI Regulation*. Oxford: Oxford Information Labs, December. https://oxil.uk/publications/2021-12-02-oxford-internet-institute-oxil-harmonising-ai/Harmonising-AI-OXIL.pdf

McGann, James (2016) *The Fifth Estate: Think Tanks, Public Policy, and Governance*. Washington: Brookings Institution Press.

McGann, James (2021a) 2020 Global go to Think Tank Index Report. Philadelphia: University of Pennsylvania Think Tanks and Civil Societies Program Global Go To Think Tank Index Reports. 18. https://repository.upenn.edu/think_tanks/18

McGann, James (eds.) (2021b) *The Future of Think Tanks and Policy Advice Around the World*. London: Palgrave/Macmillan.

McGann, James and Shull, Aaron (2018) Think tanks and emerging power networks. In McGann and Shull (eds.) *Think Tanks and Emerging Power Policy Networks*, pp. 3–14. London: Palgrave.

McKay, Amy (2012) Buying policy? The effects of lobbyists' resources on their policy success. *Political Research Quarterly*, 65(4): 908, 909.

McKinsey Global Institute (2023) The future of globalization: Think diversifying, not decoupling. *McKinsey*, 18 January. https://www.mckinsey.com/featured-insights/themes/the-future-of-globalization-think-diversifying-not-decoupling

McLauchlin, Theodore, Seymour, Lee and Martle, Simon (2022) Tracking the rise of United States foreign military training: IMTAD-USA, a new dataset and research agenda. *Journal of Peace Research*, 59(2): 286–296. https://doi.org/10.1177/00223433211047715

McNamara, Kevin (1992) Reaching captive minds with radio. *Orbis*, Winter: 23–40.

Mearsheimer, John (2014) Why the Ukraine crisis is the West's fault: The liberal delusions that provoked Putin. *Foreign Affairs*, 93(5): 77–89.

Mearsheimer, John (2018) *The Great Delusion: Liberal Dreams and International Realities.* New Haven: Yale University Press.
Medrado, Andrea and Rega, Isabella (2023) *Media Activism, Artivism and the Fight against Marginalisation in the Global South.* London: Routledge.
Meek, James (2023) That's my tank on fire. *London Review of Books*, 45(8). Megiddo, Gur and Benjakob, Omer (2022) The people who kill the truth. *The Haaretz*, 16 November. www.haaretz.com/israel-news/security-aviation/2022-11-16/ty-article-static-ext/the-israelis-destabilizing-democracy-and-disrupting-elections-worldwide/00000186-461e-d80f-abff-6e9e08b10000
Mehta, Nalin (2023) *India's Techade: Digital Revolution and Change in the World's Largest Democracy.* New Delhi: Westland.
Mehta, Pinky (2016) Sanctioning freedoms: U.S. Sanctions against Iran affecting information and communications technology companies. *University of Pennsylvania Journal of International Law*, 37(2): 763–812.
Meier, Vanessa, Karlén, Niklas, Pettersson, Therése and Croicu, Mihai (2022) External support in armed conflicts: Introducing the UCDP external support dataset (ESD), 1975–2017. *Journal of Peace Research*: 1–10. https://doi.org/10.1177/0022343322107986
Mejias, Ulises and Couldry, Nick (2024) *Data Grab: The New Colonialism of Big Tech and How to Fight Back.* Chicago: University of Chicago Press.
Mellen, Ruby, Murphy, Zoeann, Khudov, Kostiantyn and Strek, Kasia (2023) Ukraine's cultural counter offensive: The rush to erase Russia's imprint. *Washington Post*, 11 May. www.washingtonpost.com/world/interactive/2023/ukraine-russian-influence-destruction/ural.
Mendel, Iuliia (2022) *The Fight of Our Lives: My Time with Zelenskyy, Ukraine's Battle for Democracy, and What It Means for the World.* New York: Atria/One Signal.
Meng, Jing and Zhang, Shixin Ivy (2022) Contested journalistic professionalism in China: Journalists' discourses in a time of crisis. *Journalism Studies*, 23(15): 1962–1976. https://doi.org/10.1080/1461670x.2022.2135581
Menon, Shivshankar (2021) *India and Asian Geopolitics: The Past, Present.* Washington: Brookings Institution Press.
Mercille, Julien (2012) *Cruel Harvest: US Intervention in the Afghan Drug Trade.* London: Pluto.
Mervis, Jeffrey (2023) Pall of suspicion: The national institutes of health's 'China initiative' has upended hundreds of lives and destroyed scores of academic careers. *Science*, 379(6638). www.science.org/content/article/pall-suspicion-nihs-secretive-china-initiative-destroyed-scores-academic-careers
Meta (2021) *Threat Report on the Surveillance-for-Hire Industry.* Menlo Park: Meta.
Meta (2023) *Introducing LLaMA-A Foundational, 65-Billion-Parameter Large Language Model*, 24 February. https://ai.facebook.com/blog/large-language-model-llama-meta-ai/
Mettan, Guy (2017) *Creating Russophobia: From the Great Religious Schism to Anti-Putin Hysteria.* Atlanta: Clarity Press.
Metz, Cade (2023) 'The Godfather of A.I.' Leaves Google and warns of danger ahead. *New York Times*, 1 May.
Metz, Cade, Satariano, Adam and Che, Chang (2022) How Elon Musk became a geopolitical chaos agent. *New York Times*, 26 October.
Michels, Eckard (2002) From one crisis to another: The Morale of the French Foreign Legion during the Algerian War. In Alexander, Martin, Evans, Martin and Keiger, J. F. V. (eds.). *The Algerian War and the French Army, 1954–62*, pp. 96–99. Basingstoke: Palgrave.
Mickelson, Sig (1983) *America's Other Voice: The Story of Radio Free Europe and Radio Liberty.* Westport: Praeger.
Micklethwait, John and Wooldridge, Adrian (2022) Putin and Xi exposed the great illusion of capitalism: Unless the U.S. and its allies mobilize to save it, the second great age of globalization is coming to a catastrophic close. *Bloomberg*, 24 March.
Microsoft Research (2023) *Sparks of Artificial General Intelligence: Early Experiments with GPT-4.* Microsoft Research. https://arxiv.org/pdf/2303.12712.pdf

Miller Harris, Sarah (2016) *The CIA and the Congress for Cultural Freedom in the Early Cold War: The Limits of Making Common Cause*. London: Routledge.
Miller, Chris (2022) *Chip War: The Fight for the World's Most Critical Technology*. New York: Scribner.
Miller, Christian (2006) *Blood Money: Wasted Billions, Lost Lives and Corporate Greed in Iraq*. New York: Little Brown.
Miller, Christopher, Scott, Mark and Bender, Bryan (2022) UkraineX: How Elon Musk's space satellites changed the war on the ground. *Politico*, 8 June. www.politico.eu/article/elon-musk-ukraine-starlink/
Miller, Greg (2006) Senate: Hussein wasn't Allied with Al Qaeda. *Los Angeles Times*, 9 September. www.latimes.com/archives/la-xpm-2006-sep-09-na-intel9-story.html
Miller, Greg (2020) 'The intelligence coup of the century': For decades, the CIA read the encrypted communications of allies and adversaries. *The Washington Post*, 11 February. www.washingtonpost.com/graphics/2020/world/national-security/cia-crypto-encryption-machines-espionage/
Miller, Greg and Dixon, Robyn (2023) Wagner group surges in Africa as U.S. influence fades, leak reveals. *Washington Post*, 23 April.
Miller, Greg and Khurshudyan, Isabelle (2023) Ukrainian spies with deep ties to CIA wage shadow war against Russia. *Washington Post*, 23 October. www.washingtonpost.com/world/2023/10/23/ukraine-cia-shadow-war-russia/
Miller-Chatterjee, Manjari (2013) *Wronged by Empire: Post-Imperial Ideology and Foreign Policy in India and China*. Los Angeles: Stanford University Press.
Milton, Viola and Mano, Winston (2021) Afrokology as a transdisciplinary approach to media and communication studies. In Winston, Mano and Viola, Milton (eds.) *Routledge Handbook of African Media and Communication Studies*, pp. 256–275. London: Routledge.
Mims, Christopher (2022) Google, Amazon, Meta and Microsoft weave a fiber-optic web of power. *The Wall Street Journal*, 15 January. www.wsj.com/articles/google-amazon-meta-and-microsoft-weave-a-fiber-optic-web-of-power-11642222824
Ministry of Defence (2021) *Defence in a Competitive Age*. London: March, CP 411.
Ministry of Foreign Affairs of Japan (2015) *Announcement of Partnership for Quality Infrastructure: Investment for Asia's Future*, 21 May. www.mofa.go.jp/policy/oda/page18_000076.html
Mirovalev, Mansur (2021) In risky move, Ukraine's president bans pro-Russian media. *Al Jazeera*, 5 February. https://www.aljazeera.com/news/2021/2/5/ukraines-president-bans-pro-russian-networks-risking-support
Mishra, Stuti (2023) What India's discovery of first ever lithium deposits means for country. *The Independent*. www.independent.co.uk/climate-change/news/jammu-and-kashmir-lithium-deposits-india-gsi-b2279716.html
Mitter, Rana (2021) The world China wants: How Power will – and won't-reshape Chinese ambitions. *Foreign Affairs*, 100(1): 161–174.
Molter, Vanessa and DiResta, Renee (2020) Pandemics & propaganda: How Chinese state media creates and propagates CCP coronavirus narratives. *The Harvard Kennedy School (HKS) Misinformation Review*, 1: 1–18, https://misinforeview.hks.harvard.edu/wp-content/uploads/2020/06/Ipedits_FORMATTED_PandemicsandPropaganda_HKSReview.pdf (Special Issue on Covid-19 and Misinformation).
Monaco, Nick (2021) *Spamouflage Survives: CCP-aligned Disinformation Campaign Spreads on Facebook, Twitter, and YouTube*, Miburo, 22 December. https://miburo.substack.com/p/spamouflage-survives
Monsees, Linda and Lambach, Daniel (2022) Digital sovereignty, geopoliticalimaginaries, and the reproduction of European identity. *European Security*, 31(3): 377–394, https://doi.org/10.1080/09662839.2022.2101883
Moon, Miri (2020) *International News Coverage and the Korean Conflict: The Challenges of Reporting Practices*. London: Palgrave.

Moore, Adam (2019) *Empire's Labor: The Global Army that Supports U.S. Wars*. Cornell: Cornell University Press.
Moore, Andrew (2023) How AI could revolutionize diplomacy. *Foreign Policy*, 21 March.
Moore, Martin and Tambini, Damien (eds.) (2018) *Digital Dominance: The Power of Google, Amazon, Facebook, and Apple*. Oxford: Oxford University Press.
Moore, Martin and Colley, Thomas (2022) Two international propaganda models: Comparing RT and CGTN's 2020 US election coverage. *Journalism Practice*: 1–23.
Morgan Stanley (2020) *Space: Investing in the Final Frontier*. New York: Morgan Stanley. https://www.morganstanley.com/ideas/investing-in-space
Moriyasu, Ken and Okumura, Shigesaburo (2023) Trilateral commission calls 2023 'year one' of new world order. *Nikkei Asia*, 14 March. https://asia.nikkei.com/Politics/International-relations/Indo-Pacific/Trilateral-Commission-calls-2023-Year-One-of-new-world-order
Morozov, Evgeny (2011) *The Net Delusion: How Not to Liberate the World*. London: Penguin.
Morozov, Evgeny (2013) *To Save Everything, Click Here: The Folly of Technological Solutionism*. London: Allen Lane.
Morozov, Evgeny (2021) Chips with everything. *Le Monde diplomatique*, August.
Mosco, Vincent (2014) *To the Cloud: Big Data in a Turbulent World*. New York: Paradigm.
Moyo, Dambisa (2009) *Dead Aid: Why Aid Is Not Working and How There Is a Better Way for Africa*. Basingstoke: Macmillan.
Moyo, Last (2020) *The Decolonial Turn in Media Studies in Africa and the Global South*. London: Palgrave-McMillan.
Mozur, Paul, Xiao, Muyi and Liu, John (2022) 'An Invisible Cage': How China is policing the future. *New York Times*, 25 June.
Mozur, Paul, Zhong, Raymond, Krolik, Aaron, Aufrichtig, Aliza and Morgan, Nailah (2021) How Beijing Influences the Influencers. *New York Times*, 13 December. www.nytimes.com/interactive/2021/12/13/technology/china-propaganda-youtube-influencers.html
Mueller, Milton (2017) *Will the Internet Fragment? Sovereignty, Globalization and Cyberspace*. Cambridge: Polity.
Mueller, Milton (2020) Against sovereignty in cyberspace. *International Studies Review*, 22(4): 779–801. https://doi.org/10.1093/isr/viz044
Mueller, Tim (2013) The Rockefeller foundation, the social sciences, and the humanities in the Cold War. *Journal of Cold War Studies*, 15(3): 108–135.
Mukherjee, Rahul (2019) Jio sparks disruption 2.0: Infrastructural imaginaries and platform ecosystems in 'Digital India'. *Media, Culture & Society*, 41(2): 175–195.
Mukherjee, Rohan (2020) Chaos as opportunity: The United States and world order in India's grand strategy. *Contemporary Politics*, 26(4): 420–438.
Mulder, Nicholas (2022) *The Economic Weapon: The Rise of Sanctions as a Tool of Modern War*. New Haven: Yale University Press.
Munich Security Conference (2020) *Munich Security Report 2020 Westlessness*. https://securityconference.org/en/publications/munich-security-report-2020/
Munshi, Neil and Seddon, Max (2021) Russian mercenaries leave trail of destruction in the Central African Republic Mineral-rich country is 'perfect laboratory' for Wagner group as Kremlin extends influence in Africa. *Financial Times*, 22 October.
Murphy, Dawn (2022) *China's Rise in the Global South: The Middle East, Africa, and Beijing's Alternative World Order*. Los Angeles: Stanford University Press.
Murrell, Colleen (2015) *Foreign Correspondents and International News Gathering: The Role of Fixers*. New York: Routledge.
Muse Report (2021) *A Foreseeable Genocide: The Role of the French Government in Connection with the Genocide against the Tutsi in Rwanda*, 19 April. www.gov.rw/fileadmin/user_upload/gov_user_upload/2021.04.19_MUSE_REPORT.pdf
Mutsvairo, Bruce (ed.) (2016) *Digital Activism in the Social Media Era: Critical Reflections on Emerging Trends in Sub-Saharan Africa*. London: Palgrave Macmillan.

Myers, Steven (2022) Russia's unfounded claims of secret U.S. Bioweapons linger on and on. *The New York Times*, 4 September.
Nageswaran, Anantha and Kaur, Gurvinder (2023) Don't bet against India. *Foreign Affairs*, February.
Nakahara, Junki and Shahin, Saif (2021) All the President's media: How news coverage of sanctions props up the power elite and legitimizes U.S. Hegemony. In Davis, Stuart H. and Ness, Immanuel (eds.) *Sanctions as War: Anti-imperialist Perspectives on American Geo-economic Strategy*, pp. 77–90. Boston, MA: Brill.
Nakashima, Ellen (2010) Google to enlist NSA to help it ward off cyberattacks. *Washington Post*, 4 February.
Nakashima, Ellen (2022) WP EXCLUSIVE-Pentagon opens sweeping review of clandestine psychological operations. *Washington Post*, 19 September. www.washingtonpost.com/national-security/2022/09/19/pentagon-psychological-operations-facebook-twitter
Nalbach, Alex (1999) *The Ring Combination: Information, Power and the World News Agency Cartel*. Unpublished PhD Dissertation, University of Chicago.
Nalbach, Alex (2003) 'Poisoned at the source'? Telegraphic news services and big business in the nineteenth century. *Business History Review*, 77(4): 577–610.
National Computer Virus Emergency Response Center (2023) *'Empire of Hacking': The U.S. Central Intelligence Agency*. Beijing: National Computer Virus Emergency Response Center. http://42.81.126.83/head/zhaiyao/CIAEN.pdf
National Security Archive (2022) *National Security Archive: Iraq War*. Washington: George Washington University. https://nsarchive2.gwu.edu/NSAEBB/NSAEBB326/index.htm
National Security Commission on Artificial Intelligence (2021) *Final Report: National Security Commission on Artificial Intelligence*. Washington: National Security Commission on Artificial Intelligence. https://cybercemetery.unt.edu/nscai/20211005231038mp_/ https://www.nscai.gov/wp-content/uploads/2021/03/Full-Report-Digital-1.pdf
NATO (2021) NATO releases first-ever strategy for Artificial Intelligence. *News Release*, 22 October. www.nato.int/cps/en/natohq/news_187934.htm.
NATO (2022) *NATO 2022 Strategic Concept* (Adopted by Heads of State and Government at the NATO Summit in Madrid, 29 June). www.nato.int/strategic-concept/#StrategicConcept
NATO Advisory Group on Emerging and Disruptive Technologies (2020). *Annual Report 2020*. Brussels, Belgium: NATO. www.nato.int/nato_static_fl2014/assets/pdf/2021/3/pdf/210303-EDT-adv-grp-annual-report-2020.pdf.
Naughton, John (2021) Fear itself is the real threat to democracy, not tall tales of Chinese AI. *The Observer*, 7 March.
Neeley, Tsedal (2017) *The Language of Global Success: How a Common Tongue Transforms Multinational Organizations*. Princeton: Princeton University Press.
Negro, Gianluigi (2019) A history of Chinese global internet governance and its relations with ITU and ICANN. *Chinese Journal of Communication*, 13(1): 1–18. https://doi.org/10.1080/17544750.2019.1650789.
Negro, Gianluigi (2020) The rising role of China in the promotion of multilateral internet governance, 1994–2014. In Andreas, Fikers and Gabriele, Balbi (eds.) *History of the International Telecommunication Union (ITU)*, pp. 107–134. Berlin: De Gruyter Oldenbourg.
Negroponte, John and Palmisano, Samuel (2013) *Defending an Open, Global, Secure, and Resilient Internet*. Washington: Council on Foreign Relations, Independent Task Force Report. https://cdn.cfr.org/sites/default/files/pdf/2013/06/TFR70_cyber_policy.pdf.pdf
Negroponte, Nicholas (1995) *Being Digital*. New York: Alfred A. Knopf.
Nelson, Michael (1997) *War of the Black Heavens: The Battle of Western Broadcasting in the Cold War*. Syracuse: Syracuse University Press.
New York Times (1977) Worldwide Propaganda Network Built by the C.I.A. *The New York Times*, 26 December. www.nytimes.com/1977/12/26/archives/worldwide-propaganda-network-built-by-the-cia-a-worldwide-network.html

New York Times (2020) Distortions: Tracking viral misinformation. *New York Times*, 15 September.
Ng, Michael (2022) *Political Censorship in British Hong Kong: Freedom of Expression and the Law (1842–1997)*. Cambridge: Cambridge University Press.
Nguyen, David and Paczos, Marta (2020) Measuring the economic value of data and cross-border data flows: A business perspective. *OECD Digital Economy Papers*, No. 297. Paris: OECD.
Niblett, Robin (2018) Rediscovering a sense of purpose: The challenge for western think-tanks. *International Affairs*, 94(6): 1409–1430.
Nielsen, Rasmus Kleis and Fletcher, Richard (2020) Democratic creative destruction? The effect of a changing media landscape on democracy. In Persily, Nathaniel and Tucker, Joshua (eds.) *Social Media and Democracy: The State of the Field and Prospects for Reform*, pp. 139–162. Cambridge: Cambridge University Press.
Nilekani, Nandan (2018) Data to the people: India's inclusive Internet. *Foreign Affairs*, 97(5): 19–26.
Nilsson, Annika and Christensen, Miyase (2019) *Arctic Geopolitics, Media and Power*. London: Routledge.
Nimmo, Ben, Eib, Shawn and Tamora, L. (2019) *Cross-Platform Spam Network Targeted Hong Kong Protests 'Spamouflage Dragon' Used Hijacked and Fake Accounts to Amplify Video Content*. Graphika. https://publicassets.graphika.com/reports/graphika_report_spamouflage.pdf
NITI Aayog (2018) *Strategy for New India@75*. New Delhi: NITI Aayog.
Nitzan, Jonathan and Bichler, Shimshon (1995) Bringing capital accumulation back in: The Weapondollar-Petrodollar coalition – military contractors, oil companies and Middle East 'energy conflicts'. *Review of International Political Economy*, 2(3): 446–515.
Nocetti, Julien (2015) Contest and conquest: Russia and global Internet governance. *International Affairs*, 91(1): 111–130.
Nordenstreng, Kaarle (2012) The New World Information and Communication Order: An idea that refuses to die. In J. Nerone (ed.) *Media History and the Foundations of Media Studies*, Volume 1 of A. N. Valdivia (ed.) *The International Encyclopedia of Media Studies*, pp. 477–499. Chichester: Wiley-Blackwell.
Nordenstreng, Kaarle (ed.) (1986) *New International Information and Communication Order Source Book*. Prague: International Organization of Journalists.
Nordenstreng, Kaarle and Thussu, Daya Kishan (eds.) (2015) *Mapping BRICS Media*. London: Routledge.
NSA (2014) In Clarke, Richard, Morell, Michael, Stone, Geoffrey, Sunstein, Cass and Swire, Peter (eds.) *The NSA Report: Liberty and Security in a Changing World: The President's Review Group on Intelligence and Communications Technologies*. Princeton, NJ: Princeton University Press.
Nyabiage, Jevans (2022) China's political party school in Africa takes first students from 6 countries. *South China Morning Post*, 21 Jun.
Nye, Joseph (2019) The rise and fall of US hegemony from Wilson to Trump. *International Affairs*, 95(1): 63–80.
Nyman, Jonna (2023) Towards a global security studies: What can looking at China tell us about the concept of security? *European Journal of International Relations*, 29(3): 673–697. https://doi.org/10.1177/13540661231176990
Ó Tuathail, Gearóid (1996) *Critical Geopolitics: The Politics of Writing Global Space*. London: Routledge.
Ó Tuathail, Gearóid and Dalby, Simon (eds.) (1998) *Rethinking Geopolitics*. New York: Routledge.
O'Brien-Kop, Karen and Newcombe, Suzanne (eds.) (2021) *Routledge Handbook of Yoga and Meditation Studies*. London: Routledge.

O'Connor, Tom (2017) How ISIS Got Weapons from the US and used them to take Iraq and Syria. *Newsweek*, 14 December. www. newsweek.com/how-isis-got-weaponsus-used-them-take-iraq-syria-748468.

O'Neil, Cathy (2016) *Weapons of Math Destruction: How Big Data Increases Inequality and Threatens Democracy*. New York: Crown.

O'Sullivan, Donie and Passantino, Jon (2023) 'Verified' Twitter accounts share fake image of 'explosion' near Pentagon, causing confusion. *CNN*, 22 May. https://edition.cnn.com/2023/05/22/tech/twitter-fake-image-pentagon-explosion/index.html#:~:text=In%20the%20moments,was%20positive%20again.

O'Sullivan, Kevin (2014) A 'global nervous system': The rise and rise of European humanitarian NGOs, 1945–1985. In Marc, Frey, Sonke, Kunkel and Corinna, Unger (eds.) *International Organizations and Development*, 1945–1990, pp. 196–219. Basingstoke: Palgrave Macmillan.

Oates, Sarah (2013) *Revolution Stalled: The Political Limits of the Internet in the Post-Soviet Sphere*. New York: Oxford University Press.

Oberhaus, Daniel (2018) Hundreds of researchers from Harvard, Yale and Stanford Were Published in Fake Academic Journals. *The Vice*, 14 August. www.vice.com/en/article/3ky45y/hundreds-of-researchers-from-harvard-yale-and-stanford-were-published-in-fake-academic-journals

OECD (2019a) *Artificial Intelligence in Society*. Paris: OECD. https://doi.org/10.1787/eedfee77-en.

OECD (2019b) *Going Digital: Shaping Policies, Improving Lives*. Paris: Organization for Economic Cooperation and Development.

OECD (2020) *The AI Social Contract Index 2020: OECD AI Principles: Recommendation of the Council on Artificial Intelligence*. Paris: OECD.

OECD (2022) *How the War in Ukraine is Affecting Space Activities*. Paris: Organization for Economic Cooperation and Development.

OFCOM (2020) *Broadcast and On Demand Bulletin*. London: Office of Communication, Issue 403, 26 May.

Office of the Director of National Intelligence (2019) *Strategic Plan to Advance Cloud Computing in the Intelligence Community*. Washington: Office of the Director of National Intelligence. www.dni.gov/files/documents/CIO/Cloud_Computing_Strategy.pdf

Ogden, Chris (2022) *The Authoritarian Century: China's Rise and the Demise of the Liberal International Order*. Bristol: Bristol University Press.

Ohanyan, Anna (2022) *The Neighborhood Effect – The Imperial Roots of Regional Fracture in Eurasia*. Los Angeles: Stanford University Press.

Ohlberg, Mareike et al. (2018) *Authoritarian Advance: Responding to China's Growing Political Influence in Europe*. Berlin: Mercator Institute for China Studies (MERICS) and Global Public Policy Institute.

Ohnesorge, Hendrik (ed.) (2023) *Soft Power and the Future of US Foreign Policy*. Manchester: Manchester University Press.

Olivo, Antonio (2023) Northern Va. Is the heart of the internet. Not everyone is happy about that. *Washington Post*, 10 February.

Onuch, Olga and Hale, Henry (2023) *The Zelensky Effect*. New York: Oxford University Press.

Open Society Foundation (2023) Media freedom. https://www.opensocietyfoundations.org/voices/topics/media-freedom

Oremus, Will and Zakrzewski, Cat (2022) Big Tech tried to quash Russian propaganda. Russia found loopholes. *Washington Post*, 10 August.

Oreskes, Naomi and Conway, Eric (2010) *Merchants of Doubt: How a Handful of Scientists Obscured the Truth on Issues from Tobacco Smoke to Global Warming*. New York: Bloomsbury Press.

Oxfam (2023) *Inclusive Language Guide*. Oxford: Oxfam International. https://policy-practice.oxfam.org/resources/inclusive-language-guide-621487/

Palmer, Lindsay (2019) *The Fixers: Local News Workers' Perspectives on International Reporting*. New York: Oxford University Press.

Pan, Chengxin, Isakhan, Benjamin, Nwokora, Zim (2019) Othering as soft-power discursive practice: *China Daily*'s construction of Trump's America in the 2016 presidential election. *Politics*, 40(1): 54–69.

Panda, Ankit (2020) *Kim Jong-un and the Bomb: Survival and Deterrence in North Korea*. Oxford: Oxford University Press.

Pant, Harsh (2016) Rising China in India's vicinity: A rivalry takes shape in Asia. *Cambridge Review of International Affairs*, 29(2): 364–381.

Pardesi, Manjeet (2022) India's China strategy under Modi continuity in the management of an asymmetric rivalry. *International Politics*, 59: 44–66.

Pariser, Eli (2011) *The Filter Bubble: How the New Personalized Web is Changing What we Read and How we Think*. New York: Penguin.

Parker, Charlie (2022) Uber-style technology helped Ukraine to destroy Russian Battalion. *Times*, 14 May.

Parker, Jason (2016) *Hearts, Minds, Voices: US Cold War Public Diplomacy and the Formation of the Third World*. Oxford: Oxford University Press.

Parmar, Inderjeet (2002) Anglo-American elites in the interwar years: Idealism and power in the intellectual roots of Chatham House and the Council of Foreign Relations. *International Relations*, 16(1): 53–75.

Parmar, Inderjeet (2014) *Foundations of the American Century: The Ford, Carnegie, and Rockefeller Foundations in the Rise of American Power*. New York: Columbia University Press.

Partos, Gabriel (1993) *The World That Came from the Cold*. London: BBC World Service and Royal Institute of International Affairs.

Patnaik, Utsa and Patnaik, Prabhat (2021) *Capital and Imperialism: Theory, History, and the Present*. New York: Monthly Review Press.

Paul, Christopher and Matthews, Miriam (2016) *The Russian 'Firehose of Falsehood' Propaganda Model. Why It Might Work and Options to Counter It*. Santa Monica, CA: RAND Corporation.

Payne, Kenneth (2021) *I, Warbot: The Dawn of Artificially Intelligent Conflict*. Oxford: Oxford University Press.

Pei, Minxin (2019) No Easy Road for US in Decoupling. *Foreign Policy*, 6 December.

Perrigo, Billy (2023) Exclusive: OpenAI lobbied the E.U. to water down AI regulation. *Time*, 20 June.

Peters, John Durham (1986) Institutional sources of intellectual poverty in communication research. *Communication Research*, 13(4): 527–559.

Petrov, Nikita (2018) Don't speak, memory: How Russia represses its past. *Foreign Affairs*, 97(1): 16–21.

Pettegree, Andrew (2014) *The Invention of News-How the World Came to Know About Itself*. New Haven: Yale University Press.

Philips, W. (2018) *The Oxygen of Amplification – Better Practices for Reporting on Extremists, Antagonists, and Manipulators Online*. New York: Data & Society Research Institute.

Phillipson, Robert (1992) *Linguistic Imperialism*. Oxford: Oxford University Press.

Phillipson, Robert (2009) *Linguistic Imperialism Continued*. New York: Routledge.

Phillipson, Robert (2017) Myths and realities of 'global' English. *Language Policy*, 16(3): 313–331.

Pigeaud, Fanny and Sylla Samba, Ndongo (2021) *Africa's Last Colonial Currency: The CFA Franc Story*. London: Pluto Press.

Piketty, Thomas (2020) *Capital and Ideology*, Arthur, Goldhammer (trans.). Harvard: Harvard University Press.
Pillai, Rajeswari and Prasad, Rajagopalan Narayan (eds.) (2017*) Space India 2.0: Commerce, Policy, Security and Governance Perspectives*. New Delhi: Observer Research Foundation.
Pisa, Michael and Polcari, John (2019) *Governing Big Tech's Pursuit of the 'Next Billion Users.'* Washington: Center for Global Development CGD Policy Paper. https://www.cgdev.org/publication/governing-big-techs-pursuit-next-billion-users
Plantin, Jean-Christophe (2021) The geopolitical hijacking of open networking: The case of Open RAN. *European Journal of Communication*, 36(4): 404–417.
Plantin, Jean-Christophe, Lagoze, Carl, Edwards, Paul and Sandvig, Christian (2018) Infrastructure studies meet platform studies in the age of Google and Facebook. *New Media & Society*, 20(1): 293–310.
Poell, Thomas (2020) Three challenges for media studies in the age of platforms. *Television & New Media,* 21(6): 650–657.
Pohle, Julia and Thiel, Thorsten (2020) Digital sovereignty. *Internet Policy Review*, 9(4): 1–19.
Pollack, Kenneth (2014) An army to defeat Assad: How to turn Syria's opposition into a real fighting force. *Brookings Institution*, 7 September.
Polyakova, Alina and Boyer, Spencer Phipps (2018) *The Future of Political Warfare: Russia the West, and the Coming Age of Global Digital Competition*. Washington: Brookings Institute.
Pomar, Mark (2022) *Cold War Radio: The Russian Broadcasts of the Voice of America and Radio Free Europe/Radio Liberty*. Lincoln, NE: Potomac Books.
Porch, Douglas (2013) *Counterinsurgency: Exposing the Myths of the New Way of War*. Cambridge: Cambridge University Press.
Poskett, James (2022) *Horizons-A Global History of Science*. London: Penguin.
Potter, Simon (2012) *Broadcasting Empire: The BBC and the British World, 1922–1970*. Oxford: Oxford University Press.
Potter, Simon (2020) *Wireless Internationalism and Distant Listening: Britain, Propaganda, and the Invention of Global Radio, 1920–1939*. Oxford: Oxford University Press.
Potter, Simon (2022) *This is the BBC: Entertaining the Nation, Speaking for Britain? 1922–2022*. Oxford: Oxford University Press.
Potter, Simon, Clayton, David, Kind-Kovacs, Friederike, Kuitenbrouwer, Vincent, Ribeiro, Nelson, Scales, Rebecca and Stanton, Andrea (2022) *The Wireless World: Global Histories of International Radio Broadcasting*. Oxford: Oxford University Press.
Pottier, Philippe (2005) GCMA/GMI: A French experience in counterinsurgency during the French Indochina War. *Small Wars & Insurgencies*, 16(2): 125–46.
Power, Marcus (2019) *Geopolitics and Development*. London: Routledge.
Power, Marcus (2000) *Aqui Lourenço Marques!!* [Lourenço Marques here!!]: 'Radio-Colonization' and cultural identity in colonial Mozambique 1932–1974. *Journal of Historical Geography,* 26(4): 605–628.
Power, Marcus and Crampton, Andrew (2005) Reel geopolitics: Cinematographing political space. *Geopolitics*, 10: 193–203.
Prestowitz, Clyde (2021) *The World Turned Upside Down-America, China, and the Struggle for Global Leadership*. New Haven: Yale University Press.
Price, Monroe (2015) *Free Expression, Globalism and the New Strategic Communication*. Cambridge: Cambridge University Press.
Prunier, Gérard (2009) *Africa's World War: Congo, the Rwandan Genocide, and the Making of a Continental Catastrophe*. Oxford: Oxford University Press.
Puri, Samir (2020) *The Great Imperial Hangover: How Empires Have Shaped the World*. New York: Atlantic Books.
Puri, Samir (2022) *Russia's Road to War with Ukraine: Invasion Amidst the Ashes of Empires*. London: Biteback Publishing.

Putnis, Peter, Kaul, Chandrika and Wilke, Jürgen (eds.) (2011) *International Communication and Global News Networks: Historical Perspectives*. New York: Hampton Press.

Qin, Amy, Wang, Vivian and Hakim, Danny (2020) How Steve Bannon and a Chinese Billionaire created a right-wing coronavirus media sensation. *New York Times*, 22 November.

QS World University Rankings (2022) *2022 QS World University Rankings Yearbook*. London: QS Quacquarelli Symonds.

Radin, Andrew, Scobell, Andrew, Treyger, Elina, Williams, J. D., Ma, Logan, Shatz, Howard, Zeigler, Sean, Han, Eugeniu and Reach, Clint (2021) *China-Russia Cooperation: Determining Factors, Future Trajectories, Implications for the United States*. Santa Monica: RAND Corporation. www.rand.org/t/RR3067

Radu, Roxana (2019) *Negotiating Internet Governance*. Oxford: Oxford University Press.

Raghavan, Pallavi, Bayly, Martin, Leake, Elisabeth and Paliwal, Avinash (2022) The limits of decolonisation in India's international thought and practice: An introduction. *The International History Review*, 44(4): 812–818.

Rainforest Action Network, BankTrack, Indigenous Environmental Network, Oil Change International, Reclaim Finance, Sierra Club, and Urgewald (2023) *Banking on Climate Chaos: Fossil Fuel Finance Report 2022*. BankingonClimateChaos.org, February.

Rajagopalan, Rajesh (2020) Evasive balancing: India's unviable Indo-Pacific strategy. *International Affairs*, 96(1): 75–93.

Ramani, Samuel (2023) *Russia in Africa: Resurgent Great Power or Bellicose Pretender?* London: Hurst.

Ramaswamy, Vivek (2021) *Woke Inc: Inside the Social Justice Scam*. London: Swift Press.

Ramesh Jairam (2005) *Making Sense of Chindia: Reflections on China and India*. New Delhi: India Research Press.

Ramzy, Austin (2018) Chinese reporter accused of slapping man at political event in Britain. *New York Times*, 2 October.

Rao, Ursula and Nair, Vijayanka (2019) Aadhaar: Governing with biometrics. *South Asia: Journal of South Asia Studies*, 42(3): 469–481.

Rashid, Ahmed (2008) *Descent into Chaos: The U.S. and the Disaster in Pakistan, Afghanistan, and Central Asia*. London: Penguin.

Read, Donald (1992) *The Power of News: The History of Reuters, 1849–1989*. Oxford: Oxford University Press.

Recorded Future (2023) *Private Eyes: China's Embrace of Open-Source Military Intelligence*. Boston: Recorded Future. https://go.recordedfuture.com/hubfs/reports/ta-2023-0601.pdf

Recorded Futures (2023) *Private Eyes: China's Embrace of Open-Source Military Intelligence*. Washington: Recorded Futures (Insikt Group). https://go.recordedfuture.com/hubfs/reports/ta-2023-0601.pdf

Reiley, Laura (2022) The USDA's new labelling for genetically modified foods goes into effect. *Washington Post*, 1 January.

Repnikova, Maria (2022a) *Chinese Soft Power*. Cambridge: Cambridge University Press.

Repnikova, Maria (2022b) Rethinking China's soft power: 'Pragmatic enticement' of Confucius institutes in Ethiopia. *The China Quarterly*, 250(2): 440–463.

Reuters (2021) African Union says Russia offers 300 million doses of Sputnik V vaccine. 19 February.

Reuters (2022) WHO chief colour skin may be why Tigray crisis not getting attention. 17 August.

Reuters (2023a) BRICS welcomes new members in push to reshuffle world order. 25 August.

Reuters (2023b) Chinese hackers spying on US critical infrastructure, Western intelligence says. May 25.

Ribeiro, Nelson and Seul, Stephanie (eds.) (2018) *Revisiting Transnational Broadcasting: The BBC's Foreign-Language Services during the Second World War*. London: Routledge.

Rice, Condoleezza (2021) Remarks to the partnership for critical infrastructure. *U.S. Chamber of Commerce*, 23 March. www.house.gov/jec/security.pdf

Richardson, Ian, Kakabadse, Andrew and Kakabadse, Nada (2011) *Bilderberg People: Elite Power and Consensus in World Affairs*. London: Routledge.

Ricks, Thomas (2006) Military plays up role of Zarqawi Jordanian painted as Foreign threat to Iraq's stability. *Washington Post*, 10 April.

Rid, Thomas (2013) *Cyber War Will Not Take Place*. New York: Oxford University Press.

Risso, Linda (2014) *Propaganda and Intelligence in the Cold War: The NATO Information Service*. London: Routledge.

Roberts, Margaret (2018) *Censored: Distraction and Diversion Inside China's Great Firewall*. Princeton: Princeton University Press.

Roberts, Sean (2020) *The War on the Uyghurs: China's Internal Campaign Against a Muslim Minority*. Princeton: Princeton University Press.

Robinson, Nathan and Chomsky, Noam (2023) The worst crime of the 21st century: The United States' destruction of Iraq remains the worst international crime of our time. *Current Affairs*, 12 May. www.currentaffairs.org/2023/05/the-worst-crime-of-the-21st-century?

Rogers, James, Foxall, Andrew, Henderson, Matthew and Armstrong, Sam (2020) *Breaking the China Supply Chain: How the 'Five Eyes' Can Decouple from Strategic Dependency*. London: Henry Jackson Society.

Rolland, Nadège (ed.) (2020) *An Emerging China-centric order: China's Vision for a New World Order in Practice*. Seattle: The National Bureau of Asian Research (NBR special report #87. August).

Roman, Nataliya, Beasley, Berrin and Parmelee, John (2022) From fiction to reality: Presidential framing in the Ukrainian comedy servant of the people. *European Journal of Communication*, 37(1): 48–62.

Roosa, John (2022) *Buried Histories: The Anti-communist Massacres of 1965–1966 in Indonesia*. Wisconsin: University of Wisconsin Press.

Rosenberg, Matthew; Confessore, Nicholas and Cadwalladr, Carole (2018) How Trump consultants exploited the Facebook data of millions. *New York Times*, 17 March.

Rosenberger, Laura (2020) Making cyberspace safe for democracy: The New Landscape of information competition. *Foreign Affairs*, 99(3): 146–159.

Rosenstiel, Tom, Buzenberg, William, Connelly, Majorie and Loker, Kevin (2016) *Charting New Ground: The Ethical Terrain of Non-Profit Journalism*. Arlington: American Press Institute.

RT (2022) German spies helping Ukraine – media. *RT*, 28 September.

RT (2023) 'Truth is our most potent weapon' – ex-US Navy technician behind pro-Russian 'Donbass Devushka' collective. *RT*, 26 April.

Rubin, Andrew (2012) *Archives of Authority: Empire, Culture, and the Cold War*. Princeton: Princeton University Press.

Rudd, Kevin (2022a) *The Avoidable War-The Dangers of a Catastrophic Conflict between the US and Xi Jinping's China*. New York: PublicAffairs.

Rudd, Kevin (2022b) The world according to Xi Jinping: What China's ideologue in Chief really believes. *Foreign Affairs*, November/December

Rühlig, Tim (2022) China's digital power: Assessing the implications for the EU. *Digital Power China Research Consortium*, January.

Ruiz, Jeanette and Barnett, George (2015) Who owns the international Internet networks? *The Journal of International Communication*, 21(1): 38–57.

Rumer, Eugene and Weiss, Andrew (2021) Ukraine: Putin's unfinished business. *Carnegie Endowment for International Peace*, 12 November.

Russell, Stuart (2019) *Human Compatible: AI and the Problem of Control*. New York: Penguin.

Russian Federation (2014) Article 18(5), Federal Law No. 152-FZ on Personal Data as Amended in July 2014 by Federal Law No. 242-FZ on Amendments to Certain

Legislative Acts of the Russian Federation for Clarification of Personal Data Processing in Information and Telecommunications Networks.

Ryan, Fergus, Bogle, Ariel, Ruser, Nathan, Zhang, Albert and Impiombato, Daria (2021) *Borrowing Mouths to Speak on Xinjiang*. Perth: Australian Strategic Policy Institute, Policy Brief, Report no. 55.

Ryan, Missy (2022) U.S. races to track American arms in heat of Ukraine War. *Washington Post*, 1 November.

Sachs, Wolfgang (2020) The age of development: An obituary. *New Internationalist*, February.

Sachs, Wolfgang (ed.) (2010 [1992]) *The Development Dictionary: A Guide to Knowledge as Power*. London: Zed Books.

Sadeghi, McKenzie and Arvanitis, Lorenzo (2023) *Newsbots: AI-Generated News Websites Proliferating Online*. New York: NewsGuard.

Sadowski, Jathan (2020) *Too Smart: How Digital Capitalism is Extracting Data, Controlling Our Lives, and Taking Over the World*. Cambridge, MA: The MIT Press.

Sahlins, Marshall (2015) *Confucius Institutes: Academic Malware*. Chicago, IL: Prickly Paradigm Press.

SAI (2022) *2022 State of US Semiconductor Industry*. Washington: Semiconductor Industry Association.

Said, Edward (1978) *Orientalism*. London: Routledge & Kegan Paul.

Said, Edward (1993) *Culture and Imperialism*. London: Chatto & Windus.

Sakwa, Richard (2021) *Deception: Russiagate and the New Cold War*. Lanham, MD: Lexington Books.

Sanger, David, Barnes, Julian and Conger, Kate (2022) As tanks rolled into Ukraine, so did Malware. Then Microsoft entered the war. *New York Times*, 28 February.

Sarkar, Jayita (2022) *Ploughshares and Swords: India's Nuclear Program in the Global Cold War*. Ithaca: Cornell University Press.

Satariano, Adam (2019) How the Internet travels across the oceans. *The New York Times*, 10 March.

Satia, Priya (2018) *Empire of Guns-The Violent Making of the Industrial Revolution*. New York: Penguin Press.

Satia, Priya (2020) *Time's Monster: History, Conscience and Britain's Empire*. Cambridge, MA: Harvard University Press.

Saunders, Frances Stonor (2013) *The Cultural Cold War: The CIA and the World of Arts and Letters*. New York: The New Press.

Savell, Stephanie (2023) *How Death Outlives War: The Reverberating Impact of the Post-9/11 Wars on Human Health*. Providence, RI: Watson Institute, Brown University.

Sawhney, Pravin (2022) *The Last War: How AI Will Shape India's Final Showdown with China*. New Delhi: Aleph Books.

Scahill, Jeremy (2007) *Blackwater: The Rise of the World's Most Powerful Mercenary Army*. New York: Nation Books.

Schaap, Fritz (2023) Ethiopia after the Civil War: A Fragile peace in the wake of unspeakable horrors. *Der Spiegel*, 5 April.

Schaffer, Ronald (1988) *Wings of Judgment: American Bombing in World War II*. Oxford: Oxford University Press.

Scharnberg, Harriet (2016) The A and P of propaganda: Associated Press and Nazi photojournalism. *Zeithistorische Forschungen/Studies in Contemporary History*, 13: 1–28.

Scharre, Paul (2023) *Four Battlegrounds: Power in the Age of Artificial Intelligence*. New York: W. W. Norton.

Scheck, Justin and Gibbons-Neff, Thomas (2023) Stolen valor: The U.S. volunteers in Ukraine Who Lie, Waste and Bicker. *The New York Times*, 25 March (Top of Form Bottom of Form).

Schiffrin, Anya (2011) *Bad News: How America's Business Press Missed the Story of the Century*. New York: The New Press.

Schiller, Dan (2011) *How to Think about Information*. Champaign, IL: Illinois University Press.
Schiller, Herbert (1992) *Mass Communication and the American Empire*, updated ed. New York: Westview Press (Originally published in 1969).
Schindler, Seth and DiCarlo, Jessica (eds.) (2023) *The Rise of the Infrastructure State: How US–China Rivalry Shapes Politics and Place Worldwide*. Bristol: Bristol University Press.
Schlesinger, Arthur, Jr. (1965) *A Thousand Days: John F. Kennedy in the White House*. Boston: Houghton Mifflin.
Schmidt, Eric and Cohen, Jared (2010) The digital disruption: Connectivity and the diffusion of power. *Foreign Affairs*, November/December.
Schmidt, Eric and Cohen, Jared (2013) *The New Digital Age: Reshaping the Future of People, Nations and Business*. London: John Murray.
Schmitt, Eric (2022) Pentagon plans to set up a new command to Arm Ukraine, officials say. *New York Times*, 29 September.
Schmitt, Eric and Koettl, Christoph (2021) Remote C.I.A. Base in the Sahara steadily grows. *New York Times*, 8 March.
Schneider, Florian (ed.) (2021) *Global Perspectives on China's Belt and Road Initiative Asserting Agency through Regional Connectivity*. Amsterdam: Amsterdam University Press.
Schoon, Alette, Mabweazara, Hayes, Bosch, Tanja and Dugmore, Harry (2020) Decolonising digital media research methods: Positioning African digital experiences as epistemic sites of knowledge production. *African Journalism Studies*, 41(4): 1–15.
Schucan Bird, Karen and Pitman, Lesley (2020) How diverse is your reading list? Exploring issues of representation and decolonisation in the UK. *Higher Education*, 79: 903–920
Schwirtz, Michael and Kramer, Andrew (2022) Blast on Crimean bridge deals blow to Russian War effort in Ukraine. *New York Times*, 8 October.
Schyns, Camille (2023) *The Lobbying Ghost in the Machine: Big Tech's Covert Defanging of Europe's AI Act*. Brussels: Corporate Europe Observatory.
Scott, Martin, Wright, Kate and Bunce, Mel (2023) *Humanitarian Journalists Covering Crises from a Boundary Zone*. London: Routledge.
Scott-Smith, Giles (2002) *The Politics of Apolitial Culture: The Congress for Cultural Freedom, the CIA and Post-war American Hegemony*. London: Routledge.
Scott-Smith, Giles and Lerg, Charlotte (eds.) (2017) *Campaigning Culture and the Global Cold War: The Journals of the Congress for Cultural Freedom*. London: Palgrave.
Seaman, John (2020) *China and the New Geopolitics of Technical Standardization*. Paris: French Institute of International Relations.
Searcey, Dionne, Forsythe, Michael and Lipton, Eric (2021) Race to the future: A power struggle over Cobalt Rattles the clean energy revolution. *New York Times*, 20 November.
Seely, Bob, Varnish, Peter and Hemmings, John (2019) *Defending Our Data: Huawei, 5G, and Five Eyes*. London: Henry Jackson Society.
Segura, María Soledad and Waisbord, Silvio (2016) *Media Movements: Civil Society and Media Policy Reform in Latin America*. London: Zed Books.
Seymour, Richard (2019) *The Twittering Machine*. London: The Indigo.
Shah, Nishant, Puthiya-Purayil, Sneha, and Chattapadhyay, Sumandro (eds.) (2015) *Digital Activism in Asia Reader*. Lüneburg: Meson Press.
Shahsavari, Shadi, Holur, Pavan, Wang, Tianyi et al. (2020) Conspiracy in the time of corona: Automatic detection of emerging COVID-19 conspiracy theories in social media and the news. *Journal of Computational Social Science*, 3(2): 279–317.
Shambaugh, David (2015) China's soft-power push: The search for respect. *Foreign Affairs*, 94(4): 99–107.

Shanker, Thom and Schmitt, Eric (2004) Pentagon weighs use of deception in a Broad Arena. *New York Times*, 13 December.

Shapiro, Jeremy (2020) Introduction: Europe's digital sovereignty. In Carla Hobbs (ed.) *Europe's Digital Sovereignty: From Rule Maker to Superpower in the Age of US-China Rivalry*, pp. 6–13. London: European Council on Foreign Relations.

Sharma, Kiran, Bharadwaj, Sanskrita and Mahmud, Faisal (2023) Bangladesh, Brahmaputra serve as proxy for Sino-Indian conflict: China, India dams stoke tensions as region's most vulnerable suffer. *Nikkei Asia*, 26 July.

Sharma, Ram Sewak (2020) *Making of Aadhaar: World's Largest Identity Platform*. New Delhi: Rupa.

Sharma, Umang (2023) Eight countries open 50 special rupee vostro accounts in 6 months to trade in INR. *FirstPost*, 6 March.

Shen, Hong (2016) China and global internet governance: Toward an alternative analytical framework. *Chinese Journal of Communication*, 9(3): 304–324.

Shi-Kupfer, Kristin and Ohlberg, Mareike (2019) *China's Digital Rise: Challenges for Europe*. Berlin: Merics.

Shiller, Robert (2019) *Narrative Economics: How Stories Go Viral and Drive Major Economic Events*. Princeton: Princeton University Press.

Shirk, Susan (2022) *Overreach-How China Derailed Its Peaceful Rise*. New York: Oxford University Press.

Shirky, Clay (2010) *Cognitive Surplus: Creativity and Generosity in a Connected Age*. New York: Penguin.

Shirky, Clay (2011) The political power of social media. *Foreign Affairs*, 90(1): 28–41.

Shom, Raka (2006) Interdisciplinary research and globalization. *Communication Review*, 9: 1–36.

Shome, Raka (2016) When postcolonial studies meets media studies. *Critical Studies in Media Communication*, 33(3): 245–263.

Shome, Raka (2017) Going South and engaging non-Western modernities. *Media Theory*, 1(1): 65–73.

Shuster, Simon (2023) Inside Zelensky's plan to Beat Putin's propaganda in Russian-occupied Ukraine. *Time*, 22 June. https://time.com/6288904/ukraine-russia-propaganda-counteroffensive-zelensky/

Siddiqa, Ayesha (2017) *Military Inc.: Inside Pakistan's Military Economy*, 2nd ed. London: Pluto Press.

SIGAR (2018) *Counternarcotics: Lessons from the U.S. Experience in Afghanistan*. Washington: Special General Inspector for Afghan Reconstruction (SIGAR).

SIGAR (2021) *What We Need to Learn: Lessons from Twenty Years of Afghanistan Reconstruction*. Washington: Special General Inspector for Afghan Reconstruction (SAGAR).

SIGAR (2022) *Collapse of the Afghan National Defense and Security Forces: An Assessment of the Factors That Led to Its Demise*. Washington: Special Inspector General for Afghanistan Reconstruction (SIGAR).

Silberstein-Loeb, Jonathan (2014) *The International Distribution of News*. New York: Cambridge University Press.

Simon, Felix and Camargo, Chico (2021) Autopsy of a metaphor: The origins, use and blind spots of the 'infodemic'. *New Media & Society*, 25(8).

Simons, Josh (2023) *Algorithms for the People-Democracy in the Age of AI*. Princeton: Princeton University Press.

Simpson, John (1991) *From the House of War: John Simpson in the Gulf*. London: Arrow Books.

Simpson, Patricia, and Duxies, Helga (eds.) (2015) *Digital Media Strategies of the Far Right in Europe and the United States*. Lanham, MD: Lexington Books.

Singer, P. W. (2008) *Corporate Warriors: The Rise of the Privatized Military Industry*. Cornell: Cornell University Press.

Singer, Peter and Friedman, Allan (2014) *Cybersecurity and Cyberwar: What Everyone Needs to Know*. New York: Oxford University Press.

Singh, J. P. (2017) *Sweet Talk: Paternalism and Collective Action in North-South Trade Negotiations*. Stanford: Stanford University Press.

Sinha Palit, Parama (2023) *New Media and Public Diplomacy-Political Communication in India, the United States and China*. London: Routledge.

Siong, Olivia (2022) *What Happened before Hu Jintao Was Escorted Out of Congress? CNA Captured Rare Footage in Lead-Up*. Singapore: Channel News Asia. www.channelnewsasia.com/asia/hu-jintao-what-happened-former-president-escorted-out-congress-cna-video-3023251

SIPRI (2023) *SIPRI Yearbook 2023: Armaments, Disarmament and International Security*. Stockholm: Stockholm International Peace Research Institute, Oxford University Press.

Siqi, Cao (2022) 'Exclusive: Evidence of US monitoring 45 countries, regions exposed by Chinese cybersecurity experts for the 1st time'. *Global Times*, 23 February.

Sivasundaram, Sujit (2020) *Waves Across the South: A New History of Revolution and Empire*. Chicago: University of Chicago Press.

Sivasundaram, Sujit, (2020) *Waves Across the South: A New History of Revolution and Empire*. London: William Collins.

Slater, Dan (2004) *Geopolitics and the Post-Colonial: Rethinking North – South Relations*. Oxford: Blackwell.

Slaughter, Anne-Marie (2009) America's edge: Power in the networked century. *Foreign Affairs*, 88.

Sluga, Glenda and Clavin, Patricia (eds.) (2016) *Internationalisms: A Twentieth-Century History*. Cambridge: Cambridge University Press.

Smith, Anthony (1980) *The Geopolitics of Information: How Western Culture Dominates the World*. London: Faber and Faber.

Smith, Brad (2017) The need for a digital Geneva convention. *Microsoft Blogs*, 14 February. https://blogs.microsoft.com/on-the-issues/2017/02/14/need-digital-geneva-convention

Smith, Brad and Browne, Carol Ann (2019) *Tools and Weapons: The Promise and the Peril of the Digital Age*. New York: Penguin.

Smith, Gary (2023) *Distrust: Big Data, Data-Torturing, and the Assault on Science*. New York: Oxford University Press.

Smith, Leonard (2023) *French Colonialism: From the Ancien Régime to the Present*. Cambridge: Cambridge University Press.

Soldatov, Andrei and Borogan, Irina (2015) *Inside the Red Web: The Struggle Between Russia's Digital Dictators and the New Online Revolutionaries*. New York: Public Affairs.

Soldatov, Andrei and Borogan, Irina (2017) *The Red Web: The Kremlin's Wars on the Internet*. New York: PublicAffairs. (Updated edition, original published in 2015.)

Soldatov, Andrei and Borogan, Irina (2017) *The Red Web: The Kremlin's Wars on the Internet*. New York: PublicAffairs. (Updated edition, original published in 2015.)

Som, Lalita (2022) *State Capitalism: Why SOEs Matter and the Challenges They Face*. Oxford: Oxford University Press.

Sosin, Gene (1999) *Sparks of Liberty – An Insider's Memoir of Radio Liberty*. University Park, PA: Penn State University Press.

Special Competitive Studies Project (2023) *Offset X: Closing the Detterence Gap and Building the Future Joint Force*. Washington: The Special Competitive Studies Project.

Sreberny, Annabelle and Khiabany Gholam (2010) *Blogistan: The Internet and Politics in Iran*. London: I. B. Tauris.

Srinivasan, Janaki (2022) *The Political Lives of Information: Information and the Production of Development in India*. Cambridge, MA: MIT Press.

Srnicek, Nick (2017) *Platform Capitalism*. Cambridge: Polity.

Stahl, Roger (2010) *Militainment, Inc*. New York: Routledge.

Standage, Tom (1998) *The Victorian Internet: The Remarkable Story of the Telegraphy and the Nineteenth Century's On-Line Pioneers*. New York: Bloomsbury.

Starkman, Dean (2014) *The Watchdog That Didn't Bark: The Financial Crisis and the Disappearance of Investigative Journalism*. New York: Columbia University Press.
Starosielski, Nicole (2015) *The Undersea Network*. Durham: Duke University Press.
Starr, Harvey and Siverson, Randolf (1990) Alliances and geopolitics. *Political Geography Quarterly*, 9(3): 232–248.
State Council Information Office (2021) *China: Democracy That Works*. Beijing: The State Council Information Office of the People's Republic of China. www.news.cn/english/2021-12/04/c_1310351231.htm
Stauber, John and Rampton, Sheldon (2003) *Weapons of Mass Deception: The Uses of Propaganda in Bush's War on Iraq*. New York: Tarcher/Penguin.
Stearns, Jason (2022) The War that Doesn't Say its Name: *The unending conflict in the Congo*. Princeton: Princeton University Press.
Stefan, Cristina (2016) On non-Western norm shapers: Brazil and the Responsibility while Protecting. *European Journal of International Security*, 2(1): 88–110.
Stein, Jeff (2014) Inside the CIA's Syrian rebels vetting machine. *Newsweek*, 10 November.
Steinmetz, George (2023) *The Colonial Origins of Modern Social Thought: French Sociology and the Overseas Empire*. Princeton: Princeton University Press.
Stephens, Philip (2021) *Britain Alone: The Path from Suez to Brexit*. London: Faber.
Stern, Philip (2023) *Empire, Incorporated: The Corporations that Built British Colonialism*. Cambridge, MA: Harvard University Press.
Stevenson, Alexandra and Lee Myers, Steven (2021) How Peng Shuai went from 'Chinese princess' to silenced #MeToo accuser. *New York Times*, 22 November.
Stewart, Susan (ed.) (2012) *Democracy Promotion and the 'Colour Revolutions'*. London: Routledge.
Stiglitz, Joseph (2017) Toward a taxonomy of media capture. In Schiffrin, Anya (ed.) *In the Service of Power: Media Capture and the Threat to Democracy*. Washington: Center for International Media Assistance.
Stiglitz, Joseph and Bilmes, Linda (2008) *The Three Trillion Dollar War: The True Cost of the Iraq Conflict*. New York: Norton.
Stone, Diane (2013) *Capturing the Political Imagination: Think Tanks and the Policy Process*. London: Routledge.
Stone, Randall (2011) *Controlling Institutions: International Organizations and the Global Economy*. New York: Cambridge University Press.
Submarine Telecoms Forum (2022) *Submarine Telecoms Industry Report 2020/2021 Edition*. https://subtelforum.com/products/submarine-telecoms-industry-report/.
Suleyman, Mustafa (with Michael Bhaskar) (2023) *The Coming Wave: Technology, Power, and the Twenty-first Century's Greatest Dilemma*. New York: Crown.
Sunak, Rishi (2017) *Undersea Cables: Indispensable, Insecure*. London: Policy Exchange.
Supran, Geoffrey, Rahmstorf, Stefan and Oreskes, Naomi (2023) Assessing ExxonMobil's global warming projections. *Science*, 379: 153.
Svartvik, Jan and Leech, Geoffrey (2016) *English – One Tongue, Many Voices*, 2nd ed. London: Palgrave.
Szewczyk, Bart (2021) *Europe's Grand Strategy: Navigating a New World Order*. London: Palgrave-Macmillan.
Tabuchi, Hiroko (2022) Inside the Saudi strategy to keep the world hooked on oil. *New York Times*, 21 November.
Tagliacozzo, Eric (2022) *In Asian Waters: Oceanic Worlds from Yemen to Yokohama*. Princeton: Princeton University Press.
Takagi, Koichiro (2022) *The Future of China's Cognitive Warfare: Lessons from the War in Ukraine*. Washington: War on the Rocks.
Talmacs, Nicole (2020) Africa and Africans in *Wolf Warrior 2*: Narratives of trust, patriotism and rationalized racism among Chinese university students. *Journal of Asian and African Studies*, 55(8): 1230–1245.

Tamkin, Emily (2020) *The Influence of Soros: Politics, Power, and the Struggle for an Open Society*. London: Harper.
Tang, Min (2019) *Tencent: The political economy of China's surging Internet giant*. New York: Routledge.
Tang, Min (2020) Huawei versus the United States? The geopolitics of exterritorial Internet infrastructure. *International Journal of Communication*, 14: 22.
Tanwar, Raghuvendra and Kadam, Umesh (eds.) (2022) *India: The Mother of Democracy*. New Delhi: Indian Council for Historical Research.
Tao, Tian, Cremer, David and Chunb, Wu (2016) *Huawei: Leadership, Culture and Connectivity*. New Delhi: Sage.
Tarnoff, Ben (2022) *Internet for the People: The Fight for Our Digital Future*. London: Verso.
TASS (2022) Multipolar World Order Evolving Globally, Process Irreversible — Putin. TASS, 30 June. https://tass.com/politics/1473813.
Tatsumi, Yuki, Kennedy, Pamela and Li, Jason (eds.) (2019) *Disinformation, Cybersecurity, & Energy Challenges*. Washington: Stimson Center.
Taylor, Adam (2022) With NAFO, Ukraine turns the trolls on Russia. *Washington Post*, 1 September.
Taylor, Mark Zachary (2016) *The Politics of Innovation: Why Some Countries Are Better Than Others at Science and Technology*. Oxford: Oxford University Press.
Taylor, Philip (1997) *Global Communications, International Affairs and the Media since 1945*. London: Routledge.
Taylor, Philip (2003) *Munitions of the Mind: A History of Propaganda from the Ancient World to the Present Era*, 3rd ed. Manchester: Manchester University Press.
TechAccord (2019) Cybersecurity Tech Accord. https://cybertechaccord.org/uploads/prod/2019/03/2018report.pdf
Telegeography (2021) *The State of the Network 2021*. https://www2.telegeography.com/hubfs/assets/Ebooks/state-of-thenetwork-2021.pdf
Teng, W. (2019) Third world. In Christian, Sorace, Ivan, Franceschini and Nicholas, Loubere (eds.) *Afterlives of Chinese Communism: Political Concepts from Mao to Xi*, pp. 281–285. London: Verso.
Thakur, Vineet (2019) An Asian drama: The Asian relations conference, 1947. *The International History Review*, 41(3): 673–695.
The Dawn (2013) Malala Inc: Global operation surrounds teenage campaigner. *The Dawn*, 11 October. www.dawn.com/news/1048971
The Trilateral Commission (2022) *A New Spirit of Capitalism: Toward More Sustainable and Inclusive Economies*. London: Hurst.
The Virality Project (2022) *Memes, Magnets and Microchips: Narrative Dynamics Around COVID-19 Vaccines*. Stanford Digital Repository. v1.0.1 https://purl.stanford.edu/mx395xj8490
THES (2023) World University rankings 2024: China creeps closer to top 10. *Times Higher Education Supplement*, 27 September.
Thibaut, Kenton (2022) *China's Discourse Power Operations in the Global South*. Washington: Atlantic Council.
Thiel, David and McCain, Miles (2022) *Gabufacturing Dissent: An In-Depth Analysis of Gab*. Stanford, CA: Stanford Digital Repository.
Thomas, Amos Owen (2021) *Shadow Trades: The Dark Side of Global Business*. London: Sage.
Thussu, Daya Kishan (2007) *News as Entertainment: The Rise of Global Infotainment*. London: Sage.
Thussu, Daya Kishan (2013a) *Communicating India's Soft Power: Buddha to Bollywood*. New York: Palgrave/Macmillan.
Thussu, Daya Kishan (2013b) De-Americanizing media studies and the rise of 'Chindia'. *Javnost – The Public*, 20(4): 31–44.

Thussu, Daya Kishan (2018) Globalization of Chinese media: The global context. In Thussu, Daya Kishan, De Burgh, Hugo and Shi, Anbin (eds.) *China's Media Go Global*, pp. 17–33. London: Routledge.
Thussu, Daya Kishan (2019) *International Communication: Continuity and Change*, 3rd ed. New York: Bloomsbury Academic.
Thussu, Daya Kishan (2021) BRICS de-Americanizing the internet. In Thussu, Daya Kishan and Nordenstreng, Kaarle (eds.) *BRICS Media: Reshaping the Global Communication Order?*, pp. 280–301. London: Routledge.
Thussu, Daya Kishan (ed.) (1998) *Electronic Empires – Global Media and Local Resistance*. London: Arnold.
Thussu, Daya Kishan (ed.) (2009) *Internationalising Media Studies*. London: Routledge.
Thussu, Daya Kishan and Nordenstreng, Kaarle (eds.) (2021) *BRICS Media: Reshaping the Global Communication Order?* London: Routledge.
Tol, Gönül (2023) *Erdoğan's War: A Strongman's Struggle at Home and in Syria*. New York: Oxford University Press.
Tong, Zhang (2023) China launches world's fastest internet with 1.2 terabit per second link, years ahead of forecasts. *South China Morning Post*, 14 November.
Tooze, Adam (2018) *Crashed: How a Decade of Financial Crises Changed the World*. New York: Viking.
Tooze, Adam (2018) *Crashed: How a Decade of Financial Crises Changed the World*. London: Viking.
Toru, Kurata (2020) Development of the Hong Kong pro-democracy protest into a 'New Cold War': Shift from opposing the Fugitive Offenders (Amendment) Bill to opposing the Hong Kong National Security Law. *Asia-Pacific Review*, 27(2): 94–108. https://doi.org/10.1080/13439006.2020.1835304
Towns, Armond (2022) *On Black Media Philosophy*. Los Angles: California University Press.
Trisko Darden, Jessica (2019) *Aiding and Abetting: U.S. Foreign Assistance and State Violence*. Los Angeles: Stanford University Press.
Tsui, Lokman (2015) The coming colonization of Hong Kong cyberspace: Government responses to the use of new technologies by the umbrella movement. *Chinese Journal of Communication*, 8(4): 1–9.
Tsygankov, Andrei (2009) *Russophobia: Anti-Russian Lobby and American Foreign Policy*. New York: Palgrave Macmillan.
Tuathail, Gearóid and Agnew, John (1992) Geopolitics and discourse: Practical geopolitical reasoning in American foreign policy. *Political Geography*, 11(2): 190–204.
Tucker, Joshua and Persily, Nathaniel (eds.) (2020) *Social Media and Democracy: The State of the Field, Prospects for Reform*. Cambridge: Cambridge University Press.
Tudoroiu, Theodor (2024) *The Geopolitics of the Belt and Road Initiative*. London: Routledge.
Tudoroiu, Theodor and Kuteleva, Anna (eds.) (2022) *China in the Global South: Impact and Perceptions*. New York: Springer.
Tufekci, Zeynep (2017) *Twitter and Tear Gas-The Power and Fragility of Networked Protest*. New Haven: Yale University Press.
Turse, Nick and Speri, Alice (2022) How the Pentagon uses a secretive program to Wage Proxy Wars: Exclusive documents and interviews reveal the sweeping scope of classified 127e operations. *The Intercept*, 1 July.
Tworek, Heidi (2019) *News from Germany: The Competition to Control World Communications, 1900–1945*. Cambridge, MA: Harvard University Press.
Tylecote, Radomir and Clark, Robert (2021) *Inadvertently Arming China? The Chinese Military Complex and Its Potential Exploitation of Scientific Research at UK Universities*. London: Civitas: Institute for the Study of Civil Society.
UK Government (2021) *PM Launches New Initiative to Take Green Industrial Revolution Global*, 1 November. www.gov.uk/government/news/pm-launches

UK Government (2023) Integrated review refresh 2023: Responding to a more contested and volatile world. *Policy Paper*, 13 March.
Ukraine Should Investigate Forces' Apparent Use; Russian Use Continues. New York: Human Rights Watch.
Umejei, Emeka (2020) *Chinese Media in Africa: Perception, Performance, and Paradox*. Maryland: Rowman and Littlefield.
UN Human Rights Commission (2021) *Spyware Scandal: UN Experts Call for Moratorium on Sale of 'Life Threatening' Surveillance Tech*, 12 August. https://www.ohchr.org/en/press-releases/2021/08/spyware-scandal-un-experts-call-moratorium-sale-life-threatening#:~:t
UNCTAD (2019) *Digital Economy Report 2019-Value Creation and Capture: Implications for Developing Countries*. Geneva: United Nations Conference on Trade and Development.
UNCTAD (2021) *Digital Economy Report 2021-Cross Border Data Flows and Development: For Whom the Data Flow*. Geneva: United Nations Conference on Trade and Development.
UNCTAD (2022) *Digital Economy Report 2021*. Geneva: United Nations Conference on Trade and Development.
UNCTAD (2023) *BRICS Investment Report*. Geneva: United Nations Conference on Trade and Development.
UNDP (1999) *Human Development Report*. United Nations Development Programme. Oxford: Oxford University Press.
UNDP (2022) *New Threats to Human Security in the Anthropocene: Demanding Greater Solidarity*. New York: United Nations Development Programme (Special Report).
UNEP (2022) *The Closing Window-Climate Crisis Calls for Rapid Transformation of Societies: Emissions Gap Report 2022*. Nairobi: United Nations Environment Programme.
UNESCO (2021) *UNESCO Science Report: The Race against Time for Smarter Development*. Paris: United Nations Educational, Scientific and Cultural Organization.
UNESCO (2022) *Minding the Data: Protecting Learners' Privacy and Security*. Paris: United Nations Educational, Scientific and Cultural Organization.
Üngör, Çağdaş (2022) *China Is Playing by Turkey's Media Rules*. Washington: Carnegie Endowment for International Peace.
Üngör, Çağdaş (2022) *China is Playing by Turkey's Media Rules*. Washington: Carnegie Endowment for International Peace.
United Nations (2019) *The Age of Digital Interdependence: Report of the UN Secretary-General's High-level Panel on Digital Cooperation*. New York: United Nations.
United Nations (2020) *UN Tackles 'Infodemic' of Misinformation and Cybercrime in COVID-19 Crisis*. www.un.org/en/un-coronavirus-communications-team/un-tackling-%E2%80%98infodemic%E2%80%99-misinformation-and-cybercrime-covid-19
Unver, Akin and Alassaad, Hassan (2016) How Turks mobilized against the coup. *Foreign Affairs*, 14 September.
Urban, George (1997) *My War within the Cold War*. New Haven, CT: Yale University Press.
Uren, Tom, Thomas, Elise and Wallis, Jacob (2019) *Tweeting through the Great Firewall: Preliminary analysis of PRC-linked information operations against the Hong Kong protests*. Canberra: The Australian Strategic Policy Institute, Issues paper, Report No. 25/2019.
US Congressional Research Service (2021) *Department of Defense Contractor and Troop Levels in Afghanistan and Iraq: 2007–2018*, February. https://fas.org/sgp/crs/natsec/R44116.pdf
US Department of Defense (2020) *Office of the Under Secretary of Defense (Comptroller)*. https://comptroller.defense.gov/Portals/45/Documents/defbudget/fy2021/FY21_Green_Book.pdf

US Department of Defense (2021) Defense primer: Department of defense contractors. *Congressional Research Service*. https://crsreports.congress.gov/product/pdf/IF/IF10600.
US Department of Justice (2019) Promoting public safety, privacy, and the rule of law around the world: The purpose and impact of the CLOUD act. *White Paper*, April. Washington: Department of Justice.
US Department of State (2022) *Limits in the Seas: No. 150 People's Republic of China: Maritime Claims in the South China Sea*. Washington: Office of Ocean and Polar Affairs, Bureau of Oceans and International Environmental and Scientific Affairs U.S. Department of State.
US Department of State (2023) *2023 Hong Kong Policy Act Report*, 32. Washington: U.S. Department of State, Bureau of East Asian and Pacific Affairs.
US Government (1997) *A Framework for Global Electronic Commerce*. Washington: The White House.
US Government (2018) *National Cyber Strategy*. Washington: White House.
US Government (2021) *Final Report: National Security Commission on Artificial Intelligence*, March. www.nscai.gov/wp-content/uploads/2021/03/Full-Report-Digital-1.pdf
US Government (2023a) *Annual Threat Assessment of the U.S. Intelligence Community*. Washington: Office of the Director of National Intelligence. www.intelligence.senate.gov/sites/default/files/documents/unclassified_2023_ata_report.pd
US Government (2023b) *U.S. International Trade in Goods and Services, December and Annual 2022*. Washington: United States Bureau of Economic Analysis. https://www.bea.gov/news/2023/us-international-trade-goods-and-services-december-and-annual-2022
US Government (2023c) *U.S. Direct Investment Abroad: Balance of Payments and Direct investment position data*. Washington: United States Bureau of Economic Analysis. https://www.bea.gov/international/di1usdbal
USAGM (2022) *Truth over Disinformation: Supporting Freedom and Democracy – The USAGM 2022-2026 Strategic Plan*. Washington, DC: United States Agency for Global Media.
Vaidhyanathan, Siva (2011) *The Googlization of Everything*. Berkeley: University of California Press.
Vaidhyanathan, Siva (2018) *Antisocial Media: How Facebook Disconnects Us and Undermines Democracy*. New York: Oxford University Press.
van der Putten, Frans-Paul, Meijnders, Minke, van der Meer, Sico and van der Togt (eds.) (2018) *Hybrid Conflict: The Roles of Russia, North Korea and China*. Amsterdam: The Netherlands Institute of International Relations 'Clingendael'.
van der Vlist, Fernando and Helmond, Anne (2021) How partners mediate platform power: Mapping business and data partnerships in the social media ecosystem. *Big Data & Society*, 8(1): 1–16.
van Noort, Carolijn and Chatterje-Doody, Precious (2023) Visualizing China's belt and road initiative on RT (Russia Today): From infrastructural project to human development. *Eurasian Geography and Economics*, 64(4): 431–459.
Varadarajan, Latha (2010) *The Domestic Abroad: Diasporas in International Relations*. Oxford: Oxford University Press.
Varrall, Merriden (2020) *Behind the News: Inside China Global Television Network*. Sydney: Lowry Institute. www.lowyinstitute.org/publications/behind-news-inside-china-global-television-network#_edn70
Vertin, Zach (2019) *A Rope from the Sky-The Making and Unmaking of the World's Newest State*. New York: Pegasus Books.
Vila Seoane, Maximiliano (2020) Alibaba's discourse for the digital Silk Road: The electronic World Trade Platform and 'inclusive globalization. *Chinese Journal of Communication*, 13(1): 68–83.
Vine, David (2015) *Base Nation: How U.S. Military Bases Abroad Harm America and the World*. New York: Metropolitan Books.

Vines, Stephen (2021) *Defying the Dragon: Hong Kong and the World's Largest Dictatorship*. London: Hurst.
Viola, Lora Anne (2020) *The Closure of the International System: How Institutions Create Political Equalities and Hierarchies*. Cambridge: Cambridge University Press.
Voeten, Erik (2021) *Ideology and International Institutions*. Princeton: Princeton University Press.
Volkmer, Ingrid (2014) *The Global Public Sphere: Public Communication in the Age of Reflective Interdependence*. Cambridge: Polity.
Von Eschen, Penny (2004) *Satchmo Blows Up the World: Jazz Ambassadors Play the Cold War*. Cambridge, MA: Harvard University Press.
Vukovich, Daniel (2020) A sound and fury signifying mediatisation: On the Hong Kong protests, 2019. *Javnost – The Public*, 27(2): 200–209.
Wadhwa, Vivek and Kop, Mauritz (2022) Why quantum computing is even more dangerous than artificial intelligence. *Foreign Policy*, 21 August.
Waisbord, Silvio (2019) *Communication: A Post-Discipline*. Cambridge: Polity.
Walker, Andrew (1992) *A Skyful of Freedom: 60 Years of the BBC World Service*. London: Broadside Books.
Walker, Christopher (2018) What is 'sharp power'? *Journal of Democracy*: 9–23.
Walker, Darren (2018) Old money, new order-American philanthropies and the defense of liberal democracy. *Foreign Affairs*, November/December.
Walter, Nathan, Cohen, Jonathan, Holbert, Lance and Morag, Yasmin (2020) Fact-checking: A meta-analysis of what works and for whom. *Political Communication*, 37(3): 350–375.
Walton, Calder (2023) *Spies: The Epic Intelligence War between East and West*. New York: Abacus.
Waltzman, Rand (2017) The weaponization of information – the need for cognitive security. *RAND*. www.rand.org/pubs/testimonies/CT473.html
Wang, Dong and Tanner, Travis (eds.) (2021) *Avoiding the 'Thucydides Trap': US-China Relations in Strategic Domains*. London: Routledge.
Wang, Jisi (2021) The plot against China? How Beijing sees the New Washington consensus. *Foreign Affairs*, 100(6): 48–57.
Washington Post (2020) What did Xi Jinping know about the coronavirus, and when did he know it? Editorial Board. *Washington Post*, 19 February.
Washington Post (2023) How Russia turned America's helping hand to Ukraine into a vast lie. Editorial Board. *Washington Post*, 29 March.
Wasserman, Herman (2018) Power, meaning and geopolitics: Ethics as an entry point for global communication studies. *Journal of Communication*, 68: 441–451.
Watson, Alan, (1993) *Legal Transplants: An Approach to Comparative Law*, 2nd ed. Athens: University of Georgia Press.
Watts, Stephen, Johnston, Trevor, Lane, Matthew, Mann, Sean, McNerney, Michael and Brooks, Andrew (2018) *Building Security in Africa: An Evaluation of U.S. Security Sector Assistance in Africa from the Cold War to the Present*. Santa Monica: RAND Corporation. www.rand.org/content/dam/rand/pubs/research_reports/RR2400/RR2447/RAND_RR2447.pdf.
Weaver, Kent (1989) The changing world of think tanks. *Political Science and Politics*, 22(3): 563–578.
Webb, Alban (2014) *London Calling: Britain, the BBC World Service and the Cold War*. London: Bloomsbury Academic.
Weber, Cynthia (2006) *Imagining America at War: Morality, Politics, and Film*. London: Routledge.
Weber, Isabella (2021) *How China Escaped Shock Therapy: The Market Reform Debate*. London: Routledge.
Weir, Patrick (2020) Networked assemblages and geopolitical media: Governance, infrastructure and sites in BBC radio. *Geopolitics*, 2(54): 937–967.

Weisman, Jonathan and Shorey, Rachel (2022) Fueled by billionaires, political spending shatters records again. *New York Times*, 4 November.
Weiss, Jessica Chen (2022) The China Trap: U.S. Foreign policy and the perilous logic of Zero-Sum competition. *Foreign Affairs*, 101(5): 40–58.
Wen, Yun (2020) *The Huawei Model: The Rise of China's Technology Giant*. Chicago: University of Illinois Press.
Wenzlhuemer, Roland (2013) *Connecting the Nineteenth-Century World-The Telegraph and Globalization*. Cambridge: Cambridge University Press.
Westad, Odd Arne (2017) *The Cold War: A World History*. London: Penguin.
White House (2019) *Executive Order on Maintaining American Leadership in Artificial Intelligence*. Washington: The White House.
White House (2020) *Remarks by President Trump, Vice President Pence, and Members of the Coronavirus Task Force in Press Briefing*. Washington: The White House.
White House (2021a) *Fact Sheet: President Biden and G7 Leaders Launch Build Back Better World (B3W) Partnership*. Washington: The White House.
White House (2021b) *United States Space Priorities Framework*. Washington: The White House.
White House (2022) *Fact Sheet: President Biden and G7 Leaders Formally Launch the Partnership for Global Infrastructure and Investment*. Washington: The White House.
White House (2023a) *National Cybersecurity Strategy*. Washington: The White House.
White House (2023b) *The Spirit of Camp David: Joint Statement of Japan, the Republic of Korea, and the United States*. Washington: White House, 18 August. https://www.whitehouse.gov/briefing-room/statements-releases/2023/08/18/the-spirit-of-camp-david-joint-statement-of-japan-the-republic-of-korea-and-the-united-states/
White, Duncan (2019) *Cold Warriors: Writers Who Waged the Literary Cold War*. New York: Little, Brown.
Whitlock, Craig (2021) *The Afghanistan Papers: A Secret History of the War*. New York: Simon & Schuster.
WHO (2020) *Novel Coronavirus (2019-nCoV) Situation Report – 13*. Geneva: World Health Organization.
Wilford, Hugh (2008) *The Mighty Wurlitzer: How the CIA Played America*. Cambridge, MA: Harvard University Press.
Wilkins, Karin and Enghel, Florencia (2013) The privatization of development through global communication industries: Living proof? *Media Culture & Society*, 35(2): 165–181.
Willetts, Peter (2011) *Non-Governmental Organizations in World Politics: The Construction of Global Governance*. London: Routledge.
Wilson, Scott and Warrick, Joby (2011) Assad must go, Obama says. *Washington Post*, 18 August.
Windrich, Elaine (1992) *The Cold War Guerrilla: Jonas Savimbi, the US Media and the Angolan War*. New York: Greenwood Press.
Winkler, Carol, ElDamanhoury, Kareem, Dicker, Aaron and Lemieux, Anthony (2019) Images of death and dying in ISIS media: A comparison of English and Arabic print publications. *Media, War & Conflict*, 12(3): 248–262.
Winkler, Jonathan (2009) Information warfare in World War I. *Journal of Military History*, 73: 845–867.
Winseck, Dwayne (2017) The geopolitical economy of the global internet infrastructure. *Journal of Information Policy*, 7: 228–267.
Winseck, Dwayne and Pike, Robert (2007) *Communication and Empire: Media, Markets, and Globalization, 1860–1930*. Durham, NC: Duke University Press.
Wolfe, Audra (2018) *Freedom's Laboratory: The Cold War Struggle for the Soul of Science*. Lanham, MD: John Hopkins University Press.
Wolfson, Todd (2014) *Digital Rebellion: The Birth of the Cyber Left*. Chicago, IL: University of Illinois Press.

Wong, Audrye (2021) How not to win Allies and influence geopolitics: China's self-defeating economic statecraft. *Foreign Affairs*, 100(3): 44–53.
Wong, Brian (2022) *The Tao of Alibaba: Inside the Chinese Digital Giant that is Changing the World*. New York: PublicAffairs.
Wong, Edward and Ismay, John (2022) U.S. aims to turn Taiwan into Giant Weapons Depot. *New York Times*, 5 October.
Wong, Hayley (2023) Top Russian technical university campus in China's Hainan island to focus on aviation and aerospace. *South China Morning Post*, 4 April.
Wong, Joshua and Ng, Jason (2020) *Unfree Speech: The Threat to Global Democracy and Why We Must Act, Now*. New York: Penguin.
Woodward, Bob (2004) *Plan of Attack*. New York: Simon & Schuster.
Woolley, Samuel (2020) *The Reality Game: How the Next Wave of Technology Will Break the Truth*. New York: PublicAffairs.
World Bank (1998) *Knowledge for Development, World Development Report 1998–1999*. Washington: World Bank Publications.
World Bank (2018) *Information and Communications for Development 2018: Data-Driven Development*. Washington: World Bank.
World Bank (2021) *The State of Economic Inclusion Report 2021: The Potential to Scale*. Washington: World Bank.
World Bank (2023) *World Development Report 2023: Migrants, Refugees and Societies*. New York: World Bank.
World Data Lab (2023) *Internet Poverty Index*. https://internetpoverty
World Economic Forum (2022) *Earning Digital Trust: Decision-Making for Trustworthy Technologies*. Geneva: World Economic Forum.
World Intellectual Property Organization (2021) *China Leads the World in AI Related Patent Filing*, 28 September. www.wipo.int/about-wipo/en/offices/china/news/2021/news_0037.html.
WTO (1998) *Annual Report 1998*. Geneva: World Trade Organization.
Wu, Tim (2016) *The Attention Merchants: The Epic Scramble to Get Inside Our Heads*. New York: Knopf.
www.lrb.co.uk/the-paper/v45/n08/james-meek/that-s-my-tank-on-fire?
Xia, Cai (2022) The weakness of Xi Jinping how Hubris and Paranoia Threaten China's future. *Foreign Affairs*, 101(5): 85–107.
Xinhua (2015) *The Issuance of Opinions on Strengthening the Construction of New – Type Think Tanks with Chinese Characteristics by the CPC General Office and State Council General Office*. Beijing, China: The State Council of the People's Republic of China.
Xinhua (2021a) Why the U.S. is 'No. 1' in eight aspects of COVID-19 response, Chongyang Institute, Taihe and Intellisia (2021) *'America Ranked First'?! The Truth about America's fight against COVID-19*, August. www.xinhuanet.com/english/2021-08/09/c_1310117724.htm
Xinhua (2021b) Xi stresses improving China's international communication capacity. *Xinhua*, 1 June.
Yablokov, Ilya and Chatterje-Doody, Precious (2021) *Russia Today and Conspiracy Theories: People, Power and Politics on RT*. London: Routledge.
Yaffa, Joshua (2022) Inside the U.S. Effort to Arm Ukraine. *New Yorker*, 17 October.
Yang, Guobin (2016) *The Red Guard Generation and Political Activism in China*. New York: Columbia University Press.
Ye, Min (2020) *The Belt and Road and Beyond: State-Mobilized Globalization in China 1998–2018*. Cambridge: Cambridge University Press.
Yellinek, Roie and Chen, Elizabeth (2019) The '22 vs. 50' diplomatic split between the West and China over Xinjiang and human rights. *China Brief*, 19(22): 2–19.
York, Jillian (2021) *Silicon Values: The Future of Free Speech under Surveillance Capitalism*. London: Verso.

Yousafzai, Malala (with Christina Lamb) (2013) *I Am Malala: The Girl Who Stood Up for Education and Was Shot by the Taliban*. London: Weidenfeld and Nicolson.

Yu, Shirley (2019) The belt and road initiative: Modernity, geopolitics and the developing global order. *Asian Affairs*, 50(2): 187–201.

Zajec, Olivier (2022) 'If we refuse to use them, why do we have them?' A third nuclear age may be dawning in Ukraine. *Le Monde Diplomatique*, April.

Zaller, John (1992) *The Nature and Origins of Mass Opinion*. New York: Cambridge University Press.

Zarakol, Ayse (2022) *Before the West: The Rise and Fall of Eastern World Orders*. Cambridge: Cambridge University Press.

Zegart, Amy (2023) *Spies, Lies, and Algorithms: The History and Future of American Intelligence*. Princeton: Princeton University Press.

Zeitchik, Steven (2021) Fearful of political criticism, China won't show the Oscars live. *Washington Post*, 4 April.

Zeng, Jing and Schäfer, Mike (2021) Conceptualizing 'dark platforms.' COVID-19-related conspiracy theories on 8kun and Gab. *Digital Journalism*, 9(9): 1321–1343.

Zerback, Thomas and Holzleitner, Johannes (2017) Under-cover: The influence of event- and context-traits on the visibility of armed conflicts in German newspaper coverage (1992–2013). *Journalism*, 19(3): 366–383.

Zerofsky, Elisabeth (2022) How the Claremont institute became a nerve center of the American Right. *The New York Times Magazine*, 3 August.

Zerofsky, Elisabeth (2023) Poland's war on two fronts. *New York Times Magazine*, 4 April.

Zhai, Keith and Wei, Lingling (2021) China lays plans to tame E-Commerce Giant Alibaba. *The Wall Street Journal*, 12 March.

Zhang, Albert and Wallis, Jacob (2021) *Trigger Warning: The CCP's Coordinated Information Effort to Discredit the BBC*. Canberra: International Cyber Policy Centre, Australian Strategic Policy Institute.

Zhang, D., Mishra, S., Brynjolfsson, E., Etchemendy, J., Ganguli, D., Grosz, B., Lyons, T., Manyika, J., Niebles, J. C., Sellitto, M., Shoham, Y., Clark, J. and Perrault, R. (2021) *The AI Index 2021 Annual Report*. Stanford: AI Index Steering Committee, Human-Centered AI Institute, Stanford University.

Zhang, Han (2021) China's troll king-how a tabloid editor became the voice of Chinese nationalism. *Guardian*, 14 December.

Zhang, Xiaoling and Schultz, Corey (2022) Communicating China to the world: Representations, reception, and effects. In Zhang, Xiaoling and Schultz, Corey (eds.) *China's International Communication and Relationship Building*, pp. 1–12. London: Routledge.

Zhang, Xiaoling, Wasserman, Herman and Mano, Winston (eds.) (2016) *China's Media and Soft Power in Africa: Promotion and perceptions*. London: Palgrave Macmillan.

Zhao, Suisheng (2022) The US – China rivalry in the emerging Bipolar World: Hostility, alignment, and power balance. *Journal of Contemporary China*, 31(134): 169–185.

Zhao, Youzhi (2015) The BRICS formation in reshaping global communication: Possibilities and challenges. In Nordenstreng, K. and Thussu, D. K. (eds.) *Mapping BRICS Media*, pp. 66–86. London: Routledge.

Zheng, Sarah (2020) China's Wolf Warrior diplomats battle on Twitter for control of coronavirus narrative. *South China Morning Post*, 23 March.

Zhou, Wenxing (2023) Think tanks with Chinese characteristics. *International Sociology*, 38(2).

Zhu, Xufeng (2013) *The Rise of Think Tanks in China*. London: Routledge.

Zollmann, F. (2019) Bringing propaganda back into news media studies. *Critical Sociology*, 45(3): 329–345.

Zondi, Siphamandla (ed.) (2022) *The Political Economy of Intra-BRICS Cooperation: Challenges and Prospects*. Cham: Springer.

Zoubir, Yahia and Tran, Emilie (2021) China's health Silk Road in the Middle East and North Africa amidst COVID-19 and a contested world order. *Journal of Contemporary China*: 1–16.

Zuboff, Shoshana (2019) *The Age of Surveillance Capitalism*. New York: Profile Books.

Zygar, Mikhail (2023) *War and Punishment: Putin, Zelensky, and the Path to Russia's Invasion of Ukraine*. New York: Scribner.

INDEX

Note: Page numbers in **bold** indicate a table on the corresponding page.

5G, mobile telephony 59–61, 89–90, 98, 145–148, 155, 158, 176, 186
6G technology 59, 147

Abraham Accords 143
Adani, Gautam 22
Aditya Birla Group 22
Advisory Commission on Public Diplomacy 116
Aerospatiale 52
Afghanistan: China and 175; DynCorp 127; Al-Jazeera 101; post-9/11 war zones 103; Taliban's takeover 22; US failure to bring democracy 115–116; Western media coverage 116
Afghanistan National Security Forces (ANSF) 115
Africa: anti-colonial movements 41; apartheid system 14; BBC broadcast 43; British-dominated cable routes 31; Chinese aid to Africa 177; coverage of Russian invasion 118; decolonization 119; digital transformation strategy 93; Europe relationship 64; Francophonie Africa 120; Lusophone Africa 46; Russian security presence in 168; Sino-globalization 176–177; 1992 US military intervention in Somalia 119
Afrokology 192
Agenda for Sustainable Development 184

Agreement on Basic Telecommunications Services 49
Ahmadinejad, Mahmoud 77
Ahmed, Abiy 118
Airbus Defence and Space (European Aeronautic Defence and Space Company) 52
Alcatel Submarine Networks 54
Al-Hurra (The Free One) 44
Alibaba 12, 60–61, 78, 85, 87–89
Alibaba Cloud 88
Alipay 89
Al Jazeera 22, 65, 70, 101, 111, 117, 139
Allen, George 43
Allende, Salvador 104
Al Qaeda 106, 108, 110, 114–117, 119
Amazon 158, 160; and digital capitalism 78–79, 85–88, 92; as a 'hyperscale company' 56–57; as a major US digital corporation 51–52, 57, 98, 148, 189; user of international bandwidth 54
Ambani, Mukesh 98
American Broadcasting Corporation (ABC) 39
American Civil Liberties Union 142
American Civil War 29
American Forces Network (AFN) 35–36
American National Security Commission on Artificial Intelligence 160
Amílcar Cabral movement 46

Amnesty International 71, 135, 139, 152, 159
Ant Group, Alibaba's 89
Anti-Vax Watch 155
Apple 57, 78, 85, 95, 142, 150, 164
Arab Spring 22, 76–77, 145
Argentina 176
Aron, Raymond 193
Artemis programme 60
artificial intelligence (AI) 1; 2023 AI Index Report 163; AI-powered biometric and digital surveillance 159; ChatGPT 163; China as AI Superpower 160; cybernetic control strategies 162; dangers of 161–164; digital deepfakes 162; EU's regulation on AI 166; globalization of 159; information weaponization on steroids 158–159; Made in China 2025 plan 160; Meta, free access to the AI 165; mind dominance 161; OECD/G20 AI Principles 165; regulation 164–166; surveillance of Uyghur population in Xinjiang 161; weapon of math destruction 163
Asia Infrastructure Investment Bank (AIIB) 170
Asia-Pacific Gateway (APG) 55
Assange, Julian 150
Associated Press (AP) 33
Association for the Advancement of Artificial Intelligence 164
Association of Southeast Asian Nations (ASEAN) 18, 175
Atlantic Council 63
Attlee, Clement 35
Austin, Lloyd 102
Australian Institute of International Affairs 64
authoritarian disinformation 153–155
Avaaz 75, 110, 155
Aziz, Tariq 106
Al-Azmeh 192

Baerbock, Annalena 14
al Baghdadi, Abu Bakr 109
Bajpai, Kanti 171
Balandier, Georges 193
Ballmer, Steve 86
Bandung Conference 191
Bannon, Stephen 156
Baudrillard, Jean 105
BBC: in African countries 43; Arabic Service 41; charity BBC Media Action 71; coverage of the Xinjiang issue 180; global network of relay stations 36; Overseas Service 35; radio broadcasting 34; World Service 36; during World War II 35
BeiDou 58
Beijing's Global Megaphone 179
Belt and Road Initiative (BRI)11–12, 58, 60–61, 89, 95, 96, 144, 147, 171; Africa 176–177; agreement with Germany's national news agency 179; Belt and Road News Network 178; CCP-aligned media 180; communicating Sino-globalization 177–179; deal with the Taliban regime 175; expansion of Confucius Institutes 177; Gulf Cooperation Council (GCC) 175–176; Latin America and the Caribbean (LAC) 176; media 178–179; The Middle East 175–176
Berman, Edward 41
Berque, Jacques 193
Bezos, Jeff 86
Bharti Telecom 22, 187
Biden, Joseph 2, 5, 102, 125–126, 137, 144, 146
Bill and Melinda Gates Foundation 70, 155
Bils, Sarah 150, 151
bin Laden, Osama 109, 115–106
#BlackLivesMatter 77
Bloomberg Billionaires Index 86
Bloomberg TV 10, 17, 65, 80, 86, 162
Boeing 52, 102
Boorstin, Daniel 107
Borrell, Josep 168
Boston Consulting Group 65
Bourdieu, Pierre 193
BRICS (Brazil, Russia, India, China and South Africa) 17–18, 58; decentralized internet infrastructure 174; and de-dollarization 172–173; and internet 173–174; intra-BRICS infrastructure 58; Media Summits 59; and multilateral institutions 169–172; Sino-Russian collaboration 170; 2023 summit 17, 169; undersea cable' network 58
Brin, Sergey 86
British Telecom 49
Broadband Commission for Sustainable Development 189
Broadcasting Board of Governors (BBG) 44
Brookings Institution 24, 62–63, 71, 113

Index **255**

Build Back Better project 185
Bundesnachrichtendienst (BND) 133
Bureau of International Narcotics and Law Enforcement Affairs 127
Burns, John 107
Burns, William 10, 128
Bush, George W. 106–108, 127, 148

Cable and Wireless (Britain) 54
cables: British supremacy 30; fibre-optic cables 55, 60–61; increase in world trade 31; military operations 30–31; PEACE cable project 61; radiotelegraphy 31; subsea cables 55; transatlantic cable 29, 31; transpacific cable 31–31, 55; undersea telecommunication cables 26, 50, 53–55; wireless telegraphy 32
C4ADS 153
Cai Xia 174
Caixin media group 178
Cambridge Analytica scandal 87
Cambridge University Press 69
Canadian Institute of International Affairs 64
Capella Space 132
capitalism: authoritarian 174; cyber 88; foundations' of 40–41; free-market 38, 40, 48; industrial 46; platform 82, 88; surveillance 89–90; woke 195; *see also* digital/digitally enabled capitalism
Carnegie Endowment for International Peace 63, 71, 112, 157
Castell, Manuel 51, 57, 74
Cato Institute 71
Catz, Safra 160
CCP virus 156
Center for American Progress 114
Center for Countering Digital Hate 155
Center for Economic and Policy Research 114
Center for International Media Assistance 71, 104
Center for a New American Security 102, 153, 159
Center for Strategic and International Studies 63–64, 102, 148
Central Intelligence Agency (CIA) 10, 14, 36, 38–40, 104, 114, 116, 128, 133, 141–142, 141–143, 145–146, 150
Central Treaty Organization (CENTO) 104
CERN 56
Chakraborty, Dipesh 193

Chambers, John 82
Chandrayaan-3 58, 187
Change.org 75
ChatGPT 164
Chavez, Hugo 151
Chekhov Publishing House 41
Cheney, Dick 127
China: as AI Superpower 160; collaborating with Russia 60; cyberthreats from 137–140; developmental geopolitics 183; digital 'Cold War' 23–27; exploratory rover on the moon and one on Mars 59; National Space Administration 60; provider of emergency financing 184; role as a global data extractor 96; Sino-Russian collaboration 58, 170; Sino-Soviet split of 1968 37; spying 143; version of the internet 87–88; *see also* Belt and Road Initiative (BRI); BRICS
China: Democracy That Works 182
China-Arab States Cooperation Forum (CASCF) 178
China Global Television Network (CGTN) 3, 20, 157, 176, 180–182, 185
China Institute of Cyberspace Strategy 160
China Mobile 54–55, 60–61, 90
China-Pakistan Economic Corridor (CPEC) 12, 175
China Radio International 19–20, 36
China Telecom 54, 60–61, 61
China Unicom 54, 61
Chinese Communist Party (CCP) 90, 139, 145–146, 156, 174, 177
Chomsky, Noam 100, 108, 163
Chow, Alex 2
Chuhai (going overseas) 88
CITIC Telecom 60–61
Civilian Research and Development Foundation 132
Clarifying Overseas Use of Data (CLOUD) Act, 2019 92
Clean Green Initiative 185
'Clean Network' initiative 92, 148
Clearview AI 133
Clingendael 154
Clinton, Bill 120
Clooney, George 118, 128
Clyburn, Mignon 161
Cognitive Domain Operations, concept of 161
Cognitive Trade Advisor, IBM's 163
Cohen, Jared 94, 149

Colour Revolution 77, 145
Committee on the Peaceful Uses of Outer Space, UN 37
Compagnie Generale de Telegraphie Sans Fil (TSF) 30
Competition Commission of India 98
The Conference of Nationalist Organizations of the Portuguese Colonies (CONCP) 46
conflict management, privatization of 126–128
Confucius Institutes (CI) 73, 176–177
Congress for Cultural Freedom (CCF) 38
'Connect Africa' initiative 185
Connelly, Matthew 141
content providers 54–55
Convention on the Law of the Sea undersea cables 54
Corporate Europe Observatory 166
Council on Foreign Relations 64
Covid-19 13, 21, 92, 95; and geopolitical implications 27, 169; a global pandemic 12–13, 178; as a global 'infodemic' 130, 154–157; vaccine 168, 175
'Crisis Evidence Lab' at Amnesty International 152
critical geopolitics 7–8
cross-border data, countries with **24**
cryptocurrency 98, 139
cultural diplomacy 38, 44, 46
Curtis, Adam 49
cyber capitalism 88
cybersecurity 23, 90, 97, 137–140
Cybersecurity Tech Accord 140
cyber sovereignty 59, 88, 90–98
cyberspace 19, 90, 96, 137–138, 140, 173; commercial 142; Indian 97–98; Russian 96–97, 121; Sino- 95
Cyberspace Administration of China 59, 60, 89, 95

da Silva, Lula 170
Data Security Law, China 96
Dear World: A Syrian Girl's Story of War and Plea for Peace (Bana al-Abed) 113
decolonization 41, 44, 46, 119; of communication studies 190, 191–192
de-dollarization 17, 90, 172–173
de-globalization 12, 27, 174–175
Der Derian, James 8, 23, 165
deregulation 48, 51, 81
Deutsche Telekom 94

Development Finance Corporation (DFC) 185
digital 'Cold War' 23–27
digital colonization 83
digital/digitally enabled capitalism 26, 78–83, 86–89, 92, 162; 24/7 81; censorship-related issues 88; definition 78; digitally deliverable services 79; digital universalism 83; Network Readiness Index 81–82; platform capitalism 82; seven super platforms 78; shadow trades 80; splinternets 92; transnational power elite 81; *see also* capitalism
Digital Diplomacy Team 140
Digital Economy Report 2021, UNCTAD's 78, 82
digital empires 85–87
Digital Geneva Convention 140
digital imperialism: commercial infrastructure 84; commercial non-regulation' and 'anti-censorship 93; cyber exceptionalism 91; cyber governance 93; cyber libertarianism 91; cyber sovereignty 59, 88, 90, 94–98; data as global public good 92–93; data extraction, monopolization and monetization 83; data localization 93; FAIR data principles 92; governance of cross-border data flows 93; 'multi-stakeholders' approach 93; platformization of infrastructure 84; rifts in transatlantic digital alliance 94–95; Schengen Routing 94; 'soft touch' imperialism 83; splinternets 92; sustainable internet 96–97
Digital Silk Road (DSR) 11, 26, 60–61, 144, 147; areas of focus 60–61; maritime domain 61
Digital Threat Analysis Center 154
Digital Trade Restrictiveness Index 95
digital universalism 83
The Discovery of India (Nehru) 8
Dorsey, Jack 149
Dow Jones 80
DuckDuckGo 156
Dugin, Alexander 7
DynCorp International 127

Eastern Telegraph Company 30
Echelon 141, 181
Edelman Trust Barometer 69

Egypt 76
Electronic Frontier Foundation 159
electronic imperialism 36
electronic World Trade Platform (e-WTP) 89
el-Sisi, Abdel Fattah 76
Encounter, magazine 39
Enron Corporation 80
epistemic communities 70, 73, 103, 110, 112; and global communication 19, 61–62, 131; role of 26, 76, 114
Erasmus Mundus projects, EU's 68
Erdogan, Tayyip 78
Esper, Mark 102
Ethiopia 118, 177
Eurasia Group 23, 65
European Council on Foreign Relations (ECFR) 58, 64
Europe TV 178–179
Evanina, William 144
ExxonMobil 188

Facebook 20, 52, 85, 86, 87, 140, 163; and democracy 76, 85; disinformation 145, 154–157; global influence 87, 97, 134–135, 179–180; as a major US digital corporation 51, 57, 77–78, 147–148; as a major user of international bandwidth 54–55; and surveillance 150–151; *see also* Meta
Fairness and Accuracy in Reporting (FAIR) 92, 114
FASTER cable system 55
Federal Communications Commission (FCC) 50
financial intelligence 65, 79–80
First Look Entertainment 71
Five Eyes intelligence network 139
Food and Agriculture Organization (FAO) 169
Ford Foundation 38–39, 41, 68, 70
Fortem Technologies 132
Forum of China and the Community of Latin American and Caribbean States (China-CELAC Forum) 178
Forum on China-Africa Cooperation (FOCAC) 178
Fraser Institute 81
Freedom House 71, 77, 179
Freedom to Write Index 69
Fukuyama, Francis 5
Future of Life Institute 164

G-7 11, 16–17, 66, 164; summit 75
G-8 17
G-20 18, 66, 171
Gaidar, Yegor 49
Gates, Bill 86
GATS Fourth Protocol on Basic Telecommunications Services 49
General Agreement in Tariffs and Trade (GATT) 49
General Agreement on Trade in Services (GATS) 49
General Data Protection Regulation (GDPR) 83
genocide 119, 191; cultural 180; in southern Sudan 104; Rwandan 120; Uyghur genocide 180
GeoEye-1, 142
Germany 6, 15, 16, 31, 32, 68, 94, 122, 167
Ghani, Ashraf 117
Global Daily, Sustainable Development Goals news aggregator site 70
Global Data Alliance 84
Global Data Security Initiative 96
Global Development Watch 70
Global Information Infrastructure (GII) 28, 50
Global Initiative on AI and Data Commons 93
Global Investigative Journalism Network (GIJN) 153
Global Investment and Infrastructure Partnership Plan 185
Global Legal Action Network 153
Global Media Partnerships portfolio 70
Global Positioning System (GPS) 52
Global Social Justice Movement 75
Global System for Mobile Communication (GSMA) 85
Global Xpress satellite series 51
GLONASS 58
Goebbels, Josef 34
Google 85, 87, 94, 95, 98, 152, 166; and AI 158, 161–163; internet-based communication 86, 132, 194; as a major US digital corporation 51, 77, 78, 92; as a major user of international bandwidth 54–57; and surveillance 142, 148–150
Google Cloud AI 161
Google Earth 142, 152
Google Maps 86, 142, 152
Government of National Accord (GNA) 110

GRAIN 189
The Great Rivalry: China vs. the US in the 21st Century, 2021 report 160
Gülen, Fethullah 78
Gulf Cooperation Council (GCC) 169, 175–176
Guo Wengui 156

Harvard International Summer School 41
Harvard University Press 69
hashtag activism 77
Haushofer, Karl 6
Havas Agency 32
Hengtong Group 61
Henry Jackson Society 123, 148
Heritage Foundation 66, 71, 102, 114
Herman, Edward 100, 131
Higher Education World University Rankings 69, 73
Hinrich Foundation 65–66, 84
Hinton, Geoffrey 162
Hitler, Adolf 34
Hong Kong 2–4; 2019 anti-China protests 145; Hong Kong Watch 181
Hongyun satellite project, China 58
Hoover Institution at Stanford University 67–68
Horvitz, Eric 160
hostage diplomacy 146
Huawei 54, 59, 60, 61, 89, 146–147
Hudson Institute 64
Hughes 52
Hu Jintao 181
Human Rights Watch 70–71, 150, 160
Huttenlocher, Daniel 158
Hutu regime 120

India 12, 22, 24, 79, 89, 97–98, 104, 113; Aadhaar 186; AI policies 165; and China, relationship 170–171; digital public infrastructure 186–187; global multipolarity 18; Indo-Russian collaboration in space technology 58; model 185–187; presidency of the G-20 in 2023 171; public-utility approach 187; sustainable digitization and development 188–189; *see also* BRICS
Indian Space Research Organization (ISRO) 187
Industrial Revolution 28
Influence and Perception Management Office 149
Institute of Contemporary Arts 41

Institute of Geopolitics, University of Munich 6
intellectual infrastructure 19, 67–68
International Accounting Standards Board 69
International Association for Cultural Freedom 39
International Civil Aviation Organization (ICAO) 170
International Committee of the Red Cross 68
International Consortium of Investigative Journalists (ICIJ) 3, 150, 152–153
International Crisis Group 71
International Cyber Policy Centre of the Australian Strategic Policy 145
International Electrotechnical Commission 69
International Fact-Checking Network 71, 152
International Fund for Public Interest Media 71
International Institute for Strategic Studies 64, 65, 138
International Intellectual Property Alliance 19
International Maritime Satellite Organization (Inmarsat) 51
International Military Training Activities Database-USA (IMTAD-USA) 119
International Monetary Fund (IMF) 17, 48, 75, 169, 173
International Organization for Standardization 69
International Radiotelegraph Union (IRU) 33
International Telecommunications Satellite Organization (Intelsat) 51
International Telecommunications Union (ITU) 49
Internet Corporation for Assigned Names and Numbers (ICANN) 56
Internet Exchange Points (IXPs) 55–56
internet infrastructure: 'code' and 'content layers,' US domination of 56–57; data-related, land-based 55; fibre-optic submarine cables 51; internet age 53–56; satellites 52–53
Internet of Things (IoT) 59, 84, 90, 98, 158
Internet Research Agency 128, 136
internet service providers (ISPs) 56
IPv6 protocols 90

Iran 14, 22, 44, 105, 106, 137, 156, 175; BRICS summit 17, 19; disinformation 23, 134; geopolitical discourse 73, 111, 117, 149, 169, 190; state-controlled communication system 75–76, 81; surveillance 143, 145
Iran International 22
Iraq 42, 110, 114, 119; Al Qaeda and ISIS 106, 109; geopolitical impacts 108–109; mass destruction, weapons 106–107; strategic communication 105–107; televised toppling of Saddam statue 107–109; videos of 'precision bombings' 101, 105; media narrative 113
ISIS 108–110, 114, 117
Islamophobia 115
Israel 42, 143, 151, 159, 169

JAM trinity (Jan Dhan-Aadhar-Mobile) 186
Japan 24, 55, 81, 185
Jassy, Andy 160
JD 60
Jio Platform 98
Joint Warfighting Cloud Capability 158

Kaplan, Robert 103
Karzai, Hamid 117
Kaspersky 97
Kenyatta, Jomo 46
Kissinger, Henry 158
Kjellén, Rudolf 6
Knight Foundation 70
Kol Israel, Arabic service of 42
Konrad Adenauer Foundation 65
Korea Expose 140
Kristol, Irving 39
Kumar, Deepa 115
Kyoto Protocol 188

Lai, Jimmy 3
Landsat system 52
Latin America and the Caribbean (LAC) 176
lethal autonomous weapons systems (LAWS) 158
Libya 104; 108, 109–111, 127
Li Congjun 59
Li-Meng Yan 156
Liscovich, Andrey 132
'Living Proof' campaign 72
Li Wenliang 12
Lockheed Martin 52, 102, 142

Logistics Civil Augmentation Programme 127
Loral 52
Lowenthal, Mark 152
LSE Ideas 68
Luce, Henry 39
Lumumba, Patrice 104

MAAAMT grouping (Microsoft, Apple, Amazon, Alphabet, Meta and Twitter) 85, 87
MacArthur Foundation 70
MacBride Commission 45
Mackinder, Halford 6
Macron, Emmanuel 18, 58, 137
Mahan, Alfred 6
Mail.ru 96
Malala 113
Mamdani, Mahmood 104, 119
Mangalyaan 58
Marconi Wireless Telegraph Company 30–31
Matlock, Jack 16
Mattis, James 102, 153
Maxar 52, 132, 142, 153
McChesney, Robert 83
McGann, James 66
McKinsey Global Institute 25, 65
Médecins Sans Frontières 69
Medvedchuk, Viktor 123
Meta 133, 157, 165; international submarine cable system 54–55; surveillance 142–143; as US internet giant 51–52, 57, 85–86, 92, 98; *see also* Facebook
metaverse 98
#MeToo 77, 181
Miburo 154–155
Microsoft 85, 86, 140, 158; and AI 160, 163, 165–166; cyberwarfare 132, 138, 154; as a major US digital corporation 51, 57, 78, 88, 92, 148, 189; as a major user of international bandwidth 54–55
Middle East Broadcasting Networks (MBN) 44
Milburn, Andrew 127
Military and Security Developments Involving the People's Republic of China 2022 161
Military Information Support Operations 148
Ministry of Print and Propaganda, Italy 34
Misinformation Review in 2020 156

Modi, Narendra 78, 171
Mohseni, Said 117
Molfar 132
Moore, Andrew 85, 126, 161, 163
Morse, Samuel 29
Moyo, Last 192
Mozart Group 127
MQ-9 Reaper drones 143
Mubarak, Hosni 76
multipolarity, era of 10, 18, 169
Munich Security Report 2020 167
Musk, Elon 52, 76, 86, 132, 137, 164
Muslim Brotherhood 22, 76
Mussolini, Benito 34
My Lai massacre, 1968 149

NASA 52, 187
National Broadcasting Corporation (NBC) 4, 39
National Computer Virus Emergency Response Center, China 145
National Cybersecurity Strategy 23, 137
National Cyber Strategy of the United States 91
National Defense Strategy 102
National Endowment for Democracy (NED) 5, 71, 77, 104, 131
National Geospatial-Intelligence Agency (NGA) 141
National Informatics Centre 139
National Intelligence Law 146
National Security Agency (NSA) 91, 132, 150
National Space Administration, China 60
National Standards Strategy for Critical and Emerging Technology 164
National Union for the Total Independence of Angola (UNITA) 43
NATO 54, 102, 154; expansion of 15–16; invasions 109–110, 141; powers 125, 132, 137, 158
NEC 54
Nehru, Jawaharlal 8, 46
Netherlands Institute of International Relation 154
Network Readiness Index 81–82
new developmentalism 193
New Development Bank (NDB) 169
New Directions Publishing Corporation 41
New World Information and Communication Order (NWICO) 26, 45, 84, 190, 191; anti-colonial communication 46; MacBride Commission Report 45; 'Soviet-inspired' Third World design 46
Next Generation Artificial Intelligence Development Plan (China) 160
Niblett, Robin 63
Nikkei Asia 80, 138, 184
no-cost software 75–76
Non-Aligned Movement (NAM) 44
non-governmental organizations (NGOs) 75
Nordic Africa Institute 64
North Atlantic Fellas Organization (NAFO) 124, 135
North Korea 139
Northrop Grumman 52, 102
Novorossiya 7
NSO Group 143
NTT 54
Nuclear Suppliers Group 170
Nyerere, Julius 43

Obama, Barrack 111–112, 146, 171
Office of Cuba Broadcasting 44
Ogaden conflict 168
Omidyar, Pierre 71
open source intelligence (OSINT) 152–153, 161, 163
'open skies' policy 49
Open Society Foundation 70
Open Society Institute 77
Open Society University Network 71
Operation Barkhane 120
Operation Desert Storm 105; live broadcast 101
Operation Enduring Freedom 115
Operation Inherent Resolve 111
Operation Iraqi Freedom 106
Operation Just Cause 100
Operation Turquoise 120
Oracle 160
Organization for Economic Co-operation and Development (OECD) 50, 84, 93, 164–165
Organization for the Prohibition of Chemical Weapons (OPCW) 111
Oslo Freedom Forum 2, 71
Outbrain 86
Overseas Development Institute 63
Oxfam 64, 183
Oxford Analytica 65
Oxford University Press 69

Pacific Light Cable Network 55
Page, Larry 86
Pahlavi, Shah Mohammad Reza 104
Palestine Liberation Organization 42
Paley, William 39
Panama Papers scandal 3, 150
Paris agreement 5, 188
Pax Americana 105, 167–168
Pearson 68
Penn, Sean 125
Pentagon leak 150–151
People's Liberation Army (PLA) 137, 161
Pew Research Center 69
Phillipson, Robert 62
Pinochet, Augusto 41
Planet Labs 132–133, 153
platform capitalism 82, 88
Poland 16, 37, 122, 137
policy infrastructure 56–57
Portulans Institute 81
Prendergast, John 128
Press Freedom Defense Fund 71
PricewaterhouseCoopers 65
Prigozhin, Yevgeny 128
Prince, Erik 127
Private Eyes: China's Embrace of Open-Source Military Intelligence 161
privatization 26, 48, 51–52, 81, 126–127
propaganda 14, 23, 31, 144; China 20, 154–157, 179, 182; disinformation 148, 149; geopolitics of 33–37, 44, 113, 159, 178–179; hate 75, 109, 116; India 152; pro-Trump 136; pro-Western 40; Russia 21, 151; Ukraine 26, 123–125, 131, 133; US 3, 42–43, 100, 149, 161, 188
Public Radio International 70
publishing industry 68–69
Pugwash 39
Pulitzer Center on Crisis Reporting 70–71
Putin, Vladimir 10, 14, 18, 91, 114, 123, 128, 133, 159, 173
Pyongyang 139

QAnon 156–157
Qin An 160
QUAD (Quadrilateral Security Dialogue) 24

Radio Bari 34
radio broadcasts 33–34
Radio Corporation of America (RCA) 30
Radio Farda 44
Radio Free Asia 3

Radio Free Europe (RFE) 36–37, 43–44, 134
Radio Free Iraq 43
Radio Habana 38
Radio Liberty (RL) 36–37, 43–44, 134
Radio Moscow 34, 37–38, 43
Radio Sawa 43
Radio Sulawesi 43
Radio Tanzania 43
radiotelegraphy 31
Radu, Roxana 99
Rainforest Action Network 188
RAND Corporation 63–64, 102
Raytheon 52, 102, 142
RedAlpha 139
Reed Elsevier 68–69, 194; ScienceDirect platform 69
Reith, John 35
Reliance Group 22, 54
RELX 194
Reporters sans frontières 69
'Restore Hope,' US military intervention in Somalia 119
Reuters 17, 32, 33, 39, 42, 68, 80, 172
Rice, Condoleezza 106
Richthofen, Ferdinand von 11
Right Livelihood Award 112
Roberts, Ian 163
Robinson, Nathan 108
Rockefeller, David 40–41, 70, 81
Rockefeller Foundation 41, 70
Roscosmos 60
Rosenberger, Laura 57–58, 58
Roskomnadzor 97
Royal Institute of International Affairs 64
Royal United Services Institute (RUSI) 63
RT 20–23
Rumsfeld, Donald 16, 107
RuNet 96, 121
Russell, William Howard 29
Russia 9–10, 91, 93; authoritarian disinformation 153–155; BRICS (*see* BRICS); cyber-activities 133; cyberspace 96–97, 121; cyberwars 136–137; intervention in Africa 168; intervention in Syria 21; RT 20–23; Russia-Africa Summit, 2019 168; Russkiy Mir 9; Volunteer Corps 135; *see also* Ukraine, Russian invasion of
Russia 1985–1999: Trauma Zone (Curtis) 49
Russophobia 14
Rwandan genocide, 1994 120

Sachs, Wolfgang 183
Sandworm 136
satellites 52–53
Satia, Priya 46–47
Satyarthi, Kailash 113
Saudi Arabia 114, 175, 176
Saunders, Frances Stonor 38, 39, 40, 41
Schmidt, Eric 94, 158, 160
scorecard diplomacy 69
Semiconductor Industry Association (SIA) 25
Shanghai Cooperation Organisation (SCO) 18, 169
Single Intelligence Analysis Capacity, EU 144
Skyroot Aerospace 187
slacktivism 77
Smith, Brad 132, 140
Snowden, Edward 91, 150
Society for Worldwide Interbank Financial Telecommunication (SWIFT) 14, 54
Soros, George 70–71, 77
Soros Economic Development Fund of the Open Society Foundation (OSF) 70
South African Institute of International Affairs 64
South Atlantic Inter Link (SAIL) 61
Southeast Asia Treaty Organization (SEATO) 104
Space Imaging 142
SpaceX 52, 76
Spamouflage 145, 154
Special Rupee vostro Account (SRVA) 187
Sputnik satellite 13, 21, 37, 168
spying: Advanced spy satellites 141; BeiDou Navigation Satellite System 144; ByteDance tool 144; China 143–145; commercial cyberspace companies 142; cross-platform spam network 145; cyberweapons 143; digital silk road 144; Five Eyes 141; intelligence agencies and communication technologies 141; PSYOPS 141; satellite imagery industry 142; Spamouflage Dragon, cross-platform spam network 145
spyware diplomacy 143
standards development organizations (SDOs) 173, 174
Stanford Institute for Human-Centered Artificial Intelligence 163–164
Stanford Internet Observatory 156
Stanley, Morgan 53
State Plan for Informationization in the Period of the 13th Five Year Plan 59
Stiglitz, Joseph 81
Stockholm International Peace Research Institute (SIPRI) 64, 101
Strategic Plan to Advance Cloud Computing in the Intelligence Community 158
submarine cable network 53–54; fibre-optic cables 55
Submarine Telecoms Industry Report 2021 53
Sukarno 42–43, 46, 104
Sulzberger, Arthur Hays 39
Summit for Democracy 2
Sunak, Rishi 53–54
SunCalc 152
sustainable internet 96
Syria Campaign 112
Syrian Archive 153
Syria 108–114

Taboola 86
Taiwan Semiconductor Manufacturing Company (TSMC) 25, 146
talking back, strategy of 20, 181
Tat-8 53
Tata Communications 22, 54
Tata Group 22
Taylor & Francis Group 69
Team Jorge 151
Telefunken 30
TeleGeography 54
Telegram 2, 21, 29, 155–156; disinformation 135–136, 151; for propaganda 122, 124, 128, 131
Telegraph Agency of the Soviet Union (TASS) 34
telegraphy 6, 29, 31–32, 33; *see also* cables
Telstra 54
Telxius 54
Tencent 11, 60, 78, 87–89, 88
TenPay 89
TE SubCom 54
think tanks: Al Jazeera's Center for Studies 65; Australian 90, 179–180; Berlin-based 12; British 64; Chinese 72–73, 157; Chinese Think Tank Index 73; competitions 65; conservative 188; European 61, 65, 147; financial media organizations 65; free marketeers 65; French 174; functions 67; India 58; legitimizing geopolitical agendas

66–67; 'national high-end think tanks 72; number of think tanks by country, 2020 **63**; top ten think tanks 67; US 10, 20, 61, 66, 102, 109, 114, 133, 143, 157, 179
Thomson Reuters 68
Thucydides Trap 192
Tigrayan People's Liberation Front 118
TikTok 87, 89, 95, 139, 144–145
TinEye or Google Images 152
Tourist (2021) 128
Transparency International 71
TRT News 22
Trump, Donald 3, 66, 102, 136; and Covid-19 pandemic 13, 156–157; global financial crisis 90, 185; and the media 4–6, 85, 116, 123; strategic intelligence 138, 145
The Truth about America's Fight against Covid-19 157
Tsinghua 1, 73
Türkiye 19, 111, 169, 179
Twitter 20, 87, 92, 123, 133, 136, 149; audiences 21–22; as communication 75–78, 124, 132, 134, 140, 157, 179–180; disinformation 135, 145, 151, 154, 155, 162; and Elon Musk 86, 137; and Trump 4, 85
20–21, 75–78, 85–87, 92, 123–124, 132–137, 140, 145, 149, 151, 154–155, 157, 162, 179–180

Ukraine Digital Verification Lab 133
Ukraine, Russian invasion of 13–16, 21, 100, 167; anti-Ukraine discourse and disinformation in media 121–122; block of SWIFT 13; coverage of exodus of students 122–123; coverage of volunteers to join International Legion 125; digital warfare 130–135; military censorship 122; Ukrainian blast on Crimean Bridge 123; Zelensky's address at Cannes film festival 125–126
Umbrella Movement 2
UNCTAD 79, 82, 92–93, 95
UNESCO 5, 23, 45, 56, 92, 189
Unified Payments Interface (UPI) 186
UN Industrial Development Organization (UNIDO) 170
United Arab Emirates 15, 110, 127, 172, 175
United Nations Development Programme (UNDP) 49

United States 5, 14–15, 186–188; Africa Command (AFRICOM) 119; Agency for Global Media (USAGM) 44; Agency for International Development (USAID) 77, 103; Air Force's Defense Meteorological Satellite Program 52; Centers for Disease Control and Prevention 155; Cold War 36–46; Council on Foreign Relations 91; digital capitalism 78–79; digital imperialism 90–92; Foreign Intelligence Surveillance Act 142, 150; Ford Foundation 38–39, 41, 68, 70; invasions of Afghanistan 115–118; invasions of Iraq 105–109; National Security Strategy 10; National Cybersecurity Strategy 23; satellites 52–53; semiconductors 25; Telecommunications Act 50, 147; think tanks 10, 20, 61, 66, 102, 109, 114, 133, 143, 157, 179; US-China Economic and Security Review Commission 20, 144; US Information Agency (USIA) 36; US-led communication infrastructure 51–53, 57–60; Utilizing Voice of America (VOA) (*see* Voice of America (VOA)); wars in Africa 119–120
United States Space Priorities Framework, 2021 52
universities 67–68
Uppsala Conflict Data Program (UCDP) 101
Uyghur Human Rights Project 180

Vaidhyanathan, Siva 86–87
venture colonialism 10
Verizon 54
Vietnam War 42, 106, 108, 149
virtual reality (VR) 90
Vkontakte (Vk.com) 96, 156
Voice of America (VOA) 35–26, 134; anti-communist propaganda, Korean War (1950–1953) 36; Cold War US propaganda 36; expansion of international radio broadcasting 37
Voice of Free Indonesia 43
Voice of Jihad 116
Voice of the Patriotic Militiamen's Front 42
Volt Typhoon 138–139
von der Leyen, Ursula 15, 21
Vulkan files 136

war on terror 8, 116–117, 148
Warsaw Pact 36

WeChat 88–89, 145, 180
Weibo effect 138, 145
Wendt 165
Western Union Telegraph Company 30
Westlessness 167
White Helmets 112
WikiLeaks 150
Wisner, Frank 40
Wolff, Bernhard 32
Wolff agency 32
Wolf Warrior 2 (2017) 181
Wolters Kluwer 68–69
Wong, Joshua 2
World Administrative Radio Conferences, ITU's 37
World Bank 48, 49, 75, 84, 169
World Economic Forum 84
World Health Organization (WHO) 5
World Internet Conference 59
World Radiocommunication Conferences (WRC) 50
World Radio Conference in Washington in 1927 33
World Social Forum 75
World's Opinion Page 70

World Trade Organization (WTO) 13, 18, 26, 48–50, 59, 75, 171
World Wide Web 56, 74
Wozniak, Steve 164
Wuhan Institute of Virology 155
Wuhan Military Games 155

Xi Jinping 10, 11, 72, 89, 160, 174, 177, 178
Xinhua news agency 19, 21, 157, 176, 179

Yale University Press 69
Yandex (the search engine) 96–97, 97
Yanukovych, Viktor 15
Yellow Vests' movement 155
Yeltsin, Boris 49

Zapatista National Liberation Army 74
Zeitschrift für Geopolitik (Journal for Geopolitics) 6
Zelensky, Volodymyr 15, 21, 123–126, 130–131, 133, 162
Zhao Lijian 139
ZTE 60, 146
Zuckerberg, Mark 86